D0830304

COMPARATIVE
POLITICS

The Little, Brown Series
in Comparative Politics

Under the Editorship of
GABRIEL A. ALMOND
JAMES S. COLEMAN
LUCIAN W. PYE

AN ANALYTIC STUDY

COMPARATIVE
POLITICS SECOND EDITION

System, Process, and Policy

Gabriel A. Almond

Stanford University

G. Bingham Powell, Jr.

University of Rochester

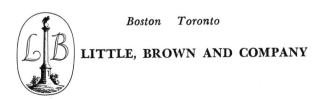

Boston   Toronto

LITTLE, BROWN AND COMPANY

LIBRARY OF CONGRESS CATALOG CARD NO. 78-50406

ISBN 0-316-03498-3

9 8 7 6 5 4 3

MV

Published simultaneously in Canada
by Little, Brown & Company (Canada) Limited

PRINTED IN THE UNITED STATES OF AMERICA

Preface

THE TWELVE YEARS which have elapsed since the publication of the first edition of *Comparative Politics* have been highly productive years for political science research and theory. In the first edition we spoke of an intellectual revolution in the study of comparative government. This revolution consisted of a fourfold innovative search for (1) a more comprehensive coverage of the variety of human experiments with politics, (2) a more realistic and less formal-institutional approach to political description and analysis, (3) greater rigor and precision in our descriptive and theoretical efforts, and (4) more adequate theoretical frameworks to encompass and order this growing body of knowledge. We are fortunate in being able to draw in this edition upon many of the fine studies produced in pursuit of these goals in the last decade.

This book is not a marginally revised edition. It has been rewritten from first to last. We have attempted to incorporate the newer literature of the discipline of comparative politics as it begins to move into the 1980s. Yet the reader familiar with the first edition will recognize the clear continuities in the present version. The intellectual structure in the earlier work has been more fully elaborated, and analytic approaches proposed then are more completely implemented now.

We spoke of three levels of political functions in the 1966 edition. In this book the three-level approach has provided the organizing principle of the work as a whole. After an introductory discussion of political culture and political structure in Part I, we proceed from *system* analysis in Part II to *process* analysis in Part III to *policy* analysis in Part IV. In Part I we define what we mean by political culture and political structure, and specify their varieties and forms. We then discuss in Part II the principal system maintenance and adaptation functions of socialization, recruitment, and communication. In Part III we define and elaborate on the conversion or process functions of interest articulation, aggregation, policy making, and implementation. This part deals with the varieties of political structures that formulate and combine political demands and supports, convert them into authoritative policies, and implement them in the domestic and foreign environment. We describe and analyze such structures as interest groups, political parties, political executives, legislatures, and bureaucracies.

Part IV, dealing with policy, represents the most notable change in the book. This aspect of politics — capabilities, outputs, and outcomes — was treated briefly in one chapter in the first edition. In the present book we treat output and outcome in separate chapters and introduce rich empirical materials descriptive of the political performance of varieties of political systems — advanced industrial and developing ones, democratic and authoritarian ones. A chapter on political development discusses the dilemmas and strategies of third world nations in system, process, and policy terms. A final chapter deals with the important question of evaluating the political characteristics of nations, again in system, process, and policy terms.

This threefold analytic structure enables the reader to move easily and logically from institution to institution and from process to process without losing the essential thread of connection and meaning. In a discussion of political parties, for example, the reader is not simply confronted with descriptive detail but is led back to the socioeconomic and political phenomena which help explain the characteristics of a particular party system on the one hand, and led forward to some of the policy consequences of that party system on the other. The same approach illuminates our discussions of political socialization, recruitment, policy making, and implementing processes and institutions. It is our intention to sustain the reader as he seeks to see the connection among the human meanings of political processes.

The new edition also reflects intellectual growth in the way it deals with problems of explanation, understanding, and interpretation of political phenomena. In the first edition we stressed sociological, anthropological, and psychological modes of analysis, seeking to explain the characteristics of politics in terms of constraining social structural and cultural conditions. In the present edition, the political system as often becomes the independent variable and the social and international environment the dependent one, as we elaborate our treatment of public policy. Our discussion of policy and its consequences leads us to adopt a political economy approach in a fuller sense of the term, dealing with political structure and process from a creative perspective and elaborating the consequences of political choice.

Thus, from a methodological point of view, the second edition provides an interface for political phenomena with the analytic approaches of sociology, psychology, and anthropology on the one hand and economics and philosophy on the other. Only this full range of analytic modes makes it possible to capture the significance of the realm of politics, that which shapes and constrains it, but more importantly the moral opportunities and potentialities which it holds out to humanity.

Gabriel A. Almond
G. Bingham Powell, Jr.

Acknowledgments

THE AUTHORS express their gratitude to students and teachers who used the first edition of this book and passed on their suggestions and criticisms to us. The present book benefited greatly from careful readings and comments at various manuscript stages from Professors James Bill, L. Gray Cowan, Henry Ehrmann, Eric Nordlinger, Jeffrey Obler, Lynda W. Powell, Richard Rose, and W. Phillips Shively. The chapter on political development owes much to the case studies of political-economic development done by graduate students in Political Science 211 at Stanford University in the winter of 1976. We are particularly grateful to Lois Renner of the Stanford Department of Political Science who handled the many manuscript typings and revisions with patience, thoughtfulness, and care.

Gabriel A. Almond
G. Bingham Powell, Jr.

Contents

PART I

Introduction

CHAPTER I

An Overview

IT MAY BE HELPFUL to introduce at the outset the principal concepts we use in this book. They will be elaborated and illustrated in later chapters. But here they are presented in compact form and in logical order so that they may serve as a guide to what follows, as a way of relating the various chapters to one another. We shall also spell out more fully our approach to comparative analysis and its uses in description and theory in comparative politics.

THE POLITICAL SYSTEM

The principal concept is the political system. The term *political system* has become very common in the titles of recent texts and monographs in comparative politics. The older works used such terms as *government, nation,* or *state* to describe what we call a political system. The new terminology involves more than a change in style; it reflects a new way of looking at politics. It includes some new names for old things and some new terms that refer to activities and processes not formerly recognized as aspects of politics.

The older terms — *state, government, nation* — are limited by legal and institutional meanings. They direct attention to a particular set of institutions usually found in modern Western societies. If one believes that the study of these institutions is the proper and sole concern of comparative politics, one can avoid many problems, including the thorny question of limiting the subject matter of the discipline. But the costs of such an approach are high. The role played by formal governmental institutions, such as legislatures and courts, varies greatly. In many societies, particularly non-Western ones, they may play a less important role than other institutions and processes will. And in all societies, their role will be shaped and limited by informal groups, political attitudes, and a multitude of interpersonal relationships. If political science is to deal

3

effectively with political phenomena in all kinds of societies, regardless of culture, degree of modernization, and size, a more comprehensive framework of analysis is needed.

To use *political system* as our most general term does not mean that we view the older language as obsolete. *State, government,* and *nation* are useful to refer to more limited or special aspects of politics. State connotes institutional specificity, authority, and legitimacy. Government has slightly different formal-legal-institutional connotations. A nation is a political system in which the citizens share a sense of historic identity and destiny. We shall use these terms when we discuss these specific aspects of political systems and political development. But the concept of political system has acquired such wide currency because it directs attention to the entire scope of political activities within a society. It is also an ecological concept, emphasizing the interactions between the political sphere and the environment.

THE DISTINCTIVENESS OF POLITICS

What is the political system? How are its boundaries defined? What gives the political system its special identity? Many political scientists have dealt with these questions; and although the precise language of their definitions varies considerably, there is some consensus. Common to most definitions is the association of the political system with legitimate physical coercion. Easton speaks of the "authoritative allocation of values"; Lasswell and Kaplan, of "severe deprivations"; Dahl, of "power, rule and authority." [1] All these definitions imply the rightful power to punish, to enforce, to compel. We agree with Max Weber that legitimate force is the thread that runs through the action of the political system, giving it special importance and coherence as a system.[2] The political authorities, and only they, have some generally accepted right in a given territory to utilize coercion and to command obedience based upon it.

Thus, the demands that enter the political system are all related to legitimate physical compulsion, whether they call for war or for the taking of real property for recreational facilities. The policies of the political system are also related to legitimate compulsion, however remote the relationship may be. Thus, public recreational facilities are

[1] David Easton, *The Political System* (New York: Alfred A. Knopf, 1953), pp. 130 ff.; David Easton, *A Framework for Political Analysis* (Englewood Cliffs: Prentice-Hall, 1965), pp. 50 ff.; Harold Lasswell and Abraham Kaplan, *Power and Society* (New Haven: Yale University Press, 1950); Robert A. Dahl, *Modern Political Analysis* (Englewood Cliffs: Prentice-Hall, 1963), pp. 5 ff.

[2] See Max Weber, "Politics as a Vocation," in *From Max Weber: Essays in Sociology,* ed. H. H. Gerth and C. Wright Mills (New York: Oxford University Press, 1946), pp. 77–78.

usually supported by taxation, and any violation of the regulations governing their use is a legal offense. When we speak of the political system, we include all the interactions that affect the use of legitimate physical coercion. The political system includes not only governmental institutions, such as legislatures, courts, and administrative agencies, but *all structures in their political aspects*. Among these are traditional structures, such as kinship ties and caste groups; anomic phenomena, such as riots; and nongovernmental organizations, such as parties, interest groups, and communications media.

We are not, then, saying that the political system is concerned solely with force, violence, or compulsion; rather, its relation to coercion is its distinctive quality. Political elites and citizens are usually concerned with goals such as national expansion or security, social welfare, increased popular participation in politics, and the like. The political system is not the only system that makes rules and enforces them, but its rules and enforcements may be backed up by compulsion.

There are societies in which the accepted power to use physical compulsion is widely diffused: shared by family, clan, religious bodies, or other groups, or taken up privately, as in the feud or duel. But even these societies are political systems, and they are still comparable with those polities in which there is something approaching a monopoly of legitimate physical coercion. In any political system, moreover, when disagreement exists about the circumstances of using coercion or about the nature of the legitimate authorities, one may assume that there exists a challenge to the regime and a potentially serious political conflict.

SYSTEMS AND ENVIRONMENTS

If what we have said defines the "political" half of our concept of political system, what do we mean by "system"? A system implies some interdependence of parts and some kind of boundary between it and its environment. By interdependence we mean that when the properties of one component in a system change, all other components and the system as a whole are affected. Thus, if the rings of an automobile erode, the car burns oil, the functioning of other aspects of the system deteriorates, and the power of the car declines. Or, as another example, there are times in the growth of organisms when some change in the endocrine system influences the overall pattern of growth, the functioning of all the parts, and the general behavior of the organism. In political systems the emergence of mass parties or of media of mass communication changes the performance of all other structures of the system (although to varying degrees) and affects the system's domestic and foreign capabilities. In other words, when one variable in a system changes in magnitude or quality, others may be subjected to strains and may be transformed. The system then changes its pattern of performance, or the unruly component is disciplined by regulatory mechanisms.

A second aspect of the concept of system is the notion of boundary and environment. A system starts somewhere and ends somewhere. In considering an organism or an automobile, it is relatively easy to locate the boundary and to specify the interactions between it and its environment. In dealing with social systems, of which political systems are one class, the problem of boundary is more difficult. Social systems are made up not of individuals, but of roles. A family, for example, consists of the roles of mother and father, husband and wife, sibling and sibling. But the family provides only one set of interacting roles for its members. Each member also has roles outside the family, in schools, work places, and churches. In the same sense, a political system is made up of the interacting roles of subjects or voters with legislators, bureaucrats, and judges. As individuals expose themselves to political communication, form political interest groups, vote, or pay taxes, they shift from non-political to political roles; one might say that they enter and leave the political system.

All political systems interact with two environments, the domestic and the international. They affect and are affected by their domestic economies, their natural environments and resources, their educational and technological systems, and their ethnic and cultural systems. Thus, they penetrate their societies in very different ways and to very different extents. Communist political systems, as in the Soviet Union, directly command and control most of the economy, whereas some other political systems exert less control over economic life. Even in systems with limited political penetration, the boundaries of the polity fluctuate. They are usually greatly extended in wartime, as large numbers of men are recruited into military service, as business firms are subjected to regulations, and as internal security measures are taken. Similarly, political systems and their societies interact with their international environments, engaging in trade, diplomacy, war, communication, and cultural exchange with other political systems and international bodies.

Political systems are the means by which societies consciously formulate and pursue collective goals in their domestic and international environments. To a greater or lesser degree, political systems adopt and attempt to implement policies designed to extract resources from these environments, distribute benefits to various domestic groups and foreign countries, regulate behavior domestically, or provide for security from foreign threats. On the other hand, political systems are themselves greatly shaped by the environments in which they operate. The problems that are posed to citizens and leaders in a society, the resources available to meet those problems, the skills and values that shape collective beliefs and actions — all are affected by the domestic and foreign environments.

Table I.1 displays some of the characteristics of the domestic and foreign environments of twenty-four contemporary political systems. These twenty-four were selected because they represent different levels of economic development, different regions and cultures, and different political arrangements and ideologies; the same illustrative set of countries will appear throughout this book. We have listed these twenty-four countries by the size of their gross national products per capita in 1973. Per capita GNP is important because it is usually associated with other characteristics of the society. Societies with low per capita income typically have most people employed in agricultural occupations or in extractive ones, such as mining. They are also typically characterized by low levels of literacy, education, nutrition, and health. In consequence, political leaders in low-income societies usually desire above all to improve the living conditions for their citizens and face a multitude of demands to do just that. The preindustrial economies face serious problems of fluctuating world demand for raw materials, constraints in accumulating capital for investment in industry, and difficulties in developing the skill and efficiency of their citizens.

Wealthy societies, such as the United States, the Western European nations, the Soviet Union, and Japan, face very different problems — controlling pollution and conserving natural resources, maintaining and extending growth rates, and dealing with unemployment and inflation, for example. And they have many more economic and social resources for coping with these problems. Because of these very different environmental conditions, we shall continue to list these political systems in order of economic per capita income throughout this book.

Table I.1 also suggests some other environmental factors relevant to politics in these systems. One is the pattern of ethnic and linguistic division resulting from the cultural systems of the societies. As we shall show later, in looking at the political process in more depth, such divisions have important implications for the political issues and for the kinds of party systems and coalitions formed in these societies, as well as for the levels and types of political conflict. The last column lists some of the salient features of the international environments. The Middle Eastern nations are overwhelmingly concerned with the conflict between Israel and the Palestinians and the international ramifications of that conflict. The Eastern European nations are dominated by the Soviet Union, and their political systems are directly affected by Soviet policies, as was most dramatically underlined by the invasion of Czechoslovakia in 1968. Canada and Latin America are greatly influenced by any actions of the

Table I.1. *Selected Aspects of Environments in Contemporary Political Systems*

Political system	Domestic economic environment — 1973 per capita GNP[a]	Domestic sociocultural environments — 1965 % of literacy[b]	1965 ethnic-linguistic fractional-ization[c]	International environment — Some major threats, concerns, and involvements
USA	$ 6,200	99%	Substantial	Arms race/Oil
Sweden	6,100	100	Very low	Neutrality
Canada	5,450	99	High	Relation to USA
W. Germany	5,320	99	Very low	Common Market/Oil/East Germany
France	4,540	99	Low	Common Market/Oil
Japan	3,630	98	Very low	Relation to China/Oil
Austria	3,510	98	Very low	Neutrality
Britain	3,060	99	Low	Common Market
Israel	3,010	90	Low	Arab war threat
Czechoslovakia	2,870	99	Substantial	Relation to USSR
Italy	2,450	92	Very low	Common Market/Oil
USSR	2,030	99	High	Arms race/China
Spain	1,710	87	Substantial	Relation to Common Market
Bulgaria	1,590	85	Low	Relation to USSR
Yugoslavia	1,010	77	High	Relation to USSR
Mexico	890	65	Low	Relation to USA
Brazil	760	61	Very low	Relation to USA/Exports
Peru	520	61	High	Relation to USA/Exports
China	270	50	Very low	Relation to USSR
Egypt	250	30	Very low	Israel, Palestinians
Nigeria	210	33	Very high	Agricultural export prices
Kenya	170	23	Very high	Agricultural export prices
Tanzania	130	18	Very high	Agricultural export prices
India	120	28	Very high	China/Pakistan

Note: These systems were chosen for purposes of interest and illustration. They do not in any sense constitute a random sample of the contemporary world of nations and thus should not be used as evidence in comparative theory testing.
[a]World Bank, *World Bank Atlas* (Washington, D.C., 1975), p. 3.
[b]Charles L. Taylor and Michael C. Hudson, *World Handbook of Political and Social Indicators,* 2d ed. (New Haven: Yale University Press, 1972), pp 232–34.
[c]Ibid., pp. 271–74, based on the Soviet *Atlas Naradov Mira.* We have taken the numerical fractionalization scores and classified them on the basis of cutoff points: Very low (0–.20), Low (.21–.40), Substantial (.41–60), High (.61–80), and Very high (over .80). It should be emphasized that these do not include religious divisions, nor do they take account of the salience of the divisions of ethnicity.

United States, especially in the realm of economics. The United States and the Soviet Union are involved in an arms race. The latter is also concerned with China and its goals and stability. Western Europe must contend with both the advantages and the possible threats to culture and identity posed by the Common Market, and many of the industrial nations are worried and affected by their dependence on Arab oil. The poorest nations are deeply dependent on international prices for raw materials, and often their exports are concentrated in a few crops (see chapter XII). A political-system perspective directs attention to these environmental features and their implications for politics and public policy.

INPUTS AND OUTPUTS

Systems theory usually divides interaction between a system and its environment into three phases: input, conversion, and output. Any set of interacting parts — that is, any system — affected by factors in its environment and seeking to affect them may be viewed in this fashion. The inputs and outputs are transactions between the system and its environment. The conversion processes are internal to the political system. When we talk about the sources of inputs — their number, contents, intensity, and how they enter the political system — and about outputs — their number, content, and how they leave the political system and affect other social systems — we shall, in effect, be talking about the boundaries of the political system.

Figure I.1 shows a schematic view of the political process from a systems point of view. Inputs of demands and supports enter the political system from the environment. Perhaps inflation has reduced the real income of certain groups in the population. When such an economic change is converted into demands for public policy or for changes in political personnel, there is an interaction between the economy and the polity. The economic situation causes certain attitudinal reactions, which are converted into demands made to trade union leaders and other lobbyists. These leaders in turn press for particular legislative and executive actions. Somewhere in this process a boundary from one system to another is crossed. On the "other side" of the political system these demands may result in policy outputs, such as taxation, welfare payments, or wage and price controls. These outputs may produce changes in the environment, called outcomes, which in turn may affect the political system, as when successful price controls check inflation, reducing the demands for action. This process is called "feedback." [3]

David Easton, the first political scientist to analyze politics in explicit

---

[3] See chap. XII for a more complete discussion of output, outcomes, and feedbacks.

Figure I.1. *A Systems Perspective on the Political Process*

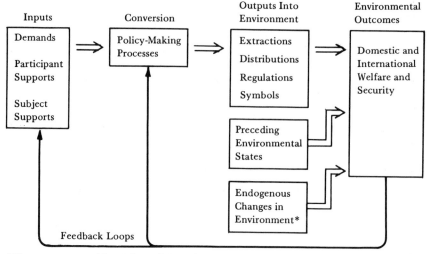

*Changes not caused by actions of the political system itself.

system terms, distinguishes two types of inputs into the political system: *demands* and *supports*.[4] Let us look at some of the types of demands made on the political system: (1) demands for distribution of goods and services, such as demands for minimum-wage and maximum-hour laws, educational opportunities, recreational benefits, roads, and transportation; (2) demands for the regulation of behavior, such as provision for public safety, controls over markets, and rules pertaining to marriage, health, and sanitation; (3) demands for greater or lesser taxation and for other forms of resource extraction; (4) demands for communication of information, such as demands for the affirmation of norms, for the communication of policy intent from elites, or for the display of the majesty and power of the political system in periods of threat or on ceremonial occasions; (5) demands for participation in the political process or for greater equity of representation for social groups, that is, demands for the right to vote, to hold office, to petition government, or to organize political associations; and (6) demands for greater stability and order, for a lessening of violence or conflict in the society, or, alternatively, for more positive adaptation and response to new values, challenges, and opportunities. A political system may face these sorts of demands in many combinations, forms, and degrees of intensity.

4 David Easton, "An Approach to the Analysis of Political Systems," *World Politics* 9 (April 1957): 383–400; for a fuller elaboration see, *A Systems Analysis of Political Life* (New York: John Wiley, 1965).

A second type of inputs it supports:

Inputs of demands are not enough to keep a political system operating. They are only the raw material out of which finished products called decisions are manufactured. Energy in the form of actions or orientations promoting and resisting a political system, the demands arising in it, and the decisions issuing from it must also be put into the system to keep it running.[5]

Two major classes of supports may be distinguished. First, there are political resource supports, the inputs of participant efforts to support leaders and groups who are engaged in making policies or who are seeking to gain public office and make public policy. Voting, participating in a campaign, and fighting for a given political faction are all examples of such supports. These are often tied to policy demands, but they need not be; for example, a citizen may vote for a party out of affection for its symbols or a sense of duty. Another example would be when peasants give aid and comfort to guerrilla groups out of fear or kinship identity, rather than dissatisfaction with the government.

A second major class of supports can be called subject supports or compliance: the provision of money or goods and services in response to authoritative policies of the legitimate political system. Examples of this class are (1) material support, such as payment of taxes or other levies, and the provision of services, such as labor on public works, jury duty, or military service; (2) obedience to law and regulations; and (3) attention paid to governmental communication and the manifestation of deference or respect for authority, symbols, and ceremony. Generally speaking, demands and political resource supports affect the policies adopted in the system, whereas subject supports provide the resources that enable a political system to extract, regulate, and distribute — in other words, to carry out its policies.

We do not wish to leave the impression, of course, that inputs come only from the society of which the political system is a part. Inputs are typically generated internally by political elites — kings, presidents, ministers, legislators, and judges. They may also come from the international system in the form of threats, invasions, controls, and assistance from foreign political systems. The flow of inputs and outputs includes transactions between the political system and components of its domestic and foreign environments. Therefore, inputs may come from any one of the three sources: the domestic society, the political elites, or the international environment.

Outputs may be said to include four classes of transactions initiated by the political system. These usually correspond fairly closely to the

[5] Easton, "Approach to the Analysis of Political Systems," p. 390.

subject supports listed, and they may or may not be responsive to demands. The classes of outputs are (1) extractions, which may take the form of tribute, booty, taxes, or personal services; (2) regulations of behavior, which may take a variety of forms; (3) distributions of goods, services, opportunities, honors, statuses, and the like; and (4) symbolic outputs, including affirmations of values, displays of political symbols, and statements of policies and intents. These outputs may or may not achieve the desired domestic and international outcomes. In chapters XI–XIII we shall be discussing some of these output-outcome relationships and the strategies for achievement, as well as evaluation of what is achieved.

STRUCTURE AND CULTURE

The terms *structure* and *culture* also have central importance in our analytical scheme. When we speak of the structure of a political system, we are referring to the activities that make up that system — activities that have a certain regularity of behavior, intention, and expectation. Thus, in a court, the structure includes interactions among the judge, jury, prosecuting and defense attorneys, witnesses, defendant, and plaintiff. Of course, not all the activities of these persons are political: each acts in a variety of other spheres. Thus, a judge may also act as a father, a deacon, a member of the Masonic Lodge. When that judge is performing regularized judicial activities, we say that he is acting in his political *role* as judge. All social systems, including political systems, are made up of roles. The individual members of a society usually perform roles in many social systems besides the political system — in families, businesses, churches, and social clubs, for example.

Thus, one of the basic units of political systems is the political role. And a set of roles is a structure. A judgeship is a role; a court is a structure of roles. We are using the terms *role* and *structure* rather than *office* and *institution* to emphasize the actual behavior of the individuals involved in politics and the actual performance of the political institution. Both *office* and *institution* may refer to formal rules, such as those presumed to govern the behavior of judges and juries, or to some mode of behavior toward which the citizens might wish them to aspire. *Role* and *structure* refer to the observable behavior of individuals. Legal rules and ideal norms may affect that behavior, but they rarely describe it fully.

Beginning with the concept of role as one of the basic units of a political system, we may speak of a structure (for example, a legislative body) as consisting of related and interacting roles and of the political system as a set of interacting structures (for example, legislatures, electorates, pressure groups, and courts). In chapter III we shall discuss more fully the concepts of role and structure and shall investigate some of their identifying properties as well as some of the dynamics that shape them. In the subsequent chapters we shall consider many kinds of structures including electorates; interest groups; competitive, corporatist, and hierarchic parties; bureaucratic agencies; legislative assemblies; monarchic, presidential, politburo, cabinet, and military executives.

There is another principal dimension that runs throughout this book: the concept of political culture. Everyone knows that there is more to individuals than their behavior over a given period of time. In the same sense, there is more to a political system than may be clearly manifested over a given period of time. For example, Italy under Fascism appeared to be a quite formidable and powerful political system. It repressed opposition, held massive and impressive parades, and defeated the Ethiopians. But then it had great difficulty coping with the Greeks, and it began to collapse in Africa when whole army divisions retreated and surrendered without much of a fight. By simply observing Italian politics during this period we would not have been able to predict the Italian political system's ability to carry out its policies. Had we known more of the mood and attitude of the Italian population, more of the morale and commitment of its soldiers, more of the resoluteness of its officers and of the capacity for policy making of its political elites, we might have been able to predict the viability of this political system when confronted with unusual pressure and opposition.

In studying any political system, therefore, one needs to know its underlying propensities, as well as its actual performance over a given period of time. We call these propensities (the psychological dimension of the political system) the *political culture*. It consists of the attitudes, beliefs, values, and skills that are current in a population. But regional or ethnic groups or social classes that make up the population of a political system may have special propensities or tendencies. We call these special propensities *subcultures*. Similarly, there may be traditions and attitudes current in the different roles, structures, and subsystems of the political system. Thus, French military officers or bureaucratic officials may have a special subculture that differentiates them from French politicians, for example, in their preferred policies, their support for the regime, and their attitudes about proper forms of participation in politics. In chapter II we shall discuss more fully the different aspects of political culture.

LEVELS OF FUNCTIONING: SYSTEM, PROCESS, AND POLICY

Having introduced the basic conceptual building blocks of our analysis — system and environment, inputs and outputs, structure and culture — we turn logically to consider the *functions* of political systems. The functioning of any system may be viewed on three different levels. We shall call these the system level, the process level, and the policy level. Major sections of this book are organized around these different levels. Although some sort of sequence must be followed in discussing them, we must emphasize that these are levels, or perspectives, not sequential stages. To illustrate them most appropriately, we would use transparent overleafs, for the three levels operate simultaneously.

THE SYSTEM LEVEL

The system level involves the system maintenance and adaptation functions. For an automobile to perform efficiently on the road, parts must be lubricated, repaired, and replaced. New parts may perform stiffly; they must be broken in. In a political system the incumbents of various roles (diplomats, military officers, tax officials) must be *recruited* to these roles and learn how to perform in them. New roles are created or old ones changed as circumstances change. Similarly, attitudes must be shaped, sustained, or changed in the political culture of the society; this is called *socialization*. And both attitude formation and continuing behavior depend on the *communication* of information between individuals. Political life is a form of social behavior, and all social activity depends on communication. In chapters IV–VI we shall discuss these system-level functions.

THE PROCESS LEVEL

The next level of the political system is the process level. Inputs of demands and supports are converted into outputs of authoritative policies through a conversion process. For analytic purposes, we may think of this conversion process as consisting of four functions. The first function is *interest articulation*. At this stage interest groups and individuals express demands for policy change or continuation. Such demands are often tied to promises of political support, as groups offer their votes or financial resources in exchange for desired policies. A labor union, for example, may agree to work for the political party that adopts its views on full employment.

The second function is *interest aggregation*. At this stage the many demands expressed in interest articulation are aggregated into a smaller number of major policy alternatives. These alternatives become "major" because substantial political resources — votes, money, media attention, armed force — are mobilized behind them. At this stage the important political contenders appear, defined by their mobilization of political resources, and they bargain with one another and join together to form political coalitions. Competitive parties may seek to mobilize electoral resources behind their policy proposals; noncompetitive parties seek to organize the backing of powerful subgroups; military organizations may seek the backing of regional commanders.

The third function is *policy making*. Each political system has a "constitution," a set of ongoing rules that define the sites of political power and the nature of the resources necessary for a coalition to make authoritative policies. These formal and informal constitutional rules may define a majority vote of the legislature and the signature of the President as necessary for policy making, as in the United States; they may require a majority of the Politburo or its most influential members, as in the Soviet Union; or they may involve only the decision of the military council or supreme leader. At the policy-making stage the authoritative goals of the political system are enacted according to those rules.

The final stage in the conversion process is *policy implementation.*[6] It is all very well for the Congress to vote more taxes or for the dictator to decree land seizures and the expansion of the army. But these policies must be implemented, typically through bureaucratic agencies, although interest groups, parties, courts, and other structures may also be involved. The policy programs must be combined with the subject-support resources extracted from citizens, resources such as tax monies. In chapters VII–X we shall discuss the four conversion process functions.

THE POLICY LEVEL

The last level of analysis is that of policy performance or, simply, policy.[7] At this level we are focusing on the behavior of the political system as a whole as it relates to other social systems and to the environment. As we have already indicated, the *outputs* of the implemented policies may be characterized as involving resource extractions, distributions of goods and services, regulations of behavior, or communication of symbols and information. We shall discuss and compare the outputs of different political systems in chapter XI. But the policy level includes a policy perspective on each stage in the conversion process, as well as attention to outputs themselves. Many political structures have policy specialties, for example, and one can analyze political coalitions according to their policy concerns. Indeed, if we do not apply the dual perspectives of process *and* policy to each part of our analysis, we shall forget much of what politics is truly about.

[6] In the first edition of this book we discussed six conversion functions. Here we retain the same basic scheme, but for simplicity have combined policy application and adjudication into a single implementation function; and on reflection have decided that communication is best considered a system function.

[7] In this edition we go beyond the "capabilities" analysis of the first edition, separating output from outcome, and including an approach to the evaluation of the performance of the political system.

We need to reemphasize, too, that the policy level is also concerned with the *outcomes* that are the consequences of the policy outputs. As we shall show in chapters XII and XIII, it is a long step from the adoption and even implementation of policies designed to increase economic performance or to equalize income distribution to actual achievement of these goals. The outputs of the political system interact with the previous state of the environment and with other events taking place simultaneously within it. An increase in educational expenditures, for example, may be diminished by bureaucratic inefficiency and corruption; the effects of the expenditures may be marginal, if the population is largely illiterate; and rapid population increases may mean that the expenditures per pupil are actually declining.

The policy analysis will also be concerned with the *feedback* effects by which successful or unsuccessful efforts to change the environment have consequences for a new round of political inputs. For example, as net expenditures for each pupil decline, parent groups may articulate new demands for further increases in the education budget. Such feedback effects send continuing waves of political demand and support interactions through the conversion process. They will also have system-level effects as new policy attitudes and new positive or negative opinions of the regime itself are formed, and as new leaders emerge to shape and respond to these attitudes.

INTERACTION OF THE THREE LEVELS

These points recall to us the perspective from which we began our discussion of the three levels: the need to deal with the political system as a system. In our sections and chapters we may discuss individual levels and specific functions and structures. But these are always interacting simultaneously. Indeed, the stability of the system itself depends on a dynamic balance among all three levels. If the same structures (such as competitive parties, elections, and a legislature) are to go on performing the same functions (such as interest aggregation and policy making) over time, such synchronization must be achieved between system, process, and policy levels. If the synchronization breaks down, then strains appear and new leaders may be recruited. These leaders may use the existing structures to create new structures, as a Hitler who is pledged, once elected, to do away with democracy; or they may lead efforts to adapt and rebuild the system, as an Adenauer or a de Gaulle. Or existing elites may change their attitudes and role performance, as when the military intervenes and takes over control of the conversion functions. We shall discuss the implications of all three functional levels for the dynamics of change.

COMPARATIVE ANALYSIS OF POLITICAL SYSTEMS

The approach to comparative politics that we have thus far presented gives us a basis for comparative analysis. Without going too deeply into the philosophical and methodological issues, we want to comment on the implications and possibilities of comparative analysis, in particular on the distinct elements of description and theory building.

COMPARATIVE DESCRIPTION

It is no simple matter to describe and compare systems of political life that are very different from each other in size, formal arrangements, customs, and policies. The difficulty can be likened to the bewilderment that often overcame explorers encountering new cultures. First, there was the problem of translation, finding language equivalents for describing local arrangements. Initially, the local term was often used. Later, on the basis of apparent goals and internal arrangements, it might be agreed that many of the terms for certain types of leader could be roughly translated as "chief" or "headman" whereas others might be translated as "king." In a similar way one can classify political structures according to ostensible functions and internal relationships; otherwise comparison is virtually impossible. One is left with the facts that in Germany there is an organization called a Bundestag; in the United States, an organization called a Congress; in Britain, an organization called a Parliament. An essential step is to classify these, at least in terms of their goals and arrangements, as legislative assemblies.

But a structure's self-designation according to function may be highly misleading as one attempts to compare political systems. As many political observers in different parts of the world have discovered, structures that look the same may indeed work very differently. To describe and compare adequately, therefore, one needs to know how the structures function in the political system. Our use of what is called *structural-functional* analysis is designed to confront this problem explicitly. We ask the question directly: What structures are performing the functions of interest articulation, policy making, and so on in each political system? This structural-functional problem must be faced by all serious students of comparative politics, even if they do not solve it the way we do. They may face it implicitly by looking only at systems where roughly the same structures are performing the same functions, as in confining comparative analysis to competitive parliamentary democracies or Soviet-style Communist regimes. Or they may face it by using some other structural-functional scheme. But if they ignore the problem, by assuming that legislative assemblies will be alike and can be studied comparatively in many systems without regard to actual functions, they are bound to get into trouble. The legislature in Mexico and that in the Soviet Union perform very different functions from the American Congress, and any useful and sophisticated analysis will rapidly come to grips with that fact.

BUILDING THEORIES IN COMPARATIVE POLITICS

When we have defined our political terms, or concepts, we can use those concepts to compare different political systems. And our ability to make comparisons in turn allows us to formulate theories.[8] Concepts and comparisons are not theories; they are based on definitions and definitional relationships. Theories are based on empirical observation and may be empirically tested. They state the relationships that have been observed between conditions and patterns in political life, and accumulate credibility as evidence appears to support them. Thus, the concepts in this book may be used in formulating theories. As they are related to empirical study and research on political systems, they act as the framework for theory building. And we believe that the approach we have chosen and the concepts we are using can accommodate a great many theories. Within this framework many apparently unrelated theories and generalizations can be related and their usefulness enhanced.

As we look at political functions and processes at all three levels of analysis, we will attempt to draw on some of the recent theories in comparative and American politics. Occasionally, we will also propose some theories of our own. Comparative analysis is, of course, crucial in generating scientific theories, as it offers settings and relationships unfamiliar to the expert in any single area. Any empirical science has a certain conservative bias; its theories must accumulate around existing events. Genuine comparative analysis of the widest range of known present and historical cases is the best protection available against such blinders on human possibilities.

Comparative analysis is also invaluable in testing the credibility of political theories. Political systems cannot be put in the laboratory, where their relationships and settings can be varied and checked. Hence, the comparison of natural variations in wealth, literacy, international

---

8 Our views on the philosophy of science are necessarily greatly simplified and abbreviated in this context. For the reader interested in some of the issues, we recommend the following works: Carl G. Hempel, *The Philosophy of Natural Science* (Englewood Cliffs: Prentice-Hall, 1966); Robert T. Holt and John E. Turner, *The Methodology of Comparative Research* (New York: Free Press, 1970), esp. chaps. 1–2; Thomas S. Kuhn, *The Structure of Scientific Revolutions* (Chicago: University of Chicago Press, 1970); Adam Przeworski and Henry Tuene, *The Logic of Comparative Social Inquiry* (New York: John Wiley, 1970); Arthur L. Stinchcombe, *Constructing Social Theories* (New York: Harcourt Brace Jovanovich, 1968); Sidney Verba, "Some Dilemmas in Comparative Research," *World Politics* 19 (1967); Gabriel A. Almond and Stephen Genco, "Clouds, Clocks, and the Study of Politics," *World Politics* 29 (July 1977).

tension, culture, party systems, and the like is a major method of testing theories. It is not our purpose in this book to test theories that have been proposed. Here we will be concerned with providing the comparative framework for the building and testing of theories.

POLITICAL DEVELOPMENT

A major concept that we have thus far touched upon only in passing is political development. Historically we can observe general trends in recent centuries toward increased secularization in the culture and increased differentiation in the structure of political systems. In chapters II and III we shall elaborate on these concepts that define the level of political development and, indeed, shall use them in chapter III as the basis for a typology of political systems. But here we shall introduce them briefly and suggest their relationship to social modernization and political change.

SECULARIZATION

Secularization is a process of attitude change, whereby people become more oriented to cause-and-effect relationships they can see in the world around them. It is closely bound up with the development of technology and science and the spread of education and communications media. In the secular culture individuals tend to believe in their ability to shape their environment, and they adopt courses of action to help them do so. We may illustrate this concept by comparing a political leader in a modern democracy with one in a traditional or primitive African political system. When running for office, for instance, a modern democratic political leader will gather substantial amounts of information about the constituency that he hopes will elect him. He makes estimates of the distribution and intensity of demands of one kind or another; he uses creative imagination to identify a possible combination of demands that may lead to his receiving a majority of votes in his constituency. A village chief in a tribal society operates largely with a given set of goals, which have developed and been hallowed by custom, and with a given set of means of attaining those goals. He owes his own position, in many cases, to combinations of physical characteristics and inheritance. The secularization of culture requires that these traditional orientations and attitudes give way to more dynamic decision-making processes involving gathering information, evaluating information, laying out alternative courses of action, selecting a course of action from among these possible courses, and testing whether or not a given course of action is producing the consequences intended.

In the discussion of cultural patterns, too sharp a line is often drawn between societies characterized by traditional cultures and those charac-

terized by modern cultures. The fact is that strongly secular elements
exist in traditional cultures, and traditional elements persist in the most
modern of cultures. A major empirical observation that follows from the
study of both types of societies is this: all political systems have mixed
political cultures, but they differ in the relative dominance and mixture
of the components.

DIFFERENTIATION

The structural aspect of political development is differentiation. In
differentiation roles change and become more specialized or autonomous,
new types of specialized roles are established, or new specialized structures and subsystems emerge or are created. Specialized organizations for
collecting taxes, training officials, communicating messages, maintaining
order, mobilizing support, and the like are introduced or split off from
earlier structures. When we speak of role differentiation and structural
differentiation, we refer not only to the appearance of new types of roles
and the transformation of older ones; we refer also to changes that may
take place in the relationship between roles or between structures. Thus,
for example, courts were established as separate structures long before
they acquired independence or autonomy from other structures of the
political system. In speaking of the developmental aspect of role and
structure, then, we are interested not only in the emergence of new types
of roles or the atrophy of old ones, but also in the interactions between
roles and structures.

When we use the developmental concepts of structural differentiation
and cultural secularization, we do not assert that there is any inevitable
trend in these directions in political systems over time. If we examine
the histories of political systems, it becomes quite clear that regressions
or reversals occur commonly. Thus, the Roman Empire reached a very
high level of structural differentiation and cultural secularization, then
fell apart into a large number of less differentiated and less secularized
political systems. It is now also clear, as we shall discuss in chapters II
and III, that there are important limits to the developmental process.

THE HYPOTHESIS OF POLITICAL DEVELOPMENT
AND POLICY CAPACITY

The concepts of political development are especially interesting and
important because of a widely discussed theory about the consequences
of structural and cultural development for public policy. A structurally
differentiated political system with a secularized political culture will
have an increased capability to shape its domestic and international
environments. Whether it will, in fact, expand its policy performance is
a matter of conscious choice for the policy-making coalitions. But a de-

veloped political system has the possibility of adopting policies that can more effectively change the environment. Most policy makers would like to be able to improve economic productivity, increase life spans through disease control, enhance internal and international security, and the like; achievement of cultural secularization and structural differentiation makes it possible for them to do so.

MODERNIZATION AND DEVELOPMENT

It should be clear from our definition that socioeconomic modernization and political development are not the same thing. The exposure of populations to modern technology and culture usually does have a secularizing influence. But the forces of economic and social change do not necessarily produce political development, although they seem everywhere to produce a powerful *desire* for political changes that will improve environmental conditions. And, on the other hand, political development has sometimes taken place under conditions other than those of economic and social transformation.

The events that may lead to political development come from the international environment, from the domestic society, or from political elites within the political system itself. A political system may be threatened by a rival nation or invaded by it. In confronting this challenge, it may find that it needs more resources and more effective ways of organizing and deploying its resources — a standing army, for example, or an officialdom to collect taxes. It may have to adapt itself structurally, that is, develop new roles, if it is to survive. If the international threat continues over a long period of time, the system may have to adapt itself culturally, inculcating values of militance and acquiring the skills and values associated with warfare. The challenge may come from internal change in the society of which the political system is a part. Thriving commerce and manufactures may create a middle class that demands to be heard in the formulation and implementation of public policy. Growth of communication and transportation may increase the desires of the poor for a better life, both absolutely and relatively to their more fortunate fellow citizens. The political elites themselves may confront the political system with a challenge as they seek to increase the resources available to them for the purpose of constructing impressive buildings or monuments, or of creating a military force capable of conquering neighboring political systems, or of enhancing the welfare of their people.

The impulses for political development involve some significant change in the magnitude and content of the flow of inputs into the political system. *Development* results when the existing structure and culture of the political system are unable to cope with the problem or challenge without further structural differentiation and cultural secularization. It is also possible for a decline in the flow of inputs, an imbalance between support and demand inputs, or a significant change in demands to result in negative or regressive "development." The capabilities of the political system may decline or be overloaded; roles and structures may atrophy; the culture may regress to a more traditional pattern of orientation. History provides many examples of the decline of empires and their breakup into less differentiated and less secularized components.[9] Transitional and developed societies also may find their differentiated modern structures collapsing or becoming functionally irrelevant when environmental strains become too great. Typically, in such cases, the period of collapse or transition is marked by violence and challenges to legitimacy, as groups use whatever resources are available to them in the struggle to control or survive.[10]

We need some way of talking about these challenges that may lead to political development, these changes in the magnitude and content of the flow of inputs that put the existing culture and structure under strain. As a beginning, we might suggest five types of problems for or challenges to a political system. The first of these is the problem of penetration and integration; we call it the problem of *state building*. The second type of system-development problem is that of loyalty and commitment, which we call *nation building*. The third problem is that of *participation*, the pressure from groups in the society for having a part in the policy making of the political system. The fourth problem is that of *economy building*, the use of the political system to increase the productive capacity of the domestic economy and to make these goods and services available to the society. The fifth challenge is that of *distribution*, or welfare, the pressure from the domestic society to employ the power of the political system to redistribute income, wealth, opportunity, and honor.

In chapter XIII we shall discuss in more detail these challenges as they confront political systems in the contemporary world. Social and economic modernization has had great impact on political systems because exposure to modern world culture and participation in contemporary international trade and communications, as well as deliberate ideo-

[9] See Samuel P. Huntington, "Political Development and Political Decay," *World Politics* 17 (April 1965); Samuel P. Huntington, *Political Order in Changing Societies* (New Haven: Yale University Press, 1968); S. N. Eisenstadt, *The Political Systems of Empires* (New York: Free Press of Glencoe, 1963).

[10] See especially Huntington, *Political Order in Changing Societies*, chaps. 1, 4. Huntington emphasizes that when agreement on the legitimate means of resolving conflicts and making policy breaks down, each group employs any means available to it, the most spectacular and effective of which is typically the use of armed force by the military. See pp. 196 ff.

logical mobilization, have tended to bring all of these challenges to bear simultaneously. The desperate effort of political leaders to devise strategies for meeting these challenges through manageable development policies is the primary topic of our developmental analysis. The bitter tradeoffs that must be often made between different political goals in implementing such strategies is a major concern in our concluding comments on political evaluation.

POLITICAL GOODS

One final concept must be introduced in our preliminary overview: political goods. All too often political analysts attempt to avoid the problem of evaluating political systems. Such attempts are usually only superficially successful. Although descriptions and analyses in comparative politics may not contain such terms as "good" and "bad," the very focus upon one level or one set of problems over another tends to involve implicit value choices. Our own earlier analysis has been criticized, not inappropriately perhaps, for its tendency to emphasize values of stability and order. Our interest in conflict and stability, their causes and consequences, often led us to look at problems from a perspective in which the maintenance of the existing system loomed large. At the same time, our interest in citizen participation and autonomy often led to criticism that we valued democratic processes at the expense of other goods.

In our opinion, the best way of dealing with the values implicit in choosing problems and perspectives is a straightforward look at *all* types of political values. Although we cannot, of course, deal with every cultural and structural nuance that may itself be valued, we shall attempt in our concluding chapter explicitly to consider classes of goods that are associated with the different levels of analysis of the political system. Thus, it seems clear that both order and stability, on one hand, and creative adaptation and response to changing conditions, on the other, are goods associated with the system level of analysis. They are goods that are often in short-run conflict with each other, and naturally the choice between them may be a source of dismay to individuals or a source of conflict between groups. Participation in the political process, compliance with and support for political directives, and justice and equity before the law are all values, or goods, associated with the process level of analysis of the political system. Welfare, security, and liberty are goods at the policy level, each with components that must be given careful consideration. These domestic goods also have their counterparts in the international arena, and the sacrifice of goods in one area or at one level for the gains at another, domestic or international, is a frequent value choice faced by political leaders.

We shall attempt in our concluding analysis to outline some of these types of goods and to suggest lines of preliminary investigation of the conflicts between their realization in the long run and the short run. For though some of these goods may be more precious to some individuals, and other goods to other individuals, and though the forms most desired may vary across cultures, many of these goods will be simultaneously desired. We can also attain a more balanced evaluation as observers by considering which goods are being produced by different political systems and to what degree. For example, we can see empirically whether sacrifices in liberty are being traded off against gains in stability and security. As such efforts to incorporate an evaluative perspective into a scientific analytic framework are not common, we shall be making little more than a beginning in this effort. But we consider it our obligation to make the effort, and we hope that our readers will make their own contributions and, at least, will see their own values in a broader comparative perspective.

CHAPTER II

Political Culture

POLITICAL CULTURE is the set of attitudes, beliefs, and feelings about politics current in a nation at a given time. This political culture has been shaped by the nation's history and by the ongoing processes of social, economic, and political activity. The attitude patterns that have been shaped in past experience have important constraining effects on future political behavior. The political culture affects the conduct of individuals in their political roles, the content of their political demands, and their responses to laws.

Through the use of public opinion surveys one can discover the attitudes that citizens bring to the political arena, or that keep them from that arena. We can thus anticipate their responses to new circumstances. Through elite interviews, public statements, speeches, and writings, as well as from past behavior, one can get some impressions of the attitudes, goals, and strategies that guide political elites in their conduct. In viewing these attitudes as propensities that may affect future behavior, one must not forget that they are themselves affected, in a dynamic process, by the political experiences of the society.

Political culture shapes the actions of individuals performing political roles throughout the political system. At the same time, the opportunities and pressures established by the existing political structures will shape that culture. Culture and structure, attitude and behavior, interact with each other continuously, as individuals learn and act, and learn through action.[1] It is useful to look at both culture and structure and to

---

[1] Brian Barry, and others, have criticized much political cultural analysis for failing to give adequate stress to the interactive and interdependent relationship between culture and structure. Brian Barry, *Sociologists, Economists, and Democracy* (London: Collier Macmillan, 1970), pp. 48 ff. Perhaps the best introduction to the concept of political culture is the essays in Lucian W. Pye and Sidney Verba, eds., *Political Culture and Political Development* (Princeton: Princeton University Press, 1965).

discover the pattern of attitudes that underlies, shapes, and is shaped by
the ongoing activities of political life. In approaching any specific political system, one should develop a map of the most important contours
of its political culture and a corresponding map of its structures and
functions. As we discuss each of the political functions, and as we analyze
performance, we shall keep returning to the effects of political culture.

CONCEPTS FOR THE ANALYSIS OF POLITICAL CULTURE
COMPONENTS OF INDIVIDUAL ORIENTATION

We may distinguish three components of an individual's attitudes
toward political objects: cognitive, affective, and evaluative.[2] Individual
orientations toward any political object may be viewed in terms of these
three components. Thus, an individual may have relatively accurate knowledge of the working of the political system, its leading figures, and the
current policy problems. This knowledge would be the cognitive component of orientation toward the system as a whole. He might, however,
have feelings of rejection toward the system; perhaps his family and
friends have long harbored such attitudes. He would be unlikely to respond favorably to demands upon him by the authorities. This is the
affective component. Finally, he may have some moral evaluation of the
system. Perhaps his democratic norms lead him to evaluate the system
as not sufficiently responsive to political demands, or his ethical norms
lead him to condemn the level of corruption.

These three components of political orientations are related. In order
to form an evaluation of the political system, one must have some knowledge of it. Knowledge of politics may be shaped by and may also shape
feelings about politics. But although these components shape each other
in various ways, they may be separately affected by the processes that
form individual attitudes. Some studies suggest, for example, that experiences in early childhood, other things being equal, have more effect
on later feelings and commitments in politics than they have on the
adult's knowledge or evaluation of the political system. The latter
change more rapidly as a result of adult learning.

CONSISTENCY ACROSS POLITICAL ORIENTATIONS

Thus far, we have been considering one political orientation at a
time. However, one of the most important aspects of an individual's
orientation to politics is the relationship between different attitudes:
the general amount and type of consistency or, as it is often called, "con-

[2] For the origins of these categories, see Talcott Parsons and Edward A. Shils, eds.,
Toward a General Theory of Action (Cambridge: Harvard University Press, 1951),
pp. 58 ff.

straint" in the citizen's view of the political world.[3] This aspect can be most easily understood by considering a citizen's attitudes toward different policy issues. If his views on one type of issue, such as foreign policy, are unrelated to his views on another issue, such as the extent of governmental intervention in the economy or racial integration, we say that his policy propensities are unconstrained. This means that we cannot predict his attitudes on one set of issues by knowing his attitudes on another set of issues. It means also that changes in one set of opinions are not going to affect his opinions on other issues. If preferences on one issue are related to those on all the other issues — for example, by knowing the citizen's position on welfare, we can also predict his position on civil rights and military intervention abroad — we say that his attitudes are highly constrained, that he possesses a highly consistent set of preferences.

If most citizens have very consistent sets of policy attitudes and if these fit together in the same way, then the entire policy preference map of the political culture can be represented by a summary dimension — such as a right-to-left continuum. In Italy, for example, Barnes found that citizens who favored income redistribution also tended to oppose the activity of the Catholic church in politics and to take a leftist foreign policy position. Most citizens could identify themselves, and be identified, as occupying a consistent right, center, or left position on the nation's spectrum of policy issues.[4]

Studies of American policy preference, on the other hand, have tended to find much less issue constraint, especially in the 1950s.[5] Indeed, American studies of cross-attitude consistency of citizens' opinions initially suggested that only political leaders might have the information and skills to develop consistent preference systems.[6] But it is now clear that the nature of policy problems, especially their penetration into the lives of average citizens, the choices that seem available to citizens, and changes in education and general interest can increase or decrease citizen attitude consistency. Nie and Anderson showed that attitude consistency in the United States declined in the 1950s from its level in the depression

[3] One of the first and best discussions of constraint is Philip Converse, "The Nature of Mass Belief Systems," in David Apter, ed., *Ideology and Discontent* (New York: Free Press, 1964).

[4] Samuel H. Barnes, "Left, Right, and the Italian Voter," *Comparative Political Studies* 4 (July 1971), pp. 157–75.

[5] Converse, "Nature of Mass Belief Systems"; Angus Campbell et al., *The American Voter* (New York: John Wiley, 1960); Philip E. Converse, "Attitudes and Non-Attitudes," in Edward Tufte, ed., *The Quantitative Study of Politics* (New York: Addison-Wesley, 1971).

[6] See Converse, "Nature of Mass Belief Systems."

years, but rose again in the 1960s in response to pressing problems and to the clearer choices offered by parties and candidates.[7]

Although we have used policy attitudes across issues as our example of constraint, the concept of constraint is important in looking at all the aspects of the policy map. We very much want to know whether or not citizens' propensities toward participation in the political process are affected by their perceptions of policy issues and alternatives. Can we predict that the issue extremists are more likely to participate in politics, for example, than those who take moderate policy positions? Similarly, we are interested in the constraint between the citizens' propensity to obey the laws and their views of how well the government is performing.

ATTITUDE DISTRIBUTIONS AND SUBCULTURES

There is a good deal of variation across nations in the distribution of political attitudes among different groups in their populations. Most Americans may agree on their evaluation of the Constitution, for example, or on a few issues, such as the desirability of avoiding nuclear war and preventing famine. Most French citizens may share a common affection for France as a nation and culture. Most Nigerians may agree that economic development is a desirable national goal, along with the elimination of disease and starvation. In such cases we may speak of this as a general element of "the American political culture," or "the French political culture," or "the Nigerian political culture."

On many issues, however, citizens may disagree on the importance of a national problem, the best solution to a crisis, the best type of government for the nation, or the relative importance of political stability, an end to inflation, and national security. In such cases we must describe the distribution of attitudes among the citizens in the nation. There are many ways in which opinions on even a single issue, or the orientations toward even a single object, can be distributed. We can suggest the general range through a pair of extreme examples.

Figure II.1 shows distributions of opinion on an important policy issue in two political cultures: a highly consensual culture and a polarized culture. The vertical axis shows the percentage of citizens who favor each position on the issue. The horizontal axis shows the positions on the issue, as a right-to-left continuum. For simplicity we can label these

---

[7] Norman H. Nie with Kristi Anderson, "Mass Belief Systems Revisited," *Journal of Politics* 36 (September 1974); 541–91; and Norman H. Nie, Sidney Verba, and John Petrocik, *The Changing American Voter* (Cambridge: Harvard University Press, 1976), chaps. 8, 9, 11. Also see the review of American and comparative findings by Philip Converse, "Public Opinion and Voting Behavior," in Fred I. Greenstein and Nelson W. Polsby, *Handbook of Political Science*, vol. 2 (Reading, Mass.: Addison-Wesley, 1975).

Figure II.1. *Consensual and Polarized Distributions of Preference in the Political Culture*

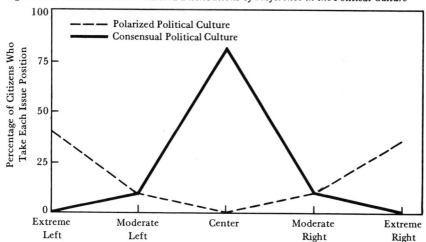

Note: It is assumed that only one salient dimension exists and that all citizens have a clear, preferred position.

positions as ranging from extreme radical to extreme conservative. In the consensual culture, the distribution of opinion is a narrow "bell" or even a "spike," with most citizens holding a single opinion. In the graph we represent that opinion as being at the moderate center; but it might well be at an extreme, as when most citizens favor introducing social security or maintaining peace.

In the polarized policy culture, most citizens fall at the extremes, in a U-shaped distribution of preference. Some important differences between these two policy cultures are obvious. In the consensual culture, there is general agreement on appropriate policy on this key issue; most procedures for selecting political leaders will yield an elite policy subculture that is like the majority; most citizens will be happy with the adoption of policies reflecting that consensus. But in the polarized culture there is sharp disagreement; minor differences in the way leaders are selected could easily result in a chief executive with opinions very different from those of the majority; *any* policy that is chosen will make a large number of citizens unhappy.[8]

Although we have used an issue example, the problem of distribution applies to any political orientation. Indeed, citizens may be in more

[8] See the further discussion of the implications of polarized and consensual distributions in chap. IX. For an empirical description of increased polarization in American policy propensities between 1956 and the early 1970s, see Nie, Verba, and Petrocik, op. cit., pp. 142–44, and chaps. 12, 18.

agreement on policy than on their role in the political process or on the best type of political system. French and Italian citizens have historically been in more disagreement on the type of regime — monarchy, Communist or Fascist government, democracy — than on many concrete policies. People in Northern Ireland and in Lebanon are in more disagreement on the political structure of the state itself than on economic policies. And there have typically existed sharp differences within some nations on the orientations to citizen roles, some highly involved and others virtually ignorant of the existence of the nation-state. As we have already suggested in the discussion of constraint, distribution patterns may either be similar across various issues and orientations or show great diversity, with polarization on one issue and agreement on others.

When we find patterns of distribution that persist over time, we may speak of political subcultures. What we do and do not define as a separate subculture depends largely on the nature of the concerns and problems in question. An observer of American politics may view the liberal and conservative wings of the Democratic party as policy subcultures, whereas a comparative analyst might dismiss them as being so firmly within the more general American political culture as to be unworthy of separate designation. There are some subcultures of such distinctiveness that they are difficult to ignore, especially when related to enduring cleavages of language, class, religion, and caste. In a nation such as India or Nigeria these political subculture differences pose great problems for any regime.

SYSTEM CULTURE

Political authorities are legitimate if the citizens in the society are willing to obey the rules that the authorities make and implement, not merely because the citizens will be punished if they disobey, but because the citizens believe that they ought to obey. If most citizens believe in the legitimacy of the authorities, the laws can be implemented with relative ease and efficiency, and the need to spend resources on enforcement will be lessened. Moreover, if some basis of legitimacy exists, the authorities will have time and discretion to deal with social and economic problems under difficult conditions. Because it is so much easier to get compliance when citizens and elites believe in the legitimacy of the authorities, virtually all governments, even the most brutal and coercive, try to make citizens believe that political rules ought to be obeyed and that coercion can legitimately be used by the authorities to enforce them.

Political legitimacy may have many different bases. In a traditional society, legitimacy may depend on the rulers' inherited status, on obedience to certain religious customs in making and implementing their decisions, and on the scope and content of the decisions. In a modern democratic political system, the legitimacy of the authorities will depend on their being selected in competitive elections and on their following the prescribed constitutional procedures in making laws, both of which procedures presumably ensure responsiveness to citizens' demands. In other political cultures, the leaders may promise to transform citizens' lives for the better, based on their special grace, wisdom, or ideology, without responding to the specific demands of citizens.[9]

The bases of legitimacy are important because they set the rules for a kind of exchange between authorities and citizens. As soon as a political system is sufficiently differentiated to have special roles for policy makers, the question of their legitimacy becomes important. The capacity of a political system to extract resources, regulate behavior, and distribute goods and services will be shaped by the level and nature of legitimacy of the authorities. In a general sense, if legitimacy declines, performance will suffer, although coercion may be used to force the compliance of many. If a dispute arises as to which authorities are legitimate, the consequence is often civil war or revolution.

Legitimacy is a complex mixture of the procedure and substance of policy enactment by the authorities. In many contemporary societies, there is a very explicit connection between the rulers' claim that their actions and the constitution that generated them reflect citizen interests; and the time frame is a very short one. In such societies, the support for the political regime — the type of structures that perform recruitment and policy making, in particular — will be rather quickly affected by the performance of the authorities in meeting the preferences of citizens. Table II.1 shows the relative speed with which support declined in the United States and Britain, but improved in France and Germany, in response to the political experiences of these nations in the 1950s and 1960s.

In a less modern society, the claim to legitimacy may rest on much less immediate promises of beneficial performance. The belief that individuals can do little to change their circumstances places much less pressure on the political authorities. The legitimacy may well be bound up in complex religious customs and beliefs, which are strongly reinforced and which change only slowly. Nonetheless, even most traditional societies have some long-range performance expectations built into their norms of legitimacy: if crops fail, enemies invade, or floods destroy, then the

---

[9] This selection of examples is suggested, of course, by Max Weber's typology of traditional, rational-legal, and charismatic bases of authority. See *From Max Weber: Essays in Sociology*, ed. H. H. Gerth and C. W. Mills (New York: Oxford University Press, 1946), pp. 245 ff.

Table II.1. *Changing Levels of Support in Four Democratic Regimes*

American confidence in regime equity [a]		1958	1964	1968	1972	1973
Percentage of citizens rejecting the proposition that U.S. government is for the benefit of a few only.		82%	70%	58%	43%	37%

British confidence in electoral regime responsiveness [b]			1963	1964	1966
Over the years, how much do you think that having elections makes the government pay attention to what the people think?	Good deal		57%	47%	46%
	Some		32	24	26
	Not much		11	29	28
	Total		100%	100%	100%

French comparative regime evaluation [c]	1958– 4th Republic		1965– 5th Republic	
	Britain	USA	Britain	USA
French functions better than	7%	5%	25%	11%
French functions as well as	33	17	25	26
French functions not so well as	39	58	14	30
No reply	21	17	36	33
Total	100%	97%	100%	100%

German regime preference [d]	1953	1956	1960	1965
Percentage favoring democracy	57%	67%	74%	79%

[a] Nie, Verba, and Petrocik, *The Changing American Voter*, p. 278.

[b] David Butler and Donald Stokes, *Political Change in Britain* (New York: St. Martin's Press, 1969), pp. 477, 485, 501. (Answers of "don't know" and "no response" excluded.)

[c] Polls by the Institut Français d'Opinion Publique, reported in Martin Harrison, ed., *French Politics* (Lexington, Mass.: D. C. Heath, 1969), p. 118.

[d] Arnold Heidenheimer, *The Governments of Germany* (New York: Thomas Y. Crowell, 1971), p. 105.

emperor may lose the "mandate of heaven," as in imperial China; or the chiefs, their authority; or the feudal lords, their claim to the loyalty of their serfs.

NATIONAL IDENTITY

Thus far, we have assumed that the legitimacy of the community, the regime, and the authorities are equivalent. It is more useful in discussing legitimacy, however, to consider David Easton's differentiation of three levels of the political system which may receive support from its citizens.[10] The political community is the whole group of individuals who are bound together into a common political process. In the language of political development theory, the problem of support for the political community is often called the problem of national identity.

In many contemporary cases, particularly in Africa, new nations were constructed from a number of ethnic, political, and geographic subnational units that had no common political bonds and whose members by and large had little information or loyalty beyond that to the local unit. The process of nation building involves, in some respects, the dissemination of information about and commitment to the national unit. At some point in the history of any nation, as loyalty to the traditional subnational unit conflicts with national loyalties and goals, the issues of the political community are likely to become paramount, creating a major political crisis.[11] The legitimacy of the national community, the compliance it can properly command, is questioned, and separatist movements appear. Even in long-established nations, the emergence of new issues, particularly those which touch linguistic and cultural identities, may reopen the question of appropriate boundaries of the political community. Scottish and Welsh nationalism in Great Britain, Breton and Corsican separatism in France, Basque and Catalonian separatism in Spain, and Quebecois separatism in Canada are current examples.

Resolving crises of national identity may be a very difficult problem indeed. An ethnic or religious group may perceive that its whole social and religious structure is threatened by the creation of schools, the induction of young people into the army, or the building of a neighborhood industry. One form of the resolution of conflicts of community loyalty may be an intense nationalism focused around a charismatic leader, such as President Nasser was in Egypt. Another possibility is the division of the national state into two nations, as in the case of Pakistan and Bangladesh. More moderate solutions are illustrated by political systems such as Mexico, where a high degree of general system support, a single dominant party, well-accepted revolutionary symbols, and some coercion have created a measure of cohesion among groups and points of view.

---

[10] Easton, *A Systems Analysis of Political Life.*

[11] Cynthia Enloe, *Ethnic Conflict and Political Development* (Boston: Little, Brown, 1972); Douglas A. Hibbs, *Mass Political Violence* (New York: John Wiley, 1974); Eric Nordlinger, *Conflict Regulation in Divided Societies* (Cambridge: Center for International Affairs, Harvard University, 1972); Alvin Rabushka and Kenneth Shepsle, *Politics in Plural Societies* (Columbus: Merrill, 1972). Also see the essays by Myron Weiner, Clifford Geertz, Immanuel Wallerstein, and Aristide Zolberg, in Jason L. Finkle and Richard W. Gable, *Political Development and Social Change,* 2d ed. (New York: John Wiley, 1971).

REGIMES AND AUTHORITIES

Within the political community there is an important distinction between the regime and the authorities. By the regime is meant the set of structures performing political functions and the norms governing that performance. By authorities is meant those individuals who occupy roles in the regime at any one time. It is possible for citizens and key elites, such as bureaucrats and military officers, to support the regime even though they disapprove of the specific individuals in office or their policies. Or, conversely, citizens and elites may give support to individuals, but not to the structures of the regime.

In France, support for community, regime, and authorities have been unusually distinct. French citizens have had, by and large, a strong sense of national community and have been willing to suffer great hardship and danger to fight for France's national existence. Yet, support for particular regimes has been tenuous for over two centuries, with great divergence of opinion on the appropriate forms of citizen participation, policy making by elites, and recruitment of leaders. At some points, it seemed that particular individuals, such as de Gaulle in 1958–62, had more support than did the regime. Hence, in 1958, de Gaulle was called to power in a national crisis and received the support of a majority of French citizens to devise a new regime: the Fifth Republic. Similarly, at the time of independence in many new nations, the leader of the independence movement had more support than did the new form of government. A critical problem of political development in these nations has been transferring legitimacy from the individuals to the regime. President Nasser's apparent success in endowing legitimacy to his regime in Egypt greatly surprised observers, who predicted its collapse after his death. It remains to be seen if such leaders as Kenyatta in Kenya or Tito in Yugoslavia will be equally successful where so many have already failed.

PROCESS CULTURE

A second major aspect of political culture is the set of orientations toward the political process. Let us look at two examples of these orientations: (1) views of one's own influence in the political process, and (2) views of relationships with other actors.

VIEWS OF THE SELF IN POLITICS: PAROCHIALS, SUBJECTS, AND PARTICIPANTS

The first major cross-national study of political cultures introduced the terms *parochials, subjects,* and *participants* to characterize citizen differences in awareness of the political process and of their potential influence.[12] Parochials are those citizens who have little or no awareness of the political system. They have no perception of their possible influence or obligation regarding it. The definition depends, of course, on the process level one has in mind. The illiterate farmer may be ignorant of national politics, but active in village decisions. But the general concept draws attention to those citizens whose lives are concerned with nonpolitical events and who develop no sense of a relationship to the national political process. Although pure parochials are rare in economically developed nations with widespread literacy, penetrative mass media, and bureaucracies, they remain a common feature of traditional and transitional societies.

Subjects are those citizens who become part of the national political system and perceive its impact, or potential impact, on their lives. But their view of their own role in politics remains that of subjects, affected by governmental action, but not active in shaping it. They may have policy preferences, as well as positive or negative expectations about their treatment by police and administrators. They may even develop a sense of legitimacy toward, or alienation from, the regime and the authorities. But they remain passive in their orientation toward political participation.

Participants, on the other hand, develop an awareness of the input processes of the society, those which facilitate their own involvement in politics. They also develop attitudes that encourage their use of opportunities for participation. One such attitude is a sense of confidence that they can affect national political events if they try to do so. Table II.2 shows citizens' perceptions that they could do something to affect local and national decisions in nine nations. Citizens who perceive that they could do something may, indeed, be considered potential participants. Although parochials, subjects, and participants can be found in varying degrees in all nations, obviously there were many more such participant-oriented citizens in the United States and Britain in 1960 than in the other nations shown in the table. The more participant-oriented cultures in the United States and Britain in part resulted from higher levels of education and organization in these nations and in part reflected specific historical and political experiences in these cultures.[13] In most political cultures, naturally, citizens feel more confident of their ability to deal

[12] Gabriel A. Almond and Sidney Verba, *The Civic Culture* (Princeton: Princeton University Press, 1963); and see the essays in Pye and Verba, op. cit.

[13] Almond and Verba, op. cit.; Norman H. Nie, G. Bingham Powell, Jr., and Kenneth Prewitt, "Social Structure and Political Participation," *American Political Science Review* 63 (June and September 1969): 361–78, 808–32. [This periodical will hereafter be cited as *APSR*.]

Table II.2. *Participant Citizens in Nine Nations: Percentage Who Say
They Can Do Something About an Unjust Regulation*

Nation	Unjust local regulation			Unjust national regulation		
	Say they can do something	Say they can do nothing; Don't know	Total	Say they can do something	Say they can do nothing; Don't know	Total
USA	77%	23%	100%	75%	25%	100%
Netherlands	–	–	–	46	54	100
W. Germany	62	38	100	38	62	100
Britain	78	22	100	62	38	100
Austria	46	54	100	–	–	–
Italy	51	49	100	28	72	100
Venezuela (Peasants only)	29	71	100	20	80	100
Mexico (Nonrural)	52	48	100	38	62	100
Turkey (Peasants only)	67	33	100	26	74	100

Note: Citizens were asked, in their own language, what they could do if an unjust regulation were passed by their local authorities; then, what they could do if an unjust law were passed by the national legislature. For the United States, Britain, West Germany, Italy, and Mexico, results are reported in Almond and Verba, *The Civic Culture*, p. 185. Other sources: the Netherlands, Arend Lijphart, *The Politics of Accommodation*, rev. ed. (Berkeley and Los Angeles: University of California Press, 1976), pp. 152–53; Austria, "Participation and Partisanship Survey," carried out by Institut f. empirische Sozialforschung, 1969; Venezuela and Turkey peasant data cited by John R. Mathiason, "The Venezuelan Campesino," in Frank Bonilla and Jose A. Silva Michelena, *A Strategy for Research on Social Policy* (Cambridge: M.I.T. Press, 1967), p. 139, referring to a Turkish survey conducted by Frederick Frey as well as to the Venezuelan study described in the Bonilla and Michelena volume.

with local politics than with national politics. These differences are especially striking among the Turkish peasants shown in table II.2, two-thirds of whom mentioned some way in which they could try to influence local politics, although few were nationally participant-oriented.

One must keep in mind, of course, that we are here talking about political culture, not actual participation. The participant citizen, in this sense, is an individual who knows something about politics and feels he or she can be active in it. Such attitudes create a propensity for action, but other factors, such as the difficult registration laws in the United States, will also affect the levels and kinds of behavior. It is now known that participation may take many forms and that many different kinds of attitudes actually facilitate political action.[14] A sense of competence, of the kind shown in table II.2, is only one such attitude. A belief that one has an obligation to be active, as an element of good citizenship, may also be a powerful motive for some kinds of participation. In events such as a national election, in which the individual's participation is to cast one ballot among millions, it may be duty that leads to the greatest propensity to activity. In the decision to contact a leader about a problem, it may be the belief that one can be effective that is most telling. Knowledge of effective strategies of influence may be an important consideration also.[15]

As we discuss the actual participation of citizens, we can explore some of the implications of a participant culture more fully. We should note here, however, that the institutions in a political system will shape the views of citizens about the possibilities of action. There is a continuous interaction between propensities to act and available roles for political activity. In an authoritarian political system, where citizens' participation activities are limited primarily to voting for a single party's candidate, it is unlikely that many citizens will develop much confidence in themselves as able to influence national affairs. At the most they will become "subject-participants," taking advantage of opportunities to contact bureaucrats, or informal "fixers," in order to shape governmental action as it affects their lives. Their citizenship roles are confined to the political output processes. However, if the political system provides diverse means of participation in national politics — as through competitive elections and parties, as well as varied interest groups — the number of participant citizens will increase and have important effects on the number and content of demands.

VIEWS OF OTHER POLITICAL ACTORS:
TRUST AND HOSTILITY

Another relevant feature of political culture is the set of perceptions, beliefs, feelings, and judgments that people have of other political actors. What picture does an individual have of the various social groups in the society? Do individuals see themselves as members of larger social groups, such as classes, ethnic groups, regional groups, and the like? Do they identify themselves with particular parties or factions? Beyond that, how do they feel about those groups of which they are *not* members? How

[14] Sidney Verba and Norman H. Nie, *Participation in America* (New York: Harper & Row, 1972), part 1.

[15] A more complete discussion of participation and types of propensities is presented in chaps. V and VI.

much distance is perceived between the groups? How much political trust and how much political hostility exist?

The question of political trust affects the willingness of citizens to work with others for political goals and the willingness of leaders to form coalitions with other groups. In indicating the importance of citizens' views of themselves as participants, we have treated participation as an individual action. But, in fact, effective participation at a national level requires citizens to join with others. The participation strategies likely to be available will depend in part, as we shall show in later chapters, on the structure of social and political groups in the society. But it will also depend on the simple amount of trust in other actors.

For elites the question of trust and distance affects the nature of individual and intergroup negotiation. The governing of a large nation requires formation of large coalitions in order to have the votes, parliamentary majorities, or other resources necessary to make and implement political decisions. Elite coalition formation will depend in part on the preferences different groups have about salient political issues. But coalitions will also depend on the degree to which groups can trust each other to keep political bargains and be honest in negotiation.[16]

Beyond the question of trust, but related to it, is the question of dislike and hostility, an emotional component of intergroup and interpersonal relations in a society. If groups learn that they are different from each other, and especially if that sense of difference is reinforced by experiences of conflict and injustice, they may develop a strong sense of mutual hostility. This intergroup hostility can become a part of the political culture, reinforced by continuing conflict. Even minor issues may easily convert such diffuse hostility into anger and violence. As numerous studies have shown, aggressive action can be a directly satisfying response to feelings of anger, whether these feelings are displaced frustration from other sources or are occasioned by direct action of the opponent.[17] Unfortunately, aggressive action by one side is only likely to fuel the hostility and frustration of the other, increasing the probability of aggressive counteraction.

A sense of intergroup distance and hostility, then, can create a high

[16] For a discussion of issue differences and trust/hostility as two elements affecting coalition formation, see Gabriel Almond, Scott Flanagan, and Robert Mundt, eds., *Crisis, Choice, and Change* (Boston: Little, Brown, 1973), especially chap. 2. For an interesting study of an elite culture characterized by high levels of interpersonal distrust, see Marvin Zonis, *The Political Elite of Iran* (Princeton: Princeton University Press, 1971); for the opposite case, see Lijphart, op. cit., on the Netherlands.
[17] See the review by Ted Robert Gurr, "Psychological Factors in Civil Violence," *World Politics* 20 (January 1968): 245–278; and Ted Robert Gurr, *Why Men Rebel* (Princeton: Princeton University Press, 1971).

potential for political conflict and can make even a relatively routine process of political decision making difficult. Elites that genuinely dislike and distrust their opponents are more likely to bypass the usual channels of discussion and courteous consultation.[18] They are more likely to oppose compromise, as shown in table II.3. One can see from the sizes of the groups in that table that there is a higher proportion of hostile politicians in the Italian House of Deputies than in the British House of Commons. But within both British and Italian groups, the effect of hostility on conciliatory attitudes is similar.[19] Hostile and suspicious elites are likely to act more aggressively and to interpret the actions of others as threatening, although here, too, the incentives and costs created by the structural setting are important.[20] As illustrated by various tragic cases of intergroup hostility, such as the bloody civil war in Lebanon, the conflict between Protestants and Catholics in Northern Ireland, or the *Violencia* of Colombia, it may be easier to initiate the process of violence between hostile communities than to stop it. After a point, the hostility and violence feed on themselves to create a deadly cycle of reinforcement.

POLICY CULTURE

The third major feature of our political culture map is the pattern of orientations toward public policies. To understand the politics of a system, one must understand the issues and preference distributions salient to those involved. The details of issue preferences, of course, are constantly changing, as different actors and daily events alter the choices perceived as available. But in different policy areas one can generally discern the underlying stances toward political problems that unite and divide a population, shaping the substance of policy approaches and coalition formation.

At the heart of the pattern of policy propensities lies the image of the good society. How do citizens in a society view the ideal society? In a later chapter we shall discuss some general categories of political goods that have been widely used for evaluating societies, past and present.[21] It is likely that we shall find some elements of material welfare, security, and liberty, in both domestic and international arenas, valued by citizens.

---

18 For a review of some theories of hostility and elite conflict, and an empirical test in 50 Austrian communities, see G. Bingham Powell, Jr. with Rodney P. Stiefbold, "Anger, Bargaining, and Mobilization as Middle-Range Theories of Conflict Behavior," *Comparative Politics* 9 (July, 1977): 379–98.

19 Robert Putnam, *The Beliefs of Politicians* (New Haven: Yale University Press, 1973).

20 Powell with Stiefbold, op. cit.; Gurr, *Why Men Rebel*.

21 See chap. XIV.

Table II.3. *Elite Hostility and Opposition to Compromise: British and Italian Politicians*

Measure of opposition to compromise	Britain						Italy					
	Most hostile politicians			Least hostile politicians			Most hostile politicians			Least hostile politicians		
	Agree	Disagree	Total	Agree	Disagree	Total	Agree	Disagree	Total	Agree	Disagree	Total
"To compromise is dangerous because it usually leads to betrayal of our own side."	62%	38%	100% (16)	29%	71%	100% (68)	64%	36%	100% (39)	23%	77%	100% (13)
"In a situation where one side seems clearly right and the other clearly wrong, would 'stick to their guns.'"	50	50	100 (10)	29	71	100 (41)	39	61	100 (28)	11	89	100 (9)
Judged by coders to show little tendency to focus on resolving social and political conflicts.	58	42	100 (19)	27	73	100 (74)	41	59	100 (64)	21	79	100 (19)

Source: Putnam, *Beliefs of Politicians*, p. 59. Putnam's politicians are samples of British MPs and Italian Deputies. The subsample size for each group, such as hostile British politicians, is shown in parentheses. The relative sizes of the hostile and nonhostile subgroups can be seen by comparing the numbers in parentheses for any question.

They may differ, however, on whether equality of welfare or equality of opportunity is the desirable social outcome or they may disagree on the appropriate distribution of welfare in society. In some societies private property is highly valued, whereas in others, communal possessions are the rule.[22]

How the present society is perceived from the evaluative perspective is also of importance for the policy culture. Is the present society perceived as living up to the ideal standards or to some reasonable approximation of them? Or does it fall short? And, a crucial question: What are the beliefs about the individual's capacity to influence his or her fate through political action? If all social outcomes are beyond human control, then the "fit" of present society to an ideal society has little political relevance. If human action is perceived as affecting social outcomes, then there is a powerful impetus for policies that support achieved ideals and seek to attain others.

If most members of the society are satisfied with the present social system, then the course of politics is likely to run smoothly. Table II.4 shows the attitudes of citizens in six European nations and the United States toward the amount of change they believe their societies need. Note that these are evaluations of the societies, not of the political systems. Two striking points emerge. First, rather few citizens in any of these nations favor revolutionary social change, less than 10 percent even in troubled Italy. (The American question refers to radical change, rather than revolution, which is not quite comparable. But even so, few favor it.) Second, in every one of these Western nations in 1973 a majority of all citizens in all social groups favored gradual reform of present society. The United States and Switzerland showed the largest conservative blocs, favoring the society as it is, but even in these countries majorities favored gradual change. It is highly likely that different social groups have different changes in mind, and the nature of the desired changes would be a critical question for the next stage of investigation. But one can contrast this outlook, which anticipates and favors a continual process of change and adaptation of the society, with more traditional views in cultures relatively unaffected by modernization. And, equally clearly, one can contrast these responses with the intense dissatisfactions that might be expected in a nation defeated in war or suffering from very high rates of poverty and unemployment.

Given the distribution of preferences about the ideal society and the attainments and shortcomings of the present society, we are left with

22 See, for example, the fascinating accounts of differences in conceptions of property and security in the three cultures described by Ruth Benedict, *Patterns of Culture* (Boston: Houghton Mifflin, 1934); or the values emphasized in Israeli kibbutz life, as depicted in Bruno Bettelheim, *Children of the Dream* (New York: Macmillan Co., 1969).

the problem of the appropriate policies to be followed in achieving these ends. Agreement on goals does not mean agreement on policies. The nations of Eastern and Western Europe, for example, have political cultures in which most citizens are probably in agreement with the goals of increased national standards of living, improved medical care, better housing, and comfortable minimum welfare standards. But the policy strategies used to achieve these goals are very different in the Eastern European nations, in which the government extracts, and redistributes or invests over 75 percent of the national income and directly engages

Table II.4. *Support for Present Society, Gradual Reform,*
or Revolutionary Change, by Social Class

	Present society	Gradual reform	Revol. change	N
West Germany				
Middle class	17%	80%	2%	699
Working class	22	76	2	725
Farm	24	74	2	170
Italy				
Middle class	9	82	9	654
Working class	11	81	9	392
Farm	15	80	6	206
Belgium				
Middle class	11	85	4	522
Working class	20	76	4	370
Farm	24	75	2	55
Switzerland				
Middle class	23	75	2	857
Working class	32	65	2	547
Farm	46	54	1	127
France				
Middle class	9	84	7	737
Working class	15	79	6	605
Farm	13	84	4	223
The Netherlands				
Middle class	13	81	6	722
Working class	17	75	9	330
Farm	27	65	9	71
United States				
Middle class	28	63	9	603
Working class	28	59	13	682
Farm	40	55	5	88

Source: From Ronald Inglehart, *The Silent Revolution: Changing Values and Political Styles Among Western Publics* (Copyright © 1977 by Princeton University Press): Table 7-9, p. 213. Reprinted by permission of Princeton University Press. European data are from a 1970 survey, American data from a 1973 survey.

Table II.5. *Perceptions of British and Italian Politicians on
Redistribution and Class Conflict*

	Any government that wants to help the poor will have to take something away from the rich in order to do it.[a]				
	Agree strongly	Agree	Disagree	Disagree strongly	Total
British politicians (N=82)	12%	37%	39%	12%	100%
Italian politicians (N=55)	73	24	0	4	101

	Do you think that there must be conflict among social classes or can they get along together without conflict?[b]				
	Class conflict clear; No common interest	Class conflict typical	Some of both	Class harmony typical	Class harmony universal	Total
British politicians (N=36)	11%	33%	8%	31%	17%	100%
Italian politicians (N=43)	40	28	7	19	7	101

[a] Putnam, *Beliefs of Politicians*, p. 105.
[b] Ibid., p. 103. This question was not asked of all respondents.

in housing construction and heavy industry. Although Western European governments are extremely active in welfare programs, far more is left to the private sector and to complex patterns of public and private cooperation.[23]

Public policy propensities, then, are preferences about the performance of the political system: its extraction and distribution of social resources and its regulation of behavior. These preferences are intentions or strategies for achieving social outcomes through various kinds of political action. Preference differences within or across nations may result from different ideal societal outcomes, different theories about how to realize those outcomes, and different perceptions of social conditions existing in the present society. Table II.5, for example, reveals the different perceptions of British and Italian elites about what policies must be used to

[23] See chaps. XI and XII for more complete description of the policy performance and outcome differences.

help the poor and about the inevitability of conflict between social classes. The Italian politicians perceive that resources will have to be extracted from the rich in order to help the poor; the British politicians agree much less frequently or strongly, as they see cooperative class relationships to be much more possible. These differences reflect in part the differences in social conditions in Italy and Britain; Italy at the time of the survey was both a poorer country than Britain and one in which present income was much less equitably divided.[24] The differences also reflect the personal backgrounds of the Italian and British politicians. Politicians from lower-class backgrounds in both nations were more likely to see conflict as inevitable.[25] These perceptions as to how greater equality and improvement of the lot of the poor can be realized make it much more difficult to gain support for particular extractive policies in Italy than in Britain.[26] In both countries, those politicians who saw welfare policies as redistributive and class conflict as inevitable were more likely to oppose political compromise and to favor extreme positions on the right-left ideological continuum.[27] It is no coincidence that Italy has been plagued by political deadlock, policy immobility, governmental instability, and rising conflict.

As conditions change, and as experiences of other nations are learned and emulated, beliefs and assumptions about public policies may change also. A typical example is the changes in most Western nations over the last thirty years in the beliefs about rights to medical care. In most of these nations free medical care has come increasingly to be accepted as a basic right. Even in the United States, public opinion seems to have reached a virtual consensus that medical care should be within reach of individuals of all wealth and age levels, despite the once bitter debates over the issue. In chapter IV we shall discuss some of the socialization agents responsible for changing policy attitudes.

Group identifications and attitudes also can have an important impact on public policy propensities. Do minorities think of themselves as groups, with special concerns and interests in various policy areas? Americans have long been less prone to see themselves in class terms than have Western Europeans. A recent Japanese study suggested that 50 percent of voters in that nation perceive their vote in terms of occu-

[24] See chap. XII. However, the persistent economic problems and sharp conflicts between the government and the trade unions in the 1970s might well have generated a more conflict-oriented, redistributively constrained set of perceptions among British politicians toward the end of the decade.
[25] Putnam, *Beliefs of Politicians*, pp. 137 ff.
[26] See the theoretical discussion of issue perceptions and conflict by Theodore Lowi, "American Business and Public Policy," *World Politics* 16 (July 1964): 677–715.
[27] Putnam, *Beliefs of Politicians*, pp. 97–107, 121–24.

pation.[28] But ethnic differences have long been a major American policy theme, shaped by the social customs and economic situations of each new wave of immigrants, as well as by the particularly difficult problems of black-white relationships. Recent years have also seen again the increased awareness of women as a political group, with special interests in equality and security.

In the regulative areas, the essential issues often involve questions of individual freedoms and rights versus needs of security and order. In most of the Western nations, as Inglehart's comparative data suggest, a growing crime rate has led to increased citizen concern with safety of person and property.[29] How far governments should go in taking measures of crime prevention and punishment seems likely to be a salient policy area in these societies well into the future. The extent to which individual actions should be observed and regulated in the interests of controlling crime rates touches issues of the greatest political and personal importance, as indicated by the recent conflicts in the United States over wiretapping, data banks, use of evidence, "no-knock" search bills, and the right of privacy.

The imposition of health and pollution standards in the economic realm is a somewhat different regulative area. But the battles over production efficiency, on one hand, and consumer and social protection, on the other, are also likely to be long-standing. In some crucial areas, such as air and water pollution, the outcomes of these battles have important effects for many people beyond those engaged in the immediate policy conflicts.

Yet another regulative area has to do with political liberties and the rights to exercise them. As we shall point out in later chapters, the freedom to collect and distribute information, to organize dissent, to find potential political allies, and to move about are critical for all levels of political system performance. The desire for short-term stability often tempts incumbent political elites commanding political majorities or other political resources to try to suppress some of these liberties. If they can prevent people from learning about potential alternatives, or potential opposition coalitions, or can at least prevent the organization of such coalitions, the status quo may be preserved. In authoritarian regimes such controls are a matter of course, and dispute surfaces only in rare cases when controls are slightly relaxed, as in demonstrations in the Soviet Union over Jewish emigration. But even in democratic regimes the use of such tactics is well known.

[28] Bradley Richardson, *The Political Culture of Japan* (Berkeley and Los Angeles: University of California Press, 1974).
[29] Ronald Inglehart, op. cit.

A last general policy area is that of foreign affairs. Ordinarily, of course, foreign policy is far removed from the life of the average citizen, and we are interested only in the propensities of special policy and process subgroups. The conduct of foreign relations means little to citizens if it does not affect their lives. However, there can arise issues that generate intense popular involvement, as Americans are now well aware. In the early 1960s most Americans knew and cared little about Southeast Asia, so high-level political decision makers and interest groups concerned with world affairs were left relatively free to make decisions. But after tens of thousands of American lives had been lost in the jungles of South Vietnam, and after television coverage and national debate had posed the issues with increasing vigor and horror, public involvement came more directly to shape the concerns of policy makers.

In many nations, such as those of Western Europe, the international arena plays a more routinized part in their daily lives. The development of the Common Market has meant that food prices and employment have been manifestly affected by decisions taken outside their own boundaries. Indeed, the combination of greater education and media coverage, on one side, and greater international dependence in trade, on the other, has increased the salience of international events for citizens in many nations. Recent arguments in the United States over foreign wheat sales to the Soviet Union and their effect on the price of bread provide one example. The crippling effect of the Arab oil embargo on the economies of many other nations provides another.

DEVELOPMENTAL ASPECTS OF POLITICAL CULTURE

There is persuasive evidence demonstrating that wherever modern institutions and influences such as industry, education, and the mass media of communication have spread in the world, they have tended to create modern, secular-rational attitudes. Inkeles and Smith and their collaborators interviewed more than five thousand respondents in six developing countries — Argentina, Chile, India, Israel, Nigeria, and Bangladesh. Their samples included persons engaged in commercial pursuits, peasants, and industrial workers and represented ethnic, religious, regional, and other social groupings in these countries. In each country they found that factory employment, education, and exposure to the modern media of communications were strongly associated with a set of attitudes that they characterized as "individual modernity." This is the way they described this modern individual, now widely distributed throughout the world:

> He is an informed participant citizen; he has a marked sense of personal efficacy; he is highly independent and autonomous in his relations to

Table II.6. *Correlations of Education, Mass Media Exposure, and
Occupational Experience with Individual Modernity*

Variable	Argentina	Chile	Bangladesh	India	Israel	Nigeria	Median
Education	.59	.51	.41	.71	.44	.52	.52
Mass media exposure	.57	.46	.38	.56	.38	.43	.45
Factory experiences	.47	.48	.35	.34	.11	.50	.41
Number of respondents	817	929	943	1,198	739	721	

Source: Adapted from Inkeles and Smith, *Becoming Modern*, p. 266.

traditional sources of influence, especially when he is making basic decisions about how to conduct his personal affairs; and he is ready for new experiences and ideas, that is, he is relatively open-minded and cognitively flexible.[30]

Table II.6 summarizes the Inkeles-Smith findings. There is clearly a strong and consistent relationship across countries between these modernizing experiences and the secular, efficacious, and participant attitudes that composed the Inkeles-Smith individual modernity scale.

Inkeles and Smith were confirming in their empirical research what sociological theorists had been discussing since the turn of the twentieth century. The work of scholars in this vein is exemplified by the distinction between *gemeinschaft* (community) and *gesellschaft* (society) in the work of Toennies, by Max Weber's distinction between traditionality and rationality, and by Parsons's distinction of four "pattern-variables" contrasting modern and traditional cultures: (1) modern culture views objects in specific, rather than in diffuse, terms; (2) it views them in a neutral, rather than an emotional, fashion; (3) it is attuned to universal standards and concepts, rather than particularistic ones; (4) it emphasizes achievement, rather than inherited status, in evaluating worth and in recruiting individuals to social roles.[31] Secular orientations of these kinds have been present in many historical epochs, although for reasons discussed in chapter IV below, they are particularly characteristic of

[30] Alex Inkeles and David H. Smith, *Becoming Modern: Individual Change in Six Developing Countries* (Cambridge: Harvard University Press, 1974), p. 290.
[31] Talcott Parsons, *The Social System* (Glencoe, Ill.: Free Press, 1951), pp. 58–67; see also Ferdinand Toennies, *Gemeinschaft und Gesellschaft* [*Community and Society*], trans. Charles P. Loomis (East Lansing: Michigan State University Press, 1958); Max Weber, *Theory of Social and Economic Organization* (New York: Oxford University Press, 1947).

modern life.[32] Secular cultures are highly compatible with views which are open to new information — which, indeed, expect change and seek new kinds of information about new conditions.

How does attitude modernization or secularization affect the principal features of political culture that we have discussed — system, process, and policy? To begin with policy, the major impact of secularization is to indicate the possibilities for deliberate policies to control social and economic environments in desired ways. The specific objectives of this control may still vary greatly — although some objectives, such as better health and longer life, seem widely accepted — and individuals may disagree on priorities and on means of achievement. Indeed, secularization may often increase conflict, if, for example, people disagree over capitalism or socialism, as the best way to improve economic life or over full employment or minimum inflation as the better option in economic growth. But secularized political cultures will contain an awareness of active political intervention as a way of attaining individual and group objectives.

At the process level, secularization means a greater awareness of political opportunities and a willingness to use those opportunities which may improve the lot of the individual. In general, secularization has meant great increases in political participation, in part because it accompanies new views of legitimacy, and in part because it accompanies new resources for citizens, but above all because it emphasizes the ability of individuals to use opportunities to change their conditions.[33] At a minimum, secularization has meant a decline in parochial attitudes toward the political process and an increase in subject and participant roles. Even in authoritarian, one-party states, secularization has meant a more active part in the implementation of policies, as citizens respond to efforts to mobilize them in support of governmental programs.

In a secularized culture, the levels of trust and hostility will be shaped by the more immediate experiences of individuals, rather than by in-

32 For an excellent discussion of the dangers in assuming that historical and contemporary societies approximate pure "traditional" and "'modern" cultural types, see Joseph R. Gusfield, "Tradition and Modernity: Misplaced Polarities in the Study of Social Change," in Finkle and Gable, op. cit., pp. 11–26. And see Lloyd Rudolph and Suzanne Rudolph, *The Modernity of Tradition* (Chicago: University of Chicago Press, 1967); and Gabriel A. Almond and James S. Coleman, eds., *The Politics of the Developing Areas* (Princeton: Princeton University Press, 1960), pp. 20 ff.

33 This theme is sounded in most of the works on political development in the late 1950s and 1960s. See, for example, Karl W. Deutsch, "Social Mobilization and Political Development," *APSR* 55 (September 1961): 493–514; Daniel Lerner, *The Passing of Traditional Society* (New York: Free Press of Glencoe, 1958); Seymour Martin Lipset, *Political Man* (Garden City: Doubleday & Co., 1969), chaps. 2, 3; Lucian W. Pye, *Aspects of Political Development* (Boston: Little, Brown, 1966); Pye and Verba, op. cit.; and Samuel P. Huntington, *Political Order in Changing Societies* (New Haven: Yale University Press, 1968).

herited stereotypes. If new experiences of betrayal and frustration do not appear, these stereotypes should decline in a secularized setting. Subcultural divisions should gradually break down. But, as we have already suggested, one must not be too quick to associate secularization with bargaining and accommodation. First, although choosing accommodative strategies may be a rational decision in some circumstances, choosing a belligerent or nonaccommodative posture may be rational in others, as conflict theorists such as Schelling have argued.[34] For example, minorities may find strategic conflict tactics essential for bargaining leverage or mobilization of support.[35] Second, in a highly conflictual political environment, individuals will quickly learn distrust, will have experiences that lead to anger and hostility, and will act to reinforce that cycle. In such circumstances, it may be the accommodative views and trust that represent the nonsecular elements.

At the system level, secularization typically means the weakening of standards of legitimacy based on custom and charisma and the increasing importance of government performance as a basis of legitimacy. Belief in the divine may continue, but rulers in a secularized culture will have to act on the maxim that God helps those who help themselves. Their claim to the obedience of subjects cannot rest on the idea that through their descent from a line of kings, or through the offering of a religious rite, they will secure the blessings of the gods for their obedient subjects. Of course, legitimacy in even secularized cultures can vary greatly, in terms of the time given leaders to respond, largely based on the previous performance record of the regime and the authorities. But at least in the secularized democracies, the leash on which leaders are kept seems to get shorter with more pervasive secularization.

In a very general sense, there has been a historical association between the extent of secularization and increased political performance. This association seems reasonable. Secularization means an awareness of the possibility of controlling the social and economic environment. It means recruiting leaders on the basis of their ability to improve governmental performance and participating to influence authorities in favor of such performance. Further, it means the continuing formation of organizations, the invention of techniques designed to improve performance, and their evaluation in terms of the success of governmental efforts to produce desirable social outcomes. Across a wide historical and contemporary spectrum of societies, it does seem that political systems with more secular cultures, and with the accompanying structural specialization

---

[34] Thomas C. Schelling, *The Strategy of Conflict* (Cambridge: Harvard University Press, 1960).

[35] See the discussion and literature cited in chap. VII. Also see Powell with Stiefbold, op. cit.

and differentiation discussed in chapter III, have been able to produce more political goods and to control their environments more successfully.

It is difficult, after all, for the specialized structures of a modern bureaucracy or a scientific research organization to operate effectively in a society that treats individuals according to birth or ethnicity, rather than according to their achievement potential. The implementation of political policies will be shaped by considerations arising from diffuse family or tribal relationships. The bureaucracy will find it difficult to penetrate and overcome the traditional rules of the society in the short run, no matter how rational the new regulations may seem to those who promulgate them. The inefficiencies resulting from such traditional attitudes toward politics are problems widely discussed in the literature dealing with new nations and traditional cultures.

Despite the apparent advantages of secularization for performance, one must be aware that there are important circumstances under which secularization is neither necessary nor sufficient to bring increased performance, circumstances where a less secular style, in fact, has important advantages. The positive relationship between secularization and performance is only a very gross one and may hold only in a particular range. There are three general reasons for the limitation on the advantages of secularized style. First, various nonsecular beliefs may help to overcome difficulties in coordination and incentive in human action. The widespread belief that good citizens should pay taxes will promote efficient resource extraction by the government. A firm belief in the legitimacy of regime and authorities will enable a political system to weather many a social and economic storm. Collective sacrifices in the name of community or national identity may increase performance beyond what coercion and remuneration could achieve. If these attitudes are subject to short-term shifts in social welfare or economic expectation, the effects on government performance may be serious. Studies of historical development in Japan and England have often emphasized that certain attitudes of deference, obedience, and loyalty to superiors and national symbols, such as the monarch, seem to have helped the process of transition.[36] Clearly, however, other types of traditional attitudes may hinder the process.

Second, in a society containing many real differences of opinion and differences in objective circumstances, the awareness of the possibilities

---

[36] See, for example, the discussions of Japan and England by Robert E. Ward, "Japan: The Continuity of Modernization," pp. 27–82; and Richard Rose, "England: The Traditionally Modern Political Culture," pp. 82–129, in Pye and Verba, op. cit. For examples of the incompatibility of many elements in traditional cultures and political performance increases, see Apter, *Political Modernization*.

of change and the increased use of opportunities for participation may simply lead to increased political conflict. That conflict may itself limit performance. Expansion of the resources extracted and distributed by the government tends to mean more possibilities for conflict over those allocations. Indeed, historically in the West, secularization has been accompanied by increased political conflict over redistribution of wealth and income, over religious education, over political participation, and over languages to be used in governmental activity. Increased secularization in many nations, particularly those divided ethnically, has meant conflict over the distribution of the state's power to control economic well-being and social customs.

Secularization may also hinder performance when it becomes so pervasive that all values other than narrow self-interest break down. It has been argued that transitional systems are often weakened by the very intensity with which traditional values and practices are questioned and challenged in the secularization process. It would appear that only underlying agreement on some values and goals makes it possible to disagree, bargain, and compromise in other areas.[37] In addition, it seems that human beings very much need some sense of broader purpose in their lives. The widespread discontent with secularized culture expressed by the younger generation in many modern nations in the 1960s may be one manifestation of the need for broader and more firmly held values. If a secular culture generates internal discontent and erodes binding collective traditions and values, it may produce conflict and breakdown rather than effective development. Thus, secularization must be contained within some larger framework of collective restraints and norms if its consequences are to be constructive.

[37] See Sidney Verba, in Pye and Verba, op. cit., pp. 544–50.

CHAPTER III

Political Structure

LOOKING AT SOCIAL LIFE in the United States or any modern country, one finds an immense number of economic, religious, cultural, and explicitly political organizations. Examples of political organizations are the League of Women Voters, the Democratic party, the Congress of the United States, the Internal Revenue Service, and the Fifth Circuit Court of Appeals. Each of these is a structure with manifestly political purposes. The goals of these organizations are more or less specialized, respectively, to the articulation of political interests, their aggregation into policies, the enactment of laws, the implementation of tax policies, and the adjudication of legal disputes.

Table III.1 provides some examples of British political structures, including the British electorate, the Labour party, the House of Commons, and the British army. Many structures without specialized political goals perform political functions; for example, the family plays an important role in political socialization. That formal political structures in fact normally perform more than one function, despite their specialization, is suggested for the British case in table III.1.

In this chapter we shall present some concepts for the analysis and description of political structures. We shall offer guidelines for discovering the most important features of the system, process, and policy structures and of their interrelationships in order to construct a map of those structures and functions. Together with our map of the system, process, and policy characteristics of the political culture, discussed in the last chapter, this structural map prepares us to describe, explain, and compare the workings of a political system as it changes over time and also to compare it with other political systems.

BASIC CONCEPTS OF POLITICAL STRUCTURE

ROLES AND STRUCTURES

The basic unit of political structure is the individual role. A role is a

Table III.1. *Social Structures and Political Functions in Britain*

Social structure	Formal goals	Political functions performed typically[a]
Nuclear family	Child-rearing and providing companionship	(Political socialization)
Manufacturing firm	Producing economic goods for profit	(Political socialization of policy attitudes)
Confederation of British industry	Articulating interests of industry	Interest articulation, (Aggregation, Communication, Socialization)
Electorate	Selecting political leaders	Political recruitment, Interest aggregation
Labour party	Selecting political leaders and mobilizing support for Labour policies	Interest aggregation, Political recruitment, (Articulation, Communication, Socialization)
House of Commons	Making laws	Policy making, Political recruitment, Policy implementation, (Socialization, Communication, Articulation)
Cabinet	Implementing policy	Policy making, Policy implementation, (Aggregation)
Governmental bureaucracy	Implementing policy	Policy implementation, (Articulation, Aggregation, Policy making, Socialization, Recruitment, Communication)
Prison system	Incarcerating criminals	Policy implementation
Army	Providing national defense	Implementation of defense policy, (Articulation)

[a]Parentheses indicate functions performed less frequently.

regularized pattern of behavior, established by one's own expectations and actions and those of others. The idea of a role comes originally from the stage: an actor is assigned to play, for example, the role of Hamlet, which is characterized by certain actions and qualities.[1] In a social situation also, the individual may be expected to perform a role, one that is established by his or her relationships to others. There may be great variability in these expectations and the way they are fulfilled. But describing a political structure spells out a network of roles; individuals have positions in which they are expected to act in certain ways and regularly do so.

[1] See Theodore R. Sarbin, "Role: Psychological Aspects," and Ralph A. Turner, "Role: Sociological Aspects," in *International Encyclopedia of the Social Sciences* (New York: Crowell, Collier, and Macmillan, 1968), 13: 546–56.

A simple example of a political role is that of voter in a modern democracy. That role is an intermittent one; at designated times the voter goes to the polls and casts a ballot. We refer to the total collection of such voters as the electorate. The electorate is thus a large, but simple, political structure with many identical individual roles, which are intermittently performed by citizens who spend most of their lives and attention elsewhere. In Britain, as shown in table III.2, the electorate is made up of some forty million individual voter roles. In any given election about 75 percent of these individuals will go to the polls and perform their role by choosing one of the candidates nominated by other political structures: the Conservative, Labour, Liberal, and other parties.

Table III.2. *Internal Roles and Role Relationships in*
              Structures in Britain

Social structure	Number of individuals in structure	Typical time in role	Role interrelationships	
			Influence relationships	Regulative resources
Nuclear family	4+	Child: Full Adult: Varies	Hierarchic	Normative/Remunerative/Coercive
Manufacturing firm	2,000+	Full	Hierarchic	Remunerative
Confederation of British industry	ca. 90,000 firms	Leaders: Full Members: Low and Intermittent	Equalitarian (bargaining)	Remunerative
Electorate	ca. 40 million	Low and Intermittent	Equalitarian (market)	Normative/Remunerative
Labour party	ca. 6 million	Leaders: Full Activists: Half Members: Low and Intermittent	Polyarchic	Normative/Remunerative
House of Commons	635	Half	Polyarchic	Normative/Remunerative
Cabinet	20+	Full	Equalitarian (bargaining)	Normative/Remunerative
Governmental bureaucracy	ca. 1 million	Full	Hierarchic	Remunerative/Coercive
Prison system	ca. 35,000	Full	Hierarchic	Coercive (Remunerative for staff)
Army	ca. 300,000	Full	Hierarchic	Coercive/Remunerative

The parties are much more complex structures than the electorate, having differentiated leader, activist, and member roles, the first of which are specialized, full-time occupations. It is possible to analyze structure from many different levels and points of view, of course. Sometimes we refer very generally to the British electoral structure or electoral subsystem. We are then referring to all the specific structures engaged in recruiting political leaders to elected office in Britain, regardless of formal goals and internal roles. The electoral subsystem encompasses not only the electorate, but also the parties, interest groups, and other structures affecting the nomination and selection of candidates.

The analysis of specific political structures and their relationship to political functions makes it possible to describe and compare very different political systems. We defined our concept of political system, and our typology of political functions, in a way that means that all political systems must include the performance of these functions. We can therefore compare political systems by observing which political structures perform the different functions in them. The great advantage of an explicitly structural-functional approach is that it enables us to avoid the confusion between the formal goals of structures and the political functions actually performed by them.[2]

For example, the national electorates in Britain and the Soviet Union may have similar formal political goals — to recruit political leaders for the nations — and similar internal structures, such as one-citizen, one-vote. But in fact they perform very different political functions in the two nations. The Soviet electorate has little impact on national leadership recruitment, merely ratifying the selection of candidates nominated by the Communist party. The much more important function is socialization of citizens into a feeling of involvement with the regime. In Britain, on the other hand, as shown in table III.1, the electorate plays an important role in interest aggregation and recruitment, as well as in socialization of attitudes. A careful structural-functional analysis also reminds us that social structures with no overt political goals may perform important political functions and typically do so, as the family does in socialization and as informal groups do in interest articulation. Finally, although formal specialization of structures, as well as of internal roles within them, is an important modern characteristic, table III.1 indicates that many modern structures are indeed multifunctional. The House of Commons does not merely make authoritative public policy — its function here is actually quite limited — but plays a critical part in

2 Joseph LaPalombara suggests that "the important lesson" of the explicit structural-functional analysis has been "structural alternatives for functional performance and the multifunctionality of similar structures" ("Macrotheories and Microapplications in Comparative Politics," *Comparative Politics* 1 [October 1968]: 52–78).

recruiting leaders, articulating interests, communicating political messages, and the like.

INTERNAL ROLE RELATIONSHIPS

There are many possible ways to describe the internal role relationships
of political structures.[3] We shall not try to discuss these exhaustively,
but shall, instead, indicate some important characteristics that will be
useful in describing structures and explaining their performance. In
table III.2 we set forth some of the characteristics of the British political
structures introduced in table III.1. For each of the structures, we first
indicate the number of individuals involved: that is, we have a rough
measure of the sizes of the structures. The British structures range from
the nuclear family, typically a pair of adults and several children, to the
forty million citizens who are eligible members of the electorate.

The next column indicates the typical amount of time that individuals spend in the roles associated with these structures. Young children
spend virtually all their time in the family, although only a small amount
of that time may involve political learning or experiences. Voters spend
very little time performing the voting role, even if time spent in gathering information is included, and perform that role only intermittently,
when elections take place. On the other hand, average Members of Parliament spend perhaps half their time in their job as MPs, the other half
in private occupations. Party leader and government bureaucrat are
usually full-time roles, primary occupations for their incumbents. All
the latter roles, from voter to bureaucrat, are manifestly political; the
formal goals of electorates, parties, and bureaucracies are to perform
political functions. The individuals in question are manifestly involved
in politics while they perform their roles in these structures.

The last two columns in table III.2 refer to relationships between
roles in the structure. Among the many possible characteristics here, we
have shown two: the pattern of internal influence, in particular the
autonomy of the "lower" participants in the structure, and the kinds of
resources used to gain compliance. Let us consider first the patterns of
influence and autonomy. The extremes here are the equalitarian pattern,
in which all roles have formally equal influence and all individuals have
great autonomy in performing their roles, and the hierarchic. Equalitarian influence relationships may be characterized either by face-to-face
bargaining or by collective individual decisions, as in a market or an

---

[3] For a complex analysis of many aspects of political structures see Harry Eckstein
and Ted Robert Gurr, *Patterns of Authority: A Structural Basis for Inquiry* (New
York: John Wiley, 1975), especially part 2.

election.[4] In the hierarchic pattern the decisions about how lower participants are to perform their roles stem from commands made at the top.

In the British case, the relationships between voters in the electorate are formally and in some degree actually equalitarian, as are those between member firms of the Confederation of British Industry. Although the interest group has a more complicated structure, the organization leaders are not able to bind their members, who thus exercise great freedom of decision, as do individual voters. The other equalitarian structure in the table, the Cabinet, has a more complicated influence mixture. In theory the members are equal, and surely face-to-face bargaining and mutual exchange do go on between members of the Cabinet. But the Prime Minister is much more than first among equals. Although unable to command cabinet colleagues to perform their tasks in various ways, the Prime Minister has the power to appoint and remove them.

The prison system and the army are the most clearly hierarchic structures in the table. In both a clear chain of command exists; policies are made at the top and communicated downward; and the lower ranks have few resources and little decision-making autonomy. The family has a more complex mixture: relationships between parents are seldom purely hierarchic, but even in "progressive" families young children have limited voice in critical decisions about their safety and well-being. The bureaucracy and, in fact, the other large hierarchic organizations have segmented substructures; there are several chains of command in different functional or geographic divisions, loosely coordinated at the top. The head of the Treasury cannot give orders, at least not formally, to workers in the welfare office; and the army commander cannot give direct orders to naval units, even if both are part of the military structure.

Among the many possible variations and versions of structural interrelationships, we wish to single out one type as being of special interest: what Dahl and Lindblom have called "polyarchic" relationships.[5] In this pattern the lower participants periodically choose their leaders and define their general tasks. Typically, they do so by selecting among

[4] See the discussion of market, bargaining, command, and polyarchic social control processes by Robert A. Dahl and Charles E. Lindblom, *Politics, Economics, and Welfare* (New York: Harper, 1953), especially part 4. Also see Amitai Etzioni, *A Comparative Analysis of Complex Organizations* (New York: Free Press, 1961); Peter M. Blau, *Exchange and Power in Social Life* (New York: John Wiley, 1964); Eckstein and Gurr, op. cit.; and the highly interesting discussion of the choices available to lower participants in different structural settings, and their implications, by Albert O. Hirschman, *Exit, Voice, and Loyalty* (Cambridge: Harvard University Press, 1970).

[5] Dahl and Lindblom, op. cit. Also see Robert A. Dahl, *Polyarchy: Participation and Opposition* (New Haven: Yale University Press, 1971).

leaders who offer alternative directions of policy. The lower participants may even select the original "constitution" that establishes their roles. However, after the leaders have been selected, they are given important resources for command and, within constitutional limits, are able to make binding decisions from the top, about the activities of the rank and file.

The British political parties have had a polyarchic arrangement such as this throughout the last century, although they have varied in their mode of selection of party leaders and the amount of power accorded to them after selection, the role of activists and functionaries as opposed to rank-and-file members, and the like. In a very general sense, of course, the total political structure of a democratic political system is envisioned as following this polyarchic pattern, where participating citizens choose between leaders in relatively open competition, but the citizens must obey the laws made by the chosen leadership.[6]

Direct, equalitarian democracy, of either the bargaining or the market type of interchange, is virtually impossible to arrange on a continuing basis in a large structure involved in complex decision making. At best, it is possible for citizens to become directly involved in decision making on a few issues (as in the special referenda used extensively in Switzerland and in some American states) or in decentralized political subsegments (such as the Yugoslavian workers' councils or the New England town meetings).

The last column in table III.2 identifies the kinds of resources typically used to secure the compliance of the various participants in their roles in the structure. Although anything of value may be used to secure compliance, we indicate three general types of resources: coercive, remunerative, and normative.[7] When coercive resources are used, participants perform their roles under the actual or threatened use of force. The prisoner remains in prison and goes about his or her daily tasks under just such duress. The taxpayer who fails to pay his or her taxes is threatened with imprisonment. The private in the army who disobeys orders faces the stockade, or even execution. A child who disobeys may be coerced, threatened with punishment, or actually punished.

In the case of remunerative resources, individuals are paid, in cash or in kind, to perform their roles. The typical example in modern societies is the bureaucrats who work, for example, for the Treasury or the Social Security Administration for a salary. They can disobey orders at the risk of losing their jobs and the accompanying financial rewards.

Normative resources lead individuals to perform their roles because they feel that it is the "right thing to do." Citizens may vote, party

6 See Dahl, *Polyarchy*.
7 See Etzioni, op. cit.

activists work for the party, and MPs follow traditional customs because of the psychological rewards for obedience or the psychological costs of deviation. Given proper socialization into appropriate values, such normative rewards and costs can be among the most powerful means for maintaining good role performance.

Normally, political organizations use various combinations of coercive, remunerative, and normative rewards and sanctions to encourage performance. Voters may be encouraged to vote both because it is the duty of the good citizen and because they are reminded that their votes may make a difference in the selection of leaders who will provide material benefits. In some nations, such as Australia, Belgium, and Costa Rica, the voter may face a fine for failing to vote. Similarly, taxpayers are threatened with fines and imprisonment for failing to pay sufficient taxes, but they are also told that full payment is a duty of the good citizen. Indeed, in saying that "legitimate force" is the identifying characteristic of political systems, we have already suggested the mixture of coercive and normative values used to maintain internal citizen compliance in subject roles.

STRUCTURAL DIFFERENTIATION AND PERFORMANCE

One structural characteristic is so important to the general concept of political development and performance that it is worth special consideration. Many modern social structures are characterized by a high level of structural differentiation, the appearance of individual roles that are specialized to different tasks within the structure. As shown in table III.2, the electorate has minimal task differentiation; it is composed of millions of identical voting roles. The family is somewhat more differentiated, especially between the roles of parents and children. But most of the large structures organized for special political purposes manifest much higher levels of internal structural differentiation and specialization. We noted in table III.2, for example, that in the Labour party there is a great contrast among the roles of members, activists, and party officials. Within the leadership roles there is much additional specialization, with special research analysis staffs, organizing agents, candidate roles, and so forth. Within the governmental bureaucracy, of course, there is specialization into various task-oriented agencies, and individual role specialization exists at various levels within these.

Organization theorists have long been fascinated with the relationship between structural differentiation and effective performance. Their analyses suggest both the reasons that differentiation has been associated with increased capability and the limits that pertain to that relationship. To increase differentiation means to recruit individuals to more specialized roles and to create patterns of inducement that would lead them to perform these limited roles. The advantage of such differentiation is that each individual can then concentrate all his or her energies on doing one small task very well. Max Weber likened the superiority of the differentiated bureaucracy to that of the machine over individual labor, and found the reason for its adoption in many societies to be just that superior performance.[8] The superiority of the differentiated, specialized structures and the appropriate specialized rewards would seem to increase with the greater scale and complexity of the political structure.

Peter Blau has provided a contemporary summary of this organizational argument:

> Formal organizations cope with the difficult problems large scale operations create by subdividing responsibilities in numerous ways and thereby facilitating the work of any operating employee, manager, and subunit in the organization. The division of labor typifies the improvement in performance attainable through subdivision. The more completely simple tasks are separated from various kinds of complex ones, the easier it is for unskilled employees to perform the routine duties and for skilled employees to acquire the specialized training and experience to perform the different complex ones. Further subdivision of responsibilities occurs among functional divisions, enabling each one to concentrate on certain kinds of work.[9]

The relationship between structural differentiation and performance, like that between cultural secularization and performance, is very complicated. The very advantages of differentiation also create problems. In a very general sense these may be seen as problems of coordination. The creation of specialized roles may mean that various subunits will be made up of individuals performing similar tasks. But the subunits will be quite different from one another or will face different geographic or technical environments, depending on the variety of criteria of differentiation. The more such units there are, and the more specialized they become, the greater are the problems of coordinating their activities.

In Blau's study of the size and differentiation of welfare agencies, for example, he found that the larger the organization, the more internal differentiation it manifested. But the relationship between size and differentiation was a declining one; after a given size, very little additional differentiation occurred, regardless of further growth in organizational size. This relationship is shown in figure III.1. Blau argued, from evidence and theory, that the relationship reflects the fact that

8 Weber, *From Max Weber: Essays in Sociology*, ed. H. H. Gerth and C. W. Mills (New York: Oxford University Press, 1946), pp. 214–16.

9 Peter M. Blau, *On the Nature of Organizations* (New York: John Wiley, 1974), pp. 305–6.

Figure III.1. *Organizational Size and Structural Differentiation in American Welfare Agencies*

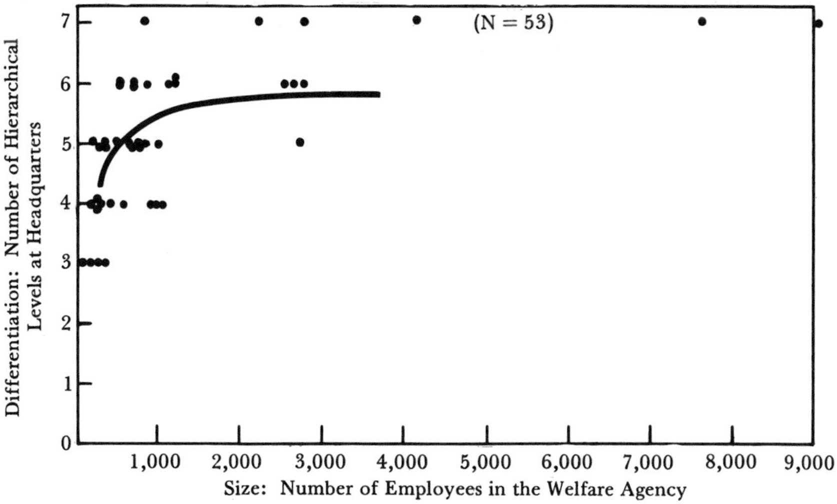

Source: From Peter M. Blau, *On the Nature of Organization*, 1974, p. 304. Reprinted by permission of John Wiley & Sons, publishers.

differentiation has both efficiency advantages, due to the specialization of tasks, and costs, due to problems of coordination. With initial growth in size, the specialization advantages lead to a sharp growth in the amount of differentiation. But as more differentiation is introduced, the difficulties and costs of coordinating the units become greater and keep further differentiations in check. Eventually, the coordination costs set a threshold, beyond which little further differentiation takes place.[10]

As Blau pointed out, his study was limited to a particular type of task and a particular aspect of the organizational situation. The relationship between differentiation and performance will be affected by the motivations of the participants, the complexity and stability of the task environment, the need for feedback and coordination in achieving the organization's goals, and the like. We could not analyze all these factors here even if adequate theory existed, but we can emphasize this implication: the advantages of differentiation represent only a very broad general tendency, one with severe limitations in many particular cases.

POLITICAL SYSTEM STRUCTURES

Just as we distinguished among the system, process, and policy aspects of culture in chapter II, so also can we divide political structure into its

[10] Ibid.

system, process, and policy aspects. System structures are those organizations and institutions which *maintain* or *change* the political structures, particularly the structures that perform the functions of political socialization, political recruitment, and political communication.

Assume first a relatively stable political system. For generations, let us suppose, individuals have been socialized through childhood and adult experience into a given set of process skills and expectations and policy preferences. As they reach maturity, some of them are recruited into specialized roles, where they are instructed or apprenticed into proper role performance. These political structures provide various benefits and costs for appropriate performance: financial reward, influence, gratifications for meeting the expectations of others, a sense of fulfillment for meeting religious obligations, or penalties for disobedience. For individuals not recruited into elite roles, there are rewards and avoidance of penalties for their appropriate playing of citizenship roles. As we saw in discussing regime legitimacy, the basis of the exchange of citizens' compliance with elite policies will vary with the political culture. In some political cultures, legitimacy may be established by birthright and the priestly sanctification of the monarch. In others, legitimacy may depend on an elaborate set of recruitment requirements — competitive elections, for example — plus maintenance of satisfactory policy performance to win the compliance of citizen groups. But the equilibrium is maintained by a synchronization of the desires of those having real and potential political resources — as defined by the existing structural arrangements — with the general pattern of policy performance.[11] Similar balances of preferences and resources are found within the various structures and subsystems.

Suppose, now, an individual is dissatisfied with the existing policy outputs. Perhaps the expectations into which he has been socialized are no longer satisfied by government policies. What he can do about it depends on his resources within the present political system and on the preferences and resources of others. He can try to put together a policy coalition to change policies within the existing political structures. If unsuccessful, he might try to change those structures themselves, perhaps through his own actions or by putting together a coalition of others with the resources to influence performance. If he is a President or Prime Minister, he might declare a state of emergency to give him the extra resources needed to change the system or its policies, as Indira Gandhi did in India in 1975. If the individual is a general, he might call out the

11 A more complete discussion of elements in synchronization can be found in Gabriel A. Almond, Scott Flanagan, and Robert Mundt, eds., *Crisis, Choice, and Change* (Boston: Little, Brown, 1973), chap. 2.

tanks to surround the Presidential Palace and National Assembly Building and might replace the old set of policy-making structures, as well as individual leaders, with others, as in the military coup in Chile in 1973. If the leader commands a legislative majority, he might put through legislation canceling free elections and perpetuating the tenure of the incumbents, as Mussolini and Hitler did in the 1920s and 1930s. Or, if he has no political resources in the existing political system, he may take to the hills or to the ghetto and form a guerrilla army to force the government into response or capitulation, as Castro did in Cuba in the 1950s.

These examples suggest, of course, that effective socialization, forming supportive attitudes and homogeneous policy preferences, would be helpful in gaining system continuity. Indeed, the leaders in most political systems do attempt to engage in such socialization, whether through the massive penetration and control of party- and state-run newspapers and television, or through the more limited stress on patriotism and good citizenship in the schools, or in the speeches of political leaders. As we shall demonstrate in the next chapter, however, many structures act as agents of attitude formation and change in a society. Changes in socialization, particularly changes in values and expectations, are a powerful source of pressures for political change. Nor can even the most effectively controlled socialization be expected to limit the ambitions and aspirations of specific individuals in powerful roles.

Most modern political systems have special organizations and institutions that regulate the performance of other political roles through the recruitment functions. They offer both opportunities and penalties in political life. In the authoritarian Communist political systems, the party officials review recruitment and performance of individuals throughout the lower levels of party and bureaucratic hierarchy. In military and personalistic authoritarian systems the pattern of recruitment and promotion is also carefully, if less thoroughly, watched from above. In the democracies, the performance of political officials is regulated through periodic elections; governmental bureaucrats are subject to civil service examination in selection and to loss of position through failure to perform duties. Chief executives who violate the rules of their office may be subject to impeachment, or to defeat in an election. Specialized regulative agencies, such as police and internal security forces, may play a continuous negative recruitment function by preventing citizens from forming illegal political organizations, such as terrorist groups. In short, the structures that perform the recruitment function are critical to system maintenance.

Obviously, this discussion, which we shall expand in more detail in chapters IV–VI does not mean that political systems never change. On the contrary, they are perpetually in a state of change. Even the most stable political systems are undergoing minor changes each day in their political cultures and political structures. When we discuss the functions of socialization, recruitment, and communication, we shall indicate how these changes come about. And larger changes are frequent as well. Military coups and internal warfare are common features of contemporary politics: over a quarter of all the "stable democracies" formed in the last one hundred years have changed at least temporarily into another regime form. There have been military coups in Chile, Brazil, France, Greece, Turkey, and Uruguay; executive coups in the Philippines and India; civil wars in Austria and Lebanon; the combination of extremist electoral victory and semilegal executive coup in Weimar Germany. Authoritarian regimes dominated by the army or hierarchical parties have been at least equally subject to major political change.[12]

But the point here is that we can understand both stability and instability through our analysis of the system functions and the structures performing them. Regimes are stable when there is a balance between the system, process, and policy preferences of their citizens, as weighted by the resources those citizens hold in the political structures, and the actual outcomes of performance. If preferences change, if resources change, if policy outcomes change, then the system may become unstable, break down, and be supplanted with another. Our analyses of socialization, recruitment, and communication will help us explain how these changes take place, whether in response to external forces creating new demands and resources or in response to continuing dissatisfaction with policy outcomes.

POLITICAL PROCESS STRUCTURES

We defined the political system as the continuing process by which those decisions backed by legitimate coercion are made and put into effect. As we examine a particular society, we ask how these policies are formed, implemented, or changed. What individuals, acting in what roles, decide how much will be collected as taxes, and from whom? What individuals, acting in what roles, actually collect the taxes, distribute the resources, and punish violations of laws? We seek to construct a map of the entire process, from the articulation of interests through the implementation of policy and its dynamic feedbacks.

In chapters VII–X we shall examine in more detail the performance of the functions of interest articulation, interest aggregation, policy making, and policy implementation. In each chapter we shall suggest types

---

12 See chaps. VIII and XIII for a discussion of the great difficulties in developing stable aggregation and policy-making structures in the less industrialized nations.

of structures that perform these functions, mention some of the implications of such performance, and provide some examples. We are interested in the informal, even hidden, structures as much as in the obvious ones, in the illegitimate as well as the legitimate. Hence, in discussing interest articulation, we are interested in the covert friendship group, cemented by old school ties or by common tribal membership, as well as in the Trades Unions Congress; we are interested in riots and armed attacks, as well as petitions and speeches. In some societies we shall find specialized political process structures whose primary formal goals are related to policy making, such as parties and legislatures. In other societies we find policy making or implementation to be a by-product of the performance of religious and economic roles by the shaman or chief. And in outlining the known possibilities, we recognize that in any new or changing society there may appear combinations of structures, or even types of structures, that we have not previously encountered.

As indicated in the examples of structures and functions in Britain (in tables III.1 and III.2), even with the development of more specialized political output structures, structures whose primary collective goal is implementation of particular types of policies, one must always take care to identify the actual function being performed. A bureaucratic agency may be a specialized organization for the implementation of, for example, health care policy; but as it implements the general policy it may collect information, listen to complaints, seek to define problems, even adopt policies with far-reaching effects not anticipated by the lawmakers. In performing these and other tasks, it is a multifunctional structure. To map accurately the political process structures, one must understand the way in which this particular goal-specialized organization performs these multiple functions.

We always bear in mind, of course, the interplay of culture and structure. Our structural-functional map is only analytically distinct from our cultural one, for attitudes, beliefs, and values shape role performance and are themselves shaped by role incentives and possibilities. In discussing citizen process propensities, for example, we referred to the parochial, subject, and participant attitudes that may characterize citizen political cultures. Clearly these terms reflect the impact of these attitudes on citizen role performance and on the citizenship role structure. And such attitudes are particularly interesting because of their effects on citizen efforts to articulate demands and citizen response to elite mobilization. But the political structures that confront citizens also shape their propensities and their role behavior. Soviet citizens have few valid participatory opportunities open to them; they develop a subject political culture and perform subject roles in part because Soviet leaders so carefully regulate communication and interest articulation, yet make massive efforts to mobilize them into ratifying the recruitment of party nominees and assisting in policy implementation.

In addition to locating the structures that perform the various functions in a society, our structural-functional map must determine the basic relationships, particularly of influence and autonomy, that exist *among* political structures. Just as role relationships within a political structure may vary from hierarchic to equalitarian, so may relationships among political structures. Naturally, of special interest is the relationship between the authoritative policy-making structures and the structures that perform interest articulation and aggregation, on one side of the process, and the implementation of policy on the other. Does the central party committee, or ruling council, or president strictly control the expression of demand and the mobilization of political resources by other structures? Does the military organization force the chief executive and party leaders to anticipate every whim of the high command, or does the bureaucracy shape authoritative policy by controlling questions raised in the legislature? Are the interest groups tied to given parties or free to switch support?

The distinction between hierarchic, "commanding" political process structures and polyarchic, bargaining ones has often been overdrawn. As we shall spell out in more detail later,[13] the relationship between process and policy, and between policy and social outcome, is far from simple. Authoritarian and democratic political systems must be evaluated by the full range of values they produce, not by structural-functional differences alone.[14] But structural-functional characteristics, including differences in differentiation and autonomy, have important consequences — or at least probable implications — for policy, process, and system goods produced under various social conditions.[15] The construction of an accurate structural-functional map will help prepare for the analysis of these relationships.

POLITICAL POLICY STRUCTURES

We have been speaking as if political process structures could be understood apart from the content of specific policies or, at least, as if the process functions were performed by the same structures for all policies. But we know from empirical studies of communities and nations that it is a serious error to assume a uniform performance of the political func-

[13] See chaps. XI and XII.
[14] See chap. XIV.
[15] See chaps. XIII and XIV.

tions in different policy areas. In fact, the structures involved in the articulation, aggregation, policy-making, and implementation functions in the area of foreign policy or national defense are typically quite different from those involved in tax policy, education, or welfare. In his study of New Haven, *Who Governs?*, Robert Dahl found quite different structures performing many of the functions in the three areas of education, urban development, and party nominations. Only the role of the mayor and a few others were involved in more than one policy area.[16] Studies of American foreign policy have found very specialized policy structures, from attentive publics of citizens especially interested in foreign policy and engaged in contacting elites and arousing public opinion, to influential private associations, specialized congressional committees, and the bureaucratic organizations of the State and Defense Departments.[17] Some of these structures are involved in other policy areas, but many of them are relatively specialized to the foreign policy area alone.

The process and policy structures can be visualized as two ways of looking at the political system. From the process point of view, one sees a variety of structures involved in, say, interest articulation or policy making in different ways and in different issue areas. From the policy point of view, one sees a variety of structures involved in shaping, say, defense policy, or welfare policy, at different stages in the policy process. The degree of process specialization and the degree of policy specialization by the specific structures of the society is an empirical question. At one extreme, the headman of a primitive, food-gathering band may perform virtually all the process functions, intermittently, and do so in all the relevant issue areas for the community. At the other extreme, in a large and very differentiated political system, there may be a different specialized structure, or perhaps many, involved in performing each functional step in each policy area. Size and complexity of the tasks and issues are two variables shaping such differentiation, but other factors are involved as well.

Policy structures often specialize in particular policy directions as well as in policy areas. Indeed, most modern interest groups, for example, are not merely issue area specialists, but advocates for a particular point of view. The National Association of Manufacturers (now amalgamated

16 Robert A. Dahl, *Who Governs?* (New Haven: Yale University Press, 1961). Of course, other studies have found much more hierarchical centralization. The problem, we stress, is one for empirical investigation.

17 See, for example, Gabriel A. Almond, *The American People and Foreign Policy* (New York: Praeger, 1960); and Raymond Bauer, Ithiel De Sola Pool, and Lewis A. Dexter, *American Business and Public Policy* (New York: Atherton Press, 1964).

with the U.S. Chamber of Commerce) and the AFL-CIO are both relatively specialized American associational interest groups, from a formal,
goal-oriented point of view; and both perform interest articulation functions primarily in the area of economic and welfare policy. But the directions of their policy propensities, and their policy efforts, are very
different; one favors probusiness policies and the other, prolabor policies.

Where policy preferences are polarized, one can usually expect to find
specific structures that are internally policy-homogeneous, but the set of
structures articulating interests in that policy area will be polarized.
Occasionally, one finds internally divided interest articulation structures
or, more commonly, interest aggregation structures, such as the American
Democratic party, with its conservative and liberal wings. But the strain
of maintaining organizational performance in a policy-polarized structure is considerable. Incentives of patronage or reward of office, or careful bargaining across issue areas, must be arranged if divergent policy
groups are to remain within the organization.[18]

By putting together our policy and process structure maps, particularly in combination with our cultural map of policy and process propensities, we are in good position to analyze the making of authoritative
decisions in a society. We can see how interests from various points of
view are articulated, what resources will be needed to put together coalitions to make the needed decisions at the aggregation and policy-making
stages, and what issue positions and structures exist for the coalitions
that shape policy outputs. With this structural-functional map of the
working policy and process structures, we should be able to explain the
basis of the Soviet Union's great expenditures on defense and education
or its repressive regulation of internal freedom. We should be able to
explain the American system's large, decentralized expenditures on education, the prominent tax loopholes in the upper income brackets, and
the subsidies to private farmers. In some policy areas the balance of resources and preferences may be quite even, and specific policy outputs
less predictable; in other areas, to know the process and policy structures
involved is to know the policy output.

THE DEVELOPMENTAL DIMENSION

Just as there is a developmental dimension in political culture, so can
one discern a developmental dimension in political structure. The appearance of increasingly differentiated and specialized political organizations
and roles, the goals and internal structure of which are purposively
directed at performing political functions, has historically been asso-

[18] See chap. VII.

ciated with the enhanced capability of political systems.[19] Such differentiation of the political structures has also tended to accompany, or to be accompanied by, cultural secularization. As we have shown in discussing secularization and differentiation in specific structures, these developmental characteristics have costs as well as benefits. It is possible that the future will see some modification of the long-term historical trends that have associated secularization and differentiation with increased political performance capability.[20] But these very general relationships, which seem to hold to some degree today and which clearly held within broad limits in the past, do provide an illuminating way of analyzing and classifying political systems.

DIFFERENTIATION OF POLITICAL STRUCTURES

In a previous section we discussed differentiation and specialization within specific modern political structures. We may now try to clarify the historical meaning of political differentiation in political systems considered as a whole. We can begin with a very simple example of a largely undifferentiated political system, such as that of the Eskimo. The Eskimos are scattered from the Bering Straits to Greenland in small communities of about one hundred inhabitants, most of them related by blood or marriage. There are only two specialized social roles of political significance — those of headman and shaman — and both are mixed roles. The shaman is the religious leader, but he can also punish those who violate taboos. In the extreme case he may order an offender exiled, which in the Arctic may mean death. The headman is a task leader, making decisions about hunting or selecting places for settlement. In matters related to political order, he is an influential bargaining leader, rather than a leader with power to command. Violations of order are handled mostly through such means as fist fights and "song duels" or, in extreme cases, family feuds. An individual who threatens the community by re-

---

[19] See the references in chap. II, above, to the long social science tradition associated with this analysis, particularly the works of Durkheim, Toennies, and Weber. We have already cited some of Toennies's and Weber's work. Durkheim's principal contribution was *The Division of Labor in Society* (Glencoe, Ill.: The Free Press, 1960). Two more recent discussions of the relationships between differentiation, capability, and development, are S. N. Eisenstadt, "Social Change, Differentiation, and Evolution," pp. 375–85; and Talcott Parsons, "Evolutionary Universals in Society," pp. 339–57, both in *American Sociological Review* 29 (June 1964).

[20] For discussion of the difficulties of performance in complex, technologically based, highly specialized and differentiated modern societies, see the essays in Leon N. Lindberg, ed., *Politics and the Future of Industrial Society* (New York: David McKay, 1976), especially the contributions by Lindberg and by La Porte and Abrams. Also see Samuel P. Huntington, "Post-Industrial Politics: How Benign Will It Be," *Comparative Politics* 6 (January 1974), pp. 163–92.

peated acts of violence, murder, or theft might be dealt with by an executioner who is given the task by the community or who assumes the responsibility for the execution with the approval of the community.

The Eskimo political system, then, has no set of roles, no structure, that is specialized for political purposes. Some of the activities of the shaman and the headman might be viewed as political or governmental activities. Some social processes, such as duels and blood feuds, might be viewed as Eskimo ways of adjudicating disputes. Other community activities may perform the political functions of communicating information, articulating different points of view, and making political decisions that have the effect of law. For comparative purposes and as political analysts, we may say that at certain times, in relation to certain problems, an Eskimo community might have been performing political functions. But the Eskimos themselves do not draw boundaries distinguishing political from religious and economic realms, let alone structural boundaries distinguishing policy-making roles from implementation roles. Examples of such *intermittent political systems* may be found among many primitive peoples.

Max Weber, in his classic typology of traditional political systems, distinguished among patriarchal, patrimonial, and feudal systems.[21] A *patriarchal* system is one in which membership is based on kinship and in which authority is exercised by the eldest male as part of his diffuse social standing. In a *patrimonial* system, an administrative staff appears, with specialized roles for the performance of governmental functions under the direct control and in the household of the ruler. One of the first significant political inventions in history seems to have been the specialized officialdom of patrimonial kingdoms.

Feudalism is defined by Weber as a system of relations of purely personal loyalty between a lord and his vassals. Both lord and vassals are patrimonial rulers; they are loosely joined by bonds of mutual obligation. In Weber's threefold classification of traditional authority, the significant dimensions of variation are structural differentiation and autonomy of parts. The feudal and patrimonial systems are more structurally differentiated than the patriarchal; and the feudal system manifests more subsystem autonomy than the patrimonial.

Patrimonial systems, with their specialized officialdoms, can be quite complex, involving several levels of authority and a variety of types of administrative officials. The administrative officials tend to be immediate

21 Max Weber, *Theory of Social and Economic Organization* (New York: Oxford University Press, 1947), pp. 341 ff.; Reinhard Bendix, *Max Weber: An Intellectual Portrait* (Garden City: Doubleday & Co., 1960), pp. 329 ff; Gunther Roth, "Personal Rulership, Patrimonialism and Empire Building in the New States," *World Politics* 20 (January 1968): 294 ff.

subordinates of the ruler, who act as personal confidants and table companions. The titles of their offices, such as chamberlain, cupbearer, and keeper of the purse, often reflect their origins in the patriarchal household. In the historical *bureaucratic empires,* such as the Egyptian, Persian, Roman, Chinese, or Incan systems, which are discussed by S. N. Eisenstadt,[22] or in the nation-states of the contemporary world, the officialdom is much more numerous and is specialized into a greater variety of functional units — tax collection agencies, welfare agencies, educational institutions, standing armies, and the like. Officials in these systems have more impersonal relations to the ruler and to each other. Such specialized output structures appear to facilitate the extraction and distribution of resources and the regulation of social behavior, at least within broad limits and with the support of appropriate attitudes. The jump from the limited specialized officialdom of the patrimonial system to the more elaborate and effective administrative apparatus of the bureaucratic empires is a second significant development.

But even as administrative roles and subsystems become more specialized, the primordial institutions of personal confidants, cronies, and table companions persist, as devices to make more direct and effective the relationships of presidents, dictators, and prime ministers to department heads, bureau chiefs, and section heads. The informal and undifferentiated roles are needed to help overcome the problems of communication and coordination created by specialization itself. Structurally, as well as culturally, all modern systems are mixed political systems.

Eisenstadt also tells us that as bureaucratic empires increase in size, conquer other political systems, and assimilate other ethnic groups, as social and occupational strata become more differentiated, as churches and religious sects become distinct from political structures, then a more or less open and legitimate process of struggle over political policy goals emerges. That is, there appear *specialized political input structures* for the articulation of political interests, the aggregation of political demands and resources, and the making of policy decisions. The emergence of such specialized input structures is typically accompanied by specialized policy and system structures, as social divisions and issues become more complex and the tasks of securing adequate personnel and compliance more formidable.

A TYPOLOGY OF POLITICAL SYSTEMS

The dimensions of cultural secularization and structural differentiation can be used to generate a developmental typology of political sys-

[22] S. N. Eisenstadt, *The Political Systems of Empires* (New York: Free Press of Glencoe, 1963).

Figure III.2. *A Developmental Typology of Political Systems*

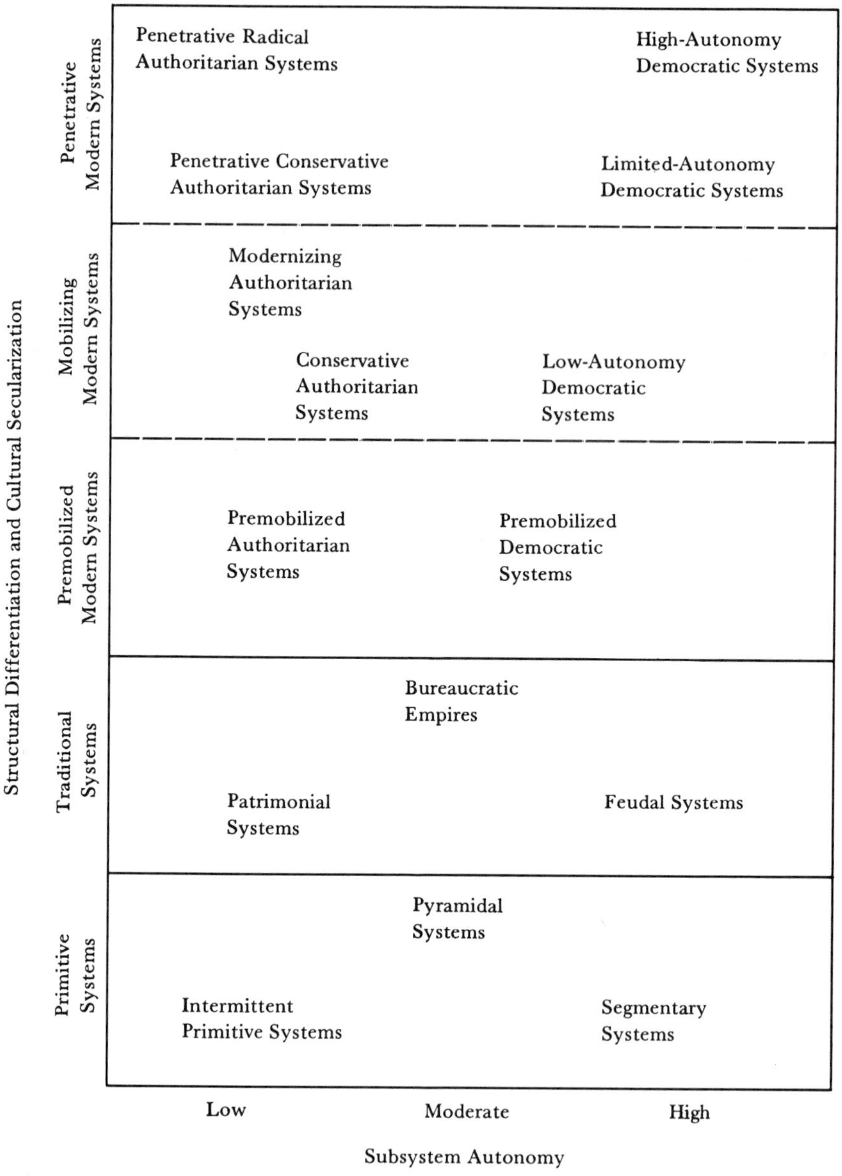

Penetrative Modern Systems	Penetrative Radical Authoritarian Systems		High-Autonomy Democratic Systems
	Penetrative Conservative Authoritarian Systems		Limited-Autonomy Democratic Systems
Mobilizing Modern Systems	Modernizing Authoritarian Systems		
		Conservative Authoritarian Systems	Low-Autonomy Democratic Systems
Premobilized Modern Systems	Premobilized Authoritarian Systems	Premobilized Democratic Systems	
Traditional Systems		Bureaucratic Empires	
	Patrimonial Systems		Feudal Systems
Primitive Systems		Pyramidal Systems	
	Intermittent Primitive Systems		Segmentary Systems

Structural Differentiation and Cultural Secularization

Low   Moderate   High

Subsystem Autonomy

tems. To do so, we combine these developmental characteristics with the dimension of subsystem autonomy. In figure III.2 we present a schematic statement of the typology. The horizontal dimension shows the level of subsystem autonomy, particularly the autonomy of the input structures.

The vertical dimension shows the degree of structural differentiation and associated cultural secularization. Although the latter two aspects of development can to some degree vary individually, we combine them for purposes of simplification and graphic presentation.

The vertical dimension, cultural and structural development, is divided into five levels. At the bottom are the primitive political systems with limited differentiation and secularization. We have grouped these primitive systems into three subtypes: (1) intermittent systems, such as the Eskimo system, which we have already discussed; (2) pyramidal systems, in which a number of groups or villages are organized in a rather loose hierarchy under a paramount chief (for instance, the Ashanti kingdom); and (3) segmentary systems, in which the units are largely autonomous but held together by minimal processes and institutions largely for the purposes of settling disputes (for example, the Alur).

In the next grouping are the traditional political systems, distinguished by differentiated governmental structures, that is, specialized structures for policy making, policy implementation, and adjudication. These include patrimonial, bureaucratic, and feudal systems, which we have already discussed.

Toward the top of figure III.2, we find three classes of modern or modernizing political systems, all of which have *both* differentiated governmental structures, such as bureaucracies, and differentiated political structures, such as interest groups and parties. In the "premobilized" type are political systems in which the modern political forms have not deeply penetrated into the society. What modern political structure and culture they have are usually concentrated among certain strata in the cities. Differentiated socialization and recruitment structures capable of sustaining continuing role performance have typically not been developed. As we shall see in examining performance and outcomes in chapters XI and XII, in such systems the capacity to extract and distribute social resources is limited. The impact of such efforts in attaining desired levels of welfare and security for the populations is also quite limited. Although in form some of these systems are more democratic and others more authoritarian, as determined by their levels of subsystem autonomy, these structural relationships tend to be quite unstable and subject to rapid change. Military and civilian coups and countercoups, legal and factual constitutional changes are quite common. Whether, at a particular point, political parties and elections are allowed or banned has perhaps less significance for life in the society than does the general fact of limited political mobilization and penetration. Such political systems as Tanzania, the Ivory Coast, and Kenya, beginning as formal democracies, have become one-party systems that only partially penetrate the underlying society.

In the next category there are "mobilizing modern systems," ones in which modern bureaucratic organizations have penetrated deeply and in which industrialization and urbanization are rather far advanced. Most of the nations of Latin America fall into this category, and they vary substantially in the extent of autonomy of their subsystems. Thus, Venezuela is on the democratic side, whereas Brazil and Peru are authoritarian. Mexico in effect has a one-party system, although other political movements are formally permitted to compete.

At the top of the diagram we are dealing with thoroughly penetrative political systems, countries in which bureaucracies and political movements reach throughout the society and economy. All of them contain highly differentiated and specialized political structures. They differ in the extent of concentration of power or autonomy of parts. On the far left are such countries as the Soviet Union and other Communist regimes, in which all political organization is under the relatively tight control of the higher echelons of the ruling parties. And at the far right are such countries as Britain, Sweden, West Germany, Japan, and the United States, in which the various parts of the political system are relatively autonomous, relatively loosely meshed. These structural characteristics have great significance for the performance of these systems and for the kinds of goals and values that they can pursue.

A classification scheme such as that presented in figure III.2, limited as it is to structural and cultural characteristics, fails to bring out some significant differences among types of regimes, particularly the modern democratic and authoritarian ones. Thus, Arend Lijphart would distinguish modern democratic systems according to their consensual and conflictual tendencies. "Centripetal," or consensual, democracies are those in which the important political movements have a large overlap in policy propensities and are loyal to the regime. The United States, Britain, the old Commonwealth countries such as Australia and New Zealand, and the Scandinavian countries would fall into this category. "Centrifugal," or conflictual, democracies are those in which important political movements are antagonistic to one another, and some important ones are opposed to the political regime itself. France, Italy, and Weimar Germany would fall into this category. Lijphart distinguishes still a third democratic form, which he calls "consociational." He is referring here to such countries as Austria, Switzerland, Holland, Belgium, and Pre-civil-war Lebanon, where the societies are divided into separate conflictual subcultures, but where historical experience and international threat have led to accommodative attitudes and arrangements among the elites.[23]

[23] Arend Lijphart, "Typologies of Democratic Systems," *Comparative Political Studies* 1 (April 1968).

On the authoritarian side, Juan Linz offers a more historically oriented classification, although on the whole his categories are similar to ours, with two main exceptions. He introduces a category of "organic-statist" regimes to refer to such political systems as Portugal under Salazar, Austria under Dolfuss, and contemporary Peru, in which authoritarian elites provide for an "organic" system of "representation" through the organization of occupational, professional, and other interest groups into corporations having some bargaining power with the state bureaucracy. He also includes a category of mixed authoritarian-democratic regimes called "racial and ethnic democracies," of which South Africa and Rhodesia are the principal contemporary exemplars. Here nonwhite majorities are governed in an authoritarian fashion, whereas the whites are governed more or less democratically.[24]

It is premature at this stage to discuss in detail the patterns of performance, outcome, and evaluative criteria that can be associated with the political systems in our typology. These are complicated problems, to which we return in our more detailed analysis of system functions, process functions, and performance in the following chapters. But this developmental approach has allowed us to classify systems in a way that will facilitate discussion of the types of problems and limitations facing different groups of systems. A specific political system that falls into one of our categories has inherited, so to speak, given types of cultural and structural arrangements from its past. The way in which leadership coalitions can deal with certain types of problems and the kinds of problems likely to appear are shaped by these historical characteristics. History does not, of course, determine the future totally, but it may well limit or exclude certain alternatives.

Suppose one were trying to predict the future career of a young graduate of a secondary school. On the basis of a few facts one could make some definite predictions about the limits and restrictions shaping the possibilities before him. If he has failed to study any mathematics, for example, one can rather safely predict that the probability of a career in science, mathematics, or engineering is very low and that if he is to begin such a career, he must choose a strategy of action that will make it possible to acquire the necessary skills. One also can predict that in the short run, if faced with certain kinds of problems, he will be incapable of solving them.

Similarly, if one knows about a set of important variables among the large number of characteristics of political systems and knows about the limits or potentials they imply, one can make some forecasts about

24 Juan Linz, "Totalitarian and Authoritarian Regimes," in Greenstein and Polsby, *Handbook of Political Science* 3: 175 ff.

political change. Thus, one knows that the ruler of a traditional empire simply cannot attain some of the system goals that may be possible for a dictator of a penetrative authoritarian system. And one can specify some of the fundamental changes that would be required if the traditional empire were to seek such goals. As we shall show, systems at different levels of differentiation and secularization, or at different levels of subsystem autonomy, encounter substantially different sets of limitations, pressures, and potentialities. Our classification contains elements of prediction and generalization, as well as the basis for a more refined development theory. In our concluding chapters we shall return to a consideration of the historical development and future strategies that lie before different types of political systems.

PART II

System Functions

CHAPTER IV

Political Socialization

POLITICAL SOCIALIZATION is the process by which political cultures are formed, maintained, and changed. Every political system has some structures that perform the political socialization function, shaping the political attitudes, inculcating the political values, and imparting the political skills of citizens and elites. In some societies the function may be performed intermittently by families, priests, and headmen carrying out their social roles, which sometimes fall into the political sphere. In other societies political socialization may be the explicit responsibility of specialized political institutions. When an authoritarian regime revises the history textbooks, or when a new nation expands its school system, the political elites are attempting to shape and control this process of political socialization.

CONCEPTS FOR SOCIALIZATION ANALYSIS
SOCIALIZATION THROUGHOUT LIFE

The first point to make about political socialization is that the process continues throughout life. Attitudes may be initially formed in childhood, but they are always being adapted as the individual goes through political and social experiences. Indeed, some major and dramatic event may provide a sudden resocialization experience for an entire nation. A great war or an economic depression can constitute a severe political shock for millions of individuals, reshaping a political culture. Involvement in a mass movement, such as the nationalist struggles prominent in the histories of many formerly colonial nations, can provide a learning experience that molds the feelings of many citizens. The participating groups acquire new conceptions of the place of politics in their lives and new goals for which they may strive.

However, though the process of attitude formation is a lifelong one, early experiences may be of great importance in several ways. On the one hand, they can initiate a process of continuous socialization that will consistently push individuals into a predictable set of orientations. Also, some kinds of attitudes seem to be formed more easily early in life, whereas others must wait for greater maturity. In our discussion of political culture we distinguished among cognitive, affective, and evaluative levels of orientations to political objects. There is considerable evidence that affective orientations, such as identification with a religious or ethnic group, are often formed early in life and exhibit considerable staying power in the face of new experiences. Cognitive attitudes are often formed later in life, in adolescent and adult years, and require the development of a more complete mental structure for knowledge about complex phenomena to be meaningful. The development of an evaluative structure involves both affective and cognitive components. Children's evaluations are largely directed by their immediate emotional reactions, whereas adults combine information and a more differentiated set of values and emotions in order to reach their evaluative positions.[1]

CONTINUITY AND REINFORCEMENT

Learning theory emphasizes that consistency is a vital element in causing reproduction of a particular attitude. If individuals receive a consistent set of messages about some political object, particularly if those messages involve their own activity, they are likely to develop a firmly held set of beliefs about that object. They become more confident, from a cognitive point of view, that their past information about the world will help them to interpret the future. On the other hand, if individuals receive varying pieces of information, they can be less confident in their assessments; the world is more uncertain; each new message must be considered for its own implications.

If citizens receive the same message from the diverse agents of socialization, the chances are high that their attitudes will be shaped in a particular way. Jennings and Niemi found that the probability that a student's attitudes would resemble those of a parent was markedly greater, on the whole range of attitudes, if both parents were in agreement.[2] Similarly, the student is more likely to hold attitudes like those of the parents if both parents and teachers are unanimous in their opinions. They conclude:

The practical implication is worth citing: if society or a given institution

---

[1] See, for example, Fred I. Greenstein, *Children and Politics* (New Haven: Yale University Press, 1965); Robert D. Hess and Judith V. Torney, *The Development of Political Attitudes in Children* (Garden City: Doubleday & Co., 1967); David Easton and Jack Dennis, *Children and the Political System* (New York: McGraw-Hill, 1969); and Richard W. Dawson, Karen S. Dawson, and Kenneth Prewitt, *Political Socialization*, 2d ed. (Boston: Little, Brown, 1977).

[2] M. Kent Jennings and Richard Niemi, *The Political Character of Adolescence* (Princeton: Princeton University Press, 1974), chap. 6.

therein desires purposely to mold its young citizens, the establishment of congruity across [socialization] agents is a prime facilitator.[3]

Similarly, stability in the political culture over time will be affected by continuity in the socialization process across agents and by those agents over time. Maximum stability of an individual's attitudes will occur when the socialization of that individual is highly continuous and reinforcing. An individual who has voted in many elections for the same political party is the most likely to establish a firmly committed partisanship.[4] Changes in affiliation tend to come among new voters and voters receiving diverse messages about parties over time. Generations are likely to have high stability of attitudes when the effect of family, school, media, and the like are the same for parents and children.

The apparent stability of political culture in many traditional societies, despite the absence of specialized political socialization roles, is due no doubt to the effect of the highly reinforcing agents of socialization in small village settings and the lack of major changes in lifestyle and circumstances across generations. In the complexity of contemporary society, with its continuing adaptation to technological change, such continuity is much less likely. The penetrative, authoritarian countries, such as the Soviet Union, have attempted to create a consistent pattern of reinforcement through controlling media and schools.

The effects of continuity in socialization also help explain the maintenance of political subcultures, particularly along lines of basic demographic cleavages in a society. Lipset and Rokkan have drawn attention to the remarkable consistency of patterns of political party support in Western Europe over half a century.[5] The political voting alignments and party support patterns of the 1960s bore amazing resemblance to those of the early 1920s in most nations of Western Europe. The resemblances seem to result from an early alignment of social and economic subgroups with particular parties and from the extensive development of organizations within these subgroups, with continuous reinforcement through voting. The organization of parties within lines of multiple social cleavages facilitated continuity in socialization. Lines of religion and

3 Ibid., p. 323.
4 See the elegant theoretical formulation and empirical test in five nations by Philip Converse, "Of Time and Partisan Stability," *Comparative Political Studies* 2 (July 1969): 139–71. Also see Paul A. Beck, "A Socialization Theory of Partisan Realignment," in Richard G. Niemi and Associates, *The Politics of Future Citizens* (San Francisco: Jossey-Bass, 1974), pp. 199–219; and Norman H. Nie, Sidney Verba, and John Petrocik, *The Changing American Voter* (Cambridge: Harvard University Press, 1976).
5 Seymour Martin Lipset and Stein Rokkan, *Party Systems and Voter Alignments* (New York: Free Press, 1967). Also see the essays in Robert A. Dahl, *Political Opposition in Western Democracies* (New Haven: Yale University Press, 1966).

social class were particularly effective, since family, church, school, and occupation would provide the same socialization cues about parties and issues linked to them.

Of course, in emphasizing the importance of continuity in explaining stability of political culture orientations, we do not wish to imply that individual and cross-generational *attitude* stability is necessarily desirable, or even stabilizing, for the political regime. As we have already pointed out in our discussion of political culture and structure, it is the fit between the propensities and the structures that affects the synchronization of resources and preferences. If and as circumstances change and new problems and new political structures are introduced, changes in the political culture must operate to keep attitudes in a balanced fit with structures.

Harry Eckstein has suggested, for example, the lack of fit between socialization patterns, culture, and the needs and expectations of the new democratic system that was set up in Germany after World War I.[6] Family, schools, political party experiences, and most formal organizations were still reinforcing a very hierarchical pattern of learning about legitimacy and processes of politics. This learning helped to limit popular acceptance of and involvement in the new political structures, which required greater participation and voluntary support. When economic and international events also failed to provide positive socialization cues about the new structures, acting rather to create more dissatisfactions, the lack of fit between culture and structure created great strain and contributed to democratic breakdown.

The continuity within subcultures has also often created problems for the political process and for system maintenance. The very continuity of forces operating within a subculture can create a sense of distance between groups, especially if reinforced by conflictual experiences, which easily support a subculture of political hostility.[7] Bargaining and accommodation become most difficult, and deadlocks and breakdown may occur.

---

[6] Harry Eckstein, "A Theory of Stable Democracy," rptd. in his *Division and Cohesion in Democracy* (Princeton: Princeton University Press, 1966). Also see Harry Eckstein and Ted Robert Gurr, *Patterns of Authority: A Structural Basis for Inquiry* (New York: John Wiley, 1975).

[7] An excellent and vivid description of such subcultural fragmentation in Weimar Germany is provided by William S. Allen, *The Nazi Seizure of Power* (Chicago: Quadrangle, 1965). A theoretical discussion and review can be found in Sidney Verba, "Organizational Membership and Democratic Consensus," *Journal of Politics* 27 (August 1965): 467–97. Description and analysis of causes and consequences of subcultural organization in Austrian politics can be found in G. Bingham Powell, Jr., *Social Fragmentation and Political Hostility* (Stanford: Stanford University Press, 1970).

ROLE SOCIALIZATION

One concept necessary for discussing the performance of the socialization function is role socialization. We have spoken of socialization as the creating or changing of attitudes toward political objects. One of the important aspects of socialization is the creation of attitudes toward roles in the political system. For the citizen, this may involve shaping of his attitudes about himself as voter, contactor of authorities, demonstrator, or as taxpayer, obeyer of the laws, and the like. For the elite actor role socialization means awareness of the set of expectations and regular, appropriate patterns of behavior expected in his role. This socialization may take the form of written rules about administrative obligations, duties, and opportunities. But it also usually involves learning about the informal expectations that others have about the role. We return below to the concept of elite role socialization, as part of the discussion of elite subcultures.

STYLES IN SOCIALIZATION PERFORMANCE

By socialization style we refer to the ways in which the structures perform the socialization function. We can, of course, make many types of style distinctions, but the contrast most commonly emphasized in socialization analysis is that between latent and manifest styles of political socialization.[8] Political socialization is manifest when it involves the open communication of information, values, or feelings toward political objects. A speech by the President informing American citizens about some foreign policy crisis, its implications, and its origins is an example of such manifest socialization. So is a father's discussion with his child about the qualities of the President or about his own intention to vote for a given political party. Widespread manifest political socialization is typically associated with a secular political culture.

Latent or indirect socialization is the transmission of nonpolitical attitudes that affect attitudes toward similar roles and objects in the political system. Such hidden socialization may occur with particular force in early experiences. For example, children may acquire certain general attitudes of accommodation or aggression toward others. Such acquired attitudes may in later life affect their attitudes toward political leaders or fellow citizens. Or early participation in family decision making, rather than strict obedience to parental decisions, may indirectly establish propensities to participate in all kinds of social activities, including political ones, and to value such participation.

---

[8] A useful review is provided by Dawson, Dawson, and Prewitt, op. cit., chap. 6, "Methods of Political Learning."

SOCIALIZATION DYNAMICS: THE YOUTH MOVEMENTS
OF THE 1960s AS AN EXAMPLE

One of the problems in studying political socialization is that so many different structures perform the function that it is difficult to sort out the particular effects of each one. As socialization is a lifelong process, one must be sensitive to the direct and indirect messages about politics being given to children and to adults as well. Because socialization can be performed by virtually any structure as it sends direct and indirect messages about politics, one must be sensitive to the interaction of many structures: family, peer group, school system, television, interest groups, work place, political parties, and government agencies. The effect of messages depends on the consistency and impact of the messages received and also on the previous opinions of the receiver, so one must be sensitive to cumulations of effect from all sources over time. Since one may be interested in many different aspects of the political culture, one must pay attention to the effects on process propensities, policy propensities, and system propensities. And it should be remembered that the interaction and feedback effects of citizens' activities result in changes in the socialization agencies themselves, which have further effects on attitudes.

To emphasize the need for a dynamic and multistructural analysis of socialization, it may be useful to provide an example of socialization dynamics before we discuss some of the individual structures involved in the process. Let us consider the efforts to explain the remarkable changes that took place in the political culture of many young people in the United States, Western Europe, and Japan in the 1960s. Any satisfying interpretation of these cultural changes must explain the unusual combination of large-scale political rebellion and cultural experimentation among young people and particularly among college students. It required an extraordinary set of socialization changes to convert the pattern of political apathy, liberal impulses, and moderate personal experimentation characteristic of young people in the 1950s into the massive and violent political mobilizations and cultural explosions of the following decade.

Table IV.1 indicates some of the general types of explanation that have been offered.[9] In the first column is the general approach; the second column shows the types of socialization agent changes suggested by that approach; and in the last column are the types of attitudinal and

[9] For sake of simplicity, we shall here emphasize the causes and explanations of youth disturbances in the United States. See Gabriel A. Almond, "Youth and Changing Political Culture in the United States," in Gordon J. Direnzo, *We the People: American Character and Social Change* (Westport, Conn.: Greenwood Press, 1977), pp. 115–47.

Table IV.1. *Alternative Explanations of the Youth Disturbances of the 1960s*

General explanatory approach	Changes in socialization agencies	Youth cultural effects explained
Life-cycle effects only	Exposure to higher education, Departure from family circle, Low stake in governmental policies directly	General policy liberalism, "Wild oats" behavior, Political apathy
Political period effects, plus life cycle	Ethnic rebellion and mass media, Vietnam War, TV, Draft; Education, Departure from family circle	Loss of legitimacy of adult authority, Sense of immediate political involvement
Socioeconomic period effects, plus life cycle	Huge increase in higher education, Increase in youth age group as percentage of population, Technical and bureaucratic character of higher education, Economic affluence, TV	Sense of generation gap and lack of history, Peer group identity and youth group experimentalism, Individual technological alienation, Rejection of materialism, Involvement
Political period effects, plus socioeconomic period effects, plus life cycle	All political and socioeconomic changes listed above	Political rebelliousness and cultural experimentalism, as listed above

behavioral changes predicted. The first row of the table shows the "life-cycle effects" type of explanation, the "boys will be boys" approach that sought initially to characterize the youth explosion of the 1960s as a familiar pattern of youthful energy and naiveté typical of adolescence. By the end of the decade such explanations were quite clearly discredited, due to their inadequacy to account for the unprecedented levels of political unrest and cultural innovation.

The second row depicts an application of Lewis Feuer's ingenious explanation, which combines life-cycle tendencies with the effects of the governmental outputs and political upheavals of the immediate political period — in the American case, the effects of the black ethnic rebellion and, increasingly throughout the decade, the Vietnam War. Given immediacy by the pervasiveness of television and, by the end of the decade, by personal and family involvement with the draft and the different protest movements, these political period effects might account for the politicization of the campuses. Feuer's historical accounts of youth movements indicate as much.[10] But there is no simple way for the black rebellion and the Vietnam War to have produced the counterculture, with its rejection of the work and achievement ethic, its communalism, its primitive and "instant" ideologies, and so forth.

Similarly, the socioeconomic period effects outlined in the third row — the youth bulge, the quantum jump in higher education, the increasingly technical nature of the curriculum and the growing impersonality in treatment of students, and the rising trend of economic growth and material affluence — all can be seen to have a causal connection to the various cultural innovations and the crises of university authority; but they cannot account for the political mobilizations of the period. Rising affluence and opportunity, as Inglehart has suggested, made the rejection of the work ethic and materialism possible and gave impetus to the search for "higher" values.[11] The rapid growth of student bodies and the decay of the traditional social structure of university life may have contributed to the commune movement, and to the stress in youth culture on "meaningful" personal relationships. The size of the youth cohort and the consequent enhancement of the role of peer group socialization, at the expense of cultural transmission through adults and authority figures, helps explain the "generation gap," the lack of a sense of history in the "now" generation, and the primitive quality of its ideological, political, and aesthetic formulations.[12] These socioeconomic period effects can help us understand Woodstock, the commune movements, and the "counter-curriculum," but not the massive political demonstrations and confrontations far beyond campus issues.

When one combines these socioeconomic and political period effects, there begins to emerge a set of independent variables capable of explaining the complex cultural shifts that went into the great youth disturbances of the late 1960s in the United States. They suggest that the political and cultural rebellions were essentially period-bound, tied to the political issues, the state of the economy, the age distribution of the population, and the educational problems of the time. Each of these two sets of period-bound developments had a distinctive relation to each of the two components of the disturbances — the socioeconomic ones with the cultural manifestations, and the political issues with the political rebellion. But in addition, the two sets of period-related causes inter-

---

[10] Lewis Samuel Feuer, *The Conflict of Generations* (New York: Basic Books, 1969).

[11] Ronald Inglehart, *The Silent Revolution* (Princeton: Princeton University Press, 1977). And see Daniel Yankelovich, *The New Morality: A Profile of American Youth in the 70's* (San Francisco: McGraw-Hill, 1974).

[12] See the discussion of peer group socialization in S. N. Eisenstadt, *From Generation to Generation* (New York: Free Press, 1956); and Dawson, Dawson, and Prewitt, op. cit., chap. 7.

acted, fed upon one another, making the political rebellion more explosive and the cultural rebellion more bizarre. The loss of legitimacy of political and social authority resulting from the ethnic rebellion and the Vietnam War weakened the moral and cultural order, or made it fair game, justifying the experimentation with new values and social arrangements. On the other hand, the youth bulge, the rapid growth of higher education, and the boom economy, combined with the immediate feedback effects from television, created volatile masses, responding quickly on a large scale to political stimuli. And initial experiences with political involvement helped create a sense of tactics and a loose cadre of political organizers that facilitated action.

The political rebellion and the cultural experimentalism both began to subside after the turn of the decade. As the ethnic mobilization lost its intensity and the American role in the Vietnam War drew to a close, the political stimuli lost their force. Participant experience levels declined as new generations entered college. And as the growth of higher education subsided and young people confronted a contracting economy, the values and expectations of American youth became more somber, even though many of the specific social beliefs of the 1960s remained.[13]

STRUCTURES PERFORMING CITIZEN SOCIALIZATION

Any political structure, or even any pattern of events, may operate as a political socialization agent for citizens, providing them with messages, implicit or explicit, that could shape their propensities for political behavior. In this section we shall discuss some of the structures that commonly perform important socialization functions in many societies. We shall begin with the family, usually the first source of attitude formation, and move outward to other types of structures, indicating the ways in which they can act to sustain or change various elements of the political culture.

THE FAMILY AS SOCIALIZATION AGENT

We have already indicated that the family may have lasting influence on some aspects of political attitudes. Jennings and Niemi, in their study of high school students and their parents, found rather high agreement between parents and children in the development of party identification and on some specific policy issues of high emotional salience and personal identity: attitudes toward school integration and school prayers.[14] Other American studies have also reported the high agreement on party

---

[13] Yankelovich, op. cit.; for a general discussion of the American setting and changes in the 1960s and early 1970s, see Nie, Verba, and Petrocik, op. cit.

[14] Jennings and Niemi, op. cit., chap. 12.

88 — Political Socialization

Table IV.2. *Associations Between Attitudes of Students and Parents in the United States and Japan*

Type of propensity	USA[a]		Japan[b]	
Process: Self in politics	Knowledge	.25		
	Interest	.11	Interest	.13
	Efficacy	.11		
Policy	Party identification	.47	Party identification	.39
	Integration	.34	Security treaty	.26
	School prayers	.29		
	Liberal vs. Conservative	.16		
	Communism	.13		
	Speech against Church	.08		
System	Trust of national government	.12	Constitutional revision	.06

Note: The statistic used as a measure of association is Tau-Beta.
[a] Jennings and Niemi, *Political Character of Adolescence.*
[b] Kabota and Ward, "Family Influences and Political Socialization in Japan." The Japanese study consisted of two waves of about sixty pairs in each wave; the average scores have been averaged for the two waves in the statistics shown here.

identification.[15] Comparative studies suggest that much depends on the clarity of the party structure and consistency of parental messages.[16] On other critical elements in the political culture, such as personal efficacy, free speech attitudes, and trust of the national government, parent-child agreement has generally been less. Table IV.2 compares parent-child agreement for teen-age students in the United States and Japan on party identification and several specific process, policy, and system propensities.

The issues on which there is high agreement between parent and child seem to be those which have salience and which are related to matters

[15] See the review in Nie, Verba, and Petrocik, op. cit., chap. 4.; and Jennings and Niemi, op. cit., chap. 2. We must not, of course, confuse agreement with socialization influence. Agreement may result from coincidental environmental and status position effects; on the other hand, socialization may have taken place, but be weakened or hidden by other factors.

[16] See Philip E. Converse and G. Dupeux, "The Politicization of the Electorates in France and the United States," *Public Opinion Quarterly,* 26 (Spring 1962): 1–23; and Jack Dennis and Donald J. McCrone, "Preadult Development of Political Party Identification in Western Democracies," pp. 115–35; and Akira Kabota and Robert E. Ward, "Family Influences and Political Socialization in Japan," pp. 11–46, both in Jack Dennis and M. Kent Jennings, eds., *Comparative Political Socialization* (Beverly Hills: Sage Publications, 1970).

of identity, such as party identification, and to the more policy-specific issues associated with race and religion, which can be shaped early in life. Matters of political trust and efficacy, on the other hand, show less agreement. One reason for the lower agreement in these areas seems to be the lack of actual political experience among the young, so development of cognitive and evaluative structures may be delayed or easily changed by personal adult experience. Various studies show, for example, that students' knowledge and awareness is much greater for federal than for state and local governments in the United States.[17] The difference seems to follow from the school emphasis on teaching about national government. Yet personal adult experience will more often be with local government and agencies. The other reason for limited specific agreement in such areas as efficacy is the diffuse and open-end nature of early learning. Jennings and Niemi conclude:

> We believe that children do acquire a minimal set of basic commitments to the political system and a realization of political membership. [But] these comprise extremely broad foundations for later growth and permutations. *Upon the generous confines of these foundations arise widely diverse value structures.* Consequently, parental dispositions are often a feeble guide as to what twelfth graders' precise global perspectives will be within the larger parameters.[18]

The nature of the relationship between the broad foundations created in childhood socialization and the more specific and complex adult value structures is a matter of continuing controversy and research.[19]

It is likely that some of the weaknesses of association between attitudes of parents and children, at least in the modern societies in which such investigations have been carried out, reflect the breakdown of the extended family structure, as well as the generally greater diversity of the environment of the child in a modern setting. The Japanese study, for example, showed that Japanese students who were family-oriented expressed attitudes much more like their parents' than did those who were not family-oriented.[20] In many traditional societies, the child grows up in an extended family; its authority structure may be either hierarchic or segmented, with authority in different areas divided between the eldest male, the father, and various female family members. But messages sent from all these adults will be highly consistent, and the family will

---

17 Greenstein, op. cit., chap. 4.
18 Jennings and Niemi, op. cit., p. 323, emphasis added.
19 Donald D. Searing, Joel J. Schwartz, and Alden E. Lind, "The Structuring Principle: Political Socialization and Belief Systems," *APSR* 67 (June 1973): 415–32.
20 Kabota and Ward, op. cit., p. 26.

take up a much greater part of the child's environment. Even learning about future occupation roles will be undertaken in the family setting, often explicitly demonstrated by relatives with special child-rearing responsibilities.

As the extended family has broken down in many modern societies under the impact of geographic mobility and other aspects of modern life, and as peer groups, the school system, radio and television, and magazines take over many of the family's old responsibilities, the impact of family socialization has probably declined. The greater equality in the nuclear family structure may also weaken socialization of specific policy propensities; as pointed out above, if the messages are less consistent, as when parents disagree, then the impact in attitude formation is less pronounced. On the other hand, more equal family relationships may act in the latent socialization of more equalitarian and participatory values. Almond and Verba found that adults reporting more active participation in family and school decision making were likely to be more politically active as adults.[21]

COMMUNITY, NEIGHBORHOOD, AND PEER GROUPS

Many of the same arguments about the role of the family in socialization apply to community and neighborhood as well. In the more traditional society the geographic isolation of most communities and their relative internal homogeneity meant that they would provide a host of cues about political life that reinforced family teaching. With the penetration of mass media and with high geographic mobility, the cues from community and neighborhood structures are less consistent, providing only one part of a diverse set of messages. These changes do not mean that community and neighborhood influences have disappeared. Growing up in the rural Midwest, Wales, or Bavaria is still a quite different experience than growing up in New York, London, or Berlin, and these differences have political consequences.

Of course, an individual's peer groups — that is, people of equal social or professional status — play an important role in shaping values and attitudes at most stages in life. Particularly where family relations are loosened in an industrial society, or where family training does not relate to a youth's social environment, one may expect the formal and informal social environments to have a considerable impact on the first views formed of politics.[22] Among adults, too, messages about politics are molded and filtered by informal discussions with friends and associates.

[21] Gabriel A. Almond and Sidney Verba, *The Civic Culture* (Princeton: Princeton University Press, 1963), chap. 11.
[22] Eisenstadt, *From Generation to Generation*; Jennings and Niemi, op. cit., chap. 9.

Table IV.3. *Children's Evaluations of the President
of the United States in Four American Subcultures*

| | General view of the president as a person | | | |
Subculture	Best in the world	Good person	Not a good person	Total
Chicagoans[a]	11%	82%	8%	101% (211)
Ohio rural whites[b]	4	77	19	100 (151)
Ohio rural blacks[b]	7	63	30	100 (43)
Appalachian whites[a]	6	68	26	100 (139)

[a] Data from Dean Jaros, Herbert Hirsch, and Frederick J. Fleron, "The Malevolent Leader: Political Socialization in an American Subculture," *APSR* 62 (June 1968): 568. The Chicago data are originally from Robert D. Hess and David Easton, "The Child's Changing Image of the President," *Public Opinion Quarterly* 14 (Winter 1960): 632–42.

[b] Data from Dean Jaros and Kenneth L. Kolran, "The Multifarious Leader: Political Socialization of Amish, Yanks, and Blacks," in Niemi and Associates, *Politics of Future Citizens*, pp. 41–62. Data for Amish are not reported here.

The first studies of mass media influence demonstrated that the political effects of mass media messages were mediated through local "opinion leaders" who were trusted by individuals who paid less direct attention to politics.[23]

Table IV.3 shows some of the pronounced subcultural differences associated with different childhood environments still operating in the United States. The Ohio black children and those in an Appalachian community obviously had more negative views of the President of the United States than did the children in Chicago and the Ohio whites. The diffuse, emotional attitudes of these grammar school children toward the symbol of highest authority in America reflect the burdens of discrimination and economic deprivation that are being conveyed by their family, peers, and community settings.[24] If such differences are created within American subcultures,[25] despite national mass media, breakdown of the extended family, and relatively uniform content of formal school curricula, how much more striking can such differences be expected to be in other national environments. In nations such as India or Nigeria,

[23] Elihu Katz and Paul F. Lazarsfeld, *Personal Influence: The Part Played by People in the Flow of Mass Communications* (Glencoe: Free Press, 1955). Also see chap. VI in this volume.

[24] See the discussion by the original sources for the data cited in table IV.3.

[25] Also see Samuel C. Patterson, "The Political Cultures of the American States," *Journal of Politics* 30 (February 1968): 187–209.

the immediate environments of children can differ by language, race, religion, custom, caste, as well as by proximity to modern life.

THE CHURCH

In Western Europe the struggle over the role of the church in the socialization process has been one of the most pervasive sources of political conflict in the last 150 years. In the nineteenth century the imperatives of technological development, and the example of the French Revolution, made mass education a central concern of nation builders. Particularly in those European nations where the Catholic church had prevailed in the Counter-Reformation of the seventeenth century, the introduction of mass education became a battleground between church and state. The reason was in part the church's belief that it must retain control over the educational system in order to expose the young to proper religious values. Liberal, and later Socialist, reformers were equally determined that young minds should be liberated from religious dogma. Although the battle was settled early in the twentieth century in many nations, the old battle lines continue to shape party alignments in Western Europe,[26] and the role of the church in education is a lively issue in such nations as Italy today.

The impact of the church in the socialization process is not, of course, limited to its role in religious schools. Rather, churches exist in order to teach a set of general values to children and adults alike. Messages preached in weekly services are one set of cues. But the institutions of Catholicism or Islam go far beyond any single type of contact and provide secondary recreational, study, and occupational groups that shape a wide set of interpersonal cues in the life of the individual. Some of these cues have political significance, either directly, as when the Italian Catholic church urged opposition to the Communist party at the polls, or indirectly, as they form values and emotional attachments to symbols, policies, and structures. The impact of secularization has lessened the role of the churches as agents of socialization, as has the impact of the many diverse messages to which a modern individual is exposed. But even today in the highly industrialized nations of Western Europe, recent studies clearly demonstrate that the best single predictors of party vote are the religious affiliation and religious activities of the citizen.[27]

SCHOOL SYSTEMS

The school system is clearly one of the most systematically powerful influences in political socialization. In the United States, Britain, Ger-

[26] Lipset and Rokkan, op. cit.
[27] See table VIII.2.

many, Italy, and Mexico, educated persons were found to be more aware of the influence of government on their lives, to pay more attention to politics, to have more information about political leaders, and to manifest more political competence.[28] These findings have been replicated in nations as diverse as Argentina, Austria, Chile, East Pakistan, India, Israel, Japan, the Netherlands, Nigeria, and Yugoslavia.[29] Of course, attaining an education reflects much more than the socialization impact of the school system. Education is related to socialization by educated parents and above all to greater social and political resources possessed by the educated in most societies.[30] Nonetheless, the role of the school system is clearly important, particularly in the provision of levels of knowledge, skill, and sense of the alternatives that encourage political activity. The school system may be particularly important for individuals from deprived family and personal environments.[31]

Schools can also play an important role in shaping other parts of the political culture map. They can strengthen or reinforce affection for the political system and can provide common symbols for the expressive response to the community and the regime, such as the national flag or the introduction of African cultural history in the schools of new African nations. They can introduce beliefs about the "unwritten rules of the political game," the appropriate standards for elites as well as for citizens, which influence conduct and the sense of legitimacy. Schools can also develop, especially among the elite, a sense of trust across political partisan lines that increases coalition possibilities. (The role of the old school tie in Britain and Japan has been often noted.) Moreover, both family and school offer particular patterns of authoritative decision making to which students are exposed. The pattern of obedience learned by the student can be related to future performance as political subject and participant.[32]

However, it is especially necessary in discussing schools to repeat the warning about political socialization that we have already voiced several

[28] Almond and Verba, op. cit., pp. 315–24.

[29] See Sidney Verba, Norman H. Nie, and Jae-on Kim, *The Modes of Democratic Participation: A Cross-National Comparison* (Beverly Hills: Sage Publications, 1971); Sidney Verba, Norman H. Nie, Ana Barbic, Galen Irwin, Henk Molleman, and Goldie Shabad, "The Modes of Participation: Continuities in Research," *Comparative Political Studies* 6 (July 1973): 235–50; Alex Inkeles and David H. Smith, *Becoming Modern* (Cambridge: Harvard University Press, 1974).

[30] An excellent brief review of the different ways in which education can relate to other social and economic resources in a society is provided by Robert D. Putnam, *The Comparative Study of Political Elites* (Englewood Cliffs: Prentice-Hall, 1976).

[31] See the findings by Jennings and Niemi, op. cit., on the effect of civics courses on black and white students (chap. 7, coauthored by Kenneth P. Langton).

[32] Almond and Verba, op. cit., chap. 11.

times: socialization outcomes depend on the interactions of all messages
and circumstances, especially on the consistency involved. Schools have
often been used by ruling groups to inculcate desired political attitudes.
But the success of such efforts is, at best, highly contingent on the setting. Soviet efforts at collective upbringing seem to have been somewhat
successful in creating adult-oriented behavior and reducing individualist
deviance among school children.[33] But the calls for obedience and the
emphasis on symbols of national unity have not prevented ethnic conflict
and fragmentation in many of the new nations. And Wylie's study of a
small French town clearly illustrated how a general attitude of contempt
and rejection toward the political system can dominate children's attitudes, even when the official school texts present quite another picture.[34]

THE WORK PLACE

Among the important individual environments for adults is the work
place. Inkeles and Smith's cross-national study of the development of
"modern attitudes," including information on national issues and leaders,
openness to new experiences, appreciation of technical skill, readiness
for social change, and personal and political efficacy, showed that occupational experiences were an influence second only to education.[35] Interestingly enough, the Inkeles-Smith study particularly emphasized the
contrast between traditional agricultural labor and modern factory experience in creating an awareness of the possibility of organization,
change, and control over nature:

> By the very nature of the forces at work in it, the factory *exemplifies* ef-
> ficacy, since in it is concentrated the power to convert obdurate materials
> into new shapes and forms far exceeding the capacity of the unaided in-
> dividual to do so. The total working of the factory affirms man's capacity,
> through organization and the harnessing of mechanical power, to transform
> nature to suit his needs. One worker we spoke to in Nigeria expressed the
> basic idea for us perfectly when, in reply to our questions about how his
> work left him feeling, he said, "Sometimes like nine feet tall with arms a
> yard wide. Here in the factory I alone with my machine can twist any way
> I want a piece of steel all the men in my home village together could not
> begin to bend at all." [36]

[33] See Urie Bronfenbrenner, *Two Worlds of Childhood: US and USSR* (New York:
Simon & Schuster, 1970); however, care must be used in interpreting the results of
such studies.
[34] Laurence Wylie, *Village in the Vaucluse* (Cambridge: Harvard University Press,
1957).
[35] Inkeles and Smith, op. cit.; and see table II.6.
[36] Ibid., p. 158.

FORMAL ORGANIZATIONS

Experience in recreational, occupational, cultural, or political organizations can also be a powerful influence on adult attitudes. Participation in collective bargaining or involvement in a union strike can be a socializing experience for worker and employer alike. Laborers who participate in a successful strike learn that they can shape the authoritative decisions being made about their future. They also gain knowledge of political techniques such as picketing. If their organization is involved in political affairs, they will receive much informal political information, perhaps even being subjected to direct mobilization campaigns by the organization's leaders.

A number of studies have shown that organizational involvement can be a major source of the attitudes that facilitate political participation, as well as increasing exposure to the mobilizing efforts of others.[37] Indeed, organizational involvement can help to overcome the inhibiting effect of lack of education on the process propensities of working-class groups.[38] We shall return to this important point in discussing recruitment to citizen participation roles in a later chapter. But we want to emphasize that the formation of voluntary organizations among various class groups can be one of the most important agents for social change and mobilization into politics. Inkeles and Smith also found, for example, that members of agricultural cooperatives had acquired "modern attitudes" more like those of factory workers than like those of other agricultural laborers.[39]

MASS MEDIA

The role of the mass media, such as television, radio, newspapers, and magazines, must also be considered in socialization analysis. One of the most obvious and important effects of the media is giving salience to political issues and events. Various studies have indicated that the emphasis placed on such problems as crime, inflation, or oil prices has led to increased citizen concern about these problems.[40] As usual, such

---

[37] Robert E. Lane, *Political Life* (New York: Free Press, 1959); Robert A. Dahl, *Who Governs?* (New Haven: Yale University Press, 1961); Almond and Verba, op. cit., chap. 10; Norman H. Nie, G. Bingham Powell, Jr., and Kenneth Prewitt, "Social Structure and Political Participation," *APSR* 63 (June and September 1969): 361–78, 808–32; Powell, op. cit., chaps. 4 and 5; Sidney Verba and Norman H. Nie, *Participation in America* (N.Y.: Harper & Row, 1972).

[38] Nie, Powell, and Prewitt, ibid.

[39] Inkeles and Smith, op. cit.

[40] An excellent review of recent extensive research in this area, and its limitations, can be found in Lee B. Becker, Maxwell E. McCombs, and Jack M. McLeod, "The Development of Political Cognitions," in Steven H. Chaffee, ed., *Political Communication* (Beverly Hills: Sage Publications, 1975), pp. 38–53. And see chap. VI.

effects are contingent on other sources of information, the setting, and previous state of opinion. But there can be little doubt that the mass media played an essential role in bringing such issues as Watergate to the attention of the American people. The media also contribute quite clearly to the general level of political information. Several British and American studies have demonstrated that increased television exposure is related to development by the electorate of more accurate information about party policies.[41] Harik's study of an Egyptian village found that half of the people had acquired their information about three government policies directly through the media.[42] There is little doubt that the mass media can constitute a major factor in increasing citizen awareness of the issues, leaders, and policy alternatives available in a society.

The impact of the mass media on long-term policy propensities and on the development of process and system propensities is a matter of greater complexity and dispute. In one of the first major studies of political development, Daniel Lerner suggested that the mass media could be important in the creation of a sense of empathy, or of identification with other people and with the prospects for better ways of life.[43] Inkeles and Smith found that mass media exposure was, indeed, an important source of a variety of modern attitudes.[44] Herbert Hyman has argued that the mass media effects can be vast and standardized enough to bring national uniformities to diverse subcultures, particularly in parochial societies.[45] And national leaders and politicians have made many attempts to mobilize regime support and introduce a sense of identification with national symbols through mass media control.

However, the use of the media as an instrument for change in fundamental cultural patterns, other than cognitive information, may be ineffective unless combined with other socialization agencies. Not only are the problems of consistency and reinforcement quite relevant, but the impersonality of mass communications creates special limitations on political socialization. For one thing, various studies suggest that frequently messages from the mass media are not received or not interpreted directly. Rather, the process is mediated through local opinion

---

[41] Becker, McCombs, and McLeod, op. cit., p. 54.

[42] Iliya F. Harik, "Opinion Leaders and Mass Media in Rural Egypt," *APSR* 65 (September 1971): 730–40.

[43] Daniel Lerner, *The Passing of Traditional Society* (Glencoe: Free Press, 1958); and see Karl W. Deutsch, *Nationalism and Social Communication* (New York: John Wiley, 1953).

[44] Inkeles and Smith, op. cit.; and see table II.6.

[45] Herbert H. Hyman, "Mass Communication and Political Socialization," in Lucian W. Pye, ed., *Communications and Political Development* (Princeton: Princeton University Press, 1963).

leaders, such as ministers, community leaders, activists, and the like, who pass on the messages of significance as they interpret them to their parishioners or constituents. Such is the well-known "two step flow" of communication as identified by Katz and Lazarsfeld.[46] Although recent studies have indicated many variations in the two-step process and have suggested that much cognitive learning may take place directly, the importance of context and of self-selection in attention cannot be denied.[47]

Indeed, people seem to pay more attention to material with which they agree and in which they have been previously interested.[48] This fact weakens the power of the media as explicit instruments for attitudinal change. Those whose attitudes and propensities might be changed are typically not paying attention. This does not mean that the media cannot play an important socialization role through reinforcing previously acquired beliefs or through increasing the sense of immediacy and salience of issues. It seems likely that television, for instance, does create a sense of immediate involvement in war and conflict. But due to self-selection tendencies, the initial effect is likely to be greatest on those already somewhat concerned. Their deepened involvement may later lead them to attempt to influence the opinions of others.

SPECIALIZED POLITICAL INPUT STRUCTURES:
INTEREST GROUPS AND PARTIES

Interest groups, such as the Committee on Political Education of the AFL-CIO (COPE), or political parties of all kinds frequently become engaged in political socialization efforts. Interest groups seek to arouse interest and support, as well as to communicate demands, and political parties attempt to mold issue preferences, to arouse the apathetic, and to find new issues as they mobilize support for candidates and coalitions. Obviously, such organizations are not always successful; they face many of the same limitations as any socialization agent. But they can have major effects, particularly as they involve individuals in political activity.

A full discussion of the types of interest groups and parties would take us too far afield of our purposes here.[49] But some of the important effects of their efforts can be indicated. One is the reinforcement of basic cultural patterns. Political parties such as the Republican and Democratic parties in the United States and the Labour and Conservative parties in Britain have much at stake in the existing political system.

---

46 Katz and Lazarsfeld, op. cit.

47 See the study and review in Harik, op. cit.

48 In general, on limitations of media effects, see Dawson, Dawson, and Prewitt, op. cit., chap. 10.

49 See chaps. VII and VIII for further examples and analysis of types of such structures.

They typically draw heavily on its traditional symbols, such as flag and country, and emphasize the positive aspects of the regime's structure. A competitive party system focuses criticism on the authorities, but frequently reinforces support of regime and community. It also keeps the citizen in constant contact with the political structures. Most individuals are concerned with politics only in quite limited ways. But a steady level of party activities, culminating in the electoral process every few years, keeps the citizen involved in citizenship, the participant role. The parties communicate information and mobilize activity.

However, not all reinforcement is stabilizing for the political system. As we pointed out earlier in this chapter, parties can attempt to create political subcultures. In Western Europe in the late nineteenth century, the Socialist parties developed an entire environment for the new working class, which was largely excluded from the traditional society. They formed not only party branches, but consumer organizations, trade unions, recreational groups, and even burial societies. Their efforts were emulated by some parties on the political right, especially the Catholic parties. Although they performed critical services for the deprived groups (even today the effects of such organization on lower-class political action can be seen [50]), the subcultural divisiveness has often created severe problems of political conflict.[51] Political parties can also draw upon subcultural divisions based on ethnicity and religion, turning latent differences into overt political issues. In such cases, the party leaders can act as political "entrepreneurs," bringing new and divisive issues to the forefront in political life. Many examples of such mobilization of cultural differences by parties can be found in developing nations, but the successful efforts by Flemish-language parties in Belgium in the 1960s are equally startling. By appealing to linguistic divisions, the small Flemish and later French parties split the traditional party system, which had lasted fifty years as a stable three-party system; aroused massive political conflict; and brought about major policy changes, including constitutional revisions.[52]

An even more dramatic example of the role of political parties in the socialization process is to be found where parties are engaged in initiating or maintaining new patterns of political culture generally. In a period of socioeconomic flux and disruption, parties that can offer political solutions are in a favorable position to woo adherents. If historical patterns

---

[50] See Nie, Powell, Prewitt, op. cit.

[51] See Verba, "Organizational Membership and Democratic Consensus"; Powell, *Social Fragmentation and Political Hostility*; Allen, op. cit.

[52] A brief, but useful, introduction to the situation in Belgium can be found in Alvin Rabushka and Kenneth Shepsle, *Politics in Plural Societies* (Columbus: Merrill, 1972), pp. 105–20.

of thinking have been shaken by new conditions, party elites may be able to introduce — and to reinforce through modes of participating and contacting — new expectations and norms of political behavior. This situation appears today in many of the less industrialized nations, where rapid social, economic, and political change may be taking place.[53]

The degree to which elites in the underdeveloped areas attempted to rely on the political party to control and order political change, particularly to provide new standards of legitimacy and orderly patterns of mobilized political participation, has been noted by almost all students of African and Asian nations. David Apter, for example, described the phenomenon as follows:

> Political movements are directly akin to religious ones. They allow people to feel purified and personally better organized, by virtue of membership. And membership itself is an informal matter. It is a matter of feelings more than party cards, loyalty rather than organization. And, because of the weak articulation of the movement, it tends to be very fragile, breaking up when some of its primary objectives have been accomplished. It is in the transformation of the movement into a party, whether of representation or solidarity, which quite often determines the constitutional future of a country and the nature of its polity; because in the institutionalization of loyalty and the institutionalization of authority, political leaders in a movement seek to transform the restless sweep of public energy, liberated by and flooding through the political sector of social life, into something more stable and permanent, so that organized beliefs about authority and government are defined and made to stick.[54]

Obviously, the ways in which political parties affect the development of political culture depend on many factors, and the attempts have met with varying degrees of success.

SPECIALIZED OUTPUT STRUCTURES: LEGISLATURES, BUREAUCRACIES, AND COURTS

Another influence is the direct contacts between citizens and the specialized output structures whose primary formal goal is to make and implement authoritative public policies. In modern societies, the wide scope of governmental activities brings citizens into frequent contact with various bureaucratic agencies. Although the scope of government intervention in daily life is not as great in the United States as in many Western European nations — or, of course, as in the Communist na-

---

[53] A good general discussion of the role of parties in the developing areas can be found in Samuel P. Huntington, *Political Order in Changing Societies* (New Haven: Yale University Press, 1968), especially chap. 7.

[54] David Apter, *The Politics of Modernization* (Chicago: University of Chicago Press, 1965), chap. 6.

tions [55] — even American citizens have sufficient direct governmental contacts to shape their evaluations. A recent study, for example, found that 72 percent of Americans interacted with at least one government agency in the preceding year, and about a third had interacted with three or more. The most frequent contacts were with tax authorities, school officials, and the police.[56] No matter how positive the view of the political system that has been taught in school, a citizen who is harassed by the police, ignored by welfare agencies, or unfairly taxed is unlikely to feel much warmth toward the authorities.

As shown in table IV.4, Almond and Verba found marked differences across their five democracies in the expectations that the citizens had of their treatment by police and bureaucrats. Italians, and particularly Mexicans, had quite dismal expectations as to equality and responsiveness of treatment. American blacks also reported quite negative expectations in these 1960 interviews. Quite likely, these expectations are in large measure a response to actual treatment patterns.

SOCIAL, ECONOMIC, AND POLITICAL OUTCOMES

Specific political experiences, such as a war or an independence movement, can have a widespread effect on political attitudes. A series of political upheavals, such as the movement for equality among American blacks, the Vietnam War, the youth protests and rebellions, the assassinations, and the shifts in party positions, all of which confronted the American public in the 1960s, can also shape the political culture. In chapter II we noted some of the many changes that have taken place in American public opinion, including the rise in attitude consistency, the decline in trust of the government, and the greater importance of issues in voting patterns.[57]

Less dramatic elements of the general social and economic environments may also have effects. Ronald Inglehart writes with great persuasiveness and imagination about the effects of economic security on the values of different generations.[58] The generations that came of age in the 1960s in the United States, Western Europe, and Japan had known only domestic peace and economic affluence, in direct contrast to the experiences of their parents with war and economic depression. Partially for this reason, Inglehart demonstrates, they seem to place a greater value than their parents did on values such as self-expression, beauty, and

[55] See chap. XI.
[56] Robert G. Lehnen, *American Institutions: Political Opinion and Public Policy* (Hinsdale: Holt, Rinehart and Winston, 1976), p. 183.
[57] See Nie, Verba, and Petrocik, op. cit., chap. 3.
[58] Inglehart, op. cit.

Table IV.4. *Expected Treatment by Government Officials and Police:*
Subgroups in the United States and Citizens in Five Nations

Expectations of treatment	Agreement in matched American subgroups (%)		Agreement in national citizen samples (%)				
	Blacks (N = 100)	Whites (N = 100)	USA (N = 970)	Britain (N = 963)	West Germany (N = 958)	Italy (N = 995)	Mexico (N = 1007)
Government officials would give equal treatment	49*	90	83	83	65	53	42
Police would give equal treatment	60	85	85	89	72	56	32
Government officials would listen and take views seriously	30	45	48	59	53	35	14
Police would listen and take views seriously	36	48	56	74	59	35	12

Source: For national citizen samples, Almond and Verba, op. cit., pp. 108–9. Analysis of the black and white differences was conducted by Dwaine Marvick, "The Political Socialization of the American Negro," *Annals of the American Academy* No. 361 (September 1965): 112–27. Marvick created black and white subgroups matched on demographic characteristics, so the figures above do not reflect the total white subsample. Interviews were conducted in 1959–60.

*That is, 49% of the black Americans responded that they expected government officials would give them equal treatment.

personal interaction. They place less emphasis on security and economic abundance, with important consequences for their relative political priorities. The differences are especially dramatic in Germany and France, least striking in Britain. Inglehart explains both similarities and cross-national differences in terms of the experiences with national economic outcomes.[59] It may be that the new and perhaps continuing confrontations with resource scarcity and economic recessions, which began in the early 1970s, will reverse these effects in future generations of citizens.

ELITE SOCIALIZATION: SUBCULTURES AND ROLE SOCIALIZATION

It has often been observed that political elites have different attitudes than the average citizen has. Since political socialization is the function shaping such attitudes, it is necessary to consider how elite socialization may differ from the socialization of citizens. There are two answers to this question. Conceptually, they are quite distinct, but in practice they are intertwined. The first answer has to do with the recruitment of elites who have sets of attitudes consistently different from the attitudes held by citizens in the population at large. The second answer has to do with the special effect of continuing role socialization on the incumbents of the elite roles.

Let us first look at recruitment, to which we shall return in the next chapter. Individuals are almost never chosen at random out of the population to become senators, presidents, generals, and dictators.[60] Rather, they in part select themselves for lower elite roles, depending on the interaction between their ambitions and the structural opportunities available. These lower roles usually constitute the channels through which some individuals are recruited to higher roles by the operation of special selection structures. The operation of both motivation and selection virtually ensures that leaders will not be randomly representative of the general society. At a minimum the leaders will be more interested, better informed, and more confident of their political abilities than the average citizen. As we shall show in the next chapter, moreover, the selection agencies will usually emphasize some distinctive criteria, depending on the elite role and the interests of the selectors. Technical capability, interpersonal skills of persuasion and leadership, loyalty to the political system, and policy preferences compatible with those of many of the selectors are among the special criteria frequently applied.

[59] Ibid.
[60] See the very large body of literature reviewed by Putnam, *Comparative Study of Political Elites,* on elite backgrounds and status in many cultures.

But even if elites were initially chosen at random, the effects of role socialization could not be ignored. Role socialization may be performed by several different types of structures. For some elite roles, especially technical and bureaucratic ones, special training or apprenticeship is required of candidates before they can actually assume a role. Thus, military officers are often given formal and explicit training at service academies, then are expected to serve a fairly long apprenticeship, working their way up through the ranks of military command before they become generals or admirals. Both the formal training and the apprenticeship serve to acquaint individuals with the duties they are expected to perform when they become commanding officers. Many civil service roles have similar socialization patterns, as do party leadership roles in some nations.

If there is no long apprenticeship and formal training period, role socialization is likely to take place through formal instruction and informal cues after the new incumbent is installed. New administrators or members of Congress are shown around their offices, told about their duties and facilities, and introduced to those with whom they must work. Often, as in the United States Senate, there are special roles whose requirements the newcomers are quietly told they must fulfill until they acquire more seniority.[61] And in all roles there is simply the effect of activity in the role, learning through unpleasant and pleasant experiences with the expectations of others. Studies of Congress suggest that there is a manifest process of role socialization through advice and warning that is designed to shortcut and simplify the painful process of learning through experience about what will work and what will not.[62]

As seen in the last chapter, structures establish sets of inducements, both rewards and costs, associated with particular roles. Individual incumbents may respond to these in various ways, and there may be various alternative roles from which they can choose, as in the "insider" and "outsider" roles so often discussed in the literature on Congress.[63] But as they learn what actions are rewarded and what actions are punished, they are being socialized into playing the role in a regular fashion.

Role socialization can be quite important for system stability, of course, especially in roles in which it is difficult to expel and replace the deviant

[61] Donald R. Matthews, *U.S. Senators and Their World* (Chapel Hill: University of North Carolina Press, 1960).

[62] See the discussion of norms adopted by members of different congressional committees in Richard F. Fenno, Jr. *Congressmen in Committees* (Boston: Little, Brown, 1973), especially chap. 3.

[63] See Ralph K. Huitt, "The Outsider in the Senate," *APSR* 55 (September 1961): 566–75; a general review of congressional norms and roles is provided in Leroy N. Rieselbach, *Congressional Politics* (New York: McGraw-Hill, 1973), chap. 6.

performer, such as a president, a general, or a Supreme Court justice. These roles have important political resources in their own right, and it may not be easy to bring inducements and sanctions to bear if the individual is determined to play the role in a different way. Hence, selection and early training will make it more likely that the structures will operate in the same way over time. Role socialization and the stable operation of structures are closely connected.

But role socialization can also be important for its effect on other political attitudes. One cannot expect that elites will think just like other citizens. In performing their jobs they receive special exposure and training that cannot help but shape their attitudes. It is unreasonable and unrealistic to expect Henry Kissinger, or any Secretary of State, or, indeed, any member of the foreign policy elite, to look at foreign affairs in the same way as the private citizen. For the one, it is a matter of daily concern, involvement, and personal decision; for the other, it is an intermittent interest at best. To take a more limited example, one cannot expect that the mayors of communities will see all community problems just as their citizens do. The mayors typically have many responsibilities for dealing with roads, sewerage, community development, and the like; their daily conduct of their office should make them more sensitive to and better informed about some problems than citizens. Of course, this does not mean that their evaluations will be based on the same criteria or even that they will be correct; there is much room for error in a complex world, for goals may vary, as well as statistics.

The effect of role socialization on a variety of political attitudes has some interesting implications for preference aggregation, as we shall see in chapter VIII. But at the moment, let us merely observe that we shall not be surprised to find various elite subcultures different from the citizen political culture at large. Moreover, the elite subculture may vary across parties, roles, and the like and at many attitude levels. In order to understand its maintenance and change, we need to examine both the recruitment process that selects individuals out of the population to become elites, and the effects of special role socialization after they enter the elite roles.

SOCIALIZATION AND POLITICAL DEVELOPMENT
CAUSES OF SECULARIZATION

We identified cultural secularization as the developmental dimension of political culture. Although all cultures contain secular elements, the secular element seems to have become much more prominent in the mix in contemporary societies. In consequence, participation has increased, legitimacy has been increasingly based on performance, and policy preferences have been directed to manifest efforts to improve the quality of life. Despite considerable variation within and across societies, these changes have been extremely widespread. The contemporary "world political culture" is notable for its secular elements.[64] Obviously, no single agent of socialization is responsible for such widespread and far-reaching alterations in cultural styles. Rather, secularization is a product of the implicit lessons of modern science and technology, which are transmitted directly and indirectly by a host of socialization agents.

The phenomenon is not new. For national leaders and young aspirants in many non-Western cultures in the nineteenth and early twentieth centuries, the essential exposure was to superior Western military technology. Leaders in Japan and the "Young Turks" in Turkey deliberately sought to introduce those elements of a secular Western culture which would equalize their nations' military capabilities. For local elites in colonized areas, secularization seemed a necessary instrument to throw off the foreign yoke. A generation of secular modernizers, determined to change their own societies and to increase independence and social capability, appeared in many non-Western nations.[65] The twentieth century has brought increasing secularization to many levels of society, however, and it is the pervasiveness that is most remarkable in the decades since World War II.

Two major elements shape the socialization process in directions that have enhanced secularization. One is the breakdown of traditional social structures and ways of life. The penetration of commercial markets, the introduction of new agricultural techniques and products, the growth of urban trading centers and manufacturing plants, the changes in mobility and population growth, and the appearance of mass media — all greatly disrupted the traditional pattern of stable transmission of cultural values to new generations. The process of social mobilization, as Karl Deutsch pointed out, made people available for political change.[66] The isolated and continuous reinforcement pattern of traditional village life became impossible.[67] The second major element was the exposure to secular elements and the possibilities they suggested: radio and films depicted alternate ways of life; merchants offered new products; the cities promised new chances to experience these. The political leadership contributed in most nations with promises of a better life through secular transformation, either to accompany or to replace old ways. The intro-

[64] Lucian W. Pye, *Aspects of Political Development* (Boston: Little, Brown, 1966).

[65] See John Kautsky, *The Political Consequences of Modernization* (New York: John Wiley, 1974), for an account of modernizer generations; and, generally, Huntington, *Political Order in Changing Societies*.

[66] Karl W. Deutsch, "Social Mobilization and Political Development," *APSR* 55 (September 1961): 493–514.

[67] See the vivid description in Lerner, op. cit.

duction of secular education created a major force designed to enhance the acquisition of secular skills.

To discuss the extent of these processes of socialization of secular attitudes does not imply uniform effect. As we have repeatedly emphasized, attitude socialization is a very complex process that depends on many sources of learning. Traditional cultures have often proved remarkably resilient and have been combined with secularized changes in many ways. But the effects of the world system changes have in general been to push toward secularization. Table II.6 showed the correlations for three major sources of secularization — education, mass media exposure, and nonagricultural occupations — in six nations. The correlations were between each source of secularized attitudes and a composite index of "modernity attitudes" developed by Inkeles and Smith. The index included information, readiness for social change, values of technical skill, and personal and political efficacy. In each country, the educated citizens, the citizens exposed to mass media, and the citizens in nonagricultural occupations were substantially more likely to hold the "modern" attitudes. Statistical analysis showed that each socialization source contributed independently, and that education and occupation were the most important.[68] Despite the resistance to secularization by those whose ways of life are threatened and destroyed, its effects are felt in virtually every contemporary society.[69]

DESECULARIZATION

Secularization is not the only trend in contemporary culture. The pragmatic, achievement-oriented quality of secularized culture, which emphasizes cause and effect, has been rejected as inadequate by many who grew up in it, as well as by proponents of values threatened by it. In various ways the disappointment with secularization has stimulated interest in Eastern religions, astrology, magic, transcendental meditation, religious revivalism, and the commune movement. Modern life seems beset by the desire for surer ultimate values and for those promoting them. This sense of the inadequacy of secularized culture to satisfy deep human needs also has a long history. Max Weber wrote movingly of the disenchantment of the modern world and the courage required for an honest life without the comforts of religious faith.[70] And about the same

[68] Inkeles and Smith, op. cit., p. 268.

[69] For a discussion of coalitions of groups affected in various ways by modernization, see Kautsky, op. cit.; and Barrington Moore, Jr., *Social Origins of Dictatorship and Democracy: Lord and Peasant in the Making of the Modern World* (Boston: Beacon, 1966).

[70] Max Weber, "Science as a Vocation," in *From Max Weber: Essays in Sociology,* ed. H. H. Gerth and C. W. Mills (New York: Oxford University Press, 1958).

time William Butler Yeats expressed the dismay acknowledged by most of the sensitive minds of the secular twentieth century:

> The best lack all conviction, while the worst
> Are full of passionate intensity.[71]

It is not our task to review the romantic movement and its contemporary descendants. We note only that as secularization has become more pervasive, and as its material achievements have alleviated the brute pressure for survival, the manifestations of disenchantment seem more widespread also.

However, disenchantment with secular culture is not the same as desecularization. The exotic movements searching for deeper meaning than secular knowledge and material plenty can supply may simply be temporary reactions. Perhaps a more serious threat is the possibility that modern society will reach a level of complexity that the average citizen will feel quite helpless to understand, let alone control. In such circumstances, the appeal of ideologies that interpret and offer simple explanations and programs of action in a complex world is manifest. This tendency may become especially serious as the complexity of contemporary society outruns the capacity of the decision-making structures and the capacity of leaders to make and implement effective public policy. In a situation in which things seem increasingly "out of control" the appeal of secularism may well decline, and new, desecularized ideologies and movements may emerge.[72] It remains to be seen whether the problems confronting modern society — scarce resources, inequality, interdependent technological complexity, population growth, pollution, and the like — can be solved or alleviated.

[71] William Butler Yeats, "The Second Coming" (first published in 1920), *The Collected Poems of W. B. Yeats.* Copyright 1924 by Macmillan Publishing Co., Inc., renewed 1952 by Bertha Georgie Yeats. Reprinted by permission of Macmillan Publishing Co., Inc., and A. P. Watt & Son.
[72] See the essays in Leon N. Lindberg, *Politics and the Future of Industrial Society* (New York: David McKay, 1976), especially the contributions of La Porte and Abrams and of Lindberg.

CHAPTER V

Political Recruitment

EVERY POLITICAL SYSTEM must have some way of filling the roles in its political structures. When specialized social roles emerge, even in the very simple structure of shaman and headman roles in the Eskimo village, there must be some means of selecting the particular individuals to fill those positions and inducing them to perform in the expected fashion. The same recruitment function must be performed in the complex roles of modern political systems. Presidents, members of Congress, party leaders, judges, voters, and taxpayers must be selected and motivated. Many individuals may wish to occupy some roles. Other roles, such as that of taxpayer, may be regarded as burdensome, but general compliance and participation are needed for the system to continue. Despite the differences, the recruitment function must be performed for each role.

The interaction between socialization and recruitment is a continuous one. An individual becomes a shaman, or a taxpayer, or a politician through a complex process of selection and influence, shaping the role through his own attitudes and expectations, yet finding those attitudes also molded by the experiences, limitations, and opportunities afforded by the role. Culture and structure influence each other through the dynamics of interaction between socialization and recruitment. In this chapter we shall develop some concepts for the analysis of the performance of the recruitment function and shall discuss some of the structures performing that function.

CONCEPTS FOR RECRUITMENT ANALYSIS
SELECTION AND INDUCEMENTS

We have already hinted at two somewhat different aspects of recruitment: the selection of individuals as role incumbents and the inducements needed to get them to play their expected roles. These two aspects come to bear in different ways on different political roles. There is little problem in finding individuals who are willing to assume offices with high social prestige and important decision-making power. The roles of general, president, or prime minister carry with them rewards that make them attractive to many individuals. The problem is choosing among many eager contenders. Recruitment involves establishing eligibility standards and selection, then encouraging the incumbent to meet performance expectations.

The rewards are not so great for many other political roles. Inducements must be offered to get individuals to leave their daily tasks, temporarily or permanently, and take up the burdens of political action. If citizens are to vote, work for a party, serve on a jury, or pay taxes, for example, they must have some incentives to do so. We can describe the structures that provide these and identify the type of incentives offered. As we outlined in chapter III, such incentives may include the chance of gaining more preferred policy outcomes, the material benefits of a city job, the normative satisfactions of acting as a good citizen, or the avoidance of penalties.

Most of the full-time political roles, of course, are in the bureaucracy. The offices of the Internal Revenue Service, the welfare agencies, the fire departments, and the school systems must be filled by recruiting tax collectors, social workers, firefighters, and teachers. The incentives for such roles in most political systems are primarily financial. The legislature appropriates funds for salaries of teachers and civil servants; these financial inducements, if adequate, attract a pool of candidates; the civil service and administration select and assign some of them on the basis of specified criteria; role performance is monitored by superiors, and continuation or promotion depends on appropriate performance. Of course, inducements for recruitment into full-time roles can also be coercive, as in the draft of citizens into military service, or normative, as in the appeal to idealism in recruiting Peace Corps volunteers.

IMPLICATIONS OF RECRUITMENT

The parts of a political system tend to be interdependent. Changes in the performance of one function are likely to influence the performance of other functions by other structures. Similarly, the levels of the system are interdependent; changes in performance at the system level affect the process and policy levels. The recruitment function is a system function; it interacts with the other system functions of socialization and communication. But a change in the performance of the recruitment function may also affect the process and policy levels.

Maintenance and change at the *system* level, as we pointed out in chapter III, is particularly a consequence of the balance between the preferences of actors controlling political resources and the policy outcomes of system performance. When there is a good fit between the expectations of those who have power and influence and the outcomes of system performance, the system is synchronized, and the maintenance of the present arrangements should be a simple matter. If preferences, resources, or policy outcomes change without continuing the balance, then stable support will be jeopardized. Socialization is important because preferences are important, and the preferences result from socialization. Recruitment is important because not all preferences are equal, and recruitment helps determine who will have political resources. The recruitment structures draw in or exclude different population groups; they put individuals with different preferences in key political roles; and they regulate the use of military force by the general, executive power by the president, or judicial review by the courts. The formation of roles and recruitment of individuals into them is crucial to the distribution of political resources and, hence, to system maintenance, adaptation, or breakdown.

At the *process* level, the recruitment function determines the inclusiveness of the political system and the representativeness of those who will hold political roles. Universal eligibility for citizen and elite roles has, indeed, become so common in many modern systems that one can too easily forget the bitter struggles waged for expansion of the voting franchise and for the rights of minorities to be eligible to vote or to hold political offices.[1] But the major struggle in the West for the past two hundred years has been over the rights of citizens to be recruited to all the political roles in modern systems. And even today, there are many nations in which large groups are excluded from the right to vote or hold office — South Africa is a prominent example — and many more systems in which recruitment to process roles is in principle open to all, but in practice heavily biased for and against various groups. The recruitment structures have a major impact on such representativeness, both in the roles that are created and in the selection to them.

Recruitment also affects public *policy* performance. It has three ways of doing this. First, recruitment can have a major effect on public policy through the enhanced policy capability, as competent and trained personnel are recruited to specialized roles in developed political systems. Second, recruitment affects policy as individuals with different preferences are recruited to fill major roles. Even without regime-level changes, such recruitment can change policies significantly. A recent comparative study has shown how changes in personnel occupying top roles, such as premier and president, are typically reflected in statistically significant

---

[1] Peter Gerlich found that internal or external violence was a major circumstance in over 70% of the 94 steps of franchise extension in the 15 European nations he studied. Peter Gerlich, "The Institutionalization of European Parliaments," in Allan Kornberg, *Legislatures in Comparative Perspective* (New York: David McKay, 1973), pp. 94 ff.

budget changes.[2] And finally, the nature of the recruitment structures can have a continuing role in promoting greater responsiveness on the part of elites to citizen policy preferences.

The basic concept of a modern democratic political system is that citizens can control elites through periodic elections. On one hand, the citizens can choose among competing candidates, selecting those whose preferences are most like their own or in whom they have the most trust. On the other hand, the existence of the elections enhances elite responsiveness through the anticipation of electoral sanctions. The authors of *Federalist* 57 presented this argument nearly two hundred years ago, in discussing the pressure on elected rulers:

> Before the sentiments impressed on their minds by the mode of their elevation can be effaced by the exercise of power, they will be compelled to anticipate the moment when their power is to cease, when their exercise of it is to be reviewed.[3]

The potential power of electoral sanctions is so great that competitive electoral structures usually become deeply involved in interest aggregation and even policy making. The desire to attain or retain political office leads candidates to organize into parties and to develop policies to offer to the electorate.[4] Although elitist theorists have often scoffed at free elections as a device for either selection or control,[5] the reluctance of authoritarian rulers to introduce them and the empirical evidence obtained in democratic systems suggest their potential in shaping the outlines of public policy.[6]

---

[2] Valerie Bunce, "Elite Succession, Petrification and Policy Innovation," *Comparative Political Studies* 9 (April 1976): 3 ff.

[3] See the discussion of this theme in Heinz Eulau and Kenneth Prewitt, *The Labyrinth of Democracy* (Indianapolis: Bobbs-Merrill, 1973), p. 219.

[4] See chap. VIII.

[5] For example, Gaetano Mosca, *The Ruling Class* (New York: McGraw-Hill, 1939), chap. 10; and see C. Wright Mills, *The Power Elite* (New York: Oxford University Press, 1956).

[6] For some empirical evidence as to the effect of competitive elections on the responsiveness of political leaders, see the following: Eulau and Prewitt, op. cit., chap. 22; Warren E. Miller and Donald E. Stokes, "Constituency Influence in Congress," *APSR* 57 (March 1963): 45–56; Kenneth Prewitt, *The Recruitment of Political Leaders* (Indianapolis: Bobbs-Merrill, 1970); Sidney Verba and Norman H. Nie, *Participation in America* (New York: Harper & Row, 1972), chaps. 18 and 19; Gerald Pomper, *Elections in America* (New York: Dodd, Mead, 1968); John W. Kingdon, *Congressmen's Voting Decisions* (New York: Harper & Row, 1973); Susan B. Hansen, "Participation, Political Structure, and the Process of Linkage," *APSR* 69 (December 1975): 1181–99; G. Bingham Powell, Jr., with Lynda W. Powell, "Analysis of Citizen-Elite Linkages," in Sidney Verba and Lucian Pye, eds., *The Citizen and Politics* (Stamford, Conn.: Greylock, 1978); Samuel H. Barnes, *Representation in Italy* (Chicago: University of Chicago Press, 1977). And see the review in Robert D. Putnam, *The Comparative Study of Political Elites* (Englewood Cliffs: Prentice-Hall, 1976), chap. 6.

RECRUITMENT TO CITIZEN ROLES

Citizens' roles in the political process fall into two major categories: participant roles and subject roles. Participant roles are those in which citizens make some attempt to influence the ongoing process of policy making. Subject roles are those in which citizens are involved in the implementation of policies. In table V.1 we offer a typology of the citizen participant and subject roles typically found in modern political systems.

It is characteristic of citizen roles, of course, that they occupy only a rather small amount of time and energy. Indeed, the citizen may be performing, intermittently, a number of different roles, such as interest group member, contactor of authorities, voter, and taxpayer. Verba and Nie found, for example, considerable specialization in the type of participant role that citizens in the United States tend to fill, and they found only 11 percent of their American sample to be "complete activists," performing all types of participant roles.[7] The range of available participant roles is smaller in an authoritarian system, where autonomous interest groups and competitive voter roles are usually excluded. Table V.1 illustrates, however, the range of roles available for modern political systems.

TYPES AND FREQUENCY OF PARTICIPATION

Let us first discuss the roles that are specialized to citizen participation in the making of public policy.[8] Interest articulation roles are those in which citizens attempt to make demands about desired public policies known to others and to political elites. They include the "parochial contactor" and the active interest group member. The parochial contactor role involves the expression of a narrow personal or family interest, usually as an appeal to some bureaucratic official or politician. These roles are to be found in virtually all political systems. Since they do not challenge the incumbents or their general policies, such roles are even permitted in authoritarian political systems, where they may be, indeed, the only legitimate form of citizen participation. Verba, Nie, and their associates found the parochial contactor to be a distinctive role in each of the seven political systems they investigated.[9] Such individual contacting

---

7 Verba and Nie, *Participation in America,* chap. 4.

8 The typology refers to goals and expectations associated with the role by the citizen, not to its structural-functional performance in successfully articulating interests, aggregating resources, and the like.

9 Sidney Verba, Norman H. Nie, and Jae-on Kim, *The Modes of Democratic Participation* (Beverly Hills: Sage Publications, 1971); and Sidney Verba, Norman H. Nie, Ana Barbic, Galen Irwin, Henk Molleman, and Goldie Shabad, "The Modes of Participation: Continuities in Research," *Comparative Political Studies* 6 (July 1973): 235-50.

Table V.1. *Typology of Citizen Participant and Subject Roles in Modern Political Systems*

Participant roles	Subject roles
Interest articulation roles	*Provider of resources*
Parochial contactor	Taxpayer
Active interest group member[a]	Military conscript
Interest aggregation roles	*Recipient of resources*
Voter in competitive election	Welfare recipient
Campaign activist	Social security recipient
Policy-making roles	*Recipient of behavior regulations*
Voter in referendum	Law-abiding citizen
Member of self-managment council or	Parent sending children to school
town meeting	Manufacturer observing health and
	safety regulations
	Recipient of symbols
	Giver of pledge or loyalty oath
	Voter in noncompetitive election

[a] See chap. VII for a more complete discussion of the types of interest groups and interest group roles.

required neither special political conditions nor individual advantages often associated with other roles. Only about 4 percent of the Americans were pure parochial contactors, who performed no other participatory roles.

Table V.2 presents survey data indicating the frequency of citizen involvement in some of the types of interest articulation roles in seven nations. The first two rows report the frequency of the parochial contacting, the percentage of citizens who had contacted government officials about personal or family problems in the last three years. As one can see, these personal contacts take place in every political system, although the frequency varies greatly, from a small percentage of citizens in Nigeria to a very large percentage in the Netherlands.

The role of active interest group member refers to many types of interest groups. A detailed exposition of group types and tactics is postponed until chapter VII. As we shall show, interest groups may involve their members in a variety of constitutional and coercive actions in their attempts to press political demands. Such actions include contacting party and bureaucratic officials, appealing for attention through the mass media, speaking at legislative sessions, staging demonstrations and strikes, and engaging in riots and other violent assaults. The surveys in question did not, for the most part, ask about the illegal or unconventional forms of group-based actions. But the next three rows in table V.2

Table V.2. *Percentage of Citizens Participating in Seven Nations*

Participant role	Austria	India	Japan	Netherlands	Nigeria	USA	Yugoslavia
Interest articulation roles							
Contact local official on family problem	16	12	7	38	2	7	20[a]
Contact extralocal official on family problem	14	6	3	10	1	6	
Contact local official on group problem	5	4	11	12	2	14	11
Work through informal group on community problem	—	10	15	16	32	30	
Participate actively in formal group taking part in community affairs	9	7	11	15	28	32	57[a]
Interest aggregation roles							
Vote in competitive national election	96	59	72	78[b]	66	72	No competitive national elections or campaigns
Belong to party in competitive party system	28	6	4	13	Parties illegal at this time	8	
Work for party in competitive election	10	25	25	10		26	

Sources: Verba, Nie, and Kim, *Modes of Democratic Participation*; Verba, Nie, Barbic, Irwin, Molleman, and Shabad, "Modes of Participation."
Note: Responsibility for fitting question responses to role types is solely that of the present authors. Surveys were conducted over a three-year period in the late 1960s.
[a] Yugoslavian question did not distinguish local from extralocal contacts, nor did it distinguish formal from informal groups.
[b] Netherlands question was about local election voting, as national voting was compulsory at that time.

nonetheless provide some information about group interest-articulation activity as performed by citizens.

From 2 percent to 14 percent of the citizens in these nations did contact a local official about some social or group problem. The studies show clearly that such group problem-contacting is closely linked to various forms of group action, such as working through a group to help solve a community problem, which is shown in the following row of the table. Work through such informal local groups was a frequent form of political participation in these nations, with 10 to 32 percent of the citizens having engaged in such activity. Finally, a slightly smaller fraction of citizens, except in the United States, were active members of a formal group that takes part in community affairs, such as the P.T.A., a fraternal group, or a farm organization. In the United States, such active membership in associational groups was the most common form of citizen participation other than voting, with almost one-third of the citizens so involved. We do not know from the surveys, of course, just what types of activities the groups engaged in, but it is very likely that some form of interest articulation was a frequent action, as groups drew attention to group and community needs. The survey in Yugoslavia did not distinguish between formal and informal groups, but the combined roles involved over half the citizens.

Table V.2 also shows the two common types of citizen policy-aggregation roles: voting and campaign participation in competitive electoral systems. Interest aggregation, as we shall discuss further in chapter VIII, involves mobilizing support for major policy alternatives. In democratic political systems the competitive political parties play a critical role in the interest aggregation process, building coalitions of support groups and mobilizing support behind candidates. Citizen voting for one of the party alternatives is, of course, the most pervasive form of citizen participation, although there is very substantial variation from system to system, with reported turnout ranging from around 50 percent in Indian elections to over 95 percent in Austrian national elections. Voting was found to be a particularly distinctive dimension of participation in each of the nations studied by Verba et al., no doubt because of the ease of the role performance and of systematic mobilization.[10] Competitive campaign activity was also a distinctive factor. Campaign activities were forbidden in Nigeria at the time of the survey, as in most authoritarian political systems, but they are a critical form of citizen involvement in democratic political systems.

Table V.1 also indicates some citizen policy-making roles. As we have suggested, it is difficult for citizen involvement to be sustained in national

[10] Ibid.

decision making, except for an occasional referendum. Hence came the development of representational devices, such as parties and legislatures. But at the local level citizen involvement is more feasible, in several senses. On one hand, there are some special forms of local self-government in which very broad participation takes place; the New England town meeting, the Yugoslavian workers' council, and the apartment or house council are examples.[11] On the other hand, there exist local decision-making roles that are, in effect, part-time elite roles. Members of American city councils typically are not full-time officials, nor are local governmental policy-making roles in other political systems, such as Britain and Austria. Local decision makers must often hold down other jobs while involved in local decision making. Because these citizen-elite participation roles are rather specialized, even if not full-time, we have not included them in table V.1, but they constitute the border area between citizen and elite roles.

RECRUITMENT TO PARTICIPANT ROLES

We have had to spend some time on the typology of citizen participation roles before considering the question of recruitment, for the recruitment structures and incentives vary with the different participant roles. First, let us point out that eligibility for participant roles is typically determined by the policy-making structures of the society, themselves often operating under some sort of general constitutional constraint. Authoritarian political systems typically do not allow party competition. Even when they provide voting roles, these function as support mobilizers; the systems involve citizens only symbolically. Moreover, citizen involvement in interest groups is carefully controlled in such systems, and the activity of such interest groups is characterized by low structural autonomy. Interest groups often play important roles in authoritarian systems, but they are controlled as much as possible from above.[12] Citizen recruitment into the interest groups is also heavily controlled, being often required for members of various occupations, such as professionals, and seldom a matter of free choice.

Democratic systems also have varied eligibility requirements, particularly for voting roles, but more flexibility in individual and group decision is allowed. The United States does stand out in the difficulty of obtaining voting eligibility; at least until recent court decisions, the residence and registration restrictions made it difficult for voters who

11 See Sidney Verba and Goldie Shabad, "Workers' Councils and Political Stratification: The Yugoslav Experience" (Paper presented at the Annual Meeting of the American Political Science Association, September 1975).
12 See chap. VII.

change their residences to maintain their registration eligibility.[13] Registration requirements have been responsible in part for the low levels of American voting turnout compared to those of many European nations. In Italy, as a contrasting example, citizens receive free rail transportation home in order to vote, and in most European nations registration is automatic. In some nations, such as Belgium, Australia, Costa Rica, and Venezuela, citizens are fined or subjected to other penalties for failing to vote, creating a direct incentive for citizen involvement.

Political parties are of great importance in explaining both voting turnout and the forms of campaign participation. The parties are a dominant factor in recruiting citizens to the interest aggregation roles of voter and campaign activist. In India the parties, particularly the governing parties, have often sent out trucks to round up voters in rural areas and ensure that they get to the polls. Likewise, in the United States and in many European nations, the party organizations make elaborate efforts to contact voters and see that they get to the polls on election day. The parties also offer a variety of incentives for citizen involvement, both as voters and as campaign activists. In Austria the party organizations offer many material incentives for membership, including opportunities for access to public housing, favored treatment by government bureaucrats of the same party, automatic membership through joining occupational groups such as farmers' associations and a host of party-linked service and recreational groups. As shown by table V.2 the Austrian system has been successful in getting over a quarter of the population to become party members, which involves making regular financial contributions, and in mobilizing virtually all voters. However, as the table also indicates, working for the party has been less widespread, largely because the Austrian parties have very large organizations of virtually full-time party officials and activists, often employed by various levels of government or interest groups. Thus, voluntary intermittent citizen party work has been less encouraged.

Recruitment to the interest group roles is a more variable activity, depending largely on the type of group and the incentives it can offer. Verba, Nie et al. have combined various types of group roles into a single category characterized by a common dimension; they call such group activity "communal." [14] Active membership in formal groups that work on community problems — such as parent-teacher associations, farm

[13] See Stanley Kelley, Jr., Richard E. Ayers, and William G. Bowen, "Registration and Voting: Putting First Things First," *APSR* 61 (June 1967): 359–79. Also see Jerrold G. Rusk, "The Effect of the Australian Ballot Reform on Split Ticket Voting," *APSR* 64 (December 1970): 1220–38.
[14] Verba and Nie, *Participation in America*; Verba, Nie, and Kim, *Modes of Democratic Participation*.

organizations, labor unions, and fraternal groups — is one of the most frequent forms of citizen participation in the United States, for example. Activities in informal groups or contact of officials in a social context, which we would call nonassociational and anomic group roles, are also frequent forms of participation.

It is difficult to generalize about recruitment into such groups because they use a variety of material, emotional, and personal incentives to encourage membership.[15] Different kinds of groups can offer assistance with work and professional goals, opportunities for special kinds of recreation, assistance with neighborhood or school problems for children, and, simply, occasions for good fellowship. But once involved in such formal and informal groups, individuals are well situated to become politically active. They may be mobilized by other group members and leaders, as their group involvement opens them up to communication. But they are also in possession of ready contacts and communication channels with others of similar interests, finding it far easier to become aware of political opportunities and to persuade others to join them in interest articulation activity.

The role of group and party recruitment and the attitudes of individual citizens go far to help explain citizen participation in politics. Table V.3 shows one of the most familiar relationships in the study of participation: the greater political awareness among the better educated. In our discussion of political socialization in the last chapter we emphasized that educationally and economically advantaged citizens tend to have more confidence in their ability to influence their environment, more resources and information for action, more exposure to information, and so on. These relationships between education and social status, on one hand, and political attitudinal involvement, on the other, hold consistently in many societies, as well in Communist Yugoslavia and in impoverished India as in the United States.[16]

Yet, some of the same studies that show the consistency of the relationship between social status and participant attitudes also reveal the variability across different nations in the relationship between status and various forms of political participation itself.[17] Voting, for example, shows great cross-national differences in the tendency of the advantaged to participate more frequently. Indeed, in Austria the advantaged citizens are a bit less likely to vote, although voting participation is high for everyone. Campaign activity also varies greatly, apparently reflecting the

15 See James Q. Wilson, *Political Organizations* (New York: Basic Books, 1973).
16 See chap. IV and Verba and Nie, op. cit., pp. 339–41.
17 Verba and Nie, *Participation in America*; Verba, Nie, and Kim, *Modes of Democratic Participation*; Verba, Nie, Barbic, Irwin, Molleman, and Shabad, "Modes of Participation."

Table V.3.   *Education and Participant Attitudes: Percentage Who Say They Can Do Something About an Unjust Local Regulation*

Nation	Education level					
	Primary and less		Some secondary		Some college	
	%	N	%	N	%	N
United States	60	339	82	443	95	188
Britain	74	593	83	322	88	24
West Germany	58	792	83	123	85	26
Italy	45	692	62	245	76	54
Mexico (Nonrural)	49	877	67	103	76	24

Source: Gabriel A. Almond and Sidney Verba, *The Civic Culture* (Princeton: Princeton University Press, 1963), p. 206. Also see table II.2, for national totals in these and other nations and for discussion of the question.

differences in incentives for involvement offered by the political parties, both the material incentives available for party work and the degree to which different social groups find issues at stake that bring them strongly to back one party or another. However, *within* social groups that are linked to parties, the advantaged do tend to be the most active. Formal and informal group activity, which is strongly affected by the self-selection of citizens into activity within the group, vary somewhat less in the tendency for the advantaged to predominate in interest articulation activity.

One of the interesting facts about the countries shown in table V.2 is that Socialist Yugoslavia and the capitalist United States show rather similar patterns of participation; in both, the advantaged citizens dominate. In both nations, the party and group recruitment structures are critical. The American voluntary organizations are the most extensive among middle-class citizens and thus encourage the participation of the more advantaged. In Yugoslavia, Communist party membership is a prerequisite for many kinds of social action. But in the absence of competitive mobilization of the lower class, it seems to be the advantaged citizens who enter the party and are active within it.[18] In Austria, on the other hand, the party organizations and the strong organized associational groups pull in many lower-status citizens and discourage those citizens not properly affiliated with the parties. In both Austria and Japan the

[18] Verba and Shabad, op. cit. In some of the self-management forms of participation, Verba and Shabad found that the party was less important, but the direct impact of social status was even more pronounced. Skilled workers were more likely to join the workers' self-management councils than the unskilled, for example.

Table V.4. *Experience of Blacks and Whites in Contacting Political and*
Governmental Officials in the United States

Contacting experience	Total (N = 2,717)	White (N = 2,371)	Black (N = 346)
Have contacted political elite	30%	33%	14%
Have not contacted but:			
Feel that they can contact elite directly	43	46	34
Feel that contact with elite is possible through connections	10	8	19
Feel that they need connections but could not find them	17	13	33
Total	100	100	100

Source: Verba and Nie, *Participation in America*, p. 166. Data are from a survey carried out in 1967.

strong, purposive mobilization of the rural and labor sectors by a variety of parties and organized groups, modern and traditional, provides to some degree a counterbalance to the attitudinal advantages of the higher status citizens.

We should observe in conclusion that citizen recruitment to the parochial contactor roles does not seem to be strongly related to socioeconomic advantage in most of the societies for which we have survey data. A major question is, How do the government structures directly impinge on the life of the individual? Also important is the perceived responsiveness of officials to possible requests by the citizens. McGlen has shown that, in Austria, personal friendships and shared party membership help to determine whether a citizen expects favorable treatment; contacting in that country is affected by such expectations.[19] Verba and Nie found, as shown in table V.4, that black Americans were much less likely to contact officials than were whites and that noncontactors were likely to express the feeling that they needed, and could not find, connections to facilitate their involvement. Because blacks were much more likely than whites to see the government as relevant to the solution of personal family problems, a fact that was directly related to lower income, the sense of inability to contact was a frustrating one.[20] The institution of the ombudsman, an official whose role is to mediate citizen

[19] Nancy E. McGlen, "Strategy Choices for Political Participation: The Case of Austria" (Ph.D. diss., University of Rochester, 1974).
[20] Verba and Nie, *Participation in America*, pp. 166 ff. Also see Donald R. Matthews and James W. Prothro, *Negroes and the New Southern Politics* (New York: Harcourt, Brace & World, 1966).

complaints about governmental treatment, is designed to prevent frustration of this type.[21]

RECRUITMENT TO SUBJECT ROLES

Important as participant roles may be to policy making in democratic political systems, the most common citizen roles in all systems are subject roles. As political systems have expanded in size and in efforts to mold their social, economic, and international environments, the variety of subject roles has expanded also. In chapter XI we shall discuss the performance of political systems and attempt to describe and to compare extraction of resources, distribution of benefits, and regulation of behavior in different political systems. Each of these types of performance requires citizens to assume subject roles. Citizen compliance is essential for system performance.

One of the most pervasive of all citizen roles, and that which, more than any other perhaps, has caused citizens to resist efforts of authorities to promote compliance, is the role of taxpayer. Resources must be extracted from the society for a wide range of political performance. Modern non-Socialist societies extract from a quarter to a half of all the national income in the form of taxes and levies, whereas Socialist political systems extract from half to three-fourths of national income through taxation and profits on national industries.[22] A great variety of devices is used to compel citizens to provide the necessary resources. The United States relies heavily on direct income taxes, which are administered by an agency of the national government, the Internal Revenue Service. Individual income-earners, as well as corporations, are subject to withholding of income and must file annual statements to justify refunds or explain additional payments. Many state and local governments also tax incomes or use a host of indirect taxes, such as sales taxes. Although the primary incentive for compliance is coercion, with severe penalties provided for illegal tax evasion, a normative emphasis on obedience to the law and good citizenship supplements that coercion. In fact, some European nations have much higher levels of tax evasion than does the United States. In France, for example, tax evasion is virtually a time-honored custom, and governmental budget forecasters anticipate a substantial short fall.[23] Discrepancies between tax policy and tax collection perfor-

---

21 See Kent M. Weeks, *Ombudsmen Around the World* (Berkeley: Institute of Governmental Studies, 1973), for a description of ombudsmen staffs and jurisdiction in eleven nations. The institution of ombudsman originated in Sweden but has diffused to many other countries.

22 See chap. XI.

23 See Hugh Heclo, Arnold Heidenheimer, and Carolyn Teich Adams, *Comparative Public Policy* (New York: St. Martin's Press, 1975), chap. 7.

mance result from complex patterns of citizen attitudes and bureaucratic implementation devices. One effect has been to lead governments in Europe to use value-added taxes more frequently, in which revenue is collected from product manufacturers, who pass on costs to consumers.[24] The citizen taxpayer role is thus assumed much more indirectly and is more difficult to avoid.

Citizen roles as receivers of governmental benefits are assumed much more readily, although here, too, government agencies usually must engage in substantial public education campaigns through the mass media to inform citizens about the availability of benefits and how to receive them. Aid to the handicapped, to war veterans, to the aged, to the poor, and to other special groups takes a great variety of forms. Patterns of bureaucratic implementation typically require citizens to register or to make special applications for the benefits in question, whether these are welfare benefits, medical care, or small business and disaster recovery loans. The agency must then monitor these claims to see that only eligible citizens assume recipient roles.

Modern societies are also covered by networks of regulations. Parents, for example, are commonly required to send their children to school for a specified number of years and during certain periods of the year. Compliance is achieved through a combination of incentives and coercion. On one hand, education is emphasized as a positive benefit to children and their families. On the other hand, penalties are provided for failure to comply, unless educational requirements can be met otherwise. It is, indeed, difficult to think of occupational and other major social and economic roles in modern societies that are not somehow linked to a form of government regulation. This linkage in turn means at least intermittent assumption of or confrontation with citizen compliance roles. From traffic regulation to antitrust laws, the citizen in a complex society faces public regulatory action. Yet here, too, there is variation. In authoritarian political systems the regulation is typically more pervasive and extends to the control of internal travel, public gatherings, and public speech.

A final form of citizen subject role is of particular interest: the symbolic involvement role. Most political systems do attempt to mobilize citizen involvement with symbols of community, regime, and authorities. American schoolchildren must learn and recite the Pledge of Allegiance, and complex legal battles have been fought in the United States over the efforts of citizens to resist this requirement for religious or ethical reasons. The mass media are filled with efforts by political leaders to invoke and reinforce symbols of national history and unity.

The contemporary authoritarian systems, particularly the penetrative,

24 See chap. XI.

mobilizational, one-party states, press citizen symbolic involvement much further. In major efforts to socialize citizen attitudes through symbolic role playing, these systems typically mobilize every citizen to cast a vote for the single party's candidates on election day and to participate in parades and other political events. Many of them have instituted vast recreational programs, to further the involvement of the young, in particular, and to emphasize active citizen assumption of roles symbolically supportive of the political system. The penetrative party and bureaucratic organizations in these regimes are usually highly effective in mobilizing citizens to perform these symbolic roles, although the effect on attitudes cannot be determined. The presence of massive citizen recruitment to symbolic support roles by party and bureaucracy is one of the most distinctive characteristics of the contemporary penetrative authoritarian regime, which uses all kinds of sanctions to turn out "99 percent" of citizens to "vote" and to participate in public events.

RECRUITMENT TO ELITE ROLES
ENTRY TO ELITE RECRUITMENT CHANNELS

In most political systems the attainment of higher elite roles is based on previous performance in lesser roles, usually in the political realm, but occasionally in other social spheres as well. Unless elite recruitment is based on very strict criteria of birth and kinship, it involves at least two stages: (1) recruitment to lower roles, such as membership in legislative assemblies or local government, whose incumbents constitute a pool of potential central leaders; then (2) selection of the individuals out of that pool for higher roles.

The most common contemporary channels of recruitment are clearly the political party, the local or state government (which may overlap with party channels), the civilian bureaucracy, and the military. The importance of the party depends in part on its role in the selection of top leaders, discussed later in this chapter, and in part on its own recruitment permeability. In the American system, the national party is often merely a coalition of locally based leaders. In parts of Western Europe, party-list systems and greater internal discipline mean that long party service is necessary to enter the pool of potential national leaders. In these systems, parties receive legislative seats according to their percentage of electoral votes. Individuals win their places according to the position on the list established by the party, giving the organization substantial control over the fate of the individual candidate.[25] Most of the Soviet and Eastern European leadership also finds party membership a necessary precondition for consideration, as is true of single-party regimes in Africa and

[25] There are, of course, many variations within these types of systems, and party control is hardly uniform.

Mexico. Local government officeholding can be an indispensable way into the higher roles of the party itself in some nations, as in the Soviet Union, Sweden, West Germany, and France.

Students of American and British politics are perhaps most inclined to overlook the civilian and military bureaucracies as channels into the national elite. Quandt found that about a quarter of legislative seats in developing nations were held by government bureaucrats,[26] and this was a growing trend in many Western European nations as well, particularly in West Germany. In nations in which the military organizations play powerful roles in top-level selection and decision making, of course, the path through the military hierarchy is an important channel for elite recruitment.

The openness of such channels of elite recruitment at the lower levels are important because of the types of individuals eventually recruited to top rule-making and implementation roles. Moreover, it is particularly at the lower levels that incentives and mobilizing organizational structures come into special play by involving some types of citizens more than others. The intrinsic rewards of power and status associated with top political roles, as we have noted, make them highly attractive. Most politicians would like to be president or senator, most captains would like to be generals, most tax review officials would like to become bureau heads. The same point can be made about elite recruitment as was made about citizen participation: politicians and government officials tend to be recruited from the better educated and the economically advantaged. Putnam reports a large number of studies that support four generalizations:

1. Political leaders are drawn disproportionately from upper-status occupations and privileged family backgrounds.
2. The social backgrounds of administrative elites are at least as upper-status as those of political leaders.
3. Economic elites are usually drawn from significantly more privileged backgrounds than even political and administrative elites.
4. Higher education is a characteristic of all kinds of elites in virtually every nation.[27]

Despite drastic regime changes the educated are tremendously overrepresented in almost all elites. In fact, as Putnam argues, following a

---

[26] William B. Quandt, *The Comparative Study of Political Elites* (Beverly Hills: Sage, 1970).
[27] Putnam, *Comparative Study of Political Elites*, chap. 2. Also see the review by Anthony Oberschall, *Social Conflict and Social Movements* (Englewood Cliffs: Prentice-Hall, 1973).

long line of elite theorists, the further one goes up the elite power hierarchy, the more complete is the domination by the educated and the advantaged. Despite the log cabin myth in America (and the relative permeability of the channels), and despite the supposed commitment of Communist elites to lower-status groups, the same trend holds in these nations. In the United States, for example, only 2 percent of all Presidents, Vice-Presidents, and Cabinet members from 1789 to 1940 were manual workers or small farmers, and only a quarter were children of such workers.[28] In Eastern Europe and the Soviet Union, leaders report more humble backgrounds, but the socioeconomically advantaged by birth, and especially the educated, have clear advantages there, also. These trends are even more striking in the developing areas. Finally, we should note that although we have been concentrating on recruitment into the established elites, many studies have shown that revolutionary leaders, too, tend to be middle- or upper-class, in all political systems, and that peasant movement leaders, of which Mao Tse-tung is only the most prominent example, tend to come from the families of wealthier peasants or local professionals.[29]

Recruitment depends on more than self-selection, of course. Groups and political party organizations make substantial and continuing efforts to recruit members into their ranks and to mobilize into active participation those who meet their favored criteria. The occasionally desperate efforts by American political party organizations to develop a reliable cadre of party officials have been described in several excellent studies.[30] Studies of American party organizations have suggested that several recruitment patterns exist, ranging from the use of material incentives and a heavy emphasis on organizational continuity to the issue-oriented "amateur" pattern, which relies on short-term intense efforts to achieve special political goals.[31] Studies of membership recruitment and mobilization by voluntary associations, which contribute very disproportion-

---

28 Putnam, *Comparative Study of Political Elites*, p. 23, citing H. Dewey Anderson, "The Education and Occupational Attainment of our National Rulers," *Scientific Monthly* 40 (June 1935): 511–18.

29 Putnam, *Comparative Study of Political Elites*; Oberschall, op. cit.

30 See Samuel J. Eldersveld, *Political Parties: A Behavioral Analysis* (Chicago: Rand McNally, 1964); Lewis Bowman and G. R. Boynton, "Recruitment Patterns Among Local Party Officials," *APSR* 60 (September 1966): 667–76; Phillip Althoff and Samuel C. Patterson, "Political Activism in a Rural County," *Midwest Journal of Political Science* 10 (February 1966): 39–51; Margaret Conway and Frank B. Feigert, "Motivation, Incentive Systems, and the Political Party Organization," *APSR* 62 (December 1968): 1159–73.

31 James Q. Wilson, *The Amateur Democrat* (Chicago: University of Chicago Press, 1962); Conway and Feigert, op. cit.; John W. Soule and James W. Clarke, "Amateurs and Professionals," *APSR* 64 (September 1970): 888–98.

ately to political involvement and activity by members,[32] also indicate a variety of incentives and tactics.[33]

Various mobilization techniques and membership criteria may also interact with the distribution of resources and talent in the society in ways that directly and indirectly favor certain groups. A fascinating example is the traditional Chinese Mandarin elite, which was selected in competitive examinations. The examinations were open to all, and clearly education, rather than status, was the criterion used in the rules of selection. The civil service examinations, however, required years of preparation, and the sons of wealthy families had great advantages in being able to devote the necessary time to education. Hence, the effect of the system was to perpetuate the predominance of families already in the Mandarinate, even though the selection structure did not in principle use incumbency or status as a criterion.[34]

Many roles in the contemporary world require literacy and at least some additional education for satisfactory role performance. This is obviously true of many technical bureaucratic roles: economic advisers, managers of nationalized industry, and teachers, for example, need to be able to read, write, and do arithmetic. For this reason alone, the degree to which occupational distributions in the governmental bureaucracy are "representative" of the population is likely to be largely a function of the level of literacy and the size of the service occupation sector in the population.[35] In part for technical reasons, then, the link between education, status, and political incumbency tends to be less strong for party, legislative, and interest group roles than for civilian bureaucratic ones. The purposive goals of the groups require more stringent qualifications for effective role performance in some cases than others.

SELECTION OF ELITES

From among those who have been recruited to the lower-level elite roles, a much smaller number must be selected for the top roles. When we refer generally to elite recruitment, we often have these top-level selection structures in mind. Historically, the problem of selecting the individuals to fill the very top political roles has been a critical difficulty in maintenance of internal order and even regime persistence. Because,

[32] See the references in chap. IV.
[33] Wilson, *Political Organizations.*
[34] Putnam, *Comparative Study of Political Elites,* chap. 2.
[35] Kenneth John Meier, "Representative Bureaucracy," *APSR* 69 (June 1975): 526–42; V. Subramaniam, "Representative Bureaucracy: A Reassessment," *APSR* 61 (December 1967): 1010–19.

as we noted earlier, recruitment to high-level roles is often associated with policy formation, conflict over the assumption of these roles is pervasive. A major accomplishment of stable democratic regimes has been to regulate this conflict so that votes are mobilized rather than weapons.

In many traditional political systems, the selection part of the recruitment function was performed by diffuse family, religious, and kinship structures, following rules of hereditary succession. The son of the chief or monarch would more or less automatically inherit the throne on the demise of his parent. This system was designed to minimize conflict over succession and to minimize the potential power of selection structures. Its contemporary institutional equivalent is the seniority system, in which an organization selects a leader in quasi-automatic fashion by designating the member with longest service. The committee system in the United States Congress has long operated on a seniority basis, although occasionally with challenges, as happened in 1975, when several senior committee chairpersons were deposed. Indeed, as Robbins Burling points out in a study of succession in a variety of political systems, primitive and contemporary, the hereditary system was seldom successful in avoiding succession challenges, either.[36] Among many of the African kingdoms that he examines, succession was typically the occasion for bloody civil strife, with local chiefs and ambitious power-seekers rallying behind various princes who claimed the throne.[37] Heredity proves to be a less stable system than one might suppose, for claims of ability among royal relatives cannot be entirely ignored in times of crisis, and lines of succession are often complex. Students of British history have, of course, been well aware of this problem; the period from the War of the Roses until the consolidation by the Tudor Henry VII is a good example.

Table V.5 provides examples of selection structures operating for the chief executive roles in a number of contemporary political systems. One indication of the pervasive need to mobilize broadly based political resources behind the selection of chief executives in contemporary political systems is that political parties are important as selection structures in so many cases. The frequent appearance of parties also reflects, no doubt, the nature of legitimacy in secular cultures: the promise that actions of the rulers will be in the interests of the ruled. Of the nations in table V.5,

---

[36] Robbins Burling, *The Passage of Power: Studies in Political Succession* (New York: Harcourt Brace Jovanovich, 1974).

[37] Ibid. Robbins discusses succession in the Manchu dynasty in imperial China, in historical India, and in four African kingdoms, as well as in parts of the contemporary world.

Table V.5.   *Selection of Chief Executive in Contemporary*
            Political Systems, 1977

Nation[a]	Chief executive office	Selection structures[b]	Regime has survived succession[c]
USA	President	Party/Electorate	Very often
Sweden	Prime Minister	Party/Assembly	Very often
Canada	Prime Minister	Party/Assembly	Very often
W. Germany	Prime Minister	Party/Assembly	Often
France	President	Party/Electorate	Twice
Japan	Prime Minister	Party/Assembly	Often
Austria	Prime Minister	Party/Assembly	Often
Britain	Prime Minister	Party/Assembly	Very often
Israel	Prime Minister	Party/Assembly	Often
Czechoslovakia	Party Secretary	Party/USSR Party	Often
Italy	Prime Minister	Party/Assembly	Very often
USSR	Party Secretary	Party	Often
Spain	Monarch	Hereditary	No experience
Bulgaria	Party Secretary	Party/USSR Party	Often
Yugoslavia	President & 1st Sec'y	Party	No experience
Mexico	President	Party/Oligarchy	Very often
Brazil	President	Military/Oligarchy	Often
Peru	President	Military	Once
China	Party Chairman	Party/Military	Once
Egypt	President	Military/Oligarchy	Once
Nigeria	President	Military	Twice
Kenya	President	Party	No experience
Tanzania	President	Party	No experience
India	Prime Minister	Party/Assembly	Three

[a]Nations are ranked by level of economic development: GNP/capita in 1973 (see table I.1).

[b]The designation "party/assembly" refers to the typical parliamentary system. In these systems the parties choose leaders; competitive elections determine the strength of the parties in the national assembly; the parties in the assembly choose the prime minister.

[c]A regime is designated as having survived chief executive succession "often" if at least three such successions have taken place.

only Spain provides for heredity as a mechanism for selecting a chief executive with a major role, and it remains to be seen what powers the Spanish monarchy can retain as that country moves into its post-Franco era.

The most familiar selection structures in the table are the presidential and parliamentary forms of competitive party systems. In the presidential form, as in the United States and France, parties select candidates for nomination, and the electorate chooses between these. The Mexican system approximates this in form, but the PRI party has such predominance that the electorate's role for half a century has been one of ratifying the party's choice, which itself is achieved in a complex bargaining between party leadership factions and other national groups.

In the parliamentary form, the selection of chief executive is not accomplished directly by popular election. Rather, in one form or another the parties select leaders, and the electorate votes to determine the strength of the party in the assembly. If a single party wins a majority, its leader becomes prime minister. If no party wins a majority, then bargaining takes place to enable some prime minister to emerge who can command a parliamentary coalition majority — or at least not be defeated by one. In some cases, as has happened rather often in Italy, a Prime Minister may exist on the sufferance of a hostile assembly, which can force him from office at any time, but may refrain because no adequate replacement can win, either. In both the competitive presidential and parliamentary systems, tenure of the chief executive is periodically renewed, as new elections are held, and either a successor is selected or the incumbent is retained. As long as the party and election/assembly structures provide clear selection majorities, and as long as all actors abide by the results, these systems can work with great stability and can tie recruitment directly to policy aggregation and innovation.

Table V.5 also illustrates the role of noncompetitive parties. In Mexico, as we have noted, selection takes place through a rather open process of oligarchic bargaining within and around the PRI and the incumbent President, who cannot succeed himself.[38] Despite the somewhat closed nature of the recruitment process, the rule of no reelection does force periodic change in personnel and often in policy, and the party and the semicompetitive elections do bring about popular involvement. In the three Communist systems of the Soviet Union, Czechoslovakia, and Bulgaria, the much more controlled hierarchies of the Communist parties select the First Secretary, or equivalent. In the two Eastern European nations, some sort of negotiation or approval by the Soviet Union is also typically involved. It has been apparent, especially since the Hungarian uprising in 1956 and the Czechoslovakian intervention in 1968, that the selection systems in these nations cannot be considered independent of the Soviet Union — which is willing to intervene militarily to maintain its policy veto. The intricacies of negotiation between top party leaders in the Presidium and the Central Committee are typically not available for full analysis. But it is safe to conclude that succession is not a simple matter in these systems, which provide for no term or limitation for in-

---

[38] See the accounts in Robert E. Scott, *Mexican Politics in Transition*, rev. ed. (Urbana: University of Illinois Press, 1964); Frank Brandenburg, *The Making of Modern Mexico* (Englewood Cliffs: Prentice-Hall, 1964); and Roger D. Hansen, *The Politics of Mexican Development* (Baltimore: Johns Hopkins University Press, 1971).

cumbents. Hence, the incumbent must always be aware of the possibility of a party coup of the type that ousted Khrushchev from the Soviet leadership in 1964. As systems, however, the hierarchical party selection structures have been quite successful in maintaining themselves.

The poorer nations, as we move down the rows of table V.5, show substantially less stability, and the regimes in these nations have usually had less experience in surviving succession crises. In Yugoslavia, Tanzania, and Kenya, the national founders of the regime remain alive, and it has yet to be seen if the one-party selection structures can function in choosing a replacement. The military regimes in Peru and Nigeria are typical of military governments in many nations not shown in the table: no other structure shows signs of replacing the military command or junta in selecting leaders, but individuals have seldom remained in command for very long without a coup. In Egypt and Brazil, mixed civilian-military oligarchies have demonstrated some substantial staying power, responding to and controlling internal power factions through a mixture of involvement and coercion. India, having passed through two successions by elections and normal parliamentary procedures – from Nehru to Shastri to Indira Gandhi – seemed to be in crisis in 1975 when Gandhi declared an emergency and suspended liberties. But the election in 1977 was conducted consistently with the constitution and resulted in a third normal succession.

INDUCEMENTS FOR ELITE ROLE PERFORMANCE

As we have been arguing, the performance of the system functions is critical for the maintenance or adaptation of the system. Elite recruitment is one of these essential system functions. Traditional empires and dictatorships, for which self-perpetuation was a major goal of the rulers, seem to have focused on recruitment as the system function to be most carefully regulated. Subsystem autonomy was controlled through the careful selection of loyalists to fill the key elite roles in the military and civilian bureaucracies and through powerful inducements for continuing support in implementing the rules. The general or authoritarian dictator mixed rewards to his favorites with severe penalties for failure or disloyalty.

Modern totalitarian systems have discovered that more efficient and effective control is achieved through simultaneous manipulation of political socialization, political recruitment, and political communication flows. Efforts are made to instill loyalty in the population through socialization, to recruit activists loyal to the regime, and to limit and regulate the flow of information. But if recruitment is simply made a part of the larger pattern of control, it is hardly neglected, in either selection or inducement aspects. The selection in, say, the Soviet Union, is accomplished largely through a device called *nomenklatura:* "The term . . . refers to a list of key positions, appointment to which is under the supervision of a specific party secretariat. These officials serve as the ultimate selectors in Soviet political recruitment." [39] The filling of the top party roles themselves is accomplished, apparently, through careful bargaining among the incumbent leaders; depending on which of them control key resources at the moment, the council of top leaders may be hierarchic, segmented, or even relatively equalitarian in its internal structure.

The inducements for role performance are also carefully controlled and a complex set of inducements is created, which make it difficult for any but the topmost officials to have great autonomy in action. Normative inducements (appeal to party, national identity, and ideological values), remunerative inducements (better salaries, apartments and country homes, and freedom to travel for higher officials), and coercive inducements (tenure control or police, party, and bureaucratic observation and reports to coercive centers) are all employed to ensure maximum control over performance. In order to avoid possible intervention or coups by the police or military forces, the party penetrates these agencies at all levels. As we shall discuss in the next chapter, communication control plays a key part in limiting formation of new, unauthorized structures.

There are recruitment controls over selection and inducement in democratic systems as well. These are designed to keep the rule makers, and the would-be rule makers, in check, as well as to ensure compliance in rule-implementation roles. Control over the tenure and reappointment of elites is one important aspect of elite recruitment in democratic systems. But continuing role inducements exist as well. The Supreme Court in the American system, for example, has the authority to declare congressional rule making or presidential actions unconstitutional. And there exist impeachment procedures that can be used against the incumbents of any of the top roles, even those of President (as seen recently in the events forcing President Nixon from office) or Supreme Court Justice, if role performance strays too far beyond permissible bounds. Other democratic systems handle these inducement and selection procedures in different ways.

There is one set of political structures that is worthy of some special attention in our analysis of recruitment and, especially, elite role performance. That set is made up of the political structures with the legiti-

[39] Putnam, *Comparative Study of Political Elites,* p. 53. Also see Frederick C. Barghoorn, *Politics in the USSR,* 2d ed. (Boston: Little, Brown, 1972), chap. 7.

mate monopoly over the instruments of coercion: the military, the police, and other security forces. If it can be applied, coercion may prevail over the other political resources. Having access to weapons, training in their use, and organizations specifically designed to facilitate their application, the security forces of a society always constitute a potential threat to the regime. They can apply their organized coercion to replace the present "selectorate" and inducement structures with their own command and decision structure. As we have noted, most changes of regime are associated with violence, most overthrows of democracy with military action.

However, access to coercive resources does not automatically mean that military organizations call the tune in all political systems. The military organization in a democratic regime (or a civilian authoritarian organization, for that matter) is not organized as a rule-making or political recruitment structure. Its internal chain of command is based on obedience for security purposes, not political intervention. The structure is organized to implement rules, not to make them or choose elites. Military men take oaths of loyalty and are initially recruited to obey the legitimate authorities, not to overthrow them. Consequently, if a top general suddenly asks his subordinates to march on the capital, it may not follow that the hierarchic command structure will operate. It may break apart when military units are called upon to act outside their normal scope.

Studies of successful and unsuccessful coups by military organizations strongly suggest the difficulty, and improbability, of a coup against a regime with strong civilian legitimacy. Brazil in the late 1950s provides such an example. Despite some previous successful interventions, the military made both unsuccessful and successful attempts in the 1955–64 period. The attempts succeeded when civilian legitimacy was low (as indicated by civilian newspaper articles calling for the military to intervene) and the government's policies were feared and disputed. The attempts failed when a small number of officers tried to mobilize others without an adequate civilian base.[40]

A French case is also instructive. In the 1958 uprising, the military officers in Algeria were united around a cause that affected them deeply; the French on the mainland had little love for the republic or desire to defend it. The presence of General de Gaulle as a figure who could manage the transition to a new regime was a relief and prevented a paratroop operation against mainland France, by apparently giving the military what they wanted. In the 1962 uprising, the military was divided; some officers stood clear and refused to act against de Gaulle. And civilian forces in France united around the regime; even the Com-

[40] See Alfred Stepan, *The Military in Politics: Changing Patterns in Brazil* (Princeton: Princeton University Press, 1971).

munists called for armed resistance to defend the Fifth Republic, and all parties staged rallies and marches. The coup collapsed.[41]

Democratic governments have used various strategies in attempting to keep the military in check. None is foolproof. If the civilian population is indifferent or disaffected, even a very small military can overthrow a civilian government. Indeed, it may be easier for officers to organize discontent in a smaller military organization. Nor can all nations keep these military organizations small — there are security policy needs as well. If the military professionals come to define their duties as involving national values, and if they perceive the civilian government as unable to maintain order or occupied in the promotion of other national goals (international security, currency stability, economic growth, or whatever), then the professional military may intervene in a very professional fashion — as in Brazil in 1964. Only if the government can prevent other civilian groups from calling for military intervention, if it can avoid intervention into the military's own promotion and discipline structures, and if it can maintain a semblance of internal order and national security, will military intervention be reduced to a highly unlikely possibility.[42]

RECRUITMENT CRITERIA AND MODERNIZATION

In the study of recruitment, the major style distinction is usually between ascriptive and achievement-oriented recruitment. In the ascriptive style, individuals are chosen for particular roles because of their lineage and social status. Ascriptive recruitment may either establish a pool of candidates or select a particular individual. The ascriptive style of leadership recruitment in Saudi Arabia, for example, operates mostly at the former level; members of the Saudi royal family dominate the important elite roles in the society. At the level of selecting the particular individuals for the kingship, premiership, and the like, more achievement-oriented criteria come into play: does the individual have the technical and leadership skills necessary for good performance; do his policy preferences reflect those desired by the other important family members? In many other traditional societies, however, the line of suc-

41 For example, see the account in Claude E. Welch and Arthur K. Smith, *Military Role and Rule* (North Scituate, Mass.: Duxbury Press, 1974).

42 In general, see the bibliography in Welch and Smith, op. cit.; and in particular, see Samuel E. Finer, *Man on Horseback* (London: Pall Mall, 1962); Robert D. Putnam, "Toward Explaining Military Intervention in Latin American Politics," rptd. in Jason L. Finkle and Richard W. Gable, *Political Development and Social Change*, 2d ed. (New York: John Wiley, 1971), pp. 284–304; and Samuel P. Huntington, *Political Order in Changing Societies* (New Haven: Yale University Press, 1968), chap. 4. Also see chap. VIII.

cession to the throne and perhaps to surrounding roles, is more clearly defined by the traditional rules: the eldest child or eldest son may always inherit. Most such societies, though, have some means for ensuring reasonably good performance, either through key advisory roles or, more brutally, through elimination of unfit incumbents.

Putnam's study of political elite recruitment suggests several types of achievement-oriented criteria used in elite selection.[43] Technical expertise is the most obvious of these and becomes a matter of increased importance as elite role performance demands more complex activity intervening in other social processes. Elite roles vary, obviously, in the type of technical expertise required. The technology involved, the autonomy of the role in making decisions, and the static or changing nature of the environment all have an effect. The observation that the dominance of the educated is less pronounced in purely political roles than in bureaucratic roles no doubt reflects in part the less clearly defined technical needs of the former roles.

Skill in organization and persuasion is a second quality that, Putnam points out, is valued in top leadership roles in almost all societies. The specialized input roles require bargaining, negotiation, and mobilization of others in order to put policies together. Specific subcultures do vary in the value they place on some aspects of these skills. Putnam's study of politicians shows the different values stressed by Italian and British elites in considering what are desirable characteristics of a good party leader.[44] Although both groups mention technical skills with about the same frequency, all the Italian deputies give a great deal of weight to ideological and intellectual skills, which are not valued by the British. Among the latter, the Labour MPs emphasize interpersonal skills of conciliation and persuasion, whereas the Conservatives emphasize public inspirational ability. These differences, and others across political systems, probably give some indication of the degree to which leaders must deal in public or private forums in building coalitions, as well as the values of the subgroups and the conflict environment.

Putnam also suggests loyalty and political reliability as selection criteria used by elites in role recruitment in all political systems. Depending on the political system, of course, such loyalty may be to the personal ruler in a dictatorship, to the throne in a monarchy, to the party in a totalitarian system, or to the regime and constitution in a democracy. The choice of subordinates on the basis of loyalty to the political process structures may share equally with or be subordinate to policy loyalty and reliability. In choosing individuals to fill policy-making positions in

43 Putnam, *Comparative Study of Political Elites,* chaps. 3, 7.
44 Ibid., p. 64.

the political structure, such as President, member of Congress, Chairman of the Central Committee, Cabinet Minister, and the like, they are filling both process and policy roles. As we have already discussed, process and policy become closely connected in the recruitment process, and it is hardly surprising that recruiters seeking an achievement-oriented type should pay close attention to both functions that the role may perform.

As recruitment selectorates become oriented to various aspects of future role performance by those they select, conflicts may well arise between various criteria. One of the most famous of these conflicts is the continuing debate in Communist China and all Communist countries over the recruitment of individuals on the basis of ideological commitment and party loyalty versus recruitment on the basis of technical expertise.[45] The conflict between "Red" and "expert" criteria is especially hard to resolve in technical, but politically sensitive, areas of the military and bureaucracy. In part the matter is one of emphasis: obedience to party and conformity to ideology as opposed to efficient technical performance. In the upheavals of China in the 1960s the efficient administration of policy was often disrupted by the removal of incumbents on loyalty grounds. On the other hand, some key technical areas, such as the nuclear research teams of the army, were apparently left untouched by the controversies — the technical needs were too overriding.

Conflict may also involve differing perceptions of the needs of effective performance in different cultures and settings. Table V.6 shows the different criteria for good leadership emphasized as most important by American and Japanese elites. The Japanese values of personal warmth and sincerity are seen as essential to the good leader. The Americans emphasized honesty and equity of treatment. Both groups may well perceive accurately the differing mixtures required for effective leadership in their cultural settings.[46]

The complex interaction of ascriptive and achievement styles can be seen in all societies, but it is particularly evident in modern societies over issues of group representation. On one hand, the recruitment of family members, friends, racial groups, traditional clients, members of religious factions, residents of particular localities, and so forth seems to emphasize ascriptive criteria. But on the other hand, the purpose may be to secure the loyalty and support of key groups that are identified by such traditional criteria. This kind of creation of balanced tickets on party candidate lists is common in most modern democracies. It is also typical

45 See Herbert Franz Schurmann, *Ideology and Organization in Communist China* (Berkeley and Los Angeles: University of California Press, 1966).
46 Lewis Austin, *Saints and Samurai: The Political Culture of American and Japanese Elites* (New Haven: Yale University Press, 1975).

Political Recruitment

Table V.6. *Elite Perceptions of Traits of the Good Leader in the
            United States and Japan*

General category of trait	Specific trait	United States (N = 42)	Japan (N = 42)
Personalistic	Warmth	4.8%	26.2%
	Sincerity	0.0	16.7
	Trust	0.0	4.8
Performance	Knowledge of men	11.9	0.0
	Willingness to delegate	11.9	2.4
	Decisiveness	11.9	11.9
	Willingness to listen	9.5	16.7
Prescriptive	Honesty, Fairness, Justice	40.5	0.0
Other	Other	9.5	21.3
Totals	Totals	100.0%	100.0%

Source: Lewis Austin, *Saints and Samurai: The Political Culture of American and Japanese Elites* (New Haven: Yale University Press, 1975), pp. 22–23. Austin's samples consist of top-level business executives and government officials.

of Cabinet formation in many nations and even of the recruitment to executive and legislative roles in one-party and Communist systems. At this point much depends on the degree to which ascriptive ties tend to shape policy propensities and identifications in the society. If so, one can expect to find ascriptive ties entering into recruitment, even if the selection structures stress achievement criteria.

Although we have been emphasizing recruitment propensities at the selection stage, many of these comments are also relevant in considering the inducements offered for performance. In the secular culture, the inducements for role performance will be directed at specific and clearly defined aspects of that performance, with the clear objective of ensuring that performance follows the expected lines. We have already commented that in a secular culture the leaders are likely to be held on a shorter leash in their performance, for the criteria for evaluation become more explicit, based on knowledge and applied with more rigor.

STRUCTURAL DIFFERENTIATION AND POLITICAL DEVELOPMENT

Structural differentiation means the creation of new and specialized political roles. Over a wide range of circumstances such role differentiation has led to increased capacity and performance. At the same time, differentiation also creates its own problems of coordination and communication among the numerous specialized roles. From a dynamic, system perspective, one may ask how such differentiation comes about, for the successful creation of new roles and new structures is surely a more difficult task than merely the inducement or selection of individuals into existing roles.

There seem to be three general ways in which the introduction of new roles — particularly, but not necessarily, more specialized ones — takes place. The first, and perhaps the most frequent historically, is the *imposition* of new roles through external coercion. The large traditional kingdoms emerged as central rulers consolidated through force their control over local chieftains. The historical bureaucratic empires expanded through the conquest of various tribes and societies.[47] The conquered peoples found new subject roles imposed on them, and their leaders were forced to participate in the structures of rule and administration. Similarly, many of the political and administrative structures inherited by the newly independent colonial nations were initially imposed upon them by their colonial rulers.

Indeed, if one examines the origins of many of the structures in the set of nations listed above in table V.5, it appears that external imposition played an important role in many cases. The introduction of modern bureaucracies in most of the ex-colonial nations, such as India, Nigeria, and Kenya, took place under colonial rule. The democratic constitutions, including the electoral systems and legislative structures of West Germany and Japan, were imposed under Allied occupation after World War II. The armed forces of the Soviet Union played a critical role in introducing and sustaining Communist-party rule in Bulgaria and Czechoslovakia after World War II and in reimposing the penetrative authoritarian control in Czechoslovakia in 1968.

A second way in which structural innovation takes place is through *creative leadership,* which establishes new roles and structures in order to increase the capability of a group, a faction, or the entire society to achieve specific goals. Such efforts may respond to an external crisis, such as the threat of invasion, flood control problems, or famine. Or they may be the result of new leadership aspirations, such as the desire for conquest, religious conversion, or improvement in citizens' living standards. Leaders introduce new structural forms to meet a challenge that the existing social structures cannot handle, but the challenge may be either thrust upon them or the product of new aspirations.

In the historical state-building experiences in Western Europe, the major force seems to have been the challenge of war, both as threat and

---

47 See, for example, Burling, op. cit.; Max Weber, *Theory of Social and Economic Organization* (New York: Oxford University Press, 1947), pp. 341 ff.; S. N. Eisenstadt, *The Political Systems of Empires* (New York: Free Press of Glencoe, 1963).

opportunity. The incidence and severity of war in Europe rose sharply from the fifteenth through the seventeenth centuries. It declined somewhat in the eighteenth century, dropped sharply in the nineteenth century, only to rise catastrophically in the twentieth.[48] The crucial state-building centuries began with the sixteenth, when the incidence and magnitude of international strife almost doubled over the preceding century. The emerging states involved in this rise were France, Austria, Great Britain, Russia, and Spain. In the seventeenth century the magnitude of international strife almost tripled again, with the same countries now joined by Sweden, the Netherlands, and the German states. Prussia joined the conflict as a major force in the eighteenth century. The new size and scale of war prompted the leaders in these nations to introduce greatly increased armed forces. The need to support these forces, through the mobilization of men and materials, in turn required the development of larger and more centralized bureaucracies. To meet both internal and external threats, as well as to achieve the ambitious goals of individual leaders, the major European nations throughout this period expanded the size and autonomy of central government authorities, introducing extensive specialized bureaucratic structures for tax collection, conscription, military training, provision of food and materials, and so on.[49] These structures were developed under the pressure of war, in part through imitation of successful innovation in other states and in part through trial-and-error searches.

Of course, not only national leaders, but also leaders of subgroups, eager to achieve new rewards for themselves and their followers, have engaged in building new political structures. In the nineteenth and early twentieth centuries in Western Europe, the leaders of the newly emergent working class attempted to build labor union and party organizations that could coordinate the drive for a more equitable place in society. In the colonial nations in the twentieth centuries, such great leaders as Mahatma Gandhi and Nehru in India developed a set of mobilizing organizations to engage their peoples in a struggle for independence. And just as the setting of international war and domestic strife gave impetus to the introduction of centralized bureaucracies in Europe earlier, the guerrilla warfare organizations developed in the harsher freedom struggles of the twentieth century played and continue to play a crucial role in the political structures emergent in such nations as China, Cuba, Vietnam, and Yugoslavia.

Americans, of course, are familiar with the needs and opportunities

[48] See Quincy Wright, *A Study of War*, 2 vols. (Chicago: University of Chicago Press, 1942).
[49] See the essays in Charles Tilly, ed., *The Formation of Nation States in Western Europe* (Princeton: Princeton University Press, 1975).

for creative leadership offered by war and revolutionary struggle. The American Constitution is a classic example of the deliberate invention of new political roles, an amalgamation of ideas, imitation, and hard political bargaining among representatives to a constitutional convention. As the fate of Weimer Germany suggests, however, constitutional engineering is no simple task. The collapse of bright hopes for democratic participation in many of the ex-colonial nations confirms the lesson. Successful structural innovation was initiated by President de Gaulle in building the French presidential system, although the upheavals of 1968 suggested that structural changes without cultural and policy changes may not be enough. Mexico's Cárdenas in the 1930s combined group mobilization and coalition building with structural innovation to give the Mexican party system its present shape and to consolidate a process of civilian control over the military.[50] And in Tito's Yugoslavia, in Kenyatta's Kenya, and in Nyerere's Tanzania there exist national structures that are the product of individual or small-group creative leadership and that have yet to stand the ultimate test of surviving their individual creators.

A third major form taken by structural innovation is the *adaptation of existing structures* to new conditions. A typical example is the gradual expansion and increasing specialization of bureaucratic roles in the nineteenth and early twentieth centuries in Western Europe, as officials attempted to implement new social legislation and to cope with application of old rules to a changing society. New patterns of bureaucratic intervention developed as officials perceived new problems and new personal opportunities and tried to create ways of collecting information and of handling large, complex tasks.[51] Adaptation took place through a subtle blend of emulation of patterns tried elsewhere, invention of new modes of problem specialization, and accidental success of individuals trying out different role approaches. Due to the advantages of scale and specialization, increased differentiation was a typical result.

---

[50] See the account in Scott, op. cit.; and the essay by Wayne A. Cornelius, "Nation Building, Participation and Distribution: The Politics of Social Reform under Cárdenas," in Gabriel Almond, Scott Flanagan, and Robert Mundt, eds., *Crisis, Choice, and Change* (Boston: Little, Brown, 1973). On party institution-building more generally, see Samuel P. Huntington, *Political Order in Changing Societies* (New Haven: Yale University Press, 1968).

[51] Oliver McDonagh, *A Pattern of Government Growth, 1800–1860* (London: McGibbon and Kee, 1961); Piet Thoenas, *The Elite in the Welfare State* (New York: Free Press, 1966); Hugh Heclo, *Modern Social Policies in Britain and Sweden* (New Haven: Yale University Press, 1974). Also see the often fascinating accounts of bureaucratic adaptive efforts when faced with changing environments and difficult goals in Naomi Caiden and Aaron Wildavsky, *Planning and Budgeting in Poor Countries* (New York: John Wiley, 1974). Clearly, not all adaptive efforts are successful in improving performance.

The dramatic occasions, in short, on which a creative leader founds a new order or a group of constitution makers assembles after war or revolution has devastated the old order, are exciting historical turning points. But they must not blind one to the continuing process of imposition, adaptation, and innovation that occurs on a smaller scale continuously. The present British system is a product of the creative mobilization of middle- and working-class discontent in 1832 and the electoral reforms that the Whigs carried through in response; [52] it is also a product of countless minor political and bureaucratic accidents and personal achievements. The present Soviet system is a product of the Bolshevik victory in 1917–21 and of Lenin's and Stalin's construction of huge state and party hierarchies; it is also the product of the factory manager's efforts to meet quotas and of collective farmers' superior cultivation of the personal plots.

Particularly in a secular culture, where roles and structures are valued for their success in performance, the conscious effort to improve performance results in continuous minor structural change. Governmental reorganization takes place on a small scale all the time: interest groups are formed; party precinct committees are reconstructed or consolidated; legislative committee rules are changed. Verba and Nie found that 14 percent of the American adult population reported that they had at some time taken part in forming a new group or organization to try to solve some community problem.[53] The structures that exist in a society at any given point are the product not only of the great innovations of political leaders, but of all these small efforts of citizens to better their lives, of bureaucrats to better their position, and of party leaders to mobilize support.

[52] See G. Bingham Powell, Jr., "Incremental Democratization: The British Reform Bill of 1832," in Almond, Flanagan, and Mundt, op. cit.

[53] Verba and Nie, *Participation in America*, p. 352.

CHAPTER VI

Political Communication

POLITICAL LEADERS and political theorists alike have long recognized the implications of communications for the political system. Democratic theorists have insisted on the necessity of freedom of press and of speech in order that the people may check the activities of their rulers. Authoritarian leaders tend to dominate such institutions and to manipulate the information available to citizens. All citizens and all officeholders are dependent upon the information they receive and the effectiveness of the messages they transmit. The great historical empires, as well as modern states, have been characterized by the appearance of specialized communication structures and by the expenditure of important resources to facilitate communication. The Mongol hordes of Genghis Khan, for example, were linked by an elaborate system of mail riders (much like the American pony express), which could cross the steppes of Asia with remarkable speed. From the drummers, runners, and smoke signals of primitive tribes, through medieval heralds, to the presidential press conference and bureaucratic memo, political systems have created special communication structures and techniques to accomplish their purposes.

There are those who suggest that all of political science might be reconceptualized in terms of communication and the factors that generate messages and determine their impact.[1] As one writer has suggested, the body of potentially relevant literature for the study of communication and comparative politics is almost unlimited.[2] General systems theorists, economists, sociologists, students of the mass media, and many political

---

[1] Karl W. Deutsch, *The Nerves of Government* (New York: Free Press of Glencoe, 1963).
[2] Richard R. Fagen, *Politics and Communication* (Boston: Little, Brown, 1966).

scientists have all stressed the importance of communication processes.[3] Rather than recasting all political thought in communication terms, or considering only communication activity as a factor in understanding other political functions, we find it most useful to take a middle road. We can focus on the most general and significant flows of information in political systems, analyzing and comparing the structures that perform this basic system function of communication. In this fashion, the communication analysis gains utility as a focus integrated into our framework. The performance of the communication function does not include all other political functions, but it constitutes instead a necessary prerequisite for the performance of all these functions. We shall thus treat the political communication function as the third of our system functions, along with political socialization and political recruitment. Its performance is deeply involved in the maintenance or alteration of the political culture and structure of a society. After discussing briefly the types of structures involved in performing the communication function, we shall consider the implications of that performance for the system, process, and policy levels of political life.

TYPES OF COMMUNICATION STRUCTURES

All forms of human interaction involve communication. The mass media, such as radio and television, are only the most specialized and differentiated communication structures in a society. For comparison and analysis of political systems, it is useful to classify the structures that may perform communication functions. The presence or absence of these structures, the volume of information passing through them, and the freedom from control they enjoy have important implications for the political system. For our purposes, we may distinguish five types of structures: (1) informal face-to-face contacts, sometimes called primary communication; (2) nonpolitical social structures, such as the family, economic, or

[3] A useful recent overview is Steven H. Chaffee, ed., *Political Communication: Issues and Strategies for Research* (Beverly Hills: Sage Publications, 1975). Among earlier works, see, for example, Karl W. Deutsch, *Nationalism and Social Communication* (New York: John Wiley, 1953); Norbert Weiner, *The Human Use of Human Beings: Cybernetics and Society* (Garden City: Doubleday & Co., 1954); M. DeFleur and O. Carsen, *The Flow of Information* (New York: Harper & Row, 1958); Daniel Lerner, *The Passing of Traditional Society* (Glencoe: Free Press, 1958); J. G. March and Herbert Simon, *Organizations* (New York: John Wiley, 1958); Peter Blau and Richard Scott, *Formal Organizations* (San Francisco: Chandler Publishing, 1962); Adrian M. McDonough, *Information Economics and Management Systems* (New York: McGraw-Hill, 1963); Lucian W. Pye, ed., *Communication and Political Development* (Princeton: Princeton University Press, 1963); Wilbur Schramm, *Mass Media and National Development* (Stanford: Stanford University Press, 1964); David Easton, *A Systems Analysis of Political Life* (New York: John Wiley, 1965); C. Seymour-Ure, *The Political Impact of Mass Media* (Beverly Hills: Sage Publications, 1974).

religious groups;[4] (3) political input structures, such as political parties and other organizations more or less specialized to the input side of the political process; (4) political output structures, such as political executives, legislatures, and bureaucracies; and (5) the specialized mass media of communication, such as the press, magazines, radio, and television.

The role of *informal face-to-face contacts* in any political system should not be underestimated. Modern social science research has emphasized the degree to which informal channels of various kinds pervade the most developed communication systems. In studying the mass media and public opinion, Katz and Lazarsfeld found that the mass media did not have a direct impact on many individuals.[5] Rather, certain persons who for one reason or another had greater interest in following political events and who communicated information and opinions to friends, neighbors, and co-workers, served as opinion leaders. It was they who interpreted the information received through the media and other contacts and who directly shaped the knowledge and beliefs of others. Social status and personal gregariousness were the two characteristics singled out by Katz and Lazarsfeld as most significant in determining whether a person would assume such an opinion-leadership role in the United States.

In his study of opinion leaders and mass media in rural Egypt, Harik found a less predominant role for informal mediation of citizen learning about government policies.[6] Still, he found that 37 percent of the villagers had learned about the three policies he investigated — savings policy, family planning, and Socialism — indirectly through oral mediation of other individuals. As shown in table VI.1, such personal mediation was especially important for individuals who did not own their own radios; illiterates also seemed to rely heavily on such personal oral mediation.

In a modern political system it is easy to overlook the communications role played by *nonpolitical social structures*. But in traditional and developing societies their influence is very obvious. Tribal heads and councils of elders, the extended family, and religious leaders may play a powerful role as the initiators and interpreters of information for large sections of the nation. The role of Buddhist monks in Vietnam, Muslim religious leaders in the Middle East, and the Catholic church in Italy may be viewed in this light. Jean Grossholtz has emphasized the role of traditional community leaders in the Philippines, particularly where a

---

4 By "nonpolitical" we mean not specialized for formal political action.

5 Elihu Katz and Paul F. Lazarsfeld, *Personal Influence* (Glencoe: Free Press, 1955).

6 Iliya F. Harik, "Opinion Leaders and Mass Media in Rural Egypt: A Reconsideration of the Two-Step Flow of Communications Hypothesis," *APSR* 65 (September 1971): 731–40. And see the literature reviewed by Harik.

Table VI.1. *Direct and Indirect Flow of Communications from the*
            Mass Media in Rural Egypt

| | Means of learning about governmental policies: savings, family planning, and socialism | | | |
Characteristics of respondents	Direct reception of news through media (%)	Oral mediation through other persons (%)	Total	Number of cases
Radio owners				
Literate	73	27	100	45
Illiterate	62	38	100	29
Non-radio owners				
Literate	50	50	100	14
Illiterate	26	74	100	27

Source: Adapted from Harik, "Opinion Leaders and Mass Media in Rural Egypt," p. 733. Individuals were classified on the basis of the way in which they received information about the three issues included in the study. Only individuals who had heard of the governmental policies, 85% of the original sample, are shown in this table.

language barrier hinders more direct communication from the outside.[7] The traditional community leaders stand between the national elite and the people and may hinder or ease the transition to national unity. Moreover, among the elites themselves traditional social institutions may serve as critical communication networks that facilitate bargaining among members of the oligarchy. Astiz has described the exclusive clubs of Lima in Peru — the Jockey Club, the Club Nacional, and the Club de la Union — as communication networks for the Peruvian landed, economic, and military elite.[8]

Traditional societal structures remain important in most modern societies, constituting one of the familiar dualisms that forbid one to draw hard and fast lines between traditional and modern societies. Modern societies are permeated by traditional and informal social networks, including family, regional, occupational, and old-school-tie educational networks, which facilitate communication between individuals otherwise divided by specialized tasks or impersonal urban life. For citizens and elites alike these play important roles in their personal life. A spectacular example in the United States has been the role of the church in mobilization of American blacks into political life. Table VI.2,

[7] Jean Grossholtz, *Politics in the Philippines* (Boston: Little, Brown, 1964), chap. 9; and see Lerner, op. cit.
[8] Carlos Astiz, *Pressure Groups and Power Elites in Peruvian Politics* (Ithaca: Cornell University Press, 1969), pp. 191 ff.

Table VI.2. *Discussion of Elections at Church, as Perceived by Those Attending Church in the American South in 1961*

Discussion of elections	Whites (N = 622)	Blacks (N = 597)
Elections discussed at church	18	35
Elections not discussed	63	54
Don't know	18	10
No answer	1	1
Total	100	100

Source: Matthews and Prothro, *Negroes and the New Southern Politics,* p. 233. Matthews and Prothro reported that 77% of the blacks reported attending church with considerable regularity.

for example, reports the discussion of elections in church, as reported by whites and blacks in the South, in the Matthews and Prothro study in the early 1960s. Over a third of the black respondents reported such discussion, and 18 percent of the blacks reported that their minister had said something about which candidate should be supported. At a time when much open associational group and political party activity was foreclosed to American blacks, the churches were a critical network of political communication, particularly in areas where formal activity was difficult.[9] As the civil rights movement developed, their role was to become increasingly more important.[10]

In addition to these traditional social structures, an important role in political communication may be played by modern organizations and institutions. One obvious example is the work place; whether in factory, law office, or university, interactions with work colleagues make up a large share of individual communications, and there is no doubt that politics is a common topic of discussion. Associational groups, such as trade unions and professional associations, also play an important communications role in modern societies. Indeed, such associations frequently exist primarily for the purpose of enabling members to share common information about problems and opportunities. Although their purpose is often not primarily political, as in the case of the trade union, which was formed to secure benefits in bargaining with management,

[9] Donald R. Matthews and James W. Prothro, *Negroes and the New Southern Politics* (New York: Harcourt Brace Jovanovich, 1966), pp. 232–34.

[10] See, for example, the account in Anthony Oberschall, *Social Conflict and Social Movements* (Englewood Cliffs: Prentice-Hall, 1973), chap. 5.

their communication networks are frequently pressed into political activity. On one hand, the fact of common group interest means likely political involvement whenever that interest involves the political sphere. On the other hand, the existence of a communication network means that a ready means exists for the politically interested to approach and mobilize others for political purposes. As the costs of initial development of such organizational networks are high, the presence of communication networks formed for other purposes greatly facilitates recruitment of organization members.[11] Verba and Nie reported that in American organizations, members reported that political discussion took place in about half the organizations and that two-thirds of the organizations played an active role in dealing with community problems.[12]

The more *specialized political input structures,* such as political associations, public interest groups, and political parties, of course constitute significant communication channels in democratic political systems. With access to such specialized organizations, citizens can voice their political demands. Moreover, organized interest groups and parties provide an important channel for disseminating information about the activity of elites. Lobbyists in the capitol not only seek to influence political activities and to express the demands of their clients, but they also make sure that elite activities affecting their interests are subjected to careful scrutiny. In similar fashion, the opposition party is eager to expose the mistakes or improprieties of the incumbent administration. Parties and organized groups also can establish networks of personal contact with the people and can utilize their organizations to press an ideology or a set of issues on the populace. The ways in which political parties attempt to engage in communication for political socialization purposes were described in chapter IV.

The *specialized political output structures* are also important sources of information. The governmental structures, particularly the bureaucracy, make it possible for the political leaders to communicate directions for policy implementation to officials up and down the line, in the regions and the localities. The lifeline of communication holds the entire government structure together and makes possible coordinated implementation of policies and mobilization of societal resources. Many of the communications linking political leaders and the general public also flow through these structures. The courts and various governmental agencies are the major instruments through which redress of grievances or registra-

---

[11] See Mancur Olson, Jr., *The Logic of Collective Action* (Cambridge: Harvard University Press, 1965) and Oberschall, op. cit.

[12] Sidney Verba and Norman Nie, *Participation in America* (New York: Harper & Row, 1972), p. 176.

tion of complaints about policy implementation is undertaken, one example being the major role taken by the courts and the Justice Department in the civil rights movement in the United States. The governmental structures also supply large amounts of information of all kinds to the public as part of the effort to obtain citizen response and compliance with programs. Not only is information regarding the formal laws, such as social security regulations, disseminated through special agencies, but news releases from governmental agencies constitute one of the chief information sources for the mass media in most societies.

Political parties are typically used in coordination with governmental agencies to provide information about governmental policies in authoritarian societies, particularly those engaged in social change efforts. In his study in Egypt, Harik found that opinion leaders tended to be specialized party and governmental officials. Party leaders supplied much of the information on Socialist policy; cooperative society officials, on savings policy; physicians and party leaders, on family planning policy.[13] In the Egyptian village, at least, the specialized output structures dominated the communication channels that supplemented the mass media, themselves government controlled.

The *mass media*, including newspapers, television, radio, magazines, and books, constitute our final class of communication structures. They are the most specialized of such structures, existing primarily for the purpose of communication rather than depending upon it in the course of other activities. Given appropriate conditions of technical development and literacy (in the case of print media), the mass media are capable of transmitting information to very large numbers of people at low cost and with minimum distortion. Television broadcasters cannot be certain that an audience will interpret their words in the desired manner, but they know that the process of transmission and reception will not normally alter the words. Rumor and word-of-mouth transmission are substantially more uncertain.

As we pointed out in chapter IV, the influence of the mass media in shaping opinions depends greatly on the other agents of socialization and on the consistency of messages received, as well as on the credibility of alternative sources. But there is no doubt that the mass media are important sources of information in most societies. Harik found a majority of his Egyptian villagers had learned about government policies through the media, particularly through the radio.[14] The positive association be-

13 Harik, op. cit., pp. 735–37. Also see James N. Mosel, "Communications Patterns and Political Socialization in Transitional Thailand," in Pye, ed., *Communication and Political Development*, pp. 200–206.
14 Harik, op. cit.; and see table VI.1.

Figure VI.1. *Percentage of Americans Following Presidential Campaigns in Various Media,*
1952-72

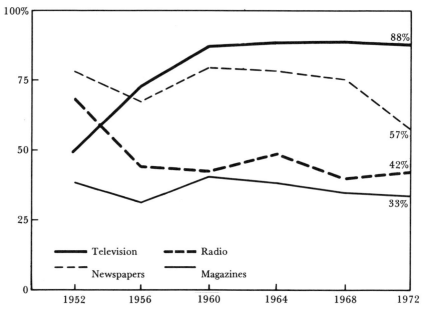

Source: Nie, Verba, and Petrocik, *Changing American Voter*, p. 274.

tween media exposure and a variety of modernity attitudes was documented for six developing nations by Inkeles and Smith.[15] Studies of national crises, such as President Eisenhower's heart attack, and the assassination of President Kennedy showed that the majority of Americans
first learned of these events through the mass media.[16] As is shown in
figure VI.1, nearly 90 percent of all Americans have been following
presidential election campaigns through television since 1960. Despite
the drop of interest in 1972, a substantial majority follows presidential
campaigns in the press and over 40 percent by radio.[17] That such atten-
tiveness is related to the acquisition of information, although not necessarily to changes in loyalty or opinion, has been well documented. The

[15] Alex Inkeles and David H. Smith, *Becoming Modern* (Cambridge: Harvard University Press, 1974); and see table II.6.

[16] P. J. Deutschmann and W. A. Danielson, "Diffusion of Knowledge of a Major
News Story," *Journalism Quarterly* 37 (Summer 1960): 345–55; B. S. Greenberg,
"Diffusion of News of the Kennedy Assassination," *Public Opinion Quarterly* 28
(Summer 1964): 225–32.

[17] Norman H. Nie, Sidney Verba, and John Petrocik, *The Changing American
Voter* (Cambridge: Harvard University Press, 1976), chap. 15.

Trenaman and McQuail study showed that increased television exposure by the British electorate was related to more accurate knowledge of party policies, although not to change in party support, a finding replicated in both Britain and the United States.[18] Above all, there seems to be good evidence that media attention to particular problems and issues has an impact on public discussion and awareness of these issues — the so-called agenda-setting role of the media.[19]

THE AUTONOMY OF COMMUNICATION STRUCTURES

In discussing the various kinds of communication structures, we have referred to the level of autonomy or of control that may be exercised over them. An autonomous communication structure is one that is free of domination either by political leaders or by particular interests in the society. Thus, to a large degree the interest groups, parties, and mass-media communication structures in such countries as the United States, Sweden, and Canada are free of tight political control. One finds neither the national governmental control nor the party control of communication media that is typical, for example, of some strongly Communist areas in France and Italy. The mass media are similarly free to disseminate information to everyone and to seek information from a multitude of sources. Recent controversies about the boundaries between press freedom and national security in the United States indicate the range of that freedom. The remarkable role of the *Washington Post* and its reporters in digging out the Watergate story and in bringing to light a vast program of government surveillance against groups and individuals suggests the influence that the mass media may exercise in politics through the acquisition and dissemination of information.

In penetrative authoritarian systems, on the other hand, these communication structures, including the mass media, are subject to a high degree of control by elites. The press, television, and radio engage primarily in "downward" information flows, released to facilitate public cooperation and support. In the Soviet Union, China, Bulgaria, and Czechoslovakia, for example, the Communist party has typically operated all the media, presenting a monolithic image of internal harmony and support except in times of leadership crisis. From the party papers to China's "revolutionary opera" the major communication flows in such

---

[18] J. Trenaman and D. McQuail, *Television and the Political Image* (London: Methuen, 1961); J. G. Blumler and D. McQuail, *Television and Politics* (Chicago: University of Chicago Press, 1969); R. D. McClure and T. E. Patterson, "Television News and Political Advertising," *Communication Research* 1 (January 1974): 3–31.

[19] See the review of this literature and findings in Lee B. Becker, Maxwell E. McCombs, and Jack M. McLeod, "The Development of Political Cognitions," in Chaffee, op. cit., pp. 38–53.

nations are primarily from the top down, with only carefully controlled flows in the reverse direction. In recent years some dissenting communication has been tolerated in Russia and other Communist countries, but it is interrupted by arrests and threats when it assumes dimensions interpreted as threatening by the regime leaders.

In other political systems a variety of less direct controls has typically been used to keep press criticism in line, even where the government does not directly operate the media. In his general account of relationships among the mass media, parties, and the governments, Seymour-Ure points out,

> Legal restrictions against the world's press range from simple excision of copy from newspapers (e.g., Rhodesia) to detailed restrictive press codes and harsh penalties (Argentina, Brazil, Greece). Economic control can be exercised through measures like government control of newsprint production or distribution (Mexico) and unfavorable fiscal arrangements (Greece).[20]

In table VI.3 we show the levels of autonomy of the mass media, in terms of their freedom to criticize their own local and national governments, in our twenty-four contemporary nations. The autonomy levels are based on judgments by expert panels, and the rating scores have been simplified here into four categories.[21] In the Communist nations (except Yugoslavia) and in Egypt, government control of the mass media is extremely close. In Spain during the Franco regime, newspapers were not government operated, but some were run by the official party, others by the Catholic church and the Catholic lay organization, *Opus Dei,* both closely identified with the regime. Opposition papers were not allowed. In the one-party states (Kenya and Mexico) and military regimes (Nigeria and Brazil) in the table, indirect controls were used to keep the press in check, but substantial autonomy was allowed. Peru is unusual in maintaining rather high press freedom. Indeed, Seymour-Ure suggests that in the absence of the party system following the military takeover, the press was allowed to speak for different interest groups earlier represented in the party system;[22] different newspapers serve as spokespersons for different groups.

Most of the Western European democracies received high ratings for freedom accorded to the mass media to engage in political criticism. In-

---

[20] Seymour-Ure, op. cit., p. 179. [Policies in Greece refer to the period of military rule from 1967 to 1973.]

[21] Data from Charles L. Taylor and Michael C. Hudson, *World Handbook of Political and Social Indicators,* 2d ed. (New Haven: Yale University Press, 1972).

[22] Seymour-Ure, op. cit., p. 186. Such relative press freedom seems to have been permitted at least for the first five or six years of direct military rule.

Table VI.3. *Autonomy of the Media in Selected*
Contemporary Political Systems

Nation	Freedom of the press and broadcasting systems to criticize their own local and national governments[a]
USA	High
Sweden	High
Canada	High
W. Germany	High
France	Moderate
Japan	High
Austria	High
Britain	High
Israel	Moderate
Czechoslovakia	Very low
Italy	Moderate
USSR	Very low
Spain	Low
Bulgaria	Very low
Yugoslavia	Moderate
Mexico	Moderate
Brazil	Moderate
Peru	High
China	Very low
Egypt	Very low
Nigeria	Moderate
Kenya	Moderate
Tanzania	Moderate
India	Moderate

Source: Adapted from Taylor and Hudson, *World Handbook of Political and Social Indicators.* The Data, from a ranking system involving multiple judges, were supplied to the *Handbook* by Ralph L. Lowenstein, Freedom of Information Center, School of Journalism, University of Missouri. Year of rating was not specified, but was presumably in the late 1960s.

Note: Nations are ranked by level of economic development: GNP/capita in 1973 (see table I.1).

[a] The Press Freedom Index in Taylor and Hudson, pp. 51-53, ranges from +4 (highest) to -4 (lowest). We have coded the data as follows for table presentation: High = +2 to +4; Moderate = 0 to +1.99; Low = -1.99 to -.01; Very low = -4 to --2.

deed, the highest ratings were received by Norway, Switzerland, and the Netherlands. Press autonomy in Italy, France, and Israel fell just below the cutoff point we used for high ratings due to a variety of government interventions and controls, whereas press freedom in Japan has been carefully guarded in the postwar era. Despite their British traditions, mass media freedom has been substantially and intermittently limited in

152 Political Communication

India, even before the sharp censorship introduced during the Declaration of Emergency period of 1975–77. Yugoslavia has much the greatest press freedom of the Socialist nations; it still ranked virtually at the borderline between low and moderate. A comparison of this table's ratings of media autonomy with the typology of differentiation and autonomy from chapter III will show a high correspondence between general subsystem autonomy and differentiation and freedom of the media.

POLITICAL COMMUNICATION: SYSTEM CONSEQUENCES

Political communication is a basic system function with many consequences for maintenance or change in political culture and political structure. One can assume, indeed, that all major changes in the political system involve changes in communication patterns, usually as both cause and effect. All socialization processes, for example, are communications processes, although communication need not result in attitude change. Similarly, the coordination and control of individuals in different organizational roles requires communication of information. Hence, establishing new socialization patterns and building new organizations both require changes in communication performance.

COMMUNICATIONS EXPANSION AND SOCIAL MOBILIZATION

Many of the developing nations of Asia, Africa, and Latin America are engaged in desperate struggles to create better lives for their peoples. These goals of development have emerged due to many forces: a gradual awareness of better conditions in other nations, the rallying cry that led to independence, the efforts of politicians to unite a new nation with themselves at the head, and the initial experience with economic development. Whatever the origins, the leaders and increasingly large parts of the populations in these areas are firmly committed to developmental goals.

Those interested in promoting development must encourage and facilitate social changes that are fundamental to the mobilization of human and natural resources. Karl Deutsch has defined social mobilization as "the process in which major clusters of old social, economic, and psychological commitments are eroded or broken, and people become available for new patterns of socialization and behavior."[23] A traditional agricultural society cannot develop the level of societal resources upon which to base improvement of living conditions. The deliberate efforts to increase mass media penetration, to launch massive educational efforts, and to build strength of a dominant political party with which to reinforce new attitudes and control their direction are largely based on this need

23 Karl W. Deutsch, "Social Mobilization and Political Development," APSR 55 (September 1961): 494.

for social mobilization, which must precede development of political and economic capabilities.

Social mobilization is in large part a communications phenomenon. Literacy, secularization of traditional ties and beliefs, employment in a wage economy, agricultural improvement, and other concomitants of mobilization involve exposure to new structures and processes of communication. As various studies have shown, such exposure can be effective. Peasants in contemporary Ghana and Kenya, for example, have substantial political information, major sources being mass media exposure and education.[24] It is this exposure to new communications sources that creates the "revolution of rising expectations." The dilemma arises from the fact that political aspirations and expectations rise much faster than the system can develop the capabilities to meet them. Information can also lead to cynicism about politicians and institutions when these are ineffective and unresponsive.[25] The resulting discontents make for a political instability often fueled by extravagant hopes built by political leaders.

The expansion of national information and awareness has created other problems as well as the aspirations that are aroused for general economic development. Before attitudes of national unity are consolidated, the various economic, geographic, and ethnic groups, becoming aware for the first time of their relationship to the rest of the nation and to the political system, can generate a host of demands that create conflicts between groups. As Deutsch wrote over fifteen years ago, the rapid expansion of communication may

> promote the consolidation of states whose peoples already share the same language, culture, and major social institutions; while the same process may tend to strain or destroy the unity of states whose population is already divided into several groups with different languages or basic ways of life.[26]

Unfortunately, these dilemmas are not easily resolved. Every success seems to sow the seeds of new problems, at least until some sort of major threshold of economic development is achieved. When India achieved its independence, for example, the groups having entry to the political system were rather few, very largely included in the Congress party and the Indian civil service. The elite was united by the independence move-

24 Fred M. Hayward, "A Reassessment of Conventional Wisdom About the Informed Public: National Political Information in Ghana," *APSR* 70 (June 1976): 433 ff.; and Joel D. Barkan, "Comment: Further Reassessment of the 'Conventional Wisdom': Political Knowledge and Voting Behavior in Rural Kenya," *APSR* 70 (June 1976): 452–55. Also see Harik, op. cit.; and Inkeles and Smith, op. cit.

25 Hayward, op. cit., pp. 445–46.

26 Deutsch, "Social Mobilization," p. 501.

ment and by the personality of Nehru. But in the decades since independence the very success of the changes in Indian life has brought more
and more groups into the political arena and has radically altered the
nature of the political elite. Competitive political mobilization has been
coupled with inability to achieve major steps forward in economic development. Indeed, the very linking to the political process of groups desiring to preserve traditional ways of life has inhibited such development,
as in the area of efficient land reform and use.[27]

REVOLUTIONARY MOBILIZATION AND
COMMUNICATIONS CONTROL

We have referred thus far to the often inadvertent changes in traditional political cultures that occur under conditions of exposure to new
communications patterns. Our discussion would be incomplete without
consideration of the deliberate efforts to change and control existing
social structures by revolutionary mobilization. The nineteenth and
twentieth centuries have seen a significant number of experiments in
the creation of new organizational structures to penetrate, mobilize, and
control various sections of traditional societies. A common thread in
those efforts which have succeeded has been the successful capturing of
communication networks.

One approach has been the cooptation of traditional social networks
and their adaptation for new purposes. Ethnically based parties, for
instance, have typically been able to draw upon existing family, tribal,
and community networks in informing group members about new political goals and coordinating political actions. A second approach has been
to train leaders and offer organizational examples in a process of building new networks where old ones were destroyed or none existed before,
as in the construction of working-class organizations in nineteenth-cen-
tury Europe. The strategies of the Communist party in China in the
1930s reflected both approaches. After initial failures, often due to
peasant resistance to fundamental change, the CCP altered its program
and organizational tactics and developed communication networks
based on local kinship groups, penetrating and transforming the traditional structures, working with them and controlling them.[28]

---

[27] See Myron Weiner, *The Politics of Scarcity* (Chicago: University of Chicago Press,
1962); and Rajni Kothari, *Politics in India* (Boston: Little, Brown, 1968); and the essay by Thomas Headrick in Gabriel A. Almond, Scott Flanagan, and Robert Mundt,
eds., *Crisis, Choice, and Change* (Boston: Little, Brown, 1973). On the basic dilemma
created by traditional groups in Indian democracy, see Barrington Moore, Jr., *Social
Origins of Dictatorship and Democracy* (Boston: Beacon, 1966), pp. 314 ff.

[28] See the account in Herbert Franz Schurmann, *Ideology and Organization in Communist China* (Berkeley and Los Angeles: University of California Press, 1968); and the
general discussion by David R. Cameron, "Toward a Theory of Political Mobilization,"
Journal of Politics 36 (February 1974): 138–71, especially pp. 146 ff.

Mass authoritarian movements that have come to power have often attempted to break down the existing social structure and to replace it by a controlled organizational hierarchy or by the dual hierarchy of party and bureaucracy. Nazi Germany and Stalin's Russia provide two obvious examples.[29] A fascinating case of the destruction and reconstruction of social communication networks in the midst of conflict, however, is the struggle for control of the villages in Vietnam, as waged by the Communist forces over a twenty-year period. According to Andrews's account of the "village war" in Dang Lao province, the party began in 1959–60 a systematic effort to eliminate traditional non-Communist village leaders through tactics of terror and coercion.[30] Large-scale assassination, kidnapping, humiliation, and terror were broadly used over a four-year period to destroy the traditional social leadership networks. Then, beginning in 1964, the party turned to the creation of a new communication and interaction network to replace the old. Information manipulation was a critical part of this process: all mail and newspapers were censored, listening to "enemy" broadcasts was forbidden, and approved radio stations and periodicals were provided in their place.[31] In addition, mass organizations were created for peasant involvement, travel was circumscribed, reform appeals were instituted, and schools were established.[32] Apparently, only in villages where Catholic or Cao Dai religious organizations provided strong personal and organizational support for individuals were the efforts at social reconstruction long resisted.[33]

The destruction of the village social framework left the villager physically unharmed but socially isolated. His leaders had been proven incapable of surmounting the problems facing the village. The traditional behavioral norms to which the villager had been accustomed no longer assured a way to attain his goals. The peasant found himself alone in a threatening and chaotic world, and in order to save himself he had to find new answers that would offer stable frames of reference. Isolated and incapable of comprehending the nature of the problem facing him, no individual or his family group could define the necessary behavior patterns required to end the

[29] See William S. Allen, *The Nazi Seizure of Power* (Chicago: Quadrangle, 1965); and Barrington Moore, Jr., *Terror and Progress* (Cambridge: Harvard University Press, 1954).

[30] William R. Andrews, *The Village War* (Columbia: University of Missouri Press, 1973), chap. 4.

[31] Ibid., pp. 110 ff.

[32] Ibid., chap. 6.

[33] Ibid., pp. 68 ff. The power of Catholic communication networks in shaping voting behavior and political attitudes in general has long been an important phenomenon in Western European politics.

disorientation. It was at this point that the Party said, in effect, "Here, do these things and act in this manner and order will be restored." [34]

Of course, not all efforts to restructure communication networks and information environments are successful. And it remains to be seen whether the structures created by the Vietnamese Communists for the purposes of revolutionary conflict can be used for purposes of social and economic development, for the Chinese experience suggests both possibilities and limitations. But it is clear that control of communication networks is virtually a prerequisite for revolutionary change. The capacity, at least in principle, of political parties to reach individual citizens and to provide communication channels to and from them is largely responsible for the prevalence of parties in societies undertaking such mobilization.

POLITICAL COMMUNICATION: PROCESS CONSEQUENCES

Popular control over political leaders is the sustaining myth of democracy. The claim of a democratic system is that "the people" can make their wishes known to officeholders and can, at regular intervals, "throw the rascals out" if the job is not being properly done. We have already suggested that the availability of autonomous interest groups, parties, and mass-media communication structures is vital in ensuring that the "will of the people" is continuously communicated to the leaders. In the subsequent chapters on interest articulation and aggregation we shall develop these themes in more detail. But a second aspect of communications in citizen influence has also been of concern to students of democracy. Without accurate knowledge of the actions of leaders and without an understanding of the relationship between those actions and popular goals, a meaningful articulation of interests and exercise of political influence is impossible. [35]

Such information is critical for several reasons. First, citizens need to have enough facts at their disposal to determine what their preferences are in a given context. Should local taxes be raised to support a new sewage disposal plant? Should national conscription be instituted to mobilize against a foreign threat? Citizens' preferences on the issues will depend in part on the health threat posed by present sewage disposal arrangements, and on the national security threat posed by the international situation. Second, citizens need to know which political leaders

[34] Andrews, op. cit., p. 132.
[35] An excellent formal account is Robert A. Dahl, *Preface to Democratic Theory* (Chicago: University of Chicago Press, 1956). A provocative treatment of citizen control problems is offered by Murray Edelman, *The Symbolic Uses of Politics* (Urbana: University of Illinois Press, 1964).

take various stands on the issues, or at least which have been in control during the immediate past, in order to communicate those preferences. If they wish to write to sympathetic officials, they must know who those officials are and how to reach them. If they intend to base their votes on the recent conduct of government, they must both evaluate that conduct and know who was responsible for it.[36] And, finally, citizens will typically be more effective in their efforts at influence and control if they join with others who are sympathetic to their position. Such group effort implies information, communication, and coordination with the actions of other citizens.

In theory the presence of individual freedom to form groups, contact officials, work for parties, and vote in competitive elections can be used to control political leaders who are periodically subject to electoral mandate — if all three sorts of information are available. And in the presence of adequate information and communication, citizens should be able to join together to form parties, interest groups, and even more coercive organizations to press demands on leaders.[37] Hence arise the efforts of penetrative authoritarian regimes to press their interpretation of national and local issues upon citizens through party and controlled press, to emphasize united national leadership and to hide internal leadership divisions when possible, and to control citizen travel, group meetings, and organizational formation.

But several factors complicate the availability of the information that would make popular control feasible even in democratic regimes. First is the technological complexity of governmental activities and the increasingly specialized knowledge necessary to understand many of them. How is the public to assess the issues involved in an administration's decision to build submarines with nuclear missiles, but not to develop faster manned bombers? How many people can judge whether the decision to build a river dam on one site rather than another is based on sound technical and economic analysis or on the consideration of landed interests in the area? What are the safety and pollution issues involved in the reliance on nuclear power plants for energy needs? The issues

36 For a discussion of such retrospective use of voting to reward and punish leadership for their performance, see V. O. Key, Jr., with Milton C. Cummings, *The Responsible Electorate* (New York: Random House, 1966); and Angus Campbell et al., *The American Voter* (New York: John Wiley, 1960), pp. 554 ff. For more recent analysis of the effect of economic fluctuations on voting for incumbents, see Gerald H. Kramer, "Short-term Fluctuations in U.S. Voting Behavior, 1896–1964," *APSR* 65 (March 1971): 131–43; and Howard S. Bloom and H. Douglas Rae, "Voter Response to Short-Run Economic Conditions," *APSR* 69 (December 1975): 1240–54.

37 As we shall discuss more completely in chap. VII, the freedom to form organizations and participate does not mean that all citizens are equally likely to do so, in part because of communication and coordination costs. Also see chap. V.

involved in many public activities may well be so complex and specialized that the public is in no position to judge whether one proposal is
better than another or even whether one outcome was the best available.
Moreover, the sheer remoteness of many political issues makes it
difficult for the average citizen to become involved at the time when
critical decisions are made. Few Americans were concerned with, or had
even heard of, events in Vietnam during those crucial years in the early
1960s when commitment to United States involvement was being steadily
expanded. About an immediate event touching his or her life, an individual is likely to hold strong opinions. But many of the great national
issues are either themselves quite remote from the life of the citizen or
are tied into remote and complex policy remedies. In such circumstances,
there is great concern that the choices made by national mass media,
particularly television, about the salience of issues and the credibility of
alternatives will unduly shape the citizens' perceptions. The impact of
the media on citizens' information about elite behavior and national
events has been well documented, at least in the short run.[38] More
speculative argument has suggested that the tendency of television, particularly in the competition for viewers in the United States, to emphasize problems and conflicts and to give them an immediacy not possible
in other media has undermined citizen confidence and even institutional
support.[39] In such fashion, the national media may sharply alter the
focus of citizen attention and may even encourage or discourage involvement in the political process itself.

It seems unlikely that the treatment by the media is more important
than the messages themselves. Where many competitive media channels
are open, the treatment by any single source will be effective only within
a total context of other messages and existing perceptions and opinions.
Despite the great speculation about the role of television in shaping
views on Vietnam, for example, Mueller's careful investigation of public
opinion and views of the wars in Korea and Vietnam showed very similar
patterns of support decline as the costs of the wars — as measured in terms
of casualties — grew.[40] Mueller specifically rejects the television hypothesis.[41] Despite the media's great short-run influence over public infor-

    [38] See Becker, McCombs, and McLeod, op. cit.; and the other essays, generally, in
Chaffee, op. cit.; Hayward, op. cit.; Harik, op. cit. Also see the analysis of the effect of
the CBS documentary on military public relations programs by Michael J. Robinson,
"Public Affairs Television and the Growth of Political Malaise," *APSR* 70 (June 1976):
409–32.
    [39] Robinson, ibid., p. 431, and the sources cited therein.
    [40] John E. Mueller, *War, Presidents, and Public Opinion* (New York: John Wiley,
1973).
    [41] Ibid., p. 167.

mation and issue salience — an influence that can have powerful effects on campaign twists, policy decisions, and the tactics of political activists — it seems probable that they were far less responsible for the major shifts in American political culture in the 1960s than were the national and international conflicts that they reported.

Yet another problem for popular control, however, is posed by the very difficulty in establishing definite cause-and-effect relationships in the world of politics. The number of factors involved in any set of political events is likely to be so complex that responsibility is difficult to assess. Students of politics are aware, for example, of the difficulties encountered in tracing down explicit responsibility for failure of Congress to enact any specific piece of legislation. The diffusion of responsibility in the American system, between President and Congress and between congressional committees, complicates the problem. But even in a majoritarian parliamentary government the relationship between government action and outcome may be difficult to trace. Although voters can and do use the device of voting against the incumbents if outcomes turn out badly, the problem of accountability becomes insoluble if all sets of incumbents perform badly. Neither of the major British parties, for example, seem to have been able to do much about the British economic crises from 1963 onward, and voters' rejection of first one and then the other may have led in the end to progressive general frustration. Indeed, as La Porte and Abrams speculate, one of the discouraging prospects of "postindustrial society" may be successive policy failures whose origins are so complex that not even the experts may be able to assess the reasons.[42]

The differences in the remoteness and technological complexity of various issues and in the ease of establishing responsibility are well known to political leaders. It seems clear that members of Congress, for example, pay close heed to their constituents on some issues, but perceive that they have much more flexibility to act on others. This reflects not so much immediate voter information, but potential salience and information if the representatives were to take particular kinds of stands.[43] The potential for competition and the presence of organized groups watching over various interests keeps successful representatives attuned to constituent preferences — as they see them — on some issues, particularly matters such as race relations, abortion, or local jobs. Still, there are

42 Todd La Porte and C. J. Abrams, "Alternative Patterns of Postindustria: The California Experience," in Leon N. Lindberg, ed., *Politics and Future of Industrial Society* (New York: David McKay, 1976), especially pp. 39 ff.

43 See Warren E. Miller and Donald E. Stokes, "Constituency Influence in Congress," *APSR* 57 (March 1963): 45–56; and John W. Kingdon, *Congressmen's Voting Decisions* (New York: Harper & Row, 1973); also see the references in chap. V, n. 6.

many general groups, such as consumers or the poor and uneducated, that often lack strong organizations to press their interests, and there are many policy issues, such as environmental ones, that may seem remote at one time, only to become overwhelmingly immediate at a time when it is no longer possible to do anything about them.

Some have argued that a high degree of elite freedom to pursue policies without citizen oversight can be beneficial to the political system. Under such conditions, it may be possible for the leaders to make and implement policy that is needed for developmental goals favored by all, but is detrimental to the short-run interests of particular groups. That is, it may be possible for the elite to take a longer time perspective than they would be permitted if the citizens were directly involved. The capability of an elite to satisfy popular demands with symbolic responses, such as minor land distribution or expropriation of foreign property "in the name of the revolution," may buy time for a decade or so of great resource investment at the expense of popular consumption. Mexico's industrialization in the 1940s and 1950s, when the relative, and probably the absolute, share of personal income received by the lowest social groups actually declined as the economy boomed, was supported by just this approach.[44]

But one must also recall that the promise to act in the best interests of the people, even if they do not perceive these interests, has been the central claim of most authoritarian rulers. Promises and symbolic gratifications may be useful in the short run, but this strategy may lead to habits of elite dominance that are not easily altered when citizen groups demand a more active policy-making role. If communication flow is more or less autonomous, elite flexibility will eventually be circumscribed, and promises must be redeemed. At this point it may be tempting for leaders to prohibit criticism and to manipulate information, rather than to allow citizen control to take effect.

POLITICAL COMMUNICATION: POLICY CONSEQUENCES

Contemporary governments typically seek to achieve major social and economic changes in their societies. In chapters XI and XII we shall describe various patterns of governmental policy efforts and the social outcomes that they achieve — and fail to achieve. One of the major debates in the general area of policy is focused on the comprehensiveness of the planning that should underlie policy efforts. Should the government, for example, develop a detailed five-year plan that establishes the

---

[44] For a description of the costs and benefits of Mexican developmental policy, and of the eventual contradictions and strains, see Roger D. Hansen, *The Politics of Mexican Development* (Baltimore: Johns Hopkins University Press, 1971).

problems and objectives to be attained through coordinated policy implementation in the intermediate future? Or should reliance be placed on much more modest and piecemeal approaches? A related debate, in various policy areas, emphasizes the costs and benefits of direct coordination versus indirect encouragement of market forces, as in the use of wage and price controls versus monetary control to check inflation or in terms of governmental operation of industry versus private sector activity. To what extent will nationalization of key industries help or hamper national economic growth?

These questions probably do not have general answers, for the policy problems are shaped by the specific environment and the capacity of the political system to use its bureaucratic agencies for extraction, distribution, regulation, and the like. But analysis of the properties of communication systems can shed light on some of the general underlying dynamics of these policy problems. For quite aside from technical problems and the question of adequately trained personnel, there are some underlying difficulties with the most obvious policy approach: the direct intervention of governmental bureaucracy and the development of comprehensive policy plans. These difficulties have to do with information distortion, both the distortions of information that reaches decision makers and the distortions in the efforts of decision makers to implement the policies that have been decided upon.[45]

Information distortion can, of course, come from many sources. But two characteristics of communication structures that have been well established in small-group research lend themselves to broad hypotheses. The first is that there are limits to the capacity of an organization to process information in a given period of time. When the volume and complexity of incoming information pass a certain point, either the organization will distort the information, or it will take longer to process it. The second hypothesis suggests that information flowing through a hierarchical structure tends to be distorted by the desires and sensitivities of the individuals with greater status and by the intimidation of those lower in the hierarchy.

Effective activities by elites in a large, centralized, and complex political system are hampered by the sheer volume of information that must be processed upward and downward through the bureaucracy. Any polit-

45 In addition to specific sources named below, a pertinent general discussion of these problems may be found in Deutsch, *Nerves of Government*, pp. 219 ff. Also see Easton, *Systems Analysis*, chaps. 8, 9, and 26; and the discussion of centralized "synoptic" decision-making patterns as opposed to those of "partisan mutual adjustment" in David Braybrooke and Charles E. Lindblom, *Strategy of Decision* (New York: Free Press of Glencoe, 1963); and Charles E. Lindblom, *The Intelligence of Democracy* (New York: The Free Press, 1965).

ical system in which the central government engages in a very wide range of activities occurring within a rapidly changing environment encounters this problem. The difficulties faced by central planners in the confused and changing social and political environments in developing nations represent an extreme case.[46] A large business organization, unwilling to decentralize, may have similar difficulties. The organizational leaders' refusal to grant autonomous decision-making authority to individuals at lower levels means that all information relevant to decisions must be communicated up the hierarchy. In the more decentralized systems, a more limited amount of information, only that relevant to particular leadership decisions, must be communicated to the top levels.

When central decision makers are responsible for evaluating all information and making all decisions, rather than for making basic policy choices alone, their effectiveness in a large and complex system is diminished by several factors. First, they can read or hear and understand only a limited quantity of information. All leaders of large organizations complain of the volume of communication crossing their desks and of the impossibility of handling it all. It is inevitably necessary to decentralize at least to the extent of letting a presidential staff, or its equivalent, dispose of much of the incoming material that seems irrelevant or unworthy of the chief executive's time.

Furthermore, as the information chain of a centralized decision-making structure involves more steps, the likelihood of error and distortion becomes multiplied.[47] Not only do lower- and intermediate-level officials have their own interests at stake, but human error is always a possibility. In addition, any communication channel is limited in the total amount of information it can receive and pass on in a given span of time. If the volume is too high for every bit of information to be passed on, some things will be intentionally or inadvertently filtered out. Otherwise there will be serious time lags in the flow of information. Just as the ticker tape on the New York Stock Exchange may run minutes and hours behind the price shifts as the volume of business mounts beyond its accustomed level, so, too, may political information systems lag.

Another problem in centralization is the increasing technical complexity of much relevant information. Leaders cannot be, even though they may be expected to be, genuine experts in all fields of military technology, cost accounting, political maneuvers, monetary inflation,

---

[46] See Naomi Caiden and Aaron Wildavsky, *Planning and Budgeting in Poor Countries* (New York: John Wiley, 1974).

[47] See Jeffry Pressman and Aaron Wildavsky, *Implementation* (Berkeley: University of California Press, 1973), chap. 3.

urban transportation, or medical care. At various points the raw data from the environment must be put in a form that can be interpreted by the top elite. This process may involve many steps, including scientific or statistical interpretation of information, analysis by experts, and translation into nontechnical terms. Each stage involves a potential for error. In such cases top officials are at the mercy of their experts except in those few fields in which they possess special competence.

As a consequence of high volumes of information and of the technical nature of much information, a very large and complex system is pushed inescapably toward a degree of decentralization or toward inefficient and irrational actions. Events within large democratic societies have emphasized these decentralizing forces. Students of governmental regulation of business in the United States and of the nationalized industries in Great Britain have, for example, noted the tendency of regulatory agencies or national administration boards to slip from government control, to become the captives of those whom they seek to administer. The sheer magnitude of the industry and the technical expertise of the "old hand" business managers and advisers overwhelm the official from the outside. In similar fashion, as students of congressional control over the Defense Department or the Office of Management and Budget have increasingly commented, it is impossible for a small leadership group to exercise effective control over a massive bureaucratic organization. Such groups can hardly manage to struggle through all the material prepared for them by the agency itself, let alone exercise really independent checks. Thus, decentralization takes place more or less inadvertently, often with the development of "counterbureaucracies," such as congressional staffs.

Volume and complexity of information and the length of communication chains constitute only one side of the problem facing leadership in complex and centralized political systems. The distorting effects of bureaucratic hierarchy may also create difficulties in gathering and disseminating information for effective policy. All large decision-making systems depend to a considerable degree on the bureaucracy to obtain and interpret information. In a bureaucracy, hierarchy and discipline are necessary for coordination of action. But bureaucratic officials are responsible to their superiors and dependent on their favors for advancement. They often develop great sensitivity to the needs and wishes of their superiors, displaying an inevitable tendency to tell powerful generals, cabinet ministers, or presidents that which they wish to hear or that which will reflect favorably on their own careers. Active and innovating Presidents of the United States, such as Franklin D. Roosevelt, have been highly sensitive to this danger of distortion and have endeavored to supplement all formal information channels with a large network of informal contacts with individuals at various points in the hierarchy.[48]

In open political systems, having many autonomous political structures and channels of communication, the elites can also utilize other information sources to help balance distortion by subordinates. Leaders read the newspapers, make personal appearances, and have polls conducted by autonomous organizations in an effort to get an unbiased understanding of popular attitudes and various sides of complex issues. However, in matters of security and in complex technological questions, particularly in times of crisis, these normal channels may cease to operate or to be relevant. Matters of national security policy in particular are typically shrouded in secrecy, and many observers suggest that political leaders become dangerously dependent on information not available for public scrutiny and discussion. Not only the desire to please, but also the special prejudices and orientations of any single agency, may distort information.

Although the differences are easy to exaggerate, the authoritarian systems face these problems of information distortion in particularly serious ways. Observers of closed political systems with ambitious policy goals, such as Nazi Germany or Stalin's Russia, have remarked on the constant, but often unsuccessful, efforts made by the ruling elites to obtain information about what is happening throughout the society. The immense scale of government activities and the efforts to accomplish far-reaching goals of economic development or military conquest, or simply the need to maintain control within the system in the face of changing conditions, create an insatiable need for information. Yet, the communications patterns that emerge in these systems are closed, nonautonomous patterns, because the elites wish to prevent the possibility of popular knowledge and activity that might lead to subversion and because the lower officials are receptive only to pressures from above, and not from below.

These closed communication structures seem to have potentially pathological tendencies, in terms of their ability to process accurate information, particularly in stress situations. Such tendencies manifest themselves as a partial consequence of the use of coercion in maintaining control over lower officials and citizens. In such cases the lower officials who staff the communications line to the elite are confronted with a difficult set of alternatives. If they deliberately distort information and are discovered, the consequences are likely to be costly. But, reporting unpleasant facts is likely to be nearly as dangerous. The man who dares hint that the leaders may have erred badly in their assessment of a situ-

[48] Richard W. Neustadt, *Presidential Power* (New York: John Wiley, 1962), pp. 156 ff.; and Deutsch, *The Nerves of Government*, op. cit., pp. 224–25.

ation is apt to have his career cut abruptly short in favor of those who convey more encouraging news. The tendency of tyrants to surround themselves with yes-men who confirm the existing beliefs of the ruler is well known. Boulding explains this phenomenon in the following terms:

> The case is somewhat analogous to that of the schizophrenic or the extreme paranoid. His sense receptors are so much "afraid" of him that they merely confirm the products of his heated imagination. The terrorized information sources of the tyrant likewise tell him only what they think will be pleasing to his ears. Organizations as well as individuals can suffer from hallucinations. It is the peculiar disease of authoritarian structures.[49]

Needless to say, the situation is reinforced by the average citizen's reluctance to tell even the lower officials anything but the formal party line. Information about popular attitudes is likely to be distorted, as are reports of the inefficiency or ineffectiveness of the actions of the reporting subordinates. Even general "scientific" information may be heavily slanted, as is apparent in the work of social scientists in the Soviet Union — and was even the case in the long-standing official support for biological theories discarded much earlier in the West.

Barrington Moore has emphasized the strenuous efforts made by authoritarian leaders to lessen their dependence on any single information source.[50] In the Soviet Union, Stalin used the secret police, the party, and the bureaucracy as checks on one another, relying on each organization to inform him of errors and deviations of the other two. But, as Apter and others have suggested, in times of stress the multiple channels are apt to reinforce distorted information, rather than to correct it.[51] In fact, this reinforcement is likely even in more autonomous systems.[52] If it is clear that the leadership is convinced of a set of facts, informants will find and pass on substantiations rather than denials of those facts.

These characteristic problems of hierarchic communication systems and long, complex communication channels suggest some limits on the use of large, centralized bureaucracies to control public policy, particularly in highly controlled authoritarian systems. The increase in control reaches a point of diminishing returns as the distortion of information and the costs of maintaining multiple information channels cut into

---

[49] Kenneth Boulding, *The Image* (Ann Arbor: University of Michigan Press, 1956), p. 101.
[50] Moore, *Terror and Progress: USSR,* op. cit., pp. 176 ff.
[51] David Apter, *The Politics of Modernization* (Chicago: University of Chicago Press, 1965).
[52] See Ole Holsti, "The 1914 Case," *APSR* 59 (June 1965): 365–78.

effectiveness. Reports of bureaucratic inefficiencies are legion in all systems with extensive governmental sectors; they are particularly spectacular in the authoritarian ones. The inefficiencies are due not only to the systematic distortions in hierarchical, upward information flow, but also to the sheer volume of problems and information in a highly centralized system. Various individuals in the upward information chain may delete or dismiss information that turns out to be most relevant to some local problem. Unable to rely on centralized planning, the local officials, held responsible for their output, turn to a "fixer" to unsnarl the clogged communication channels and to unearth necessary supplies and information. But these private arrangements have their own inefficiencies, unchecked as they are by the cost-reduction pressures of market pricing and competition. Thus, boatloads of coal may pass each other on the river, each fulfilling a private deal with a manufacturing plant in the port of origin of the other. And without a pricing mechanism, the basic information about the scarcity or value of raw materials is extremely difficult to ascertain. It should also be recalled that the elaborate, multiple information-and-control systems developed in penetrative authoritarian systems — bureaucracy, party, police — all require time and resources to fulfill their communication functions.

Measures are constantly being introduced to alleviate the costs of centralization, both through limited and imaginative forms of decentralization and through initiation of technological improvements in information processing, such as the use of computers. In authoritarian systems, however, suspicious rulers will not readily relinquish their decision-making monopolies. And all systems need some types of centralized organization to keep various parts in balance and to mobilize resources for achievement of collective goals beyond the capacity or interest of private groups. It is unlikely that any single balance of government preemption and private ownership, centralization or decentralization, direct or indirect control, is optimal for all policies in all circumstances. Continuing organizational innovation — along with an irreducible element of inefficiency — is likely to remain for the indefinite future, as all policy-making systems balance their needs of coordination and control against their needs for free-flowing and accurate communication.[53]

[53] See the comment by Blau and Scott, op. cit., pp. 242 ff., on this perennial organizational dilemma, and the remarks on the limits of differentiation in chaps. III and V, as well as the literature there cited.

PART III

Process Functions

CHAPTER VII

Interest Articulation

THE POLITICAL PROCESS is set in motion when some group or individual makes a political demand. This process of demand making is called interest articulation. Interest articulation may be performed by many different structures and in many different ways. In a very simple political system there will be no specialized structures for interest articulation. The individual members of the band or village may approach the headman or may talk with one another to express their desires and problems. In a somewhat more differentiated system, the subjects of a king may seek an audience to make their pleas. In a modern political system are found associations organized primarily to facilitate interest articulation, although interests can be articulated by and through nonspecialized structures as well.

Each of the following events is an example of interest articulation: a citizen writes his or her Representative for assistance in obtaining a small business loan; black leaders discuss fair housing policy with the President; British labor leaders protest a wage freeze at the Annual Conference of the Labour party; Israeli citizens demonstrate in front of the French Embassy protesting that country's release of an alleged Palestinian terrorist; Ulster terrorists set off a bomb in a crowded London department store.

As these examples suggest, the articulation of interests is quite a different matter from their successful conversion into authoritative policies. Each interest group faces competition from other interests, new or entrenched, active or potential, and the success of its demands will depend on the total process of interest aggregation, policy making, and policy implementation that we shall discuss in subsequent chapters. Interest articulation is only the first stage in the process. The ultimate implications for system, process, and policy depend on the other stages as well. Nonetheless, as long as one understands that interest articulation must

169

be described and analyzed in the context of the total system, one can learn much from a careful analysis of this function.

TYPES OF INTEREST GROUPS

The term *interest group* has been the object of considerable dispute among political scientists. By an interest group we mean simply a set of individuals who are linked by bonds of concern or advantage and who are aware of these shared interests. The interest group may itself be organized for continuing activity by group members, or it may reflect only their occasional involvement. Any social structure may, in fact, provide patterns of communication and preference that lead some individuals within it to form an interest group. But some social structures are more easily adapted to perform interest articulation than others, and the differing opportunities presented in political systems induce varied forms of involvement. In the subsequent discussion we shall attempt to identify some of the types of groups that most frequently perform interest articulation.

We must begin by drawing attention to the continuing importance of *individuals as articulators of their own interests,* independent of any group organization or involvement. The most clear-cut cases of such individual interest articulation involve individuals contacting government officials regarding personal and family problems, such as obtaining housing, employment, or loans. As we pointed out in chapter V, such activities remain common forms of political participation even in economically developed societies, where the large size of the governmental sector and the high levels of individual competence and education may lead to frequent personal contacting activity.[1] Individuals may also attempt to articulate their opinions on broader issues, as when they write their senator on foreign policy or approach their local zoning board about a neighborhood improvement. However, individual efforts to articulate interests on these broader issues become closely intertwined, typically, with group awareness and group activities, as we shall discuss later.[2]

Particularistic interest articulation is often associated with "machine" politics: personal networks of individual supporters established by political leaders on the basis of narrow, particularistic exchanges. These "patron-client" relationships involve the citizen's support for the indi-

---

[1] See table V.1 for data on the frequency of such participation.

[2] In a variety of nations such contacting on broader issues was strongly associated with, for example, actively participating in formal organizations involved in local affairs and working through and forming local groups (Sidney Verba, Norman H. Nie, and Jae-on Kim, *The Modes of Democratic Participation* [Beverly Hills: Sage Publications, 1971]).

vidual leader, regardless of the latter's general policies, in exchange for personal benefits of patronage and protection. Such networks of personal followings may be especially important in societies where many individuals have only the bare means of survival and where formal organizations are not very effective. But they are found in virtually all societies, at various levels, where leaders have patronage and benefits to bestow and are dependent on electoral or other forms of support. Skillful leaders may be able to build substantial networks of personal ties through subleaders and to create important political bases.[3] The Daley machine in Chicago was an example of this form of patron-client relationship in a modern democratic context. But this kind of patron-client structure, in which individual interests are satisfied in exchange for political support, is to be encountered in Communist societies as well. Students of Soviet politics have written of the personal patronage networks established by Stalin, Khrushchev, Brezhnev, and other Soviet leaders in their rise to power and of the effects of these networks on the careers of both leaders and followers.[4]

Finally, we must note, of course, that not all citizens have equal personal political resources. The party worker in a machine-run city or the peasant in a patron-dominated village may have only his vote or some campaign work to offer. The campaign contributor who could offer hundreds of thousands of dollars may receive more personal attention, as the awarding of ambassadorships has often indicated (such was the case in the United States until recent campaign law changes). The individual who occupies a critical political role, as a member of the military junta, the king's council, or the presidential Cabinet, has an even better opportunity to make her personal wishes known and interests attended. The accumulation of personal fortunes by political leaders and their immediate followers has been commonplace in less developed political systems, not uncommon in modern ones.

Beyond individual interest articulation we can distinguish four types of interest *groups* from the organizational perspective: (1) anomic,[5] (2) nonassociational, (3) institutional, and (4) associational.

[3] For an account of such personal "webs" in extreme form, and their prevalence in such societies as the Philippines, see Carl H. Lande, "Networks and Groups in Southeast Asia," *APSR* 67 (March 1973): 103–27. Also see the discussion and references to some of the literature on clientelism in the analysis in chap. VIII.

[4] See, for example, the essays in G. F. Skilling and F. Griffiths, eds., *Interest Groups in Soviet Politics* (Princeton: Princeton University Press, 1971); and see John A. Armstrong, *The Soviet Bureaucratic Elite* (New York: Praeger, 1959); Frederick C. Barghoorn, *Politics in the USSR* (Boston: Little, Brown, 1966), pp. 184 ff.; and Philip D. Stewart et al., "Political Mobility and the Soviet Political System," *APSR* 66 (December 1972): 1269–91.

[5] The term *anomic* is of Greek derivation and means irregular or lawless.

Anomic interest groups are unorganized mobs and riots, more or less spontaneous expressions of grievance or protest, quickly rising and usually quickly subsiding. It is, of course, true that many riots and demonstrations are really deliberately provoked by organized groups. But particularly where elements of a society lack organized groups or have failed to obtain adequate representation of their interests by such groups as are present, smoldering discontent may be sparked by an incident or by the emergence of a leader and may suddenly explode in unpredictable and uncontrollable ways. Although the anomic group is not organized into specialized roles for promoting its interests and maintaining continuity, direct personal interactions plus rumors and news reports of the actions of others provide momentary impetus and direction for the individuals.

James Coleman provides a good example of an anomic interest group in the eastern region of Nigeria, where women carried on much of the trading:

> The rumor that women were to be taxed . . . precipitated a women's movement that spread like wildfire through two of the most densely populated provinces. Chiefs and Europeans were attacked indiscriminately, and there was widespread destruction of property and goods, belonging mainly to trading firms. The riot was not quelled until the police, in an overwhelming show of force, killed fifty women and injured an equal number. An unusual feature was that the women, all illiterate, not only initiated but also were the only participants in the uprising. The whole affair was entirely spontaneous and received no support from either the men or the literate elements of the province.[6]

Recent events in many nations reflect the anomic forms of interest groups in action. In the Communist nations of Eastern Europe, violent, generally spontaneous protest appeared in East Berlin and Hungary in the 1950s, in Czechoslovakia in 1968 during the period of Soviet occupation, and in many Polish cities in 1970 and again in 1976, when workers demonstrated against government wage and price policies. In the United States, spontaneous political actions occurred in the aftermath of Martin Luther King's assassination and on many college campuses after the American invasion of Cambodia in 1970. Wildcat strikes, long a feature of the British trade union scene, have recently occurred more frequently in such continental countries as Italy, West Germany, and Sweden and were a major aspect of the huge upheavals in France in 1968. And in southern Italy in 1970 there was a massive uprising in Reggio Calabria

---

[6] James S. Coleman, *Nigeria: Background to Nationalism* (Berkeley and Los Angeles: University of California Press, 1958), p. 174.

after the city was not granted the politically and economically important status of regional capital.

Nonassociational interest groups are also distinguished by the absence of specialized organization. Such groups differ from anomic interest groups because they are based in commonly perceived interests of race, language, religion, region, occupation, or perhaps kinship and lineage. Because of these continuing cultural or economic ties, nonassociational groups have more continuity of interest over time than do the anomic interest groups.

There are two particularly interesting types of nonassociational interest group. One is the very large group with commonly perceived interests that has not, however, organized itself effectively along associational or institutional lines. The classic example of such a group is the consumer interest group, but many ethnic, regional, and occupational groups may also fall into this category. Mancur Olson and other theorists of social organization have suggested the special difficulties in effectively organizing such groups into associations with specialized roles.[7] The costs of involvement in time and energy are too great and the collective benefits to each member are too small to make forming organizations easy. Hence, the group may remain unorganized, and its interests may be articulated only intermittently through individuals, anomic subgroups, informal delegations, and the like. Political leaders, in deference to the potential strength of the group, particularly in electoral situations, may seek to ascertain the preferences of group members or may mobilize their support on occasion, so they are not without influence. But the activities of such groups in interest articulation are less consistent and effective than those of organized associations.

A second type of nonassociational group is the smaller, face-to-face kinship, lineage, economic, or ethnic group. Here, too, there is long-term continuity and only intermittent and specialized articulation of interests. But the smaller group built on face-to-face interactions and a clearly defined set of mutual obligations may be highly effective in some political situations and may eschew formal organization as unnecessary, illegal, or too conspicuous. Examples of such smaller-group activity include the work stoppages and petitions demanding better wages and working conditions by doctors in Mexico City in the 1960s,[8] joint requests made by large landowners to a bureaucrat for continuing a pro-

7 Mancur Olson, Jr., *The Logic of Collective Action* (Cambridge: Harvard University Press, 1965).

8 See Evelyn P. Stevens, "Protest Movements in an Authoritarian Regime," *Comparative Politics* 7 (April 1975): 361–82.

tective tariff on meats or grains, and the appeal by relatives to a government tax collector for preferred treatment for a family business. As the latter examples suggest, personal interest articulation may often be given more legitimacy and put on a more permanent basis by invoking family, kinship, village, or old school ties and interests, and leaders may similarly invoke such connections in building personal support networks. Especially in times of social change, these small nonassociational groups may be crucial links between individuals and new larger institutions.

Institutional interest groups are found within such organizations as political parties, corporations, legislatures, armies, bureaucracies, and churches. The formal parent organization has a highly differentiated role structure, but it is organized for functions other than interest articulation. Except for the degree of formal organization, the characteristics of these groups are somewhat like those of the face-to-face kinship and lineage groups. Other networks of social interaction are used to provide an organizational basis that can be pressed into service and may provide a common interest in articulating demands in the political arena. Institutional interest groups, either as whole institutional structures or as subgroups (for example, either the military establishment or special factions within it), are likely to be quite powerful because of the resources and access provided by their organizational bases.

The tendency of governmental officials to expand their organizations through the discovery of new problems and policies is common throughout the world. In his study of Brazil, for example, Schmitter discussed the way in which a variety of important issues became politicized on a national level. He found that the initial efforts to bring the issues to national attention were made not by associational interest groups, but by (1) politicians, whose tenure was being threatened, (2) economic administrators, (3) intellectuals, and (4) military officers.[9] Students of British, American, and Swedish social policy have made much the same point. Often the articulation of interests on an issue was initiated by bureaucrats whose agencies were involved in the general policy area.[10]

In authoritarian regimes, where other types of groups are more or less directly prohibited or controlled by the central institutions, institutional groups are even more important. Educational officials, party officials and factions, jurists, factory managers, officers in the various military services, and many other institutionally based groups have important in-

[9] Philippe Schmitter, *Interest Conflict and Political Change in Brazil* (Stanford: Stanford University Press, 1971), pp. 251 ff.

[10] See, for example, Olson, op. cit.; Hugh Heclo, *Modern Social Policies in Britain and Sweden* (New Haven: Yale University Press, 1974); Oliver McDonagh, *A Pattern of Government Growth, 1800–1860* (London: McGibbons and Kee, 1961).

terest articulation roles in Communist regimes.[11] And in less developed political systems, where associational groups are limited in number or are ineffective, the prominent part played by military groups, corporations, and party factions is obvious. In virtually all complex systems, in fact, some institutional groups are likely to be important, because of their communication networks, common interests, and the resource control that inevitably is their share; their regulation is, then, a critical problem.

Associational interest groups are the specialized structures for interest articulation, which are designed specifically to represent the goals of particular groups. Their organizations include a full-time staff, specialized internal roles focused around the interest articulation goals, and orderly procedures for the formulation of interests and demands. Typical examples are trade unions, ethnic associations, organizations for particular businesses or industries, associations organized by religious denominations, and associations organized to promote particular political causes, such as civic reform or foreign policy. The trade union is a particularly interesting example of a group that falls somewhere between an institutional and associational interest group; its primary goal is often negotiation with employers on the behalf of workers. However, trade unions are usually drawn into political concerns and either act directly in that sphere, using the internal machinery developed for interest representation to influence employers, or organize special political subassociations, such as the COPE organization of the AFL-CIO. The trade union and some other economic organizations may be able to shift from economic to political activity particularly easily because their basic functions involve interest representation in another sphere.

As the importance of associational interest groups in interest articulation has been recognized, they have become the object of many studies.[12] Where these groups are allowed to organize and flourish, they tend to regulate the development and involvement of other types of interest groups. Their organizational base gives them an advantage over the anomic and the large, unorganized nonassociational groups, especially because it allows them to watch over their group's interests in the day-

11 See Roman Kolkowicz, "Interest Groups in Soviet Politics," *Comparative Politics* 2 (April 1970): 445–72; Skilling and Griffiths, op. cit.; and the essays by Barghoorn and Skilling in Robert A. Dahl, ed., *Regimes and Oppositions* (New Haven: Yale University Press, 1973).

12 For an excellent early collection of associational interest group studies see Henry W. Ehrmann, *Interest Groups on Four Continents* (Pittsburgh: University of Pittsburgh Press, 1958). Also see in particular the studies by Harry Eckstein, *Pressure Group Politics* (Stanford: Stanford University Press, 1960); Joseph LaPalombara, *Interest Groups in Italian Politics* (Princeton: Princeton University Press, 1964); and James Q. Wilson, *Political Organizations* (New York: Basic Books, 1973).

Table VII.1. *Examples of Associational Interest Groups, Classified by Social*
Bases or Issue Specialization

Social base or goal	Examples
Tribal	Ibo Federal Union (Nigeria)
	Alaskan Federation of Natives (Eskimos, Indians, Aleuts)
	(United States)
Racial	Chinese American Citizens Alliance (United States)
	Congress of Racial Equality (United States)
	British West Indies Association (Great Britain)
Ethnic	Polish National Alliance (United States)
	Mexican-American Political Association (United States)
	Quebec Liberation Front (Canada)
Religious	Burma Muslim Organization (Burma)
	American Friends Service Committee (United States)
	Independent Catholic Action (France)
	Society for the Propagation of the Gospel in Foreign Parts
	(Great Britain)
Occupational-	Transport and General Workers Union (Great Britain)
professional	American Medical Association (United States)
	General Confederation of Italian Industry (Italy)
	Wheatgrowers Federation (Australia)
	General Confederation of Beetgrowers (France)
	Federation of Housewives (Japan)
Issue- or policy-	Committee for the Green Foothills (United States)
oriented	Society for the Preservation of Rural England (Great Britain)
	Temperance Alliance (Australia)
	Council on Foreign Relations (United States)
	Association for Returning Okinawa Islands to Japan (Japan)

to-day process of making and implementing public policy. They become indispensable to groups without the continuing ties of kinship or other face-to-face interactions and so have become prevalent in large, modern societies. Their relative legitimacy in openly expressing goals and presenting demands and the broad range of interests they collectively represent can also limit and control to some degree the more covert actions of institutional groups and informal cliques.

The associational groups are often classified as primarily organized either around a social group base or around a special policy interest. Table VII.1 shows some examples of associational interest groups and the diverse social and issue bases suggested by their formal titles.

TYPES OF INTEREST GROUP SUBSYSTEMS

Interest groups in advanced industrial societies constitute a subsystem of the political system. If one looks at the history of associational interest groups, it is clear that their development followed a pattern. Thus the formation of associations concerned with the condition of the working class and favoring the regulation of industry triggered the development of trade and manufacturing associations concerned with opposing or limiting such regulation. The development of trade unions concerned with collective bargaining precipitated the development of employer's federations designed to strengthen the bargaining capacity of industry. The development of a trade association in one sector of the industrial economy triggered the emergence of trade associations in other sectors. The same pattern was followed in the agricultural sector, crop by crop, so to speak, and process by process. More recently, as new issues have arisen in advanced industrial societies, environmentalists and developers, gun controllers and gun possessors have organized to support and oppose regulatory legislation.

Broadly speaking, we can differentiate among four interest group systems — ways in which interest group subsystems in advanced industrial societies are related to the policy-making process as a whole. The first of these — the *competitive* — is well represented in the United States, where interest groups operate relatively autonomously in pursuit of benefits and protections for their members. The second type may be called *nonautonomous;* in these systems, as in those of France and Italy, trade unions, peasant organizations, youth groups, and the like may be dominated by the Catholic church or by the Communist or Socialist parties. The interests of their members are subordinated to those of the institutions that dominate them. The third type of interest group system is *corporatist.* Here we have in mind a situation in which the major interest groups — business, labor, agriculture, and so on — are regularly associated with the bureaucracy, working out policy in an organized negotiatory committee process. The Scandinavian interest group subsystems are illustrative of this type. There is another version of corporatism associated with Catholic political ideology; it was implemented briefly in Austria in the 1930s, in Portugal under Salazar, and more recently in Peru. This system operates without political parties through a direct interaction between professional and occupational interest groups and the state bureaucracy. The interest groups are established by law, but at least in theory their interaction with the state bureaucracy is a two-way process. Finally there is the *statist* system of interest groups characteristic of Communism and Fascism. Here interest groups operate as "transmission belts" for party and government policy. They preempt interest articulation, ensuring that the policy of the party and governmental elite is implemented in the various spheres of the economy and society.[13]

---

[13] For a somewhat different classification scheme of types of interest group subsystems and for a more comprehensive and complete analysis of interest group theory, see the special issue of *Comparative Political Studies* 9 (April 1977) edited by Philippe C. Schmitter and entitled "Corporatism and Policy-Making in Contemporary Western Europe."

CHANNELS OF ACCESS AND TACTICS OF INFLUENCE

Most political systems permit some forms of at least very limited interest articulation by individuals. In penetrative authoritarian systems legitimate interest articulation for most citizens and groups is limited to providing information and perhaps to voicing complaints. Or the various bureaucratic and party institutional groups may approach their superiors with proposals for policy shifts within broad boundaries determined from above. In more open systems, a much greater variety of channels is provided for interest articulation, and demands for new or continuing policies may legitimately be tied to promises of electoral support.

Almost all political systems prohibit or at least carefully control and regulate the use of violence and, particularly, the coercion of policy makers. The widespread use of violence and illegitimate coercion is usually a symptom that the regime is breaking down and losing its legitimacy. The resources and channels it provides for interest articulation are being bypassed as groups turn to coercion. We shall, then, discuss the variety of legitimate or constitutional interest articulation channels that may be present in political systems before turning to coercive channels and decisions about using them.

CONSTITUTIONAL ACCESS CHANNELS

Perhaps the oldest and most traditional means of access to political elites is *personal connection*. By personal connection channels we mean the use of family, school, local, and social ties as instruments for contacting political elites. An example of such channels would be the informal communication network among graduates of the same school. In the United States, Japan, and Great Britain, the contacts and friendships among graduates of a particular university have proved to be important channels of access for the articulation of individual and group interests. In the Soviet Union, the connections formed with leaders such as Khrushchev and Brezhnev in their early days as regional administrators serve as continuing bases for the formation of factions and for individual advancement among lower-level bureaucrats and party officials.[14]

Such channels may, of course, be transitory, involving the particular personal friendship patterns of individual leaders. Each American President, for example, has brought to the presidency a circle of personal advisers and contacts; these have typically been very important avenues of access to the President during his time in office. Similarly, Lande has described the very transitory nature of the personal connections throughout the political system in the Philippines.[15] On the other hand, the

14 See Armstrong, op. cit.; Barghoorn, op. cit.; and Stewart et al., op. cit.
15 Lande, op. cit.

channels of connection may be tied to the social structure of the society; one example is traditional ethnic bonds, which may have influence over the tenure of many individual leaders. Much depends, also, on whether or not the networks of personal connection are themselves organized into wide-reaching patron-client structures, which may be tied to party machines trading votes for personal favors.[16]

Although such personal connection channels are commonly used by individuals and nonassociational groups, such as those representing ethnic or regional interests, they are important to all sorts of groups. Perhaps because messages conveyed through such channels can have a strong effect on the receiver, connections are eagerly sought by groups in all types of political systems. Studies of opinion formation have demonstrated that face-to-face contact is one of the most effective means of shaping attitudes. Where the contact occurs in an atmosphere of cordiality and friendship, the possibility of a favorable response is improved. Demands articulated by a friend, relative, neighbor, or trusted associate are much more effective than a formal approach from a total stranger. Thus, even in modern political systems one finds personal connections being developed with care, and those excluded from them may perceive themselves as notably disadvantaged in potential interest articulation.[17] And one finds lobbyists earning a living by using their personal connections with governmental officials to facilitate the representation of group interests.

Elite representation constitutes a channel of access that can be utilized very effectively by an interest group. It may take the form of the presence of a group member in the policy-making structure or of sympathetic representation by an independent elite member. Rather than having to use personal connection or formal channels to gain access, the group that has elite representation can rely on direct and continued articulation of its interests by a member involved in the decision-making structure. For example, representation of interests on a continuing, day-to-day basis on legislative committees is an advantage enjoyed by Italian labor unions and a fact lamented by the giant enterprises of Italian industry.[18] Whereas in the United States the presence of associational interest group members in Congress or the executive is frowned upon (although it exists), the legislatures of Great Britain, France, Germany, and other nations include many interest group representatives in their ranks.

Legislatures are not, of course, the only bodies engaged in decision making. Indeed, in many nations their role is only a formal one, if they

---

[16] Ibid.; and see chap. VIII.

[17] Verba and Nie, *Participation in America,* chap. 11; and see Nancy E. McGlen, "Strategy Choices for Political Participation" (Ph.D. diss., University of Rochester, 1974).

[18] LaPalombara, *Interest Groups in Italian Politics.*

are present at all. In such cases governmental institutional interest groups have particular influence, since their members often find themselves in daily contact with the active decision-making elites and usually constitute part of the elite structure directly concerned with their interests.

Elite representation may also serve as a channel for interest groups that have no other means of articulation, particularly for large nonassociational groups. In the 1830s and 1840s in Britain, certain aristocratic and middle-class Members of Parliament took it upon themselves to articulate the interests of the working class. They were not responding to channeled pressures and demands from below as much as they were acting as independent, self-appointed guardians of these neglected and suppressed interests. The work on committees and the like did much to promote the passage of factory and mines legislation. Such elite members may have a feeling for group needs and desires and may serve to communicate these interests into the decision-making structure. This channel of access often is used today in the developing areas where an effective system of associational groups and parties has yet to appear or fails to reach a majority of citizens. Representation on the basis of identifying feelings and vague indications, however, is an unreliable form of access, and articulation through it may result in considerable errors on the part of the elite.

One must also consider the numerous *formal and institutional channels of access* that exist in a modern political system. The *mass media* constitute one such access channel, although, as we have noted, the reaction created by the number of messages and by their lack of specific direction limits their effectiveness for many less important groups. Where the mass media are controlled by the political elites and messages are subject to their approval, the media are, to some degree, eliminated as a useful channel of access or reserved only for favored groups. However, in an open society the mass media are a major means of conveying political demands to decision makers.[19]

Political parties constitute a second important institutional access channel. A number of factors affect their usefulness. A highly ideological party with an ordered organizational structure, such as the Communist party, is more likely to control associated interest groups than to communicate demands that those interest groups create. Decentralized party organizations like those in the United States, whether inside or outside the legislative organizations, may respond less than individual legislators or groups of legislators. In a nation such as Britain, on the other hand, the various elements of the party organization, particularly parliamentary committees, serve as significant channels. They can articulate

[19] Also see the discussion of the mass media in chap. VI.

Table VII.2. *Choice of Bureaucratic or Party Contact Channels by British Interest Groups, by Type of Issue*

	Administrative contacts (%)	Partisan contacts (%)	Total
Broad "status group issues": Involving "the interests of social classes, racial and ethnic groups, and the providers and recipients of governmental services"	24	76	100 (25)
Narrower "pluralist issues": Involving "matters broader than individual concerns, but narrower than those of social strata"	72	28	100 (165)

Source: Table calculated from table 4, p. 587, in K. Newton and D. S. Morris, "British Interest Group Theory Re-examined," *Comparative Politics* 7 (July 1975): 577–95.

Note: Data collected in Birmingham, England. The original table breaks down these data for consumer and producer interest groups, who show very similar patterns of contact choice, although producer groups were slightly less likely (10% vs. 15%) to contact about status group issues.

demands with some prospect of influence upon the cabinet or the executive advisory group and the party in power. In nations where a single-party structure dominates the political system, as in Mexico, it may become the most vital channel for the articulation of many interests.[20]

Legislatures, cabinets, and *bureaucratic agencies* also constitute common channels of access. Standard tactics of individuals or groups using these channels include appearing before legislative committees or supplying information to individual legislators. Contacts with the bureaucracy at various levels and in different functional departments may be particularly important where considerable decision-making authority has been delegated to the agencies, where the group is more interested in shaping specific methods of implementation, or where interests are quite narrow and directly involve few citizens outside the interest group itself. Table VII.2 indicates the choice of access channels made by British

[20] Debate continues among specialists on Mexico over the extent to which the dominant party (PRI) controls the political input process. Some very influential business and financial interests seem to rely on elite representation and access to the President rather than party channels. For the two major positions on the role of the party, see Robert E. Scott, *Mexican Government in Transition*, rev. ed. (Urbana: University of Illinois Press, 1964); and Frank Brandenburg, *The Making of Modern Mexico* (Englewood Cliffs: Prentice-Hall, 1964). A more recent analysis, reviewing the debate, but emphasizing elite representation, is Roger D. Hansen, *The Politics of Mexican Development* (Baltimore: Johns Hopkins University Press, 1971). For additional general discussion of interest articulation in one-party systems, see Samuel P. Huntington and Clement H. Moore, *Authoritarian Politics in Modern Society* (New York: Basic Books, 1970), particularly the introductory essay.

interest groups in Birmingham, according to the breadth of the political issue about which the group is contacting. On broad issues — involving social classes, ethnic groups, or large numbers of recipients of governmental aid or services — the interest groups tended to approach the political parties, as in the dispute over comprehensive education. On narrower issues, likely to involve fewer other groups and less political conflict, the groups tended to turn to the appropriate administrative department.

These findings of Newton and Morris, as well as other research, suggest that it is not only the special access advantages and organizational bases of a group that shape its tactics, but also the type of political resources that must be mobilized to achieve its particular goals.[21] Party channels may be indispensable where broad interests are in conflict and substantial political resources must be aggregated to achieve — or defend — group interests.[22] But where interests are narrow, it may be far simpler and more effective to approach administrative agencies, operating within a preestablished policy framework.

The different kinds of relationships between interest groups and bureaucracies are a topic that has been well researched. The appearance of regular processes for consultation and negotiation with interest groups, such as the committees, conferences, and informal communications found in the Scandinavian and British systems, constitutes an unusually clear form of interest group access to the bureaucracy. But a multitude of less formalized relationships have been analyzed in the United States, France, Italy, West Germany, and such nations in the developing areas as Egypt, Thailand, and the Philippines.[23]

Protest demonstrations, strikes, and other nonviolent, but dramatic and direct, pressures on government are a form of access that may cross the border between constitutional and nonconstitutional channels, depend-

---

[21] K. Newton and D. S. Morris, "British Interest Group Theory Reexamined," *Comparative Politics* 7 (July 1975): 577–95.

[22] See Paul E. Peterson, "British Interest Group Theory Reexamined: The Politics of Comprehensive Education in Three British Cities," *Comparative Politics* 3 (April 1971): 381–402; Robert J. Lieber, "Interest Groups and Political Integration: British Entry into Europe," *APSR* 66 (March 1972): 53–67; Eckstein, *Pressure Group Politics;* and Theodore J. Lowi, "American Business and Public Policy," *World Politics* 16 (July 1964): 677–715.

[23] See the special issue of *Comparative Political Studies* 9 (April 1977); Francis E. Rourke, ed., *Bureaucratic Power in National Politics* (Boston: Little, Brown, 1965); Henry W. Ehrmann, *Organized Business in France* (Princeton: Princeton University Press, 1957); Gerard Braunthal, *The Federation of German Industry in Politics* (Ithaca: Cornell University Press, 1965), chaps. 9 and 10; LaPalombara, op. cit., especially chaps. 8–10; Morroe Berger, *Bureaucracy and Society in Modern Egypt* (Princeton: Princeton University Press, 1957), chap. 6; F. W. Riggs, *The Ecology of Public Administration* (New Delhi: India Institute of Public Administration, 1961); Jean Grossholtz, *Politics in the Philippines* (Boston: Little, Brown, 1964).

ing on the rules of the specific political circumstances and the activities of the demonstrators. Such demonstrations may be, as we have already noted, either spontaneous actions of anomic groups or, more frequently, an organized resort to an unconventional channel by associational or small nonassociational groups. In democratic societies, protest demonstrations may be primarily efforts to mobilize popular support, eventually electoral support, for the group's cause. The civil rights and Vietnam War demonstrations of the 1960s were prime examples of such activity. In nondemocratic societies such demonstrations may be hazardous as a channel of access and may represent extreme dissatisfaction with the alternative channels. As is shown in table VII.3, the use of antigovernment demonstrations is more frequent in democratic systems, no doubt because of the greater controls on such activity in other types of regimes.

Protest demonstrations have been aptly described as a tactic of the "powerless" groups in a society, those groups which do not themselves have access or resources to influence decision makers and hence use unconventional means of appealing for response and support.[24] As a "tactic of the powerless," protest activity is typically used as a form of participation for minority groups or young people, those who do not hold important elite roles in the political system. But within the appropriate group whose goals set the protest in motion, the same motivational structures tend to operate in protest activity as in many other forms of participation. Those with social and economic advantages and the members of other social and political organizations are the most likely to participate in protest actions. Their better information, interest, skills, and general resources facilitate involvement; organizational networks facilitate communication and coordination.

A study of black and white protesters in Milwaukee, Wisconsin, found that within both white and black communities protesters were likely to be educated and to be organization members.[25] The greater stakes of the black community, based on the ethnic group issue, and their relative poverty perhaps account for the fact that ongoing organizations were frequently at the base of their protests, whereas white protests were more often ad hoc and individually mobilized. Eisinger points out that, especially for blacks,

> most protests are organized by ongoing groups. These groups supply a ready
> leadership cadre, as well as auxiliary workers. They have other resources at
> hand as well, such as office space and mimeograph machines. In addition,

24 James Q. Wilson, "The Strategy of Protest," *Journal of Conflict Resolution* 3 (September 1961): 291–303; and Michael Lipsky, "Protest as a Political Resource," *APSR* 60 (December 1968): 1144–58. Also see Peter K. Eisinger, "The Conditions of Protest Behavior in American Cities," *APSR* 68 (March 1973): 11–28.

25 Peter K. Eisinger, "Racial Differences in Protest Participation," *APSR* 68 (June 1974): 592–606.

Table VII.3. *Antigovernment Protest Demonstrations in Selected Nations, 1958–67*

Nation	Population, 1965 (in 000s)	Demonstrations											Demonstrations per million in decade
		58	59	60	61	62	63	64	65	66	67	Total	
USA	194,572	21	12	95	165	72	202	134	211	124	115	1,151	5.9
Sweden	7,734	—	—	—	—	—	—	—	—	—	1	1	.1
Canada	19,604	1	—	1	—	6	1	7	6	1	1	24	1.2
France	48,922	8	19	35	39	1	12	9	3	—	7	133	2.7
West Germany	59,041	1	1	1	15	—	—	1	57	9	19	89	1.5
Britain	54,595	7	21	14	—	13	6	3	13	8	16	116	2.1
Czechoslovakia	14,159	1	—	—	—	2	1	—	—	—	—	4	.3
Israel	2,563	2	—	—	10	1	6	—	4	2	2	27	10.4
USSR	230,600	—	—	—	—	5	1	—	1	1	1	9	.03
Austria	7,255	—	—	—	—	—	—	—	1	—	—	1	.1
Italy	51,576	4	—	—	2	—	1	5	4	3	14	33	.6
Japan	97,960	—	3	71	9	11	3	2	2	4	2	107	1.1
Bulgaria	8,200	—	—	—	—	—	1	—	—	—	—	1	.13
Spain	31,604	1	—	1	—	17	—	—	9	7	30	65	2.1
Mexico	42,689	3	2	9	6	1	2	—	1	—	2	26	.6
Yugoslavia	19,508	—	3	—	—	—	—	—	—	—	—	3	.2
Peru	11,650	2	1	—	1	11	—	—	—	—	1	16	1.37
Brazil	82,222	3	2	5	6	1	—	—	1	4	—	22	.3
Egypt	29,600	—	—	—	—	—	—	—	5	—	—	5	.2
China	700,000	—	—	—	—	—	—	—	—	2	—	3	.004
India	486,729	4	14	6	5	—	2	1	39	27	37	135	.3
Kenya	9,365	1	3	7	3	—	1	—	—	—	—	16	.3
Nigeria	57,500	—	—	1	—	—	1	2	1	5	1	11	1.7
Tanzania	10,515	—	—	1	1	—	—	—	—	2	—	4	.4

Source: Charles L. Taylor and Michael C. Hudson, *World Handbook of Political and Social Indicators* (New Haven: Yale University Press, 1972), pp. 88-93, 295-98.
Note: Since the data for these events are available only for the 1950s and 1960s, we have listed the countries in order of their 1965 GNP/capita.

they have institutional experience and memories, both of which may be drawn upon over and over to provide guidelines and lessons for dealing with new situations.[26]

COERCIVE ACCESS CHANNELS

We distinguished earlier between the use of constitutional access channels and the use of coercive ones. This distinction is related to our general distinction between two major kinds of political resources employed in political bargaining. The decision-making structures of the regime establish regularized procedures for making authoritative rules. In an electoral-legislative regime, the appropriate resources may be votes in the national parliament. Various factions may attempt to gain control of these legislative votes through victories in national elections, bargains with winning legislators over other policy issues, persuasion, or promises of support. In a few systems, it may be permissible to buy support with direct financial promises, but usually such promises are illegal. But the rules of the game define what the decisive constitutional resources will be and establish the rules for conversion of other resources — citizen votes, wealth, organizational aid — into the decisive ones.

Most political systems place severe constraints on the use of coercion beyond the legal rights to lobby for votes, the favor of the central committee, or the support of the majority party. Political strikes, which employ coercive pressure through disrupting government performance may therefore be restricted. In some political systems, the right of key groups, such as police, bureaucrats, and postal workers, to engage in political strikes is well recognized. Italians regularly face the disruption of telephone, garbage, and mail services due to antigovernment strikes by these institutional groups. In other political systems, however, such a use of coercion against the government, even if nonviolent, is prohibited, although the level of suppression and the violence of governmental response may vary greatly.[27]

Typically, because of the complex coordination problems involved in such tactics, *strikes and obstructions* are carried out by well-organized associational or institutional groups. According to Willner, for example, public protests in Indonesia under Sukarno were largely "instigated, provoked, and planned by one or several members of a political elite," in order to test their respective strengths, gain additional support from among the ranks of the undecided, frighten others from joining opposition elements, and challenge higher authorities to see what responses

---

26 Ibid., p. 603.
27 See the comparisons of Mexico and Spain in Stevens, op. cit.

they would make.[28] Payne suggests that in Peru, violent demonstrations and riots under the civilian regimes of the early 1960s were "fully a part of the Peruvian pattern, not merely distasteful, peripheral incidents." Particularly for the labor unions, such tactics were crucial to their very survival under prevailing conditions: "To ask the Peruvian unionists to use collective bargaining and refrain from violence is tantamount to urging dissolution of the labor movement." [29]

Occasionally, in a nation with long political experience, the shared memories of "to the barricades," of various revolutionary experiences, can lead to relatively spontaneous emergence of a massive protest strike, as happened in France in 1968. In that case, the cumulative dissatisfactions of workers, based on their relative exclusion from influence for a decade under de Gaulle, and their economic dissatisfactions led to a spontaneous response among the workers and urban residents to the massive student-police confrontations and announced settlement. The traditional union and party organizers were surprised and outflanked by a nationwide strike of very large anomic groups.[30]

Strikes and obstructions have had varying effectiveness as a means of access in different political conditions and systems. In Belgium a general strike was instrumental in bringing about expansion of suffrage early in the twentieth century. French farm groups in Brittany used "direct action" tactics of obstruction, including the seizure of public buildings and the blocking of roads, to win major governmental concessions in the early 1960s.[31] Student groups have often used strikes to win concessions from campus administrators.

It is difficult, however, for minorities to use strikes and coercion in national politics unless they are supported by sympathetic electoral majorities, or unless the pressure coincides with a threat of more serious, violent upheavals. The French peasants' direct action tactics in the early 1960s were successful largely because the government was threatened by massive violence elsewhere on the political right and desperately needed peasant support. By the late 1960s, a stronger regime was able to ignore or suppress such efforts.[32] French workers and students won academic and

[28] Ann Ruth Willner, "Public Protest in Indonesia," in Ivo K. Feierabend, Rosalind Feierabend, and Ted Robert Gurr, eds., *Anger, Violence, and Politics* (Englewood Cliffs: Prentice-Hall, 1972), pp. 355–57.

[29] James L. Payne, "Peru: The Politics of Structured Violence," in Feierabend, Feierabend, and Gurr, op. cit., p. 368.

[30] However, the various organizations did play a significant role in the conflict. See Bernard Brown, *The French Revolt of 1968* (Morristown, N.J.: General Learning Press, 1970); and see Henry W. Ehrmann, *Politics in France* (Boston: Little, Brown, 1976), pp. 204–14.

[31] Suzanne Berger, *Peasants Against Politics* (Cambridge: Harvard University Press, 1972), chaps. 7–8.

[32] Ibid.

wage concessions from the 1968 upheavals, but were unable to bring down the regime. More disastrously, general strikes by workers in Italy in 1922 and Britain in 1927 not only failed, but also severely discredited the organizations that sponsored them. Moreover, these strikes, like the truckers' strike against President Allende's leftist regime in Chile in 1972, enhanced the fears and bitterness of polarized societies.

Riots, too, have had mixed success as a means of political access. There are many types of riots, some by groups with rather clear-cut common purposes, others reflecting aimless frustration. In eighteenth-century Britain there was a recognized "right to riot" among the London mob, and such riots were often directed at expressing popular disapproval of particular pieces of legislation. In contrast, the destructive "victory riots" that broke out in several American cities at the declaration of peace after World War II had no political purpose at all. But most often rioting has represented a diffuse unrest and dissatisfaction on the part of some citizen groups. In political systems that do not recognize openly any right of citizens to form interest groups and express preferences, such rioting may be one of the few cues to popular dissatisfaction.

The genuine anomic riot involves the relatively spontaneous expression of collective anger and dissatisfaction by a group of citizens living in the same geographic area. Long dismissed as an aberrant and irrational form of behavior of the riffraff of society,[33] riots vary greatly in the types of motivations involved, in the kinds of behavior observed, and in the nature of the participants, according to recent studies.[34] Most riots, in fact, follow rather distinct norms of behavior, usually learned in the customs of the particular society. (Oberschall cites as evidence the grisly data on the tendency of lynch mobs in different cultures to use distinctive and different forms of execution, such as stoning, burning, beheading, hanging, and so on.[35]) Riots often are directed against property, rather than persons, as was seen in American racial riots in the 1960s, in which most deaths were caused by troops trying to restore order, not by rioters. The participants tend to be the residents of the area, rather than transients or recent arrivals. Except for being typically younger and more often male than female, the rioters in American studies show no remarkable socioeconomic characteristics in comparison to the other residents of the riot area.[36]

---

[33] See the review of the literature on the crowd or the mob in Anthony Oberschall, *Social Conflict and Social Movements* (Englewood Cliffs: Prentice-Hall, 1973); and the essays in James F. Short and Marvin E. Wolfgang, eds., *Collective Violence* (Chicago: University of Chicago Press, 1972), especially Gary T. Marx, "Issueless Riots," pp. 47–59.

[34] Ibid.

[35] Oberschall, op. cit.

[36] See Oberschall, op. cit., and David O. Sears and John B. McConahay, *The Politics of Violence* (Boston: Houghton Mifflin, 1973).

The critical feature in determining riot participation seems to be a sharp sense of relative deprivation, an anger over the discrepancy between the way things are and the way they ought to be. When a widespread sense of intense relative deprivation exists among citizens of a city or peasants in a countryside, and when police control is inadequate, a single incident can touch off the shared frustrations, and lashing, angry collective behavior explodes. Psychological theory explains that for an angry person, the act of violence itself can be satisfying, relieving the pent-up frustration.[37] With shared angers, the citizens in a riot have motivation for their actions; with shared symbols of frustration and perceptions of grievance and with face-to-face communication networks, the ingredients of collective action are provided. If fear of sanctions disappears — when the sudden growth of the mob overwhelms the police, for example — the inhibition against illegal behavior breaks down.

In table XII.9 we present some data on the frequency of riot behavior in a number of nations. As is suggested in that table, rioting has been particularly common in ethnically divided nations, as in the United States, India, Nigeria, South Africa, and Rhodesia. However, politically troubled and immobilized systems such as Italy may also experience high levels of anomic group activity. Because rioting generally reflects a temporary breakdown in local police control, riots are more rare in the penetrative authoritarian regimes, such as the Soviet Union. Their appearance in such systems typically reflects some breakdown in the unity and control by the ruling elite, as in Hungary in 1956, Czechoslovakia in 1968, and China during the Cultural Revolution. In nations with limited development of structures for autonomous interest articulation, a limited regulatory capability, and many internal tensions, as in many Arab, African, and Southeast Asian nations, anomic interest group activities may be very common phenomena. Due to patterns of reporting in the press, the data in table XII.9 probably even understate events in these nations.

The most extreme use of coercive methods is the employment of *political terror tactics*, which include the deliberate use of assassination, armed attacks on other groups or government officials, and the provocation of bloodshed. The use of terror tactics in a political system reflects the desire of some group or groups to change the rules of the political game. Armed attacks on political opponents may be directed at historical rivals or, more frequently, at contenders who exhibit growing strength or ambition, to prevent their gaining governmental influence. They may even be undertaken with the tacit support of the authorities themselves,

---

[37] Leonard Berkowitz, *Aggression: A Social Psychological Analysis* (New York: McGraw-Hill, 1962); and see the review by Ted Robert Gurr, "Psychological Factors in Civil Violence," *World Politics* 20 (January 1968): 245–78; and, generally, Ted Robert Gurr, *Why Men Rebel* (Princeton: Princeton University Press, 1971).

as in the systematic murder and intimidation of blacks in the American South from the end of Reconstruction through the days of the civil rights movement. Undertaken with the open or covert support of local governments, terror was used by the Ku Klux Klan and other groups to maintain white domination.

Terror tactics have been frequently directed against governments themselves, either to reinforce demands for policy changes or to undermine the general legitimacy of the regime and to create an atmosphere in which a guerrilla movement can flourish. A spectacular example was the terror campaign of the OAS secret army organization against the Gaullist government in France. After de Gaulle announced his intention to give Algeria its independence, dissatisfied army officers went underground and launched a systematic campaign to force the government to change its policies. At least nine attempts were made to assassinate de Gaulle himself between 1961 and 1964. And as is shown in table VII.4 nearly three hundred attacks were made in 1962 alone at the height of the OAS efforts. More recently, kidnappings and skyjackings have been frequent tactics of guerrilla movements seeking to gain national or international attention, to obtain ransom money to finance further activity, or directly to force governments to comply with their demands. The Palestine liberation organizations, for example, have engaged in many such actions, including the seizure and murder of many Israeli athletes at the Olympic games in 1972 and the kidnapping of the oil ministers of the OPEC nations in Austria in 1976.

In the short run, the use of such tactics have frequently been successful, at least in gaining attention and ransom funds for the terrorists. Although intensive international security efforts have cut down on the incidence of such actions and tougher governmental policies have limited the frequency of success, each year seems to bring new and spectacular examples. Massive terror tactics can be launched by relatively small groups, who can thus seem to command far more resources than they could garner in any other fashion. Yet, the overall success of these tactics in bringing about policy changes has been limited. The OAS efforts were completely unsuccessful in France. The Palestinian efforts have brought their case to world attention, but have not forced the government of Israel to change positions. One problem is that the use of naked coercion so severely undermines and threatens the authority of the regime itself that it is difficult for political leaders to change policy in response to such tactics without compromising their position entirely. The use of armed attacks has, in fact, been frequently associated with military coups and interventions and with counterviolence and the escalation of conflicts.[38] Terror tactics may thus spark major structural changes in a re-

[38] See Douglas A. Hibbs, *Mass Political Violence* (New York: John Wiley, 1973).

Table VII.4. Coercive Channels of Interest Articulation: Frequency of Armed Political Attacks by Organized Groups in Selected Nations, 1958–67

Nation	Population, 1965 (in 000s)	Armed attacks by organized groups										Total	Armed attacks per millions in decade
		58	59	60	61	62	63	64	65	66	67		
USA	194,572	97	61	57	22	31	47	71	71	23	43	523	2.7
Sweden	7,734	—	—	—	—	—	—	—	—	—	—	0	0
Canada	19,604	7	1	—	—	65	9	5	4	1	3	95	4.8
France	48,922	34	18	15	110	296	3	7	1	1	1	485	9.9
West Germany	59,041	3	1	—	1	4	5	1	1	—	9	25	.4
Britain	54,595	3	4	1	2	—	—	1	2	8	5	26	.5
Czechoslovakia	14,159	—	—	—	—	—	—	—	—	1	1	2	.1
Israel	2,563	—	1	—	1	—	8	—	2	26	10	48	18.5
USSR	230,600	—	7	—	1	2	1	—	—	—	9	20	.1
Austria	7,255	—	—	—	5	—	1	—	—	—	—	6	.8
Italy	51,576	4	7	5	57	17	23	7	2	6	11	139	2.7
Japan	97,960	1	—	2	1	—	—	—	—	—	2	6	.1
Bulgaria	8,200	—	—	—	—	—	1	—	—	—	1	2	.25
Spain	31,604	—	—	6	1	18	10	12	1	6	2	56	1.8
Mexico	42,689	3	5	1	9	8	10	—	3	2	9	50	1.2
Yugoslavia	19,508	—	—	—	—	—	—	—	—	1	2	3	.2
Peru	11,650	9	2	—	2	11	13	25	49	7	—	118	10.13
Brazil	82,222	2	7	3	4	14	5	11	4	19	2	71	.9
Egypt	29,600	—	—	—	—	—	—	—	—	—	—	0	0
China	700,000	158	24	16	—	5	15	2	12	17	408	657	.9
India	486,729	31	18	64	27	4	8	18	159	78	1,100	1,507	3.1
Kenya	9,365	1	1	19	8	22	3	58	10	2	1	125	13.3
Nigeria	57,500	—	—	8	7	—	—	115	7	46	210	393	6.8
Tanzania	10,515	—	—	—	—	—	—	15	1	—	—	16	1.5

Source: Taylor and Hudson, *World Handbook*, pp. 102-8, 295-98.
Note: Countries are ranked in order of GNP/capita in 1965.

gime with low legitimacy, but these typically benefit the incumbent institutional groups — military and bureaucratic — rather than the excluded minorities.

POLICY PERSPECTIVES ON INTEREST ARTICULATION

As we pointed out in chapter III, one must look at the structures performing political functions from both process and policy perspectives. To understand the formation of policies, one must know not merely what groups articulate interests, but what policy preferences they are expressing. Many associational interest groups, for example, specialize in certain policy areas and consistently represent certain special points of view within them. The list of formal titles of associational interest groups given in table VII.1 has already suggested the tendency of such groups to organize themselves around issue-specific or group-specific bases. The concerns of other types of groups, such as institutional or anomic ones, may be less easily discerned, but are also important for the policy process.

Table VII.5 provides a three-dimensional overview of examples of interest articulation. The far left column indicates the types of interest groups that commonly articulate interests in modern societies. The next columns provide examples of interest articulation by each type of group in respective policy areas: extractive, distributive, and regulative policies in the domestic arena and a variety of examples in the international policy arena. A third dimension is provided by the asterisks, which indicate when the activity involved coercive and unconstitutional channels, rather than constitutional ones. Careful examination of each case will provide a more precise classification of the access channels, including the elite representation by black members of Congress in the United States, the use of party channels by the Italian Catholic church, and the use of terror by the French OAS. In this table we have used examples from many nations in order to suggest the variety of possibilities and to fill in all the categories with reasonably obvious cases. If we were studying the interest articulation patterns in a single nation, of course, we should attempt to build up the table showing the structures, policies, and channels being involved in interest articulation in the given nation during some particular period of time.

Although we have focused here on relatively specific policy articulations, it is possible for expressions of discontent to be much vaguer and more diffuse. Another distinction often made is the level at which the demand is made. Rather than distinguishing among output policy areas, for example, we might distinguish among demands for minor policy change, for changes in the processes of decision making and implementation, and for changes in the basic system itself, particularly in elite re-

Table VII.5. *Process and Policy Perspectives on Interest Articulation*

Types of interest groups	Examples of interest articulation in various policy areas			
	Domestic extractive policy	*Domestic distributive policy*	*Domestic regulative policy*	*International policy*
Individual interest articulation	Peasant family seeks patron's aid with tax law	Austrian worker asks party official for housing aid	U.S. family business seeks relief from pollution standards	British farmer writes against Common Market
Anomic interest groups	Nigerian women riot over 1950s rumor on taxes*	Polish workers strike over wage policies*	Venezuelan students and citizens strike against dictatorship, 1958*	U.S. students demonstrate over Cambodia policy†
Nonassociational interest groups	Mexican business leaders discuss taxes with President	Farmers in drought-stricken area ask for loans and subsidies	Soviet writers demand more freedom of speech, 1960s	Saudi Arabian royal family factions favor oil embargo
Institutional interest groups	Catholic church urges Christian party to oppose Vatican tax	Congressional black caucus demands jobs for minority unemployed	Soviet jurists ask more due process in "parasite" laws, 1960s	Politburo faction opposes Soviet missiles in Cuba, 1962
Associational interest groups	AFL-CIO president calls for U.S. tax cut in 1974	British Medical Ass'n negotiates salaries under Health Service	U.S. Retail Druggists lobby to pass Fair Trade Laws	French OAS launch terror bombing over Algeria policy, 1960s*

Note: An asterisk (*) by a particular example indicates the use of coercive, unconstitutional access channels and tactics. A dagger (†) indicates use of coercion by some elements or subgroups.

cruitment. Students of the Soviet system, for example, have used terms such as "subversive" or "integral" opposition to refer to actions calling for basic change in the Communist system, as opposed to "factional" or "sectoral" interests articulated by institutional groups on policy questions.[39]

POLITICAL DEVELOPMENT AND INTEREST ARTICULATION

We suggested that specialized structures, operating in a secular political culture, will generally increase the capability of the political system to cope with its environment. In fact, we think that such development usually occurs in response to some sort of challenge that cannot be met by the structures already performing some of the functions of the political system.

If we apply this analysis to the development of specialized and differentiated structures for interest articulation, we can see more clearly how development takes place. Interest articulation involves the expression of demands by various groups in the society. The development of specialized interest organizations increases the ability of political decision makers to learn what various groups are demanding. This information can be used to strike various bargains for the support of groups needed to sustain the regime and help its leaders seek their goals. Various kinds of challenges, therefore, might stimulate the effort to develop more specialized interest articulation structures, both groups and channels, for conveying their messages accurately. One such challenge would be the adoption by the political elites of new goals that required them to mobilize special groups into action; they then might need specialized structures in order to bargain with and activate these groups. Another challenge might come from the appearance of many new groups with demands that they wish to articulate in politics. Yet a third challenge might come when existing social and economic groups start to define some of their problems as political and wish to transmit their interests into the political system.

In fact, historically the development of specialized interest groups and specialized interest articulation channels have come in response to all these kinds of challenges. Various studies have shown, for example, that interest groups and channels for articulation have often been initially organized and established by governments interested in increasing group involvement.[40] In the United States, farm groups are a conspicuous example: development of the largest farmer's association, the Farm Bureau, was directly encouraged by the federal government, which needed a

[39] See the essays by Barghoorn and Skilling in Dahl, *Regimes and Oppositions*.
[40] See Olson, op. cit.

channel for providing information and aid to farmers. Such examples are commonplace in democratic systems and also in authoritarian systems, in which a government desiring to gain the support of various groups encourages the formation of specialized interest organizations. Political party elites have also been important in encouraging the formation of organized interest groups in order to have continuing links with group members for support. The most obvious examples are found in the Socialist and Catholic parties of Western Europe, which have often deliberately created elaborate interest group structures (trade unions, cooperatives, leisure and recreation groups), more or less linked to the parties, in order to involve group members in politics. Of course, in addition to the direct creation of groups, political elites also encourage group formation by creating bureaucratic channels or mass media through which interests can be articulated.

Indeed, one can best understand the internal development of specialized interest articulation structures by considering the choices faced by the members or leaders of interest groups. They are aware that the "group" exists, in the sense that there are a number of individuals with some interests or concerns in common. But the specialized organization of that group and the decision to use particular channels and styles of interest articulation do not follow from the existence of the group alone. Individuals must decide if there are rewards that might follow from political action, what forms of political action might be effective, how probable it is that such actions might succeed, what are the costs of undertaking them, and so forth. Only under rather specialized circumstances of reward and cost will the benefits of forming such a political organization and of using it for interest articulation be sufficient to encourage individuals to undertake it — although once the structures are created and some internal reward structure established, then it may be used for various purposes more easily. It is for this reason that institutional groups play so large a role in most systems and that many associational groups have their origin in institutional groups or settings.

Considering the political system as a whole, one can see that sharp changes in the interest articulation structures and styles are likely to follow other changes. First, changes in the *communication* structures are likely to offer opportunity for interest articulation and thus encourage development of specialized group structures. Large numbers of individuals can be made aware of common interests and appeals for coordinated support can more easily be made to them. Second, the *political culture* is important to interest articulation in several ways. Attitudes toward violence, for example, will affect the pervasiveness and permissibility of riots. The belief that the government is responsive or hostile will shape style, channel, and frequency of action. A participant culture can be more easily mobilized if opportunities are provided. And secularization may open the possibilities of new, previously untried forms of action. Finally, the distribution of *political resources* in the society is important. Representation of interests on a continuing basis is expensive and not likely to be afforded by groups and individuals on the margin of subsistence. Moreover, if groups have few political resources, they are likely to perceive that interest articulation, at least through normal channels, is a hopeless procedure, probably not worth the cost. In countries with large gaps between haves and have-nots, the normal interest articulation channels are likely dominated by the haves, while the have-nots either remain quiet or intermittently adopt violent or radical means of making their voice heard.

This consideration, even so briefly, of the sources of system change in the performance of the interest articulation function can suggest why socioeconomic modernization has such a powerful impact on political change. Such socioeconomic modernization is not by any means the only stimulus to political development — and to the challenges that may result in political decline. But most observers seem to agree that certain almost irreversible processes of social and economic change seem to drive political systems along very general, but discernible, paths of change in their own structure and culture.

The most evident of the forces of socioeconomic change are related to the industrial, technological, and scientific revolutions. The past few centuries have witnessed remarkable changes in ways of life and thought, which have been in large part associated with the economic advantages of the specialization of labor and of the adoption of new technologies to control and exploit the environment. Among the consequences of these changes has been an increasingly general belief that the conditions of life are not fixed, that they *can* be altered through human action. Associated secondarily with these changes have been urbanization and adaptation to the forms of city life, education, radical growth in communication and in interdependence of thought and economic activity, and, in most cases, real improvement in the physical conditions of life. The same socioeconomic changes have also been associated, however, with a breakdown in traditional patterns of belief and in traditional forms of family and social life. Although the individual forms taken by these changes have been varied, the general patterns have emerged with regularity in association with the spread of technology and communication.

It is these changes that make it possible, as it has perhaps never been possible before, to speak of *modern* political systems. They are modern because they rest on the consequences of socioeconomic changes that are unique and not easily reversed. These changes affect political systems in many ways. In general, they greatly increase both the need for coordinated social action in order to solve new problems and the possibility of increased political participation and political demands from members of the society.

The needs for coordinated social action arise from many sources, but the perception of all the related problems as political problems reflects something more than the changes in society. It reflects the development of a set of attitudes that defines these problems as solvable, problems that no longer need be left to fate. Examples of change in other societies and in other groups, contacts with means of influence and with control of the physical environment, and experience with government intervention as a force in everyday life — all can also create an awareness of the potential of responsible governmental action to create a new and better life. It is the common growth of such an awareness that has led S. N. Eisenstadt to suggest that the basic "legitimacy" of governments in all modern nations — nations that have experienced some of these socioeconomic changes — rests on the claim of the ruler to act in the interests of the ruled. This is as true of authoritarian as of democratic ideology.[41]

The specific means by which attitudes become part of the political culture and subsequently come to affect the structures and functioning of interest articulation are the processes of socialization and recruitment. Processes of social and economic change can directly affect several elements of political culture: level of political information, degree of political participation, feelings of political competence, and perception of the pressure or potential pressure of government on the life of the individual. These elements of political culture are affected not through some mysterious transfer process, but by the fact that social and economic development greatly increases the flow of information and contact between parts of the society and raises the level of education, wealth, and status that the individual member of the society possibly has. And a great deal of evidence exists to suggest that increases in educational level and socioeconomic status are closely related to the level of political competence.[42]

Thus, the general trends in societies experiencing modernization are those which are closely related to the rise of participant attitudes in political culture. Individuals and groups face new problems and are more likely to define old problems as deserving human solution. At the same time, the specialization of labor leads to the formation of a large number of new special interests that can be the basis for associational interest groups. The actual processes by which associational groups

41 S. N. Eisenstadt, *The Political Systems of Empires* (New York: Free Press of Glencoe, 1963); and see the notes in chaps. II and IV.

42 See chaps. IV and V.

emerge and sustain themselves are complex. However, the rise of mass media, of a more extended bureaucracy, and of other political structures provides additional channels through which emerging groups can act. The existence of such channels is in itself a stimulus for group formation, as is the greater flow of political information.

Thus, it is possible to argue that as a society undergoes economic and technological change, and as it acquires the attitudes related to these processes, both the orientation and the means of action that lead to higher levels of political interest articulation will emerge. The appearance of the problems of participation and distribution is an extremely likely consequence. The leaders may, of course, attempt to control this process, often at the same time as they stimulate it through their efforts to modernize and industrialize. This attempt at control may involve bringing special interest groups within a dominant party organization, establishing control over the flow of information, and suppressing demands and dissent. The development of complex and differentiated political structures within the political system either to accommodate or to control such new awareness and articulation is typical of modern political systems, whether authoritarian or democratic.

CHAPTER VIII

Interest Aggregation

THE FUNCTION OF CONVERTING DEMANDS into major policy alternatives is called interest aggregation. Demands become major policy alternatives when they are backed by substantial political resources. By political resources we mean such things as the votes of citizens who support candidates, the votes of legislators, the support of bureaucratic groups, and the use of armed force that may be mobilized in recruitment and policy making. For political demands to become serious policy alternatives, they have to be backed up by a sufficient proportion of whatever resources are decisive in a political system. Political aggregation, then, consists of the processes that combine demands into policy alternatives and mobilize resources behind these policy alternatives.

A political party convention engages in interest aggregation when it receives the complaints and demands of labor unions and business organizations, of ethnic groups and urban poor, and then juggles, bargains, and compromises these conflicting interests into some form of policy statement that many can support. So do the workers and voters who mobilize electoral support for that party on election day. At another point in the American political system, a legislative committee performs interest aggregation when it combines the military's plea for more defense funds and the budget bureau's opposition to additional expenditures into a single military appropriations bill.

In a nation such as the Soviet Union, interest aggregation is performed rather differently. A central group of party leaders may hear the proposals of military officers, the advice of party subordinates, and the statements of administrative officials regarding the shift from heavy industry to manufacture of more consumer goods. Information bearing on the problem may come from the buying behavior of consumers as well as from perceived international crises. During deliberations, various policy alternatives emerge, favored by different leaders and the subgroups and organizations associated with them. A leadership clique may make a bid for power behind an important figure committed to a "hard" or "soft" policy line. Or the Politburo and Central Committee may develop a more widely accepted balance of sectoral interests in response to a combination of pragmatic and ideological considerations. But in either case the coalescence of these policy factions, as defined by the grouping of various political resources behind more inclusive policy positions, is interest aggregation.

Interest aggregation is an important function, having major implications at the system, process, and policy levels. At the level of the political *system,* it is helpful to consider what kinds of political resources are being used to form the support for contenders and for policies. If contenders seek to gain power by appealing to groups with coercive resources, the stability of the system may be threatened. In Brazil in the 1950s and 1960s, for example, the appeal by civilian politicians for the military to join the conservative forces and to move against the left typically preceded military intervention. On the other hand, if major contenders concentrate their activities on building legitimate electoral coalitions and mobilizing citizen electoral support, the stability of a democratic system may be reinforced. Recent detailed analyses of the organizational activities of the Italian Communist party suggest, for example, that its efforts to build widespread electoral support and to establish a legitimate "presence" in all aspects of Italian life and all sectors of Italian society may well limit its potential for the coercive pressure and undemocratic confrontation implied by its ideology.[1]

Interest aggregation has important implications for the policy-making *process.* It serves as a major bridge between the scattered interests and resources of large numbers of groups and individuals, and the formulation of authoritative policies backed by majority coalitions. From a coalition-formation point of view, interest aggregation determines the strength and issue positions of the major contenders who will engage in policy making. If the policy-making structures themselves are not to be overburdened, interest aggregation must build a set of major alternatives that can be the basis for effective decisions. On the one hand, if interest aggregation is very fragmented, the assembly or cabinet or executive may be faced with a great variety of demands, each backed by a small proportion of the resources, and the building of decisive coalitions may be a very complex task. A common complaint about political institutions in the developing nations is that personalistic aggregation by many local

---

[1] See Sidney Tarrow, "Political Dualism and Italian Communism," *APSR* 41 (March 1967): 39–53; and the essays in Donald L. M. Blackmer and Sidney Tarrow, *Communism in Italy and France* (Princeton: Princeton University Press, 1975).

patrons and influentials makes unified policy making and policy implementation difficult.[2]

On the other hand, aggregation may result in a small number of very tightly constructed contender groups, but these groups may be bound to policies that are sharply antagonistic. A typical example is the appearance of ethnic parties built upon communal associations and intense values of religion and language; these may be very effective at mobilizing support for their policies, but may adopt mutually exclusive goals of language predominance or separatism.[3] Here, too, such aggregation structures place a very heavy burden on government. Even if there is a majority, the positions of minority groups may be so little weighed in the policy that it is impossible to retain their support for the regime itself.

At the *policy* level the pattern of interest aggregation affects the substantive content of policy. As we have already noted, extreme personalistic and small-group diffusion in interest aggregation may limit the capacity of the governmental agencies to build an adequate support basis for social changes, as in many developing nations. Fragmentation of aggregation structures into mutually antagonistic coalitions may immobilize policy making and lead to alienation of groups opposed to the status quo, as seems often to have been the case in Italy and France. On the other hand, the ability of a major contender to aggregate very substantial resources, especially if a majority, will help determine policy directions.

We shall point out in the discussion of policy outputs and outcomes in chapters XI and XII that there is a long road between policy making and social outcomes. But various studies have suggested that the aggregation stage can indeed be critical. It is perhaps harder to see the policy implications of party and electoral aggregation in the United States, because of the blurring of differences between the two major parties on many issues. But one study has shown that on social welfare issues the Democratic candidates for Congress in 1966 were almost always more liberal than their Republican counterparts and that the election of a heavily Democratic Congress would have substantially altered the potential coalitions on welfare issues.[4] Another study demonstrated that the balance between unemployment and inflation in European democracies was associated with whether or not Social Democratic parties had been

---

[2] This problem of concentrating political resources for bringing about effectively implemented policies has been discussed by many students of politics in the developing nations. See especially Samuel P. Huntington, *Political Order in Changing Societies* (New Haven: Yale University Press, 1968).

[3] See the references in chap. II, to the growing literature on ethnic conflict.

[4] John L. Sullivan and Robert E. O'Connor, "Electoral Choice and Popular Control of Public Policy," *APSR* 66 (December 1972): 1256–68.

part of governmental coalitions. The nations having experience with leftist governments were more likely to reduce unemployment, even when it meant greater inflation.[5] Still a third study pointed to a relationship between the number of years a government was controlled by Social Democrats and their leftist allies and the increase in public expenditures over a seventeen-year period.[6]

In short, interest aggregation helps shape the substantive policy outcomes. If interest aggregation creates majority or decisive support for particular policy lines, such policies are likely to be enacted. If aggregation creates several contenders, much will depend, at the policy-making stage, on their respective policy commitments made to followers in the process of aggregation and on the size and types of resources they have accumulated.

STRUCTURES PERFORMING INTEREST AGGREGATION

All groups and organizations performing interest articulation may also perform interest aggregation. In modern societies, large associational interest groups, such as the Federation of German Industry or the British Trades Union Congress, may represent a great variety of associated organizations and may combine diverse and conflicting demands into policy alternatives to present to party and cabinet. The governmental structures themselves, from assembly to military junta, commonly engage in additional aggregation before the major policy alternatives have emerged. But highly developed political systems usually have more specialized structures, for the aggregation of interests and the mobilization of resources behind the emergent proposals. Political parties are typically engaged in just these activities. In table VIII.1 we display the variety of agencies that perform interest aggregation in the set of contemporary systems we have been considering throughout this book. The table is only a very rough initial guide, for performance will vary in different issue areas. But in the subsequent pages we shall discuss the role of these and other structures in interest aggregation.

INDIVIDUAL ELITES AS INTEREST AGGREGATORS

We pointed out in the last chapter that individual leaders may be able to establish networks of individual supporters on the basis of personalistic exchanges of favors and support. Such networks may allow individual leaders to accumulate substantial political resources and hence

---

[5] Douglas A. Hibbs, Jr., "Political Parties and Macroeconomic Policy," *APSR* 71 (December 1977): 1467–87.

[6] David B. Cameron, "Inequality and the State" (Paper delivered at the 1976 Annual Meetings of the American Political Science Association, Chicago, September 1976). Cameron also found less income inequality in such systems.

Table VIII.1. *Interest Aggregation in Selected Systems, 1976*

		Extensiveness of interest aggregation by selected types of structures			
Nation[a]	*Clientelist networks*	*Associational groups*	*Competitive parties/ Assemblies*	*Non- competitive party*	*Military*
USA	Low	Mod	High	None	Low
Sweden	Low	High	High	None	Low
Canada	Low	Mod	High	None	Low
W. Germany	Low	High	High	None	Low
France	Low	Mod	High	None	Low
Japan	Mod	High	High	None	None
Austria	Low	High	High	None	Low
Britain	Low	High	High	None	Low
Israel	Low	High	High	None	Low
Czechoslovakia	Low	Low	None	High	Low
Italy	Mod	Mod	High	None	Low
USSR	Low	Low	None	High	Low
Bulgaria	Low	Low	None	High	Low
Yugoslavia	Low	High	None	High	Low
Mexico	Mod	Mod	Low	High	Low
Brazil	Mod	Mod	None	Low	High
Peru	High	Mod	None	None	High
China	Low	Low	None	High	Mod
Egypt	High	Low	None	Low	High
Nigeria	High	Mod	None	None	High
Kenya	High	Mod	None	Mod	Low
Tanzania	High	Mod	None	Mod	Low
India	High	Mod	High	None	Low

[a] Nations are ranked by level of economic development: GNP/capita in 1973 (see table I.1).

to play a significant role in shaping political alternatives. They can deliver votes or other manifestations of support from their followers because they provide each individual with personal rewards or favors. The collective interests of the followers are not being expressed, nor can they be said to constitute an interest group, because they may not perceive common interests. Rather, their resources are being aggregated through the personal exchanges built by individual leaders.

Although such personal networks are to be found in all societies, they have been especially prominent in the peasant societies in Latin America and Southeast Asia and in some industrial societies, such as Japan and Italy. In recent years political scientists, often drawing upon the work of anthropologists, have analyzed aspects of these personalistic patron-client relationships.[7] Typically, these structures involved a diffuse pattern of exchange of goods and services between patrons and clients. Patrons provided land, equipment, marketing services, loans for poor harvest years, protection from bandits (and tax collectors), and negotiations with state officials to secure public works, loans, favors, and the like. Clients provided labor for the land, personal services to the patron, and whatever political resources they possessed, including voting as directed by the patron.

Interest aggregation through personal networks has often been important for the careers of individual politicians and can help to integrate individual citizens into the society through providing them with needed benefits — especially if they exist on the margin of subsistence, as in many peasant societies. However, successful domination of interest aggregation by personal patron-client ties typically results in a rather static pattern of overall policy formation, and the ability to mobilize political resources behind unified policies of social change is difficult, depending, at a minimum, on a coalition of many factional leaders. Scott described such conditions in Southeast Asia:

> In the patron-client pattern peasants are more or less passively represented (one might even say "subsumed") in local or regional politics by their particular patrons. Political competition takes on a factional quality inasmuch as the contending units are patron-client networks quite similar to one another in class composition. For the peasants, the main social links are those which tie them to elite patrons and these links tend to reduce the social significance of the horizontal ties between peasants. The overall pattern, similar to that of Western European feudalism, is that of a disaggregated peasantry attached vertically by bonds of loyalty to agrarian elites who form the active participants in an oligarchic political order.[8]

INTEREST GROUPS: ASSOCIATIONAL, NONASSOCIATIONAL, AND INSTITUTIONAL

At least three of the types of interest groups discussed in the last chapter can act as significant interest aggregators. Nonassociational

---

[7] See especially John Duncan Powell, "Peasant Society and Clientelist Politics," *APSR* 64 (June 1970): 411–25; René Lemarchand and Keith Legg, "Political Clientelism and Development," *Comparative Politics* 4 (January 1972): 148–78; James C. Scott, "Patron-Client Politics and Political Change in Southeast Asia," *APSR* 66 (March 1972): 81–113; and Carl H. Lande, "Networks and Groups in Southeast Asia," *APSR* 67 (March 1973): 103–27. On patron-clientism in Japan, see Nobutake Ike, *Japanese Politics: Patron Client Democracy in Japan* (New York: Alfred A. Knopf, 1972), chap. 1; Taketsuyu Tsurutani, *Political Change in Japan* (New York: David McKay, 1977), chap. 2.

[8] James Scott, "The Erosion of Patron-Client Bonds and Social Change in Rural Southeast Asia," *Journal of Asian Studies* 32 (November 1972): 5.

groups based on religion, language, kinship, tribe, and the like can be used to develop policy backing among many individuals and subgroups. Either as factions within party or bureaucratic structures or as contenders in their own rights, such nonassociational groups can play an important role in aggregating interests of group members.

The structure of associational interest groups enables their leaders to learn the opinions of their members and to mobilize their activities in favor of particular policies. Whether formed on the basis of specific issue representation or on the basis of more general class or ethnic group identity, such associational groups can often mobilize considerable electoral or financial resources merely by alerting the members to matters of common interest and by coordinating their activities.

Although such associational interest groups typically function as support groups for more major political contenders, such as parties, they can on occasion wield sufficient resources to become contenders in their own right. Their support of governing coalitions may be critical, and they may become essential subsystems within political parties, able to influence or even control party policies. The power of the labor unions within the British Labour party, for example, has rested on the unions' ability to develop coherent policy positions and mobilize the voting strength of their members to support these positions. In many European nations, moreover, more or less autonomous national bodies, such as the Dutch Social and Economic Council [9] or the Austrian Chamber system,[10] may have substantial power to formulate national policies — and may directly incorporate national labor union leaders and representatives of large employer associations into their membership.

We must also note the ability of large unions or business associations to call nationwide strikes or shut down key industries and thereby to shape policy formation. In Britain in 1974 the coal miners' strike crippled the national economy, and the unions played a relatively direct role in national policy making, aggregating the powerful resources of workers in an essential economic sector. In Chile in 1972 and 1973, the long and devastating strikes by the Confederation of Truck Owners against the Allende government created and aggravated food and resource shortages throughout the nation, initially encouraging the government to bring military officers into the Cabinet and later playing an important role in the breakdown of governmental legitimacy that preceded the military coup.

Such institutional interest groups as bureaucratic and military factions

[9] See Arend Lijphart, *The Politics of Accommodation,* rev. ed. (Berkeley and Los Angeles: University of California Press, 1976).
[10] See Kurt Steiner, *Politics in Austria* (Boston: Little, Brown, 1973).

can be extremely important interest aggregators. The bureaucracy acts as a kind of interest aggregator in most societies. Although established primarily for the implementation of policies whose broad outline is established by higher authorities, the bureaucracy may negotiate with a variety of client groups to ascertain their preferences or to mobilize their support or may even be "captured" by them to represent their collective interests. The aggregation of individual and group interests into backing for new policy initiatives is often performed by institutional interest groups within the civilian or military bureaucracy. It may include arousing and coordinating client support, as well as bringing into play the resources of the institution itself.

Military interest groups have a special role as potential interest aggregators because of their monopoly, in most cases, over the instruments of violence. When and if the legitimacy of the constitutional order breaks down, the role of the military can be decisive. Many factors, some of which we discussed in chapter V, may contribute to a decline in the legitimacy of the regime and bring about military intervention. But effective military intervention requires that the military itself be able to aggregate the coercive resources they control into a united pattern of action. Studies of attempted military coups suggest that one-third to one-half of such attempts in the last decade have failed.[11] Because failure is so costly, coups are usually attempted where chances of success seem reasonable. Because the military is a hierarchical organization, in which open mobilization of members behind political goals is typically frowned upon, it is not surprising that the interests of the military institutions themselves are an essential element in many, probably most, coups. A recent study has shown that the corporate interests of the military or the ambitions of the military services or cliques of officers lay behind about three-fifths of the military coups attempted in the third world in the last decades. Only two-fifths of these coups had either liberal or conservative political goals and involved aggregation of civil as well as military interests.[12]

COMPETITIVE PARTY SYSTEMS

The political party is the specialized interest aggregation structure of contemporary societies. Political parties developed historically as the voting franchise was extended and as groups sought public office by mobilizing electoral support around policies appealing to different inter-

---

[11] See the evidence reviewed by Eric A. Nordlinger, *Soldiers in Politics: Military Coups and Governments* (Englewood Cliffs: Prentice-Hall, 1976), pp. 101 ff.

[12] William Thompson, *The Grievances of Military Coup-Makers* (Beverly Hills: Sage Publications, 1973).

ests. The degree to which they actually perform this function in different societies is, of course, a matter for empirical investigation. But most contemporary societies have some kind of party or party system.

Parties may have different goals and organizational structures, and may operate in very different political settings. Consequently, they vary greatly in their performance of interest aggregation. One must keep in mind the distinction between competitive political parties, seeking primarily to mobilize and build upon electoral support, and noncompetitive parties. The distinction does not depend on the closeness of electoral victory or even on the number of parties. Rather, it depends on the primacy of winning votes as a prerequisite for control of policy making, on one hand, and the freedom for parties to form and organize to seek those votes, on the other. Thus, there might exist a party that wins most of the votes in a given area or region, or even a given national election, but is nonetheless a competitive party. Its goals involve winning elections, either as a primary objective or as a means for policy making; its predominance at the polls is always subject to actual or potential challenge by other parties if it does not respond to the wishes of voters. Its organization thus involves arrangements for ascertaining voter preference and seeking to arouse voter support.[13]

In analyzing the role of competitive political parties in interest aggregation, one must consider not only the individual party, but also the structure of parties, electorates, electoral laws, and policy-making bodies that interact in a competitive party system. Typically, interest aggregation takes place at one or more of three levels: within individual party organizations as intraparty factions compete; through electoral competition between parties, with voters giving varying amounts of electoral support to different parties; and through party bargaining and coalition formation in the assembly or the executive or both.

Thus, each individual party develops some set of policy alternatives. Typically, these are alternatives believed to have the backing of large or cohesive groups of voters, or they may reflect continuing linkages between parties and organized interest groups, such as labor unions or business associations. In the United States the national party conventions are the focus of such development of policy positions, both through for-

---

[13] One must avoid being confused by the use of the term *noncompetitive district* as often used to describe areas where one party is strong, or the term *one-party* region used similarly by students of national politics. In our analysis, we consider a party and party system competitive if open organization and competition for valuable votes is possible, no matter how great party majorities may be in recent elections. See the discussion by Giovanni Sartori, *Parties and Party Systems* (Cambridge: Cambridge University Press, 1976), chap. 7, especially p. 218.

mation of party platforms and, perhaps more importantly, through the selection of candidates who are committed to various policy programs.[14] The parties then offer their chosen candidates for office in the electoral process. They not only present candidates, but also attempt to mobilize electoral support through rallies, mass media promotion, door-to-door campaigning, and systematic efforts to locate sympathetic voters and get them to the polls on election day. In the elections, citizens directly participate in aggregation by giving support to different parties. Such voting outcomes are converted into legislative seats or executive control — as in a presidential election — through the electoral laws.

If an individual party that is committed to some clear-cut policy positions wins control of the executive, directly or indirectly, and of the legislature, it will be able to pass desired legislation and implement policies. This has happened, for example, when Social Democratic parties committed to expansion of the government sector have won legislative control in various European nations. However, if the parties are not internally cohesive (as in the United States) or if no party wins a clear majority (as in most European elections), the final stages of aggregation take place as different parties and factions within them continue to bargain and organize coalitions within the assemblies and executives.

Interest aggregation in competitive party systems has been investigated from many points of view. We will review some of the research and discuss some of the factors that shape this process. It is necessary to consider at least five elements, which interact in complex ways: (1) the governmental structure, (2) the alternatives offered by the party system, (3) the voting behavior of the electorate, (4) the electoral laws, and (5) legislative coalition formation.

Governmental Organization. The organization of government is important because it shapes the tactics of parties in the aggregation process.[15] If policy making is nationally centralized, then the objective must be to participate in nationally strong coalitions. If there is a federal system and decentralization, parties may wish to focus on provincial control, as often happens in Canada and is typical in Switzerland. Similarly,

[14] Gerald Pomper's analysis of party platforms and the record of parties in implementing them in the United States suggests that parties do tend to keep their pledges, and platforms are not irrelevant, at least as cues to voters about party behavior (*Elections in America* [New York: Dodd, Mead, 1968], chaps. 7–10). See also Sullivan and O'Connor, op. cit.

[15] See chap. IX. And see Robert A. Dahl, *Political Oppositions in Western Democracies* (New Haven: Yale University Press, 1966), chaps. 12 and 13, for an analysis of the effect of concentration of policy-making power on the strategies used by political oppositions.

a strong executive who is elected independently of the legislature, as in the United States or the French Fifth Republic, will be a focus of party action; and the need to capture the executive will usually encourage parties to broaden their base of preelectoral support, either through general catchall policies of single parties or through the formation of preelectoral coalitions. The presence of a strong executive in the French Fifth Republic has clearly encouraged cooperation between leftist parties, for example.[16] In the true parliamentary system, in contrast, the legislative assembly will be a major focus of action, as the prime minister must have control of a majority of seats there in order to make and implement policies. Strong and disciplined parties, as in Britain, may shift the locus of policy-making activity to the executive, but legislative elections and the role of parties in mobilizing electoral and legislative support remain a critical element in interest aggregation. Where no party obtains a majority, or where internal party discipline is weak, coalition building within the parliament is essential to stable policy making. Such has typically been the case in the Scandinavian nations, Belgium, the Netherlands, and Italy.

Alternatives Offered by the Party System. If there are many parties presenting different policy alternatives, citizens are more likely to find a party representing just the combination of policy positions that they favor. Especially if there are several salient policy dimensions, such as religion and social class, cutting across each other, it is unlikely that a two-party system will offer very many citizens the combinations they individually prefer. If there are many parties, the election outcomes may create a very fragmented legislature. The legislature may reflect voter preferences, but such fragmented aggregation may make policy making quite difficult. Both students of the American Congress and students of European systems with many small parties in parliament have typically been concerned about the difficulties for coherent policy making created by party systems that bring many uncoordinated contenders into the legislature.[17] Of course, from the citizens' point of view, the worst of these possible worlds is the process in which only limited aggregation is taking place, but in which, even so, *their* most important concerns are not being presented to the electorate. One reason that interest groups play such a critical role is that they may force the party system to confront a wide range of possible voter concerns.

[16] See Frank L. Wilson, *The French Democratic Left, 1963–1969* (Stanford: Stanford University Press, 1971).
[17] Also see the discussion of party factions, and the literature reviewed there, by Sartori, op. cit., chap. 4.

The formation of the policy alternatives to be offered to the electorate by political parties is a complex problem that depends on the distributions of preferences in the society and also on the ambition, resources, and strategies of the party leaders.[18] The party leadership may choose to offer a narrow and quite specific program that seeks to mobilize the support of a very homogeneous constituency of voters. If the bloc of supporters is large enough, such a party may be able to win a clear majority and to implement the program. Or the party may appeal to a clear-cut group that is not large enough to provide legislative control but can get the party into the legislature, where it can bargain with other parties and join or shape governmental coalitions. Yet another approach is to offer a broad, catchall set of policy positions, appealing to a wide range of voters, in an attempt to build the largest possible plurality. In such a case, the party might be able to take control of the government, but its broad and ambiguous programs and its diverse internal factions mean that further intraparty or intraexecutive aggregation must take place before final policy making. American parties typically find themselves in this last situation.

Which strategy a party will select depends on the leaders' objectives, their perception of voters' preferences, their relationship with party activists, and the role of other parties. Political scientists and economists have subjected the logic of party competition to increasingly sophisticated mathematical analysis, following the pioneering work of Anthony Downs.[19] He demonstrated that with one dimension of salient issues, and with voters clustered toward the center, the logic of two-party competition in elections with high participation forces parties to adopt positions near the center of the voter distribution if they wish to win.[20] A party that strays off the center can easily be defeated in the election by an opponent that moves toward the center, winning all the voters on "its" side of the center and at the center as well. Something very much like this seemed to happen in the American presidential elections in 1964 and 1972, when first the Republican party chose a conservative candidate

[18] Two useful reviews and discussions are Dahl, *Political Oppositions in Western Democracies,* and Sartori, op. cit., chap. 6.

[19] Anthony Downs, *An Economic Theory of Democracy* (New York: Harper & Row, 1957). More recently, see the review by William H. Riker and Peter C. Ordeshook, *An Introduction to Positive Political Theory* (Englewood Cliffs: Prentice-Hall, 1973), chaps. 11 and 12. And see Morris Fiorina, *Representatives, Roll Calls, and Constituencies* (Lexington, Mass.: D. C. Heath, 1974); David Robertson, *A Theory of Party Competition* (New York: John Wiley, 1975); Sartori, op. cit., chap. 10; Gunnar Sjoblom, *Party Strategies in a Multiparty System* (Lund: Studentlitteratur, 1968); Donald Stokes, "Spatial Models of Party Competition," in Angus Campbell et al., *Elections and the Political Order* (New York: John Wiley, 1966), pp. 161–79.

[20] Downs, op. cit.

(Goldwater) and then the Democratic party chose a liberal candidate (McGovern), both of whom were defeated by middle-of-the-road candidates. In 1960, 1968, and 1976, both parties aggregated a variety of interests within their camps and nominated widely acceptable "center" candidates. As a result, the elections were extremely close. As the 1964 and 1972 elections demonstrate, party strategies are not dictated purely by strategic considerations; party activists may play a critical role, as may important issues and ideological objectives.

The strategies chosen by parties will be shaped by the clustering of voter preferences and by the number of parties. Most competitive party systems are structured by divisions of social class, religion, region, or ethnicity. Since parties seek to build group support, the opportunity to create parties or to expand them by appealing to such important group interests is inevitable. Many individual parties become closely linked to special occupational, religious, or ethnic groups, such as the Social Democratic parties and the working class, the Christian Democratic parties and active Catholics, and the Flemish- and French-language parties and their respective linguistic groups in Belgium. Other parties build across these social groups, but clear-cut factions within those parties appear, such as Southern Democrats in the United States, the labor wing of the Italian Christian Democratic party, the French and Flemish wings of all major Belgian parties. An understanding of the working of competitive party systems, and particularly of the strategies available to party leaders, requires that one locate the significant social groups in the society and identify their interests and demands.

Citizen Electoral Behavior. In working and voting for the candidates of particular parties, citizens participate directly in interest aggregation. The study of electoral behavior has been a major focus of much research in contemporary political science, and we cannot summarize the findings here. But several important points can be emphasized. It is clear that the actions of voters depend to a large degree on the alternatives provided to them by the party system. Where salient issues are linked to general social divisions of occupation, income, religion, and language, and where parties offer alternatives enabling the voter easily to identify with a particular party, then voting lines will tend to follow demographic ones.

Table VIII.2 shows the relationships between major demographic divisions and voting patterns in fifteen competitive party systems. In the Netherlands, where the traditional five larger parties have been closely linked to religion and class; in Austria and Belgium, where, respectively, two and three large parties have been identified by religious and class interests; and in the Scandinavian nations, where occupational divisions have traditionally defined clear party lines — in all these situations, large

Table VIII.2. *Party Alternatives, Social Cleavages, and Electoral
Behavior in Selected Competitive Party Systems*

Nation	Size, in millions[a]	Number of parties to account for 95% of votes[b]	Social cleavage with most explanatory power[c]	Variance in voting explained by all social cleavages[d] (%)
Netherlands	12	10	Religion	51.2 (1968)
France, 4th Republic	49	7	Religion	34.4 (1956)
Norway	4	6	Occupation	37.9 (1965)
Denmark	5	6	Occupation	27.7 (1968)
Finland	5	6	Occupation	33.2 (1966)
Belgium	9	6	Religion	34.4 (1970)
Italy	52	6	Religion	28.3 (1968)
Sweden	8	5	Occupation	37.9 (1964)
France, 5th Republic	49	5	Religion	18.7 (1971)
Australia	11	4	Occupation	14.6 (1967)
Canada	20	4	Religion	15.0 (1965)
Ireland	3	3	Region	3.1 (1969)
Austria	7	3	Religion[e]	46.0 (1969)
Britain	55	3	Occupation	12.0 (1970)
W. Germany	59	3	Religion	19.7 (1967)
USA	195	2	Religion	12.8 (1952–64 average)

[a] Charles L. Taylor and Michael C. Hudson, *World Handbook of Political and Social Indicators*, 2d ed. (New Haven: Yale University Press, 1972). Figures are for 1965.
[b] For the election closest to the date of the survey, as shown in the last column. Calculated from Thomas T. Mackie and Richard Rose, *The International Almanac of Electoral History* (New York: Free Press, 1974).
[c] Based on "AID" tree analysis of demographic characteristics and prediction of party preference or vote in the survey taken in year shown in the last column. Adapted from Richard Rose, *Electoral Behavior: A Comparative Handbook* (New York: Free Press, 1974), p. 17.
[d] Ibid.
[e] In Austria, occupation also accounted for a large additional amount of voting, beyond that accounted for by religion. In the other countries, the second cleavage accounted for substantially less voting variation than the first, although often significant.

proportions of the variability in voting behavior is explained by demographic ties. In Italy and France, too, the frequency of church attendance is a powerful guide to voting behavior, although less so in the French Fifth Republic than in the Fourth. In Austria, for example, most citizens have viewed the Austrian People's party as the better party for devout Catholics and farmers; most have seen the Socialists as better for workers.

212 *Interest Aggregation*

These perceptions are held by large majorities.[21] Such perceptions are less common and less consistent in the United States and Britain, and demographic characteristics are a less certain guide to electoral behavior. Indeed, the table suggests that in general the systems with fewer parties show more blurred divisions.

We do not wish to imply that voters respond mechanically to the claims of parties that appeal to their group memberships or that the true interests of voters always follow cleavage lines. But drawing upon the social networks created by the Catholic church or the trade union structure, parties can more easily mobilize and communicate with their constituents.[22] Moreover, voters' positions in the demographic divisions of class, religion, and so on will probably be associated with some of their issue positions and will, in any case, almost surely shape their information and communication patterns.

However, changing issues will change the attitudes of voters and their patterns of party support. In the United States, researchers in the 1950s found party identification and candidate appeal of primary importance in shaping electoral behavior, with most voters rather well committed to a given party identification. By the late 1960s new issues of war, civil unrest, and social change had become salient, and the parties were offering more distinctive, though not always more congenial, choices.[23] In response to these new issues that touched their lives and in response to the shifting sets of party alternatives, as well as in reflection of social changes themselves, American voters increasingly began to split their tickets, voting for candidates of different parties at different levels of government, and began to vote on the basis of issues rather than party identification.[24] The importance of candidates' perceived personal qualities, and of the virtues of being an incumbent and, thus, a known quan-

[21] See G. Bingham Powell, Jr., "Political Cleavage Structure, Cross-Pressure Processes, and Partisanship," *American Journal of Political Science* 20 (February 1976): 1–23.

[22] For example, see Samuel Barnes, *Representation in Italy* (Chicago: University of Chicago Press, 1977); the essays in Richard Rose, ed., *Electoral Behavior* (New York: Free Press, 1974); Leon D. Epstein, *Political Parties in Western Democracies* (New York: Praeger, 1967); the essays in Dahl, *Political Oppositions in Western Democracies;* Stein Rokkan, *Citizens, Elections, Parties* (New York: David McKay, 1970); and especially Seymour Martin Lipset and Stein Rokkan, eds., *Party Systems and Voter Alignments* (New York: Free Press, 1967).

[23] See Norman H. Nie, Sidney Verba, and John Petrocik, *The Changing American Voter* (Cambridge: Harvard University Press, 1976); and also Warren E. Miller and Teresa E. Levitin, *Leadership and Change* (Cambridge: Winthrop, 1976); Philip E. Converse, "Public Opinion and Voting Behavior," in Fred I. Greenstein and Nelson W. Polsby, *Handbook of Political Science*, vol. 4 (Reading, Mass.: Addison-Wesley, 1975); Gerald Pomper, *Voters' Choice* (New York: Harper & Row, 1975).

[24] Ibid.; and see the symposium on issue voting in the June 1972 issue of the *American Political Science Review*, including the bibliography by Kessel.

tity, remained significant, but the context of their application had altered markedly.[25]

Similarly, the traditional alignments in the Netherlands seem to be breaking down, as the old religious and class blocs are eroded by common socialization and the declining salience of religious issues.[26] French voters, too, find themselves facing quite a new set of party alignments, in addition to new issues of personal importance.[27] In Italy, religious and class divisions are still very significant, but the economic disasters of the mid-1970s gave greater salience to the class dimensions, a phenomenon apparently reinforced by the weakening of church attendance and religious organizations. The Communist party itself played an important role by calling for a "historic compromise" of Christian and Communist forces, attempting to undercut the salience of the religious dimension and also to reassure voters who feared for the safety of the democratic regime. The Communist party recorded major gains in the 1976 election, receiving nearly as much support as the Christian Democrats, over one-third of the electorate.[28]

Electoral Laws. Both the behavior of voters and the implications of their actions for interest aggregation are affected by the electoral laws. The battle for the secret ballot and the extensions of suffrage to all citizens are milestones in the development of competitive party systems. They determine which citizens will play a role in electoral aggregation. Less dramatically, the registration and polling laws in different nations continue to affect voter turnout and the types of voters who will be encouraged or inhibited. Limited polling hours and more difficult registration have contributed to the disenfranchisement of many Americans, especially the less well-off.

The complexities of electoral laws in linking voting outcomes to legislative and executive representation cannot be quickly summarized. But three features of such laws are of particular importance and affect both the immediate legislative outcomes and the long-range encouragement

[25] See especially the debate over the 1972 American presidential election in the September 1976 issue of the *American Political Science Review*.

[26] See Lijphart, *Politics of Accommodation;* and Lijphart's essay in Rose, op. cit.

[27] See Ronald Inglehart, *The Silent Revolution* (Princeton: Princeton University Press, 1977).

[28] On changing Italian voting behavior see Giacomo Sani, "Secular Trends and Party Realignments in Italy: The 1975 Election" (Paper presented at the 1975 Annual Meeting of the American Political Science Association, September 1975); also see the essays in Blackmer and Tarrow, op. cit.; Barnes, *Representation in Italy*; Sidney Tarrow, *Between Center and Periphery: Grassroots Politicians in Italy and France* (New Haven: Yale University Press, 1977); and Sidney Tarrow, "The Italian Party System Between Crisis and Transition," *American Journal of Political Science* 21 (May, 1977): 193–224.

and discouragement of parties to run and to offer alternatives to voters. The simplest feature is the presence of *cutoff provisions* for legislative representation. Designed to keep small parties out of the legislature, cutoff laws basically limit legislative representation in Germany to parties with at least 5 percent of the national vote and in Sweden to parties with 4 percent of the national vote, for example.[29] The effect of these laws may be seen in the 1969 legislatures in Germany and Italy. In Germany the neo-Nazi party won 4.5 percent of the vote and was denied any legislative representation by the cutoff law, while the Free Democrats gained just over 5 percent and became a critical coalition partner for the Socialists. In Italy, on the other hand, nine parties were represented in the legislature, a number that would have been cut to three by application of a 5 percent cutoff rule.

A second important feature is the *number of representatives in each legislative district*. In the United States, Britain, Australia, New Zealand, Canada, and Fifth Republic France, the electoral laws provide for single-member districts. In the Netherlands and Israel, the entire nation is treated as a single district. More typically, Austria and Sweden have from four to seven representatives elected at the same time from a district, whereas Italy has, on the average, twenty members in a district. In most of these latter cases voters can designate a party list for which they cast a single ballot. The most important point about the "magnitude" of districts, as Rae calls this characteristic, is that low magnitudes, especially single-member districts, can greatly distort legislative reflection of citizen voting outcomes and greatly magnify citizen voting shifts.[30] The degree of distortion and magnification will depend on the number of parties, specific voting levels, and geographic concentration of votes. A small party with wide geographic support, such as the British Liberal party, can be heavily penalized by single-member districts. They may do well in many districts, but carry few of them, as in 1974 when they won 20 percent of the vote, but captured only 2 percent of the seats in Parliament. Such effects of the electoral laws have great impact on voter and party strategic decisions, as well as on outcomes.[31] On the other hand, one can see in table VIII.3 that the French Gaullists in 1968 captured

---

[29] For a more complete explanation of various cutoff provisions, including some exceptions even in these cases, see Thomas T. Mackie and Richard Rose, *The International Almanac of Electoral History* (New York: Free Press, 1974). Unless noted otherwise, our aggregate electoral data are from Mackie and Rose.

[30] This discussion of the effects of electoral laws draws heavily upon Douglas W. Rae, *The Political Consequences of Electoral Laws* (New Haven: Yale University Press, 1967; rev. ed., 1971).

[31] For a discussion of various aspects of strategic voting and aggregation for the British Liberals, see Peter H. Lemieux, "The Liberal Party and British Political Change: 1955–1974" (Ph.D. diss., M.I.T., 1977).

Table VIII.3. *Party Alternatives, Electoral Aggregation, and Number of Postwar Governments in Selected Competitive Party Systems*

Nation	Election year	Number of parties to account for 95% of votes[a]	Largest party and % of votes[a]		Electoral laws[b]	Largest party, % of seats[a]	Number of postwar governments to 1969[c]
Netherlands	1971	12	Labor	25	PR[d]	26	10
Finland	1970	7	Social Democrat	23	PR	26	23
Belgium	1971	6	Christian Socialist	30	PR	32	15
Denmark	1971	6	Social Democrat	37	PR	40	11
Italy	1968	6	Christian Democrat	39	PR	42	20
Norway	1969	6	Labor	47	PR	49	6
France, 4th Rep.	1956	7	Communist	26	PR	27	34
France, 5th Rep.	1968	5	Gaullist	46	Majority	74	3
Sweden	1970	5	Social Democrat	45	PR	47	4
Australia	1969	4	Labour	47	Majority	47	5
Canada	1968	4	Liberal	46	Plurality	59	5
Austria	1970	3	Social Democrat	48	PR	49	6
West Germany	1969	3	Christian Democrat	46	PR	49	6
Ireland	1969	3	Fianna Fail	46	PR	52	6
Britain	1970	3	Conservative	46	Plurality	52	6

[a] Data from Mackie and Rose, *International Almanac of Electoral History*.
[b] A more detailed description of the electoral laws can be found in Rae, *Political Consequences of Electoral Laws*. In all of these cases, the proportional representation systems have multimember districts.
[c] From Michael Taylor and V. M. Herman, "Party Systems and Governmental Stability," *APSR* 65 (March 1971): 29.
[d] PR = proportional representation.

74 percent of the seats with only 46 percent of the vote. One of the most dramatic recent examples of the effects of single-member districts came in the 1976 elections in Quebec, where the *Parti Québecquois* increased its vote only from about 33 percent to about 43 percent, but jumped from only 6 seats to 70 in the 110-seat provincial legislature. The geographic distribution of the vote and the presence of several other parties splitting the Liberal support contributed to the remarkable swing in outcome.

The third major feature of the electoral laws, which is in practice usually associated with larger district magnitudes, is *proportional representation*, as opposed to *majority* or *plurality representation*. In plurality representation, the candidate with the most votes wins the representation from a district. In American single-member districts, this means the candidate's party wins one seat. In the American presidential elections, a plurality in a state means that all the state's electoral votes go to the winner. Thus, under the plurality system an individual can be elected President even though the other party's candidate wins more votes. This has happened in the United States; and, indeed, in 1976 a shift of some fifteen thousand votes in Ohio and Hawaii could have elected Gerald Ford as a minority President, despite Carter's victory in popular votes.

In proportional representation, each party is awarded a number of seats proportional to the number of votes it receives, as determined by various formulas.[32] As Rae clearly demonstrates, a proportional representational system with large district magnitudes is the most representative in converting voter choices into legislative representation. However, it also tends to encourage more parties in the legislature, both in the short run and over a long time, especially in the absence of a cutoff rule. Such effects are also suggested in table VIII.3, although electoral laws are only one relevant factor.

Rarely will one party win a majority of citizen votes. Typically it is the operation of electoral laws that "creates" one-party legislative majorities, which are often defended as having advantages for executive stability and for the voters' ability to assess party responsibility. In Rae's analysis of 117 legislative elections, he found voters giving a single party a majority of votes only 16 times, but the electoral laws created a single-party legislative majority in an additional 27 cases.[33] Both moderate-magnitude proportional representation and plurality/majority systems have operated to create majorities, as can be seen from the cases of

---

[32] A much more detailed discussion of the various approaches and their effects can be found in Rae, op. cit.

[33] Ibid., p. 74.

Canada, Ireland, France, and Great Britain in table VIII.3, but single-member districts do so more frequently.[34]

Coalition Formation in Legislatures. The electoral laws, the party alternatives, and the behavior of the electorate combine to create party representation in the legislature and the executive. At that point, interest aggregation becomes largely a process of forming legislative coalitions within and across parties. Students of American politics are, of course, familiar with the fact that an electoral majority, even if translated into a majority of legislative seats, does not necessarily mean that a party can control its representatives' votes in the legislature. Although party is the best indicator of how a member of the American Congress will vote, many legislative coalitions form and reform on various issues. Party is a telling indicator in part because of the general significance in constituency and issue terms of the party label.[35] Although party discipline is usually much stronger in other legislatures, party factions are always a problem. Parties vary in their ability to control the renomination of legislative candidates, although this is typically greater in the party-list proportional representation systems. But in any case, most legislatures find themselves without single-party majorities; a multiparty coalition must then be constructed in order to pass legislation and, in pure parliamentary regimes, to form a government. At a minimum, the government in such systems must have the tacit agreement of other parties not to vote it down.

The formation of legislative coalitions is a complex matter, effected by the specific legislative rules and the committee system, as well as by party discipline and party representation. Recent studies have revealed much, however, about the dynamics of this process.[36] Dodd's research on the durability of cabinet governments suggested two stages of analysis. The first question is whether or not the parties can bargain and form a

34 Ibid., pp. 75–76.

35 See John Kingdon, *Congressmen's Voting Decisions* (New York: Harper & Row, 1973); and Duncan MacRae, Jr., *Issues and Parties in Legislative Voting* (New York: Harper & Row, 1970). For an excellent review of the "party versus constituency" debate and a theoretical synthesis, see Fiorina, op. cit. Also see Sullivan and O'Connor, op. cit., on cross-constituency similarities in meaning of party.

36 See Robert Axelrod, *Conflict of Interest* (Chicago: Markham, 1970); Bruce Bueno de Mesquita, *Strategy, Risk, and Personality in Coalition Politics: The Case of India* (New York: Cambridge University Press, 1975); S. Groennings, E. W. Kelley, and M. Leiserson, eds., *The Study of Coalition Behavior* (New York: Holt, Rinehart and Winston, 1970); Abram de Swaan, *Coalition Theories and Cabinet Formation* (Amsterdam: Elsevier, 1973); Lawrence C. Dodd, *Coalitions in Parliamentary Government* (Princeton: Princeton University Press, 1976). The major intellectual stimulus to such coalition studies came from William H. Riker, *The Theory of Political Coalitions* (New Haven: Yale University Press, 1962).

particular type of coalition: a "minimum winning coalition." The second stage has to do with the ability of the coalition to weather various challenges and to govern effectively.

In table VIII.4 one sees the fate of cabinets of various coalition types, as reported in Dodd's comparative analysis of fifteen nations with similar parliamentary forms between 1918 and 1972. The concepts are quite straightforward. A minimum winning coalition is one whose parties control over 50 percent of the seats in the legislature, but in which the withdrawal of any single party from the coalition would cause it to lose its majority. An "undersize" coalition is one whose parties have less than 50 percent of the legislative seats, even though they make up the government and share the cabinet posts. An "oversize" coalition controls a parliamentary majority and would still do so, even if one or more parties left the coalition. As shown quite clearly in table VIII.4, the more a coalition deviates from minimal winning, the less durable the coalition.

Undersize coalition cabinets tend to be defeated in a vote or to resign in despair over their inability to govern. Oversize coalition governments tend to break up and be reformed with fewer parties, an outcome predicted by Riker's well-known theory, which develops the argument that members of such coalitions would be better off in smaller coalitions

Table VIII.4.   *Minimum Winning Coalitions and the Durability of Cabinet*
               Governments in Fifteen Nations, 1918-72

Size of party coalition in cabinet	Average durability of cabinet in months		
	No single party majority	Single party majority	All cabinets
Very oversized	7	19	9
Quite oversized	13	35	15
Oversized	25	22	25
Slightly oversized	18	30	20
Minimum winning	53	67	58
Slightly undersized	29	–	29
Undersized	17	–	17
Quite undersized	16	–	16
Very undersized	13	–	13

Source: Table adapted from Dodd, *Coalitions in Parliamentary Government*, p. 159.
Note: A minimum winning coalition has over 50% of the parliamentary seats, but the deletion of any one party from the coalition will deprive it of its parliamentary majority. If the coalition is oversized, the deletion of a party will leave it with a majority; the degree to which it is oversized depends on the percentage of seats held by the party (or parties) whose deletion would leave a majority. If the coalition is undersized, it lacks a parliamentary majority; the degree to which it is undersized depends on the percentage of seats held by the party (or parties) needed to make a majority.

where the payoffs would not have to be so widely shared.[37] One especially interesting point is that multiparty coalitions can be quite stable if they are "minimum winning," lasting about four years on the average. Indeed, Dodd shows that during some historical periods such coalitions have been more stable than single-party majority governments.[38]

If stable cabinets tend to depend on minimum winning coalitions, what factors affect the formation of such coalitions? Here the answer is less clear, for the specific goals of the various parties, their relative sizes, and the strategies and tactics of the leaders are all relevant to the analysis.[39] Dodd's study of coalition cabinets suggests three factors inhibiting the formation of minimum winning coalitions: rapid turnover in legislative representation, which affects the information parties have about each other and the familiarity of the various leaderships with each other; the fractionalization of the legislature into many parties; and the polarization of the party system.[40]

When the strength of parties in the legislature changes swiftly, it is difficult to know the present and future bargaining possibilities, and oversize coalitions seem attractive. When there are many parties, coalition building is very complicated because there are so many possible combinations. Mitra's work also suggests that the presence of many issues may be a problem associated with fractionalization.[41] When many issue dimensions cut across each other and saliences vary, no single coalition may be stable.[42] As in the early Fourth French Republic, governments may form on one issue dimension, such as the economy, only to fall as soon as the opposition can bring up an issue, such as religious schools, that divides the members of the coalition.[43]

Taken individually, these factors may not make stable cabinet government impossible. The legislatures in the Netherlands, for example, have typically been characterized by many parties and high fractionalization,

---

[37] Riker, op. cit. Also see Riker and Ordeshook, op. cit., chap. 6. Riker refers to this theory as "the size principle."

[38] Dodd, op. cit.

[39] See the discussions of coalition formation in many settings in Gabriel A. Almond, Scott Flanagan, and Robert Mundt, eds., *Crisis, Choice, and Change* (Boston: Little, Brown, 1973), especially chap. 2.

[40] Dodd, op. cit.

[41] Subrata K. Mitra, "Ideological Structure, Strategy, and Cabinet Instability" (Ph.D. diss., University of Rochester, 1976). Mitra found that unidimensionality of party positions on campaign issues was a strong predictor of cabinet stability in five Indian states. Dodd assumes unidimensionality of his multiple issues, but his fractionalization measure may tap multidimensionality also. See chap. II for discussion of single and multiple issue dimensions.

[42] Mitra, op. cit.

[43] See Duncan MacRae, *Parliament, Parties, and Society in France, 1946–1958* (New York: St. Martin's Press, 1967).

as indicated in table VIII.3. The fractionalization has typically made coalition formation difficult, and the Dutch system has often spent months without a government while the parties haggled over coalition formation. However, the low or moderate polarization and the historic stability of representation and leadership have led to the formation of rather stable governments once the coalition was formed — substantially fewer postwar governments than in France, Finland, Italy, or Belgium.

It is clear from the last column in table VIII.3 that systems with fewer parties and occasional one-party majorities (as in Norway and Sweden) have had fewer and more durable governments. On the other hand, high polarization, shifting votes, and numerous parties have been associated with governmental instability as in Fourth Republic France, Weimar Germany, Italy, and Finland.[44] In the first two cases the very high polarization and governmental instability contributed to their eventual collapse.

Competitive party systems are complex structures. In touching briefly on the effects of governmental organization, parties and their strategies, electoral behavior, electoral laws, and legislative coalition formation, we have only scratched the surface of the knowledge now available. In our later discussion of polarization we want to return to the effects of coalition building on governmental stability and policy making. But first we must consider other structures that play a major role in interest aggregation, structures that are, indeed, more predominant in the contemporary world than are competitive party systems.

NONCOMPETITIVE POLITICAL PARTIES: CORPORATIVE AND HIERARCHICAL

Noncompetitive political parties are also specialized interest aggregation structures, attempting to develop policy alternatives and to mobilize support for them. But they do so quite differently than the competitive parties and party systems we have been discussing. Here aggregation takes place only within the ranks of the party or in interactions with institutional interest groups in the bureaucracy or the military. We distinguish two major variants of the noncompetitive party, according to their degree of internal hierarchical control and their relationship with subgroups.

The Corporatist Political Party. The corporatist party permits some autonomous formation of demands within its own ranks or by associa-

---

[44] Dodd, op. cit. And see Michael Taylor and V. M. Herman, "Party Systems and Governmental Stability," *APSR* 65 (March 1971): 28–37. They found an excluded "anti-system" party a major cause of instability in cabinets, along with fractionalization.

tional interest groups associated with it. The degree of internal aggregation and open bargaining may be quite substantial and take many forms.
In Mexico the PRI (Party of the Institutional Revolution) dominates
the political process, and there has been little chance of another party
winning a national electoral victory. The PRI has maintained general
popular support since the creation of a broad coalition by Cárdenas in
the 1930s and also controls the counting of the ballots. Its actions are
not shaped by the logic of electoral competition. But the party incorpo-
rates many associational interest groups within its internal structure,
with separate sectors for labor, agrarian, and middle-class interests. In
addition to these formal corporate components, the party has typically
given informal recognition to distinct and well-organized political factions grouped behind influential political figures.

Various Mexican leaders and, above all, the incumbent President
mobilize their factions within the PRI and in other important groups
not directly affiliated with it, such as big business interests. Such bargaining is particularly important in presidential election years when a new
presidential nominee must be chosen by the party. The long-honored
tradition and legal provision in Mexico that incumbent Presidents may
not succeed themselves guarantees some turnover of elites and facilitates,
perhaps, a more open internal bargaining process. Recent discontent
has suggested, however, some of the difficulties in incorporating all interests, particularly those of the urban and rural poor who have not shared
in Mexico's general economic growth.[45]

Another interesting variation of the corporatist party is in Tanzania,
where the Tanzanian African National Union (TANU) controls nominations, but requires that two candidates be nominated in each district
for the elections. This presence of two candidates permits local interests
to form behind one or the other and encourages the party toward more
open internal aggregation. The defeat of many Cabinet members by
little-known local candidates suggests that the competition is more than
an illusion. At the same time, control over the nomination and the prohibition against parties other than the TANU obviously limit the kinds
of groups that are allowed to mobilize support.[46]

Neighboring Kenya has had a more personalistic, factionalized, and
tribal-oriented set of conflicts within the KANU party and less central
party control over candidates. But in both Tanzania and Kenya the
electoral process has contributed to substantial turnover of individual

---

[45] See the general discussion of communication problems in one-party regimes and
specific footnote references to studies of Mexico in chap. VII.

[46] Henry Bienen, *Tanzania: Party Transformation and Economic Development*
(Princeton: Princeton University Press, 1970).

elites and hence to pressure for attention to constituent needs, as well as citizen perception of elite responsiveness. In Kenya in 1969, half of the former Members of Parliament who contested seats for reelection were defeated, including five Ministers.[47] Moreover, the electoral process has played an important role in shaping competition within the elite groups. According to Bienen,

> it must be emphasized that elections counted in Kenya despite the fact that they were often highly constrained. . . . National leaders had to be able to hold their constituencies. They had to make a good showing in elections and where possible to use their influence to help their supporters win election.[48]

The mobilization of support in the corporatist one-party systems often resembles the patron-client structures discussed earlier. The party provides concrete services needed by the local patronage group and deals out such services to the patron, who is often directly incorporated as a local party leader. In return, the clients provide the local leader and his party faction with consistent voting support and can mobilize electoral activity.

Similar arrangements are also often found in local settings within national competitive party systems. The American party city machine is a well-known example. Such machines got their start by providing economic services, security, and help with bureaucratic red tape for the new immigrant groups to the American cities during the nineteenth and early twentieth centuries. Some machines of this kind, such as the Chicago organization long run by Mayor Richard Daley, remain powerful forces. With little chance of electoral defeat and a pervasive network of local ward leaders integrated into the personal face-to-face networks at the local party leader. In return, the clients provide the local leader and his structures. The long-standing governmental parties within the competitive systems of Italy and Venezuela have used their bureaucratic controls and connections with the face-to-face village networks of peasants to incorporate patron-client relations in similar fashion.[49] However, these parties remain constrained by competitive electoral systems and the dynamics discussed in the previous section.

The Hierarchical Governing Party. The hierarchical governing party, unlike its corporatist counterpart, does not openly recognize the legitimacy of internal interest aggregation, nor of aggregation by autonomous

---

[47] Henry Bienen, *Kenya: The Politics of Participation and Control* (Princeton: Princeton University Press, 1974), p. 112.

[48] Ibid., pp. 103–4.

[49] See J. D. Powell, "Peasant Society and Clientelist Politics," and the various works by J. C. Scott cited earlier.

social groups. Some limited forms of interest articulation may be permitted to controlled institutional or associational groups. But the open mobilization of support for alternative policy positions is not permitted. In such regimes as the Soviet Union and Communist China, the party is an instrument for mobilizing mass support behind the policies developed at the top level. The Chinese regime, for example, has not typically recognized the legitimacy of any large internal groups. Interest articulation by individuals, within certain bounds, may be permitted, but the mobilization of wider support before the top elite has made its decision is not.[50] The parties play important roles in the mobilization of support for policies. An unchallenged ideological focus provides legitimacy and coherence, and the party is used to penetrate and organize most social structures in its name and in accordance with centralized policies.

The hierarchical ruling party, as we have suggested, may be the focus of more internal aggregation at various levels than is legitimately recognized.[51] Internally, various groups may coalesce behind such sectoral interests as region or type of industry or behind leaders who represent policy factions. Generational differences or differences of temperament may distinguish hard-liners and soft-liners, for example, in foreign and defense policy. Either covertly, beneath the supposedly united front, or openly in times of crisis, severe power struggles may erupt, with different leaders mobilizing backing for themselves and seeking positions within the party. Succession crises are particularly likely to generate such power struggles, as demonstrated at the death of Stalin in the Soviet Union and recently at the death of Mao Tse-tung in China.

The party itself may also be challenged by other political structures and may appear as only one among several policy aggregators. A spectacular example was the period of the Cultural Revolution in China, with Mao Tse-tung apparently using the students and the army against the entrenched party bureaucracy to force a more populist policy. And the hierarchical governing parties of Eastern Europe have been constrained in their actions by pressure from the Soviet Union, which has set limits on the kinds of policy alternatives that may be considered.

As an instrument designed for unified policy mobilization, the hierarchical governing party has seemed an attractive model to many political leaders committed to massive social change. The party that was successful

[50] See Herbert Franz Schurmann, *Ideology and Organization in Communist China* (Berkeley and Los Angeles: University of California Press, 1968).
[51] See especially the essays by Skilling and Barghoorn in Robert A. Dahl, ed., *Regimes and Oppositions* (New Haven: Yale University Press, 1973); and other references to group behavior in the USSR cited in chap. VII. Also see the essay by the editors and the essay by Andrew C. Janos, in S. P. Huntington and C. H. Moore, eds., *Authoritarian Politics in Modern Society* (New York: Basic Books, 1970); and Kenneth Jowitt, "An Organizational Approach to the Study of Political Culture in Marxist-Leninist Systems, *APSR* 68 (September 1974): 1171–91.

in mobilizing a colonial people behind an independence movement, for example, might be used to penetrate and change an underdeveloped society. However, as the experience of many new nations has underlined, the creation of a genuinely hierarchical and penetrative governing party that could be used for social transformation is itself extremely difficult. The protracted guerrilla warfare that contributed to the development of the Chinese party is not easily replicated, nor is the external Soviet involvement that has played an essential role in Eastern Europe and North Korea. Indigenous Communism in Yugoslavia has taken a more decentralized and corporatist form, both as a matter of creative policy and in recognition of the party's broad linkages to local peasant supporters.[52] The stable one-party regimes in most underdeveloped nations have for the most part been involved in explicit military coalitions, as in Egypt, or are internally corporatist, as in Tanzania, Kenya, the Ivory Coast, and Mexico. The hierarchical models undertaken in some African states have proved to have limited penetrative capacity, and Nkrumah's effort in Ghana was easily toppled by a military coup.

Indeed, as the wave of coups in the single-party African systems in the late 1960s and early 1970s so conclusively demonstrated, the development of a stable corporatist party system is no easy matter, either. The relative success of the corporatist party systems in Mexico, Kenya, and Tanzania ought not to obscure the frequent failure of efforts to establish such structures in many other systems in the developing areas. Moreover, many of the corporatist systems exist in uneasy and unstable coalition with the armed forces.[53] One might tentatively assume that in Egypt, Burma, and the Congo the single-party systems play the more critical interest aggregation role on a day-to-day basis, but there is no doubt that the military is crucial in sustaining the chief executive and it predominates in affairs touching its special interests.

MILITARY GOVERNMENTS

We cannot leave our consideration of structures performing interest aggregation without some consideration of military governments. The last decade has seen the overthrow of many single-party and multiparty regimes established in the new nations following their independence. In some cases the party-based regime was replaced with another, but more frequently the new regime was based on the military, or on the military as at least one of the most important interest aggregators. Even where

---

[52] See Bogdan Denis Denitch, *The Legitimation of a Revolution: The Yugoslav Case* (New Haven: Yale University Press, 1976).

[53] In general, see the excellent discussion of "fluid parties and quasi-parties" by Sartori, op. cit., chap. 8.

civilian rule was later reestablished, the experience of successful military intervention seems to interject the military more or less permanently as a major policy contender. In Brazil the military played a critical interest aggregation role in the democratic processes before 1964, the dominant aggregating and policy-making roles after 1964. In Nigeria the collapse of democracy into civil war has resulted in continuing military rule, and the overthrow of Nkrumah in Ghana has been followed by military rule interspersed with competitive party experimentation. In Peru military governments have been the rule for a decade. And in many other nations, including Syria, Bangladesh, Indonesia, Mali, Uganda, Bolivia, and Chile, the military has become the critical, or at least a major, interest aggregator.

Table VIII.5 provides an estimate of the most important interest aggregation structure in the 118 sizable (over one million in population) independent nations in various regions of the world at the beginning of

Table VIII.5. *Regimes Classified by Predominant Interest Aggregation Structure in 1975-76*

| | Predominant type of interest aggregation structure | | | | | |
Region of world	Competitive party/ Assembly system	Noncompetitive party system	Military	Other[a]	Total	(Nations)
Atlantic	88	6	6	0	100	(17)
Eastern Europe and Northern Asia	0	100	0	0	100	(11)
Middle East (incl. Greece and Turkey)	20	20	33	27	100	(15)
Southern and Southeast Asia	36	36	19	9	100	(22)
Sub-Sahara Africa	3	48.5	48.5	0	100	(33)
Latin America	30	15	45	10	100	(20)
Total	28	35	29	8	100	
(Nations)	(33)	(42)	(34)	(9)		(118)

Source: Estimates based on a variety of sources, including Arthur Banks, *Political Handbook of the World, 1976* (New York: McGraw-Hill, 1976); and the *Statesman's Year Book, 1975-76* (New York: St. Martin's Press, 1975). Also see Sartori, op. cit., chap. 8.

Note: Only nations with over one million population are included. Atlantic region includes Western Europe, the United States, and Canada. Classification should be considered a rough estimate; see discussion in text.

[a]The "other" category includes the traditional monarchies of Saudi Arabia, Iran, Jordan, Nepal, and Morocco, as well as the primarily executive/bureaucracy-based systems of the Philippines, Paraguay, and Haiti.

1976. These figures must be taken only as a rough approximation, both because knowledge of the politics of some nations is limited and because relative importance in interest aggregation will vary with different issues and circumstances even within a single nation. But the table provides a general idea of the importance of the three major forms — competitive party/assembly systems, one-party structures, and military organizations — within the different political systems. It is perhaps most striking that systems in which the military is the predominant interest aggregator are about as common as each type of party-dominated system. Military-dominated governments are particularly frequently found in Africa and Latin America and play a large role in the Middle East.

The virtual monopoly of coercive resources held by the military organizations of a regime give the military potentially great power as a political contender. The major limitation on military organizations as contenders is, however, the fact that their internal structures are not well designed for interest aggregation across a range of issues or outside the purely coercive arena. The military structure is organized primarily to facilitate downward processing of commands involving the use of military power and is not typically set up to compromise and aggregate internal differences, or to mobilize wide support behind authoritative policy. Military organizations are not easily adapted to rally or communicate with social groups outside the command hierarchy. In these respects they lack advantages in support mobilization held by party systems. Such internal limitations may be less serious when dealing with common corporate grievances and when putting pressure on — or seizing power from — the incumbent authorities. But these limitations become a real problem in mobilizing backing for, say, economic development policy. Legitimate authority and communication that transmits the political and ideological goals of the regime to many social sectors are needed for such goals in the long run.

After some experience with intervention or with operation of a governing military bureaucracy, the military organization may well attempt to develop, at least informally, more specialized internal aggregation structures. The Brazilian military, for example, seems to have developed fairly clear-cut interest factions in the late 1960s and to have had policy formation structured by the activities carried out in these subcoalitions of officers. The military leaders may also encourage formation of a subordinate single party to assist the civilian bureaucracy in gaining support of the population for policies. However, without some fairly systematic way of aggregating internal interests or of mobilizing around a single command, the military is extremely vulnerable to countercoups from within its own ranks.

Military intervention is often undertaken to suppress polarization in society or to remedy the shortcomings of the existing party system. But unless it can develop a successful alternative to the party system, it may fall back on the use of raw force to suppress dissent. This may lead to conflicts within the military itself, to bloody preventative purges, or to immobilization in a desire to avoid internal conflict. Or its leaders may decide to return the nation to civilian rule, while continuing to play an important aggregation role in some policy areas.[54]

POLARIZATION AND DEPOLARIZATION OF INTEREST AGGREGATION

One of the most interesting and important aspects of interest aggregation is its relation to political polarization. Suppose there are several major political contenders, whether these are political parties, factions in a single-party regime, or military groups. If the contenders with most of the political resources share rather similar policy positions, polarization is said to be low. If contenders with major resources are far apart on policy preferences or are so distrustful and hostile toward each other that they are reluctant to form coalitions regardless of policies, polarization is considered to be high.[55] An extreme example of polarization is the Weimar Republic in the early 1930s, where both Communist and Nazi parties had large blocs of seats and were unwilling to form coalitions with each other or the major democratic party, the Socialists. The French Fourth Republic faced a situation nearly as serious. High polarization inhibits the ability to build stable coalitions, and policies chosen are likely to alienate groups and to tempt them to try to alter the rules of the game through force.

The level of polarization of the contenders is likely to reflect the polarization of the political culture. Deeply divided societies are likely

---

[54] The literature on the political role of military has grown rapidly in recent years. See, inter al., a review article on the Latin American literature, Abraham F. Lowenthal, "Armies and Politics in Latin America," *World Politics* (October 1974): 107 ff.; and on the African literature, Aristide Zolberg, "The Military Decade in Africa," *World Politics* (January 1973): 308 ff.; see also Catherine M. Kelleher, *Political Military Systems* (Beverly Hills: Sage Publications, 1974); Philippe C. Schmitter, *Military Rule in Latin America* (Beverly Hills: Sage Publications, 1973); Amos Perlmutter, "The Praetorian State and the Praetorian Army," *Comparative Politics* 1 (April 1969): 382 ff.; William Thompson, "Regime Vulnerability and the Military Coup," *Comparative Politics* 7 (July 1975): 459 ff.; Douglas A. Hibbs, *Mass Political Violence* (New York: John Wiley, 1973); Alfred Stepan, *The Military in Politics* (Princeton: Princeton University Press, 1971); Nordlinger, *Soldiers in Politics*; and Claude E. Welch and Arthur K. Smith, *Military Role and Rule* (North Scituate, Mass.: Duxbury Press, 1974).

[55] For a more complete discussion of polarization see Almond, Flanagan and Mundt, op. cit., chap. 2.

to produce deeply divided elite contenders, whereas consensual societies are likely to produce consensual party systems or legitimate ruling groups. However, interest aggregation is immediately responsible for the amount of polarization among the elite contenders. And elite polarization need not simply reflect the polarization in the society; it may either exacerbate or mitigate it, as resources are aggregated behind factions and parties taking various policy positions.

Consider first a relatively consensual political culture. Among citizens involved in politics, at least, most people favor issue positions within a narrow range, perhaps at the center. If interest aggregation is reflective or depolarizing, virtually all the important elite contenders will also favor positions around the center. If this is a competitive two-party system, for example, the logic of electoral competition will drive successful parties toward the center, as we pointed out earlier. In such cases, the contenders will be quite representative of the attitudes of citizens; the final policies adopted by the winning coalition will also be quite representative, as they are favored by most of the possible coalition members. It will not make too much difference which party or parties (in the multiparty case) actually form the government.

If the style of aggregation is polarizing, on the other hand, it means that the positions of the major contenders are being pulled away from the center. The party system becomes more polarized than consensual, despite citizen agreement. A minor degree of such polarization is typical in democratic systems, because the contenders attempt to differentiate themselves sufficiently to provide activists and supporters with a sense of purpose. More seriously, contenders may adopt polarizing policies in a relatively consensual society because of ideological commitments, or their sense of mutual distrust and hostility, or both. If both parties in a two-party system choose such courses of action, and if the formation of new parties is difficult because of organizational or electoral conditions, the consensual dynamics may not work effectively.[56] Moreover, the patterns of communication through party ranks may distort the images the leaders have of citizen preferences, a serious problem in authoritarian, hierarchical structures. An especially serious problem emerges if there is some ethnic or religious division and a willingness on the part of relatively small elite groups to use violence and terror to bring coercive resources into play in interest aggregation. In such cases, polarizing strategies may overwhelm citizen predispositions toward accommodation.

---

[56] Something like this seems to have been the case in Austria in the 1960s. See G. Bingham Powell, Jr., *Social Fragmentation and Political Hostility* (Stanford: Stanford University Press, 1970); Steiner, op. cit.; and Rodney P. Stiefbold, "Segmented Pluralism and Consociational Democracy in Austria," in Martin O. Heisler, ed., *Politics in Europe* (New York: David McKay, 1974), pp. 117–77.

If one considers the initially polarized society, the critical role of aggregation structures can be seen even more clearly. Aggregation that reflects citizen differences reproduces polarization among contenders, as in the citizen and elite divisions in troubled Italy, where citizens and elites alike have been deeply divided over the role of the church, social equality and income redistribution, and foreign policy.[57] A polarized style of aggregation will exacerbate and mobilize citizen differences even more extensively. Rabushka and Shepsle have suggested, for example, the role of political "entrepreneurs" in forming new parties or factions to exploit ethnic divisions in the new nations achieving independence after World War II.[58] Independence parties had typically played down ethnic differences during the struggle for independence. After independence was achieved, such parties were highly vulnerable to politicians seeking to exploit these divisions, and the more polarized style of aggregation typically led to results that satisfied the ethnic majority but severely alienated the minority. Another tragic example of polarizing aggregation is found in Northern Ireland, where terrorist campaigns and extremist leaders have been able to prevent peace, even when there seem to exist popular majorities that favor an end to bloodshed.

On the other side, depolarizing aggregation in divided societies may prevent extreme forms of conflict and sustain a potentially weak regime. In the widely discussed consociational democracy model set forth by Arend Lijphart, the various party elites make a deliberate effort to keep conflict within bounds and adopt a variety of procedural and institutional arrangements designed to accommodate their differences.[59] In the Netherlands these have included proportional participation in decision making, proportional division of benefits, secrecy and the working out of behind-the-scenes accommodative agreements, and so on. Such depolarization has also characterized Colombia at points of critical division and was elaborately developed in Austria at the top elite levels in the 1950s.[60]

A very different approach to depolarization is the solution typically attempted in military and hierarchical party regimes: one contender seizes control and imposes its will upon the society. The first steps are usually to eliminate other contenders and potential contenders and to

---

[57] See Barnes, *Representation in Italy.*

[58] Alvin Rabushka and Kenneth Shepsle, *Politics in Plural Societies* (Columbus: Merrill, 1972).

[59] Lijphart, *Politics of Accommodation,* and "Typologies of Democratic Systems," *Comparative Political Studies* 1 (April 1968).

[60] In general, see the review by Eric Nordlinger, *Conflict Regulation in Divided Societies* (Cambridge: Center for International Affairs, Harvard University, 1972).

establish a regime in which opposition party activity is suppressed. The Nazis in Germany solved the problem of polarization in Weimar in just this fashion. The extreme polarization that had developed in Chile in 1972–73 between the governing left-wing groups and the various more conservative parties in control of the legislature — which included the formation of armed groups, strikes, and land seizures — was similarly ended by a military government.

Indeed, the argument that their societies are too divided to permit the interplay of party competition is a major justification given for the imposition of one-party or military rule in many states. As many such regimes have already discovered, however, if social differences are truly deep, it will be difficult for the government to prevent polarization within its own ranks or to forestall groups from attempting to change the political system by adopting violent resistance and creating a new power contender. It is for this last reason that one-party systems typically make strong efforts to use the party organization for effective political socialization and to mitigate the cultural polarization by inculcating a common ideology and sense of identity.

INTEREST AGGREGATION AND THE DEVELOPMENTAL DIMENSION

The problem of development both affects and is shaped by the performance of interest aggregation. As we pointed out in discussing interest articulation, the tendency of social and economic modernization to expand communication levels, to increase political participation, to widen the gap between rich and poor, and generally to increase the number of autonomous demands arising from the society places growing stress on the interest aggregation structures. Effective aggregation of these diverse interests into a limited set of policy alternatives is necessary if support for the regime is to be sustained, but can be very difficult to achieve, because of the limitations on wealth and administrative capacity inevitable in nations undertaking the initial stages of economic growth. It has, in fact, proved to be nearly impossible to sustain stable competitive party systems under these conditions, for demands become nearly impossible to reconcile. Unrest and violence and eventually a breakdown of the competitive system occurred in almost all of the third world nations in the 1960s and 1970s.[61]

---

[61] The scarcity of competitive party/assembly systems in the third world is clearly shown in table VIII.5. They have virtually disappeared in Africa. In the Middle East, both Greece and Turkey have experienced intervals of military intervention, as in most of the now competitive Latin American cases. In Asia, Thailand suffered another coup in 1976; Pakistan has had repeated military intervention; Malaysia has restricted competition.

The creation of effective and stable one-party systems under these conditions has been very difficult also, and the military-based aggregation structures have been wracked by coups and purges as well. There is simply no ready structural solution to the pressures created in the process of modernization. What solutions do emerge will depend on a combination of the chosen strategy of development and the ability to create successful interest aggregation structures, both to channel demands and to mobilize compliance. As we shall discuss more fully in chapter XIII, one developmental strategy is to suppress competition and form an alliance with private middle-class interests who will push economic growth while the government maintains conditions of order. This has been the Brazilian solution, requiring only enough aggregative capacity to keep order in the military and repress potential popular insurgency.

Another approach is to repress competition, but to use the military or a civilian one-party regime to encourage both income equality and economic growth. This requires more aggregative capacity to keep interests reconciled and to mobilize support for government intervention in society and economy. Peru, South Korea, and perhaps Kenya used this strategy more or less successfully, although the military government in Peru has recently been experiencing internal conflict.

The most ambitious approach is to use aggressive interest aggregation structures to mobilize and coordinate popular backing for social change, involving, yet controlling, the activities of many social groups. The hierarchical Communist parties are the most thoroughgoing examples of this approach. Less extreme use of this strategy by corporatist parties in Mexico, Taiwan, Yugoslavia, and Tanzania has met with some success. In countries with initially low levels of development it is difficult to build a party system sufficiently independent of the localizing pressures of the society to continue social change.

We shall return to consideration of aggregation structures and development strategies in chapter XIII. At this point we can emphasize only that aggregation of resources behind stable governments is very difficult in systems undergoing major social upheavals. The tendencies for demands to outrun responsive capacity, for personalistic clientelism to fragment political resources, and for new and fragile aggregation structures to be overwhelmed by conflicting pressures are not easily controlled.

CHAPTER IX

Decision Rules and Policy Making

POLICY MAKING is the pivotal stage of the political process, the point at which effective political demands are converted into authoritative decisions. By effective demands we mean those which are advocated by political contenders who have resources — votes, seats in legislative bodies, influential positions in government and private life, money, technical knowledge and expertise, control over the media of communication, or means of coercion. The logically prior processes of recruitment, interest articulation, and aggregation will have grouped these contenders and their resources together into coalitions or potential coalitions favoring policy alternatives. Political coalitions are power-policy groupings, determined on the one hand by these prior processes and on the other by the decision rules.

DECISION RULES

The enactment and implementation of authoritative policies requires some set of decision rules — rules about rule making — determining who can do what in the enactment and implementation of policy. Decision rules include the basic grants of or limits upon authority, such as the distribution of power between central and regional units, the division of powers among governmental agencies, the protection of private rights against governmental power, and the like. They also include more specific procedural and organizational rules operative in particular agencies, such as those governing debate in legislative bodies, evidence in courts, and delegation of authority in administrative bodies. All political systems have these organizational and procedural rules, whether they are of a customary character or are formulated in explicit "constitutional" enactments, statutes, or formal regulations. Even tyrannies and highly authoritarian regimes have decision rules, though these rules may set few limits on the will of the ruler or ruling group.

The decision rules, from the perspective of groups and coalitions of groups seeking to gain political power and to make public policy, determine how the political game is played. The decision rules assign particular values to political resources and determine how policy making is to be organized, indicating, for example, who may vote for what office and what powers particular offices may exercise. In other words, the decision rules define the framework within which political contenders have to formulate their strategies and tactics and carry out their political struggles.

These decision rules are made in a variety of ways. They may simply grow out of historical practice as in the case of the British Cabinet system, or they may be the result of a conscious legislative process. The deliberate legislative process that changes the decision rules may be ordinary or extraordinary. Britain granted some federal autonomy to Scotland and Wales through a simple parliamentary statute. The original constitutions of Canada, Australia, and New Zealand were acts of the British Parliament. In the United States the written constitution may be changed only by extraordinary action calling for two-thirds majorities in both houses of Congress and for majorities in three-quarters of the state legislatures or specially elected state conventions. Countries that have written constitutions often require some extraordinary enacting process for amendments. These may take the form of a two-stage process involving both the central and local units (the United States and Switzerland), extraordinary majorities (the United States and pre-1973 Chile), or a popular referendum (Switzerland). But even in those political systems in which normal statutory processes can change the constitution, there tends to be an awareness of the importance of a parliamentary statute that changes the way policies are made. Decision rules governing the organization and procedure of specific agencies of government (such as legislative bodies, administrative agencies, and courts) are formulated by laws and statutes or by the regulations of the specific governmental agency itself.

The most fundamental of these decision rules determine (1) territorial distribution of authority among central and local units, (2) the separation and allocation of decision making to different agencies, and (3) the amount and manner of limitation on governmental powers.

TERRITORIAL DIVISION OF GOVERNMENTAL AUTHORITY

When governments are classified according to the geographic or territorial division of power, there are unitary systems at one extreme and confederated ones at the other (see table IX.1). Over 80 percent of contemporary governments are unitary, including those in democratic countries such as France, Japan, the Scandinavian nations, and most of the Communist and non-Communist authoritarian regimes. A unitary regime

Table IX.1. *Examples of Territorial Distribution of Power*

Territorially centralized ◄──────────────────────────► *Territorially decentralized*

Unitary	Formally federal	Quasi-federal	Federal	Confederal
France	USSR	Britain	USA	USA (1777–87)
Japan	Czechoslovakia	Italy	Canada	Swiss Confederation
Scandinavian	Brazil	Yugoslavia	Australia	(1813–48)
countries	Mexico		W. Germany	German Confedera-
China	Venezuela		Switzerland	tion (1813–66)
E. Germany			Austria	United Nations
Poland			India	European Economic
Rumania			Malaysia	Community
Bulgaria				
Hungary				

Sources: Ivo D. Duchacek, *Power Maps: Comparative Politics of Constitutions* (Santa Barbara, Calif.: ABC Clio Press, 1973), chaps. 4 and 5; William H. Riker, "Federalism," in Fred I. Greenstein and Nelson W. Polsby, *Handbook of Political Science* (Reading, Mass.: Addison-Wesley, 1975), 5: 93 ff.

is one in which power and authority are concentrated legally in the central institutions. Specific powers and responsibilities may be delegated to local governments and agencies, but these are subject to revocation and are usually centrally supervised.

A second category of regimes might be characterized as formally federal, but practically unitary. These would include the Soviet Union, with its fifteen union republics and other formally autonomous territorial units, and Czechoslovakia, with its provision for an autonomous Slovakia. In both of these countries the highly centralized Communist parties create a practical unitarism behind a facade of federated components. Brazilian federalism has had a long tradition and is still embodied in the Brazilian written constitution, but it is of mainly formal significance under the current military-authoritarian regime. Similarly Mexican federalism is now largely a facade, power actually being concentrated in the center.

Another class of governments may be characterized as quasi-federal. This class would include Great Britain, with its formally autonomous Northern Ireland, the powers of which have been suspended under the emergency, and with Scotland and Wales, which recently acquired differing degrees of autonomy under overall parliamentary supervision. British federalism is still too recent to treat as a stable federal system. Italy has had a formally federal system since it adopted the Constitution of 1947, and includes some twenty regions that have had long historical cultural traditions. The decentralizing provisions of the Italian constitution were only partly implemented in 1972 and have still not demonstrated much vitality. Yugoslavia is the only Communist regime in which the constituent units — the six republics — have some autonomy.

Only nineteen or twenty countries in all have federal systems in any sense of the term, but these federal systems cover about half of the land surface of the world. They include the United States, Canada, the Soviet Union, India, Australia, Brazil and Argentina.[1] In general, federalism seems to have been the constitutional arrangement adopted by countries that occupy large land masses and have regionally distinct areas with autonomous traditions and by countries that have different ethnic, linguistic, or religious groups concentrated in particular regions. The United States and Australia would fall in the first category of countries with large land masses and prior regional autonomies. Canada combines a large land mass with the ethnic particularism of the French population in Quebec. India combines a large land mass and autonomous political traditions with great ethnic-religious-linguistic diversity.

But though large size and multiethnicity seem to be associated with federal constitutional arrangements, there are large countries and multiethnic countries that have adopted unitary arrangements. China, for example, has a unitary regime. Of the smaller countries of Europe, Switzerland and Austria have federal systems, whereas Belgium and the Netherlands have unitary systems. Switzerland and Belgium are multiethnic, whereas Austria and the Netherlands are more culturally homogeneous. Thus the federal solution to the division of powers is only loosely related to size and ethnicity.

One cannot draw a hard and fast distinction between unitary and federal systems, since even in the unitary ones there is usually some delegation of authority to the local units — some power to tax or to legislate with respect to specific matters. To constitute a federal system the powers granted to the local units must not be trivial; they must be substantial. Federal systems range widely in the way in which powers are distributed. Some federal systems specifically enumerate the powers of the central government, the remainder lodging with the local units; this class includes Switzerland, West Germany, Malaysia, and the United States. Other federal systems enumerate the local powers, leaving the remainder to the central government; Canada and India are examples. Normally in federal systems there is some overlap in powers, some concurrent federal and local authority. Possible conflicts between these concurrent powers

---

[1] Compare Ivo D. Duchacek, *Power Maps* (Santa Barbara, Calif.: ABC Clio Press, 1973), p. 111; William Riker, "Federalism," in Fred I. Greenstein and Nelson W. Polsby, *Handbook of Political Science* (Reading, Mass.: Addison-Wesley, 1975), 5: 93 ff.

are usually resolved by according supremacy to the central authority. A central decision in this concurrent area supersedes a conflicting local decision. Conflicts between central and local units are usually regulated by such agencies as courts or special councils. In some federal systems, such as West Germany, the local units may be required to execute and administer central decisions.

The typical federal division of authority among central and local units assigns to the central government the power to make war, conduct foreign policy, regulate some aspects of the economy, and take some part in the provision of welfare services, while assigning to the local units some powers of maintaining internal order, regulating aspects of the local economy, and administering education, social, and health services. In federal systems both central and local governments have taxing powers. Historically, with the rise of urban industrial society and the development of highly interdependent economies, there has been a gravitation of power to the center and an attenuation of local powers. Nevertheless, there are important differences among federal systems according to the degree of this centralization, with Switzerland and Canada at the decentralized end of a continuum and West Germany and the United States at the more centralized end.[2]

Confederations differ from federations in that the central institutions, while having some formal authority, lack the means of enforcement, such as direct taxing powers and direct regulatory power. This type of system is of both historical and contemporary interest. The United States during 1777–87 operated under the Articles of Confederation, which left to the states the power to tax and directly regulate society. The Congress could make policies, but could not enforce them. Similarly, the Swiss operated under a confederated system in the period of 1813–48, and the German states operated under a loose confederation during the period of 1813–66.

In the contemporary world the most interesting confederations are the United Nations and the various regional confederations, such as the European Economic Community. The United Nations Charter commits its members to certain common policies and certain modes of resolving disputes. The Security Council and the Assembly are representative bodies charged with making decisions, and the Secretariat is charged with carrying them out. But the United Nations depends for its financing on member contributions and for the implementation of its decisions on the willingness of its members to enforce and comply with decisions made by the Security Council and the Assembly. The European Eco-

---

[2] See Duchacek, *Power Maps*, pp. 121 ff.; Riker, "Federalism," pp. 131 ff.; Robert R. Bowie and Carl J. Friedrich, *Studies in Federalism* (Boston: Little, Brown, 1954).

nomic Community, comprising nine European countries, also has policy-making and administrative agencies. In the field of tariffs, agricultural policy, and investment aid, the European Economic Community has adopted and implements common policies among the nine member nations. In other areas of public policy, the cooperation is of a more partial and ad hoc character. But even in the policy areas where a single policy is followed, the EEC depends on the voluntary compliance of its members. Consequently, we would call it a confederation, rather than a federation.[3]

SEPARATION OF GOVERNMENTAL POWERS

When governments are compared according to the concentration or separation of their powers, at any geographical level, at least four types of systems are discernible. Table IX.2 illustrates these, using our usual twenty-four nations, plus several more. In *authoritarian* regimes, such as the Soviet Union, China, Egypt, and Brazil, there is no fully settled delegation of authority to legislatures, courts, or similar structures outside the office of chief executive. In such systems, power may either be concentrated in a political bureau or military junta or, typically, consist of an uneasy balance of military factions, bureaucrats, and party leaders. But none of these groups, as they bring their political resources to bear on decision making, are faced with an accepted need to compete for autonomous citizen support. Such systems, as we saw in chapter III, vary greatly in the extent to which they permit autonomy of other social systems in the society or strive to control all aspects of political and social life. But in all of them the rules of governmental decision making involve a concentrated focus on executive action.

Parliamentary regimes, such as those of Britain, Canada, West Germany, and Japan, are characterized by a combination of political executive and a directly linked, significant legislature. In most such regimes, the political executive, usually called a cabinet or council of ministers, is selected from the assembly and holds office only as long as it can command the support of a majority in the assembly. In some countries, such as West Germany, a positive replacement of one party government with another is required, in a "constructive" vote of no confidence in the government. In all these systems the prime ministers and cabinets have clearly settled spheres of authority.

Governmental powers are the most sharply separated in *presidential* regimes, of which the United States is the outstanding example. The principal characteristics of the presidential system are that political

[3] Ernst B. Haas, *The Obsolescence of Regional Integration Theory* (Berkeley: Institute of International Studies, 1975), pp. 72 ff.

Table IX.2.   *Concentration and Separation of Powers*
               in Contemporary Political Systems

Concentrated ←			→ Separated
Authoritarian	*Parliamentary*	*Mixed parliamentary-presidential*	*Presidential*
Czechoslovakia	Sweden	France	USA
USSR	Canada	Finland	Venezuela
Spain (through	W. Germany		Chile (to 1973)
1975)	Japan		
Bulgaria	Austria		
Yugoslavia	Britain		
Chile (post 1973)	Israel		
Mexico	Italy		
Brazil	India		
Peru			
China			
Egypt			
Nigeria			
Kenya			
Tanzania			

Note: Within each category, nations are listed in order of 1973 GNP/capita. For illustrative purposes, several additional cases are added to our standard 24 countries.

executives are independently elected, hold office for their legal term whether or not they are supported by the legislature, and have substantial rule-making and implementing powers.[4] Yet, in the true presidential system, the assembly retains a major share of policy-making authority and is also electorally responsible. Chile, prior to the military coup in 1973, was a genuine presidential regime with power divided between an independently elected executive and a legislature. A number of other "presidential" regimes in Latin America and elsewhere more closely correspond to the authoritarian regime described above, as does Brazil. Mexico, although formally presidential, is nearly authoritarian, as the executive dominates the assembly in all elements of the policy process, and the degree of competition for citizen support has been very limited under the domination of the PRI party. Similarly, Tanzania has been very strongly dominated by the presidency under Nyerere, although under a successor the system might move toward a more even balance of assembly participation.

---

[4] See Duchacek, *Power Maps*, chaps. 6 and 7; Anthony King, "Executives," in Greenstein and Polsby, op. cit., 5: 173 ff.

France under the Fifth Republic is a *mixed parliamentary-presidential regime*. Presidents of France are elected by popular vote, hold office for a seven-year term whether or not they are supported by the National Assembly, and have substantial powers. French Prime Ministers are appointed by and may be removed by the President, and yet they depend also on a majority in the National Assembly. Thus far in the Fifth Republic, the system has been sustained by a National Assembly majority supportive of the President. The real test of the system may occur when this majority dissolves and a contest occurs between the President and the National Assembly over the appointment of a Prime Minister and a Council of Ministers.

In a parliamentary system the cabinet or council of ministers is constituted from the leaders of the majority party or from the majority coalition of parties in the parliamentary assembly. A single party or coalition of parties controls both the political executive and the legislature. In the presidential system there is always the possibility that different political parties will control the political executive and the legislature. The assumption is that policy making is more expeditious in the parliamentary system than in the presidential, where deadlocks are more possible. Although this is normally the case, the majority party in parliamentary systems may be seriously divided, and part of it may oppose the cabinet, thus complicating and delaying the legislative process. Where a coalition of parties is required because no one party has a majority, similarly, there is a possibility of conflict among the parties in the coalition both in the legislature and the executive. Thus, there is no hard and fast conclusion that one can draw about the relative efficiency of parliamentary and presidential systems. Their workings and efficiency depend on the characteristics of the party system.

LIMITATION OF GOVERNMENTAL POWERS

The concept of separation of powers is usually associated with clear institutional and legal divisions between the political executive, legislative, and judicial agencies of government, and it is closely related to another important concept in political theory, that of constitutionalism.[5] Systems in which the powers of various governmental units are defined and limited by written constitution, statutes, or custom are called *constitutional regimes*.[6] Constitutional regimes also typically restrict govern-

---

[5] For a good recent analysis of the separation of powers doctrine see M. J. C. Vile, *Constitutionalism and the Separation of Powers* (Oxford: Clarendon Press, 1967); and Henry J. Merry, *Montesquieu's System of Natural Government* (West Lafayette, Ind.: Purdue University Press, 1970).

[6] For an excellent discussion of constitutionalism see Harvey Wheeler, "Constitutionalism" in Greenstein and Polsby, op. cit., 5: 1 ff. Also Carl J. Friedrich, *Limited Government: A Comparison* (Englewood Cliffs: Prentice-Hall, 1974).

Table IX.3. *Limitation of Powers by Courts*

Courts not independent	Independent courts	Judicial review of governmental powers
USSR	Britain	USA
China	Belgium	W. Germany
Eastern European countries	Netherlands	Italy
		Canada
Brazil		Austria
Chile		Japan

mental power as such. Citizens' rights — like a fair trial and freedom to speak, petition, publish, and assemble — are protected against governmental interference except under unusual and specific circumstances. The courts can be crucial institutions in the limitation of governmental power. If the courts are not independent, it is difficult, if not impossible, to prevent excesses of power and to protect individual rights.

Governments may be divided into those, at one extreme, in which the power to coerce citizens is nearly unlimited by the courts; at the other extreme are systems in which the courts not only protect the rights of citizens but also can police other parts of the government to see that their powers are properly exercised (see table IX.3). The United States is the best example of a system in which political power is limited by the courts. Its institution of judicial review allows the federal and state courts to rule that other parts of the government have exceeded their powers. Most constitutional regimes have independent courts that protect citizens against the improper implementation of laws and regulations, but may not overrule the assembly and the political executive. The substantive rights of citizens in these systems are protected by custom, self-restraint, and political pressure, rather than by judicial process.

Judicial review of actions by the legislature and executive used to be an American "peculiarity" much debated and criticized by constitutional lawyers and political theorists. The main argument against it was that it gave substantial political power to an agency — the judiciary — that was supposed to be politically neutral. But the collapse of constitutional regimes in Germany, Italy, and Japan and the world experience with tyranny in the 1930s and 1940s led to a widespread imitation of American practice.[7] Thus the constitution of Japan, which was prepared under

---

[7] See Henry Ehrmann, *Comparative Legal Cultures* (Englewood Cliffs: Prentice-Hall, 1976), pp. 138 ff.

the American occupation and actually drafted by the occupation authorities, specifically provides for a Supreme Court with power to rule on the constitutionality of all laws, orders, and regulations. In practice the Japanese Supreme Court has overturned some administrative regulations, but has not as yet declared any major pieces of legislation unconstitutional.[8] The German constitutional court has been more "activist." [9] Those countries which have recently adopted some form of judicial review usually depart from the American practice of a federal judiciary appointed for life. In Japan, judges of the Supreme Court, though appointed by the Cabinet, may be recalled by popular election at the end of ten years. The Federal Constitutional Court of Germany is composed of sixteen judges, half elected by the lower house and half elected by the upper house of the West German Parliament. And the Italian Constitutional Court is appointed by the President of the Republic, the Parliament, and the Italian highest court of appeals; its members serve twelve-year terms. These new judicial institutions, however, have developed differently from the American. The tradition of judicial review of statutes is not as thoroughly established except in the German constitutional court. In most of these nations the courts perform other functions than the American system permits, such as providing advisory opinions, supervising referenda or presidential and parliamentary elections, and the like.[10]

Most modern constitutions contain guarantees of rights and liberties, some of which specify limits on the exercise of governmental powers, whereas others elaborate the duties and obligations of governments to their citizens. Duchacek summarizes these constitutional provisions under six categories:

(1) Guarantees of personal liberty, right to privacy, freedom of thought, right to equality, and minority and women's rights. . . .
(2) Right to social progress and happiness.
(3) Right to impartial justice.
(4) Freedom of expression and the right to be informed.
(5) Right of access to decision making through the intermediary of political parties and universal suffrage.
(6) Right to formulate specific group demands and form interest groups for this purpose.[11]

[8] Nobutake Ike, *Japanese Politics* (New York: Alfred A. Knopf, 1972).
[9] Lewis Edinger, *Politics in Germany* (Boston: Little, Brown, 1977), pp. 308–12; Arnold Heidenheimer, *The Governments of Germany* (New York: Crowell & Co., 1966), pp. 161 ff.
[10] See Duchacek, *Power Maps,* 214 ff.
[11] Ivo Duchacek, *Rights and Liberties in the World Today* (Santa Barbara, Calif.: ABC Clio Press, 1973), pp. 40 ff.

There has been a historical trend in the development of these conceptions of rights. In the eighteenth and nineteenth centuries the rights that were specified in constitutions, statutes, and regulations were restrictions on government power; they usually were formulated in negative terms, as in the First Amendment of the American Constitution:

> Congress shall make no law respecting an establishment of religion, or prohibiting the free exercise thereof; of abridging freedom of speech, or of the press; or of the right of the people peaceably to assemble, and to petition the government for a redress of grievances.

More recently, written constitutions have come to include positive rights and opportunities, as in the right to equality, social progress, and happiness (see items 1 and 2 of Duchacek's list). They have also become far more detailed and specific, elaborating the rights of political party and interest group membership, the right to be informed, the rights to an education or employment, and the like. Written constitutions in Communist countries stress these social rights, whereas liberal democratic constitutions stress prohibitions on government invasion of citizen rights.[12]

Needless to say, there are wide discrepancies between rights specified in written constitutions and rights that are realized. Genuine protections of rights and liberties, the real limitation of governmental power, depends on some separation of governmental powers, particularly an independent system of courts, and on free and competitive elections.

The great majority of countries in the world today are authoritarian. Only around thirty countries can properly be classed as democracies;[13] the remaining hundred or so are some variety of authoritarian system. From the point of view of our discussion of the distribution of and limits on power, these authoritarian regimes tend to be unitary in fact, if not in law; power is concentrated rather than separated; and the courts in most cases are not independent. But this tells us what authoritarian regimes are *not*. As we indicated in chapter III, this large group of regimes can be classified according to their system, process, and policy characteristics.[14] Some of them are quite loosely organized regimes with substantial traditional limits on the exercise of political power (Saudi Arabia); others are relatively pluralistic, permitting some groups and interests to participate in policy making (Mexico); still others are quite dynamic, highly organized and mobilized, with decision making sharply

---

[12] Ibid., pp. 43 ff.
[13] See Juan Linz, "Authoritarian Regimes," in Greenstein & Polsby, op. cit., 3: 180–81.
[14] Ibid., pp. 278 ff. And see chaps. XIII and XIV.

concentrated at the center and no effective limits on the exercise of power (the Soviet Union).

POLICY MAKING: HISTORICAL PERSPECTIVE

The idea of policy making and its formal institutionalization are relatively recent developments. Although primitive and traditional political systems normally provide for enforcement and adjudication, it is more difficult to explicate the processes that formulate general policies themselves. It is the very essence of traditionality that policy making be problematic and extraordinary. The ancient codes of law were credited to great lawgivers, such as Hammurabi, Moses, Solon, or Lycurgus, who either codified the traditional rules — in other words, "declared" them — or transmitted laws charismatically as intermediaries for deities or as men of extraordinary virtue and wisdom. The making of laws was viewed as an extraordinary event.

Policy making in the traditional and primitive political systems tends to be either a charismatic process or a slow, incremental process of the accumulation of tradition, which is in part a derivative of day-to-day enforcements and adjudications. It is possible for outsiders to distinguish the policy-making function in such political systems and to describe the structures that engage in it. Members of most traditional or primitive societies, on the other hand, would not admit the legitimacy of a policy-making function as we understand it. They might acknowledge the legitimacy of a prophetic representation of the will of the deity or a magical communication with extranatural powers, but they would not acknowledge the legitimacy of a process whereby new rules are made by specific institutions and deliberative processes.

In the simpler intermittent political systems, the structure or institution involved in the making of general decisions may be the group of adult males in the band or village, or the lineage elders intermittently meeting as a council, or those holding specialized roles, such as the village head or the magical leader. These groups and individuals are the codifiers and repositories of the political system's traditions, which they bring to bear on problems arising out of the activities of the community or out of its interactions with other communities. Each action involves bringing out of memory the appropriate principles, customs, or standards, and each time these traditions are invoked in specific contexts something may be added and something left out so that the traditions are adapted or changed.[15]

---

[15] Adamson Hoebel, *The Law of Primitive Man* (Cambridge: Harvard University Press, 1954), p. 285.

In patrimonial kingdoms, the policy-making structures may consist of political rulers such as kings, councils of officials, and individual officials, who either declare what the law is or adapt and modify it as they confront specific cases. In these political systems there may also be prophets and lawgivers who are active primarily in times of conflict and threat and who may reaffirm traditional rules or transmit new rules attributed to extranatural forces.

In his treatment of the historical bureaucratic empires, Eisenstadt uses the rulers' pursuit of autonomous goals as one of the criteria defining these systems. In this larger-scale, differentiated political system (for example, the Persian and Roman empires), which Eisenstadt views as transitional to modern political systems, one begins to get a differentiated policy-making function.[16] Similarly, in some of the ancient and medieval city-states, there was an explicit legislative process lodged in a legislative body or bodies.

The policy-making function as such in Britain did not become fully differentiated until the fifteenth and sixteenth centuries. The Magna Carta represented an effort on the part of the nobility to maintain the validity of the ancient feudal freedoms and customs against the efforts of King John to develop new powers of taxation and regulation. It was justified as a declaration of *the* law, rather than an enactment of new law.[17] In the interaction between Kings and Parliaments in Britain during the thirteenth, fourteenth, and fifteenth centuries, one can observe the gradual differentiation of a general policy-making function. The process began as a series of bargains in which the King acquired the right to impose specific tax measures in exchange for the redress of specific grievances. In this centuries-long interplay of demand and response, the power of Parliament to enact statutes slowly became legitimate, an appropriate function to be performed by "the King in Parliament." Similar struggles over the differentiation of a policy-making function are to be observed in the history of continental European countries such as France and Prussia, although the process and the institutional results differed substantially from the British pattern. The Kings acquired the policy-making power and not "the King in Parliament."

The long history of the emergence of the British Parliament is one of struggle over the location of the policy-making power and over questions concerning which elements in the society ought to be represented. The struggle between King, Lords, and Commons continued until the eight-

---

16 S. N. Eisenstadt, *The Political Systems of Empires* (New York: Free Press of Glencoe, 1963).

17 F. W. Maitland, *The Constitutional History of England* (Cambridge: Cambridge University Press, 1963), pp. 90 ff.

eenth century, when the statutory power of the houses of Parliament was formally legitimated and established. But if the struggle was settled formally, it continued politically as the King and powerful aristocrats sought to control Parliament through family, patronage, and electoral manipulation. In the nineteenth century the emergence of mass politics and disciplined parties shifted the locus of struggle to electoral competition, and the contemporary pattern of policy making by Cabinets based on party majorities in the House of Commons appeared.

Throughout this long history, however, the houses of Parliament, with rare though important exceptions, tended to be legitimators and modifiers of policies rather than policy makers. In the early period the initiation and formulation of statutes came from the King and his officials, and these were modified and authorized in the houses of Parliament. In the later period the initiation and formulation of general policies came from the higher civil service, the Ministers and the Cabinet. Thus, the bodies that one thinks of as being the specialized legislative structures have never been the policy makers in the full sense of that term.

THE POLICY-MAKING PROCESS
POLICY AND IMPLEMENTATION

Policy making and policy implementation are continuous processes. It is difficult to establish a boundary where the one ends and the other begins. Political executives and legislators cannot always anticipate the conditions that will obtain when the policy that they have enacted reaches the point of implementation. Normally they will accord or delegate some discretion to the officials charged with the enforcement of a law. Traffic police enforcing a regulation do not simply enforce the law automatically; they have a range of discretion and may construe the rules of traffic safety differently in good or bad weather. It is usual for policy makers to delegate to specialized administrative agencies the power to issue regulations consistent with statutory enactments. These regulations are "subpolicies" falling within the framework of goals and means established by the general policy. These administrative regulations outnumber the statutes many times over. The operative tax legislation in a given country may occupy a few volumes; the tax regulations may occupy many volumes. When President Carter ordered his department heads to read and approve all the regulations emanating from their departments in the interest of clarity and simplicity, it was soon apparent that even this degree of oversight was an impossibility, so large was the daily flow of subpolicy making.

What we usually mean when we speak of policy making — as opposed to implementation — are the broader, direction-setting and means-providing phases of this continuous process. It would include the authoritative formulation of goals by the appropriate governmental authorities: for example, the decision to regulate factory safety, the assignment of authority to an agency to make and implement those regulations, and the provision of funds necessary for their implementation. Policy making, to be sure, continues beyond this as administrative authorities make new and revise old regulations and as operating officials apply these regulations in specific contexts. But for analytic convenience we draw the line somewhere between broad discretionary decisions and narrower ones.[18]

ISSUE AREAS AND POLICY SPECIALIZATION

The notion that a country has a single, homogeneous policy-making process is an abstraction. Policy-making processes operate differently in response to different kinds of issues. In his trailblazing study of the politics of New Haven, Dahl demonstrated that different political groupings were involved in decision making on different issues. This theory of policy specialization by issue area would seem to have some general validity. Thus, in American national government, all policy making would involve some pattern of accommodation between the executive and the Congress, but different parts of the executive and the Congress would be involved in the making of foreign policy, defense policy, tax policy, welfare policy, energy policy, and so on. And the structure of policy making would tend to differ in these specialized areas. The process for making foreign policy would be more centered in the executive; that for tax and welfare policy, more in the Congress.

The increasing importance of these policy specializations in modern government is suggested by recent developments in the British Cabinet system. British constitutional theory would hold that the Cabinet is the most important collective policy maker; but with the increased load and technical character of modern public business, most of the actual policy making is done by the responsible Ministers, their higher civil servants, and a specialized Cabinet committee. In recent years Cabinet action has tended to devolve upon its Committees on Defense, Home Affairs, Housing, Prices and Incomes, Europe, Social Services, Energy, and the like.[19] The Cabinet as a corporate body for the most part simply ratifies the decisions brought to it by its committees. Even in the centralized Communist regimes there is a similar pattern of specialization, with particular government ministries acting in conjunction with specialized de-

[18] See Frank Goodnow, *Politics and Administration* (New York: The Macmillan Co., 1900); also John G. Grumm, "The Analysis of Policy Impact" in Greenstein and Polsby, *Handbook of Political Science*, 6: 444–45.

[19] John Mackintosh, *The British Cabinet* (London: Methuen, 1968), pp. 511 ff.

partments of the Party Secretariat and with committees of the Politburo.[20]

Consequently, the task of characterizing a policy-making process is not the simple one of describing the grants of authority to particular agencies, but rather an attempt to discern by empirical investigation the variety of ways in which various institutions of politics and government combine in the production of specialized policies. General characterizations of individual countries and comparisons among countries have to summarize and abstract from this variety of policy-making processes.

POLICY COORDINATION AND CONTROL: THE BUDGET

New policy making, as in the fields of environmental protection or energy conservation, constitutes only a small part of governmental action. For the most part, policy making and administrative agencies are involved in adapting old policies (tax reform or welfare reform, for instance) and implementing them. One of the most important devices of modern government intended to maintain or change priorities in governmental action, to coordinate the various areas of governmental action, and to improve its efficiency is the budget. Centralized budget making in the United States, which is about half a century old, developed in response to two principal problems. As the modern welfare and service state came into being during the last century, the problem of estimating and balancing revenues and expenditures became increasingly complex. Only by focusing these processes in a single agency was it possible for the modern state to relate expenditure to revenue and to review its priorities and allocations periodically. Second, the increasing size of the public sector of national economies — which accounts for one-third to one-half of the gross national product in most modern market economies — has meant that the composition and size of public revenue and expenditure have substantial effects on the general state of the economy. Large expenditures and budget deficits have substantial effects on employment, inflation, and investment decisions. Similarly, tax policies affect investment incentives, consumption levels, and productivity. Thus, the need for central review and control over revenue and expenditure has led to centralized budget agencies and to the institution of annual budgets. Budget making has become one of the most important policy decisions made by governments. This case is presented with great cogency by Aaron Wildavsky:

> Since funds are limited, a budget becomes a mechanism for allocating resources. If receiving the largest returns for a given sum of money is stressed,

[20] Frederick C. Barghoorn, *Politics in the USSR* (Boston: Little, Brown, 1972), pp. 202 ff.

or if the push is toward obtaining desired objectives at the lowest cost, a budget may become an instrument for pursuing efficiency. When efforts are made to make money grow, as it were, by considering spending a form of investment, budgets become means for securing economic growth. Expenditures are economically rational insofar as they add to (rather than detract from) a nation's wealth. To the extent that governments take money from some people in the form of taxes and give it to others who benefit from the expenditures, budgets become engines of income distribution. Of course, it is imperative to assess the direction of the distribution: does the money go from the rich to the poor or vice versa? . . . Budgets with predictive value may be seen as expressing the part played by government in national life, as the most operational expression of national priorities in the public sector. Compared to party platforms and most legislative laws, inclusion in the budget carries a higher probability of concrete action. Little can be done without money, and what will be tried is embedded in the budget. If one asks who gets what the government has to give? then the answers for a specific moment in time are recorded in the budget. If politics is regarded as conflict over whose preferences are to prevail in the determination of policy, then the budget records the outcomes of this struggle.[21]

The making of the budget in democratic countries involves an interplay between the political executive, the higher civil service, and the legislature, but this interplay varies from one country to the next. In Britain the budget developed by the Chancellor of the Exchequer has a high probability of being enacted by Parliament in the form presented by the Cabinet. This tends also to be the case in such countries as France, West Germany, and Japan. The United States is an exception in the division of the budget-making power between the political executive, the higher civil service, and the Congress, particularly its Appropriations, Ways and Means, and recently formed Budget committees.

The important variables that affect budget making, according to Wildavsky, are the predictability of the economic and political environment and the level of economic development in particular countries. During the 1950s and 1960s, when most of the advanced industrial countries experienced steady and substantial economic growth, they enjoyed what economists refer to as a "fiscal dividend"; that is, revenues increased even without increasing taxes, since wages, incomes, and profits were increasing. Thus funds were available for new programs or for increases in expenditures on already existing programs without the need for raising the level of taxation. Declining rates of growth create difficulties. To increase expenditures for one program means reducing it for others.

---

[21] Aaron Wildavsky, *Budgeting: A Comparative Theory of Budgetary Processes* (Boston: Little, Brown, 1975), pp. 4–5.

Poor countries with primarily agricultural, subsistence economies, which are often dependent on single commodities for exports and foreign exchange, have small economic bases from which to extract resources and are vulnerable to fluctuations in world prices for raw materials. Hence their revenues are necessarily low and unpredictable.

Aaron Wildavsky contrasts budgetary controls in rich and stable societies with those of poor and unstable societies. In advanced industrial societies where the political and economic environments are relatively stable, policy makers tend to adopt what he calls "incremental budgeting." By incremental budgeting he means that "past decisions determine most future expenditures . . . so present choice focuses on adding or subtracting a small percentage (the increment) over the existing base. It is not the increment but the base that is crucial, for it signifies acceptance of the past." [22] Although the examples he uses of incremental budgeting are all from advanced, industrial, democratic countries — the United States, Japan, France, and Great Britain — he argues that the Soviet Union, being both rich and predictable, also engages in incremental budgeting (insofar as one can judge from information available on these processes).

On the other hand, Wildavsky tells us,

> in poor countries we find repetitive budgeting under which budgets are made and remade throughout the year amid endless strategic byplay. Poverty leads them to delay lest they run out of money; uncertainty leads them to reprogram funds repeatedly to adjust to the rapidly changing scene. Poor countries do not know where they are now, and the budget does not help them learn where they will be next year. Most in need of stable budgets, they are least able to secure them. Poor countries lack the redundancy that wealth makes possible — the duplication that provides a margin of safety to cope with emergencies, the overlap to compensate for imperfect arrangements — and that is essential for reliable performance. The combination of poverty and uncertainty is devastating; these countries have little to spend because they are poor, and they find it hard to spend wisely because they are uncertain.[23]

What Wildavsky indicates in this contrast between budget making in rich and poor countries is that in the former, policy tends to be continuous and effective; such policy changes that occur are marginal — incremental or decremental. In poor countries there simply is not much effective policy making at all. There would appear to be little that governments with both limited and uncertain resources can do to effect

[22] Ibid., p. 10.
[23] Ibid., p. 11.

innovation and change.[24] What he recommends for poor countries is a lowering of expectations, a general policy of belt-tightening, and a "continuous" budgeting of resources that takes into account their poverty and uncertainty and makes possible some control over governmental expenditures.

One problem with Wildavsky's theory of budgets and policy making is that it lacks a historical dimension. Budgeting has not always been incremental in Western industrial countries, and it need not be, and sometimes is not, repetitive and ineffective in poor countries. World War I sharply raised public expenditure in Western countries, which did not return to its prewar level in the postwar period. World War II had similar budgetary consequences.[25] The introduction of public welfare programs as a consequence of critical elections producing working-class-oriented governments may similarly change the level and distribution of public expenditure sharply and not incrementally.[26] Among poor countries revolutionary changes may significantly alter the level and composition of public expenditure.

Wildavsky's comparison of budget-making policy in rich and poor countries captures these processes in static terms and views the budget as the *cause* of policy. But the budget as a financial summary of the policies and implementations of polities has also to be viewed as the *effect* of politics both domestic and international. Whereas "normal" politics in rich and poor countries tends to produce incremental or repetitive budgeting, "abnormal" politics may produce reallocative budgeting.

LEADERSHIP AND POLICY MAKING

The structural arrangements and decision rules of a political system may be viewed as a set of constraints upon decision making and as creating an organizational framework for political processes. The problems and challenges that arise in the domestic and international environments may be similarly viewed as setting constraints upon and offering opportunities for policy making. But neither the one nor the other *explains* policy. The structural and decisional arrangements tell us something of *how* policy may be made; and the environmental challenges tell us something of *what kind* of policy may be made. But the full explanation requires a dynamic, creative component that, operating in relation to the framework of structure and process, confronts challenges and opportuni-

---

[24] See also Naomi Caiden and Aaron Wildavsky, *Planning and Budgeting in Poor Countries* (New York: John Wiley, 1974).

[25] Alan Peacock and Jack Wiseman, *The Growth of Public Expenditure in the United Kingdom* (Princeton: Princeton University Press, 1961), chap. 4.

[26] Ibid., pp. 70 ff.

ties with policy choices or decisions. This creative component of leadership may be individual or collective, and it may occur within the political system or outside it; within the established organizations of the political system it may occur in the political executive, in the legislature, in the higher civil service, and even on occasion in the courts. It may occur in ordinary or in extraordinary times.

History is full of examples of individual leaders who have been identified with major structural and policy innovations. Central roles in political systems are generally understood to accord a range of discretion to their incumbents. The American presidency, the British prime ministership, the Russian first secretaryship of the Central Committee have their strong and weak variants. How the role will be played by the incumbent is in part determined by the problem context in which the political system finds itself and by the balance of resources aggregated by the political contenders. But it will also be significantly determined by the intelligence, imagination, and character of the incumbent. The leader can both respond to and help shape the mobilization of support for policies. Both a Hoover and a Roosevelt confronted an America in depression; their policy and leadership approaches were in sharp contrast. Bismarck, Caprivi, Hohenlohe, and von Bülow held the German imperial chancellorship in succession, but managed external and domestic affairs in very different ways. An Asquith and a Lloyd George made war with different energies and qualities of imagination. The impact of specific leaders on policy may change over time and not simply because the contextual pressures change. They may learn and become more adept, or their leadership qualities may deteriorate and their effectiveness decline.

A recent study of eight historical crisis episodes suggests the importance of the leadership variable in explaining political structural and policy change.[27] In table IX.4 the role of leadership in these eight historical episodes is characterized as either weak or strong, collective or individual. During the sequence of crises leading up to the enactment of the Reform Act of 1832, which introduced major changes in parliamentary representation in Britain, strong collective leadership was exercised by the Whig and Radical leadership in the House of Commons. The Duke of Wellington played a strong and critical, but temporary, individual role in creating the short-lived coalition that passed the Catholic Emancipation Act in 1829, an event that set the stage for the alignments for electoral reform in the 1830s. The Reform Act itself was essentially an outcome of collective bargaining among Whigs, Radicals, and moder-

[27] Gabriel A. Almond, Scott Flanagan, and Robert Mundt, eds., *Crisis, Choice, and Change* (Boston: Little, Brown, 1973).

Table IX.4. *Leadership in Eight Historical-Political Crises*

Nation and date	Leading actors	Leadership properties
Britain, 1832		
1826	Whigs, Tories	Weak collective
1829	Duke of Wellington	Strong individual
	Whigs	Strong collective
1832	Whigs, Radicals	Strong collective
Britain, 1931		
June 1931	MacDonald	Weak individual
August 1931	MacDonald	Weak individual
France, 1871		
1870	Napoleon III	Weak individual
1871	Thiers	Strong individual
	Communards	Weak collective
1873	Monarchists	Weak collective
	Thiers	Strong individual
Germany, 1918		
1914	Imperial government	Weak collective
1917	Military leadership	Weak collective
1918-20	Social Democrats	Weak collective
Mexico, 1930s		
June 1935	Cárdenas	Strong individual
1936-38	Cárdenas	Strong individual
Japan, 1868		
1863-65	Shogunate	Weak collective
1867	Peripheral houses	Strong collective
Japan, 1930s		
1925	Parties	Weak collective
1932-36	Military-bureaucracy	Strong collective
India, 1960s		
1960-64	Nehru	Strong individual
1964-67	Congress party elite	Strong collective

Source: Adapted from Almond, Flanagan, and Mundt, *Crisis, Choice, and Change,* p. 640.

ate Tories, although within their ranks one or two leaders, such as Lord Grey, were prominent. In the depression crisis of 1931 in England, the Labour Prime Minister, Ramsay MacDonald, had the initiative at the two phases of the crisis, failing to join forces with the Liberals around a program of public works, and finally joining forces with the Conservatives at the cost of dividing the Labour party. Here the lack of political leadership helps explain the decline in Labour party fortunes and the postponement of British welfare reforms.

In the French crises leading to the formation of the Third Republic, first a poorly informed and rash Napoleon III challenged a more powerful Prussia, incurring disastrous defeat and enemy occupation. In the chaotic outcome the left-wing leaders took to the streets in Paris without regard to their support in the rest of France; and the skillful conservative leader, Adolphe Thiers, succeeded in isolating and finally destroying them. In the conservative mood that followed, three rival groups of monarchists frittered away their support, making it possible for Thiers to launch the conservative Third Republic.

In World War I the German imperial government and the military leaders both manifested weak collective leadership as Germany faltered in defeat, stubbornly persisting in constitutional forms and military goals that were in conflict with their needs for wide popular support. In the immediate postwar crisis the Social Democratic leadership failed to take the moderately revolutionary steps that might have given the Weimar Republic a solid chance to succeed.

The Cárdenas era in Mexico dramatically illustrates the importance of creative individual leadership in political change. As Cornelius points out,

> Cárdenas entered the presidency of Mexico while the reins of power were still firmly in the hands of conservative elites almost diametrically opposed to him in issue preferences. He succeeded in freeing himself of their tutelage, mobilizing the latent demands and supportive power of peasants and workers, restructuring the rules of political competition, disengaging the military from the active role in top-level political decision making, and effecting the transfer of power to a hand-picked successor by using political machinery of his own creation. . . . Such a performance cannot be understood or explained except by reference to the leadership and problem-solving propensities of the man primarily responsible for structuring the dynamics of conflict and development in Mexico during this period.[28]

The two Japanese crises — the Meiji Restoration of the 1860s and the collapse of parliamentary government in the 1930s — were both dominated by collective leadership. In the Meiji Restoration the Shogunate failed to take the steps needed to confront the international threat and to modernize and mobilize Japanese resources. The new regime, dominated by the outlying feudal houses, took the resolute steps needed for moving Japan on a modernizing course. In the 1930s Japan's party leaders failed to root their organizations in popular support and thus collapsed under the pressure of a military leadership that had mobilized the countryside.

India in the 1960s weathered a serious language crisis under the

28 Ibid., p. 395.

skillful leadership of Nehru and Shastri and an economic crisis and famine through the effective bargaining tactics of the Congress party leadership. Both crises were accompanied by large-scale disorder and rioting, but were resolved without any significant change in the Indian political structure.

Though policy-making leadership is normally associated with the very top level of the political executive, there are many illustrations of the fact that it may occur farther down the executive administrative line and in legislative bodies. Individual ministers or department heads may have substantial autonomy. Under the leadership of a strong and capable Cabinet officer, for example, an agency in the American executive branch may be able to use congressional connections, administrative discretion and competence, and the technique of ignoring undesirable presidential requests to attain a highly autonomous position. Richard Fenno has provided us with a fascinating account of the "political fiefdom" established by Jesse Jones, as the head of Roosevelt's Reconstruction Finance Corporation. Within limits, Jones was able to ignore certain of Roosevelt's proposals, to overcome financial cuts that the Bureau of the Budget attempted to impose over the RFC, and generally to operate the RFC as an independent force in its own area of competence.[29] On occasion Secretaries of State in the American system may acquire great autonomy. Thus Henry Kissinger in the Nixon and Ford administrations tended to make the controlling foreign policy decisions. British Cabinet Ministers may similarly exercise great autonomy in their specialized policy-making areas, as is described in Richard Crossman's fascinating account of the role of individual Ministers in British policy making in the 1960s.[30]

Similarly, bureaucratic agencies and higher civil servants may acquire substantial powers in their special spheres. J. Edgar Hoover for a number of decades could resist control of the F.B.I. by the President and the Attorney General and could manipulate the Congress. The Central Intelligence Agency has also operated autonomously, sometimes committing the United States to a foreign policy course independently of the political executive and legislative agencies. Richard Crossman records with frustration his efforts to control his own ministry (Housing and Urban Affairs) in opposition to the views of his permanent secretary. He became aware of a network of higher civil servants throughout Whitehall, a network that in some circumstances could fight the British Prime Minister and Cabinet to a standstill.[31]

[29] Richard F. Fenno, Jr., *The President's Cabinet* (Cambridge: Harvard University Press, 1959), pp. 234–47.
[30] Richard Crossman, *Diary of a Cabinet Minister* (London: Macmillan & Co., 1975).
[31] Ibid.

Finally, leaders in legislative bodies and committee chairpersons may enjoy significant influence in their particular spheres of policy making. Here the most dramatic examples are from American experience, in which powerful committee chairs have in the past tended to dominate legislation within their jurisdiction. Committees of the German Bundestag, the Italian Chamber of Deputies, and the French National Assembly, though not as powerful as their American counterparts, take an active and substantial part in the policy-making process.

The phenomena of political leadership should remind one that politics is not a fixed, calculable, causal process. The regularities and "laws" of politics are tendencies and propensities that constrain choices and limit creativity and innovation. But the leadership variable has the potential of moving political systems in new directions, radically changing the basic decision rules or alignment of resources — as Lenin did in Russia in 1917, as Kemal Atatürk did in Turkey in the 1920s, and as Cárdenas did in Mexico in the 1930s — or transforming the content of public policy — as Roosevelt did in the United States of the 1930s or as Adenauer did in the Germany of the 1950s.

CHAPTER X

Governmental Structures and Their Functions

A GOVERNMENT is a set of policy-making and policy-implementing structures with binding authority over a particular population in a particular territory. Governmental structures provide the more or less stable authoritative framework within which political action takes place. The political system's basic decision rules define their organization and powers.

In authoritarian regimes there are often single monopolistic parties that have to be viewed as parts of the government, as is the case, for example, in Communist regimes. Communist parties have explicit, authoritative policy-making and policy-implementing functions. Indeed, they are the top governmental agencies — the Politburo is more powerful than the Council of Ministers; the Central Committee is more powerful than the Supreme Soviet; and the Secretariat of the Central Committee oversees the work of the ministries and the bureaucracy. In democratic systems political parties are not part of the government, though they may organize and take control of it, forming the cabinet or council of ministers, and constituting majority and opposition in the legislative assembly. Their control, however, is contingent upon winning in competitive elections. The government is a framework of legitimate "authorities." Parties and other groups seek to gain control over these authorities and to enact and implement their policies through them.

It has long been understood that governmental agencies — though specialized in many ways — are multifunctional. Executive agencies make policy as well as enforcing and adjudicating it; legislative agencies participate in the implementation of policy (through the power of investigation, for example) as well as participating in policy making; and courts sometimes make policy as well as adjudicating it (that is, in the power of judicial review of legislation). Thus the division of labor among governmental agencies is quite complex, though it is possible, as we shall suggest later, to describe empirically the functions performed by these government agencies in different countries and to draw some conclusions about their general characteristics.

The functional differences among government agencies are related to differences in their structures and procedures. Political executives typically contain small numbers and are either hierarchically or collectively organized (as in a presidency or a cabinet). Legislative bodies are typically medium-sized (ranging in the hundreds of members) and collectively organized; bureaucracies are large (ranging in the hundreds of thousands or even millions in large countries) and hierarchically organized.

Anthony King points out that governmental agencies differ in their procedures:

> Legislatures go in for public debate. They usually discuss a bill or motion with a view to arriving at some collective decision. Their elaborate rules are designed both to ensure orderly debate and to specify the means by which the final decisions shall be taken; similar rules ("parliamentary procedure") tend to be adopted by any body wishing to function in a debate/ decision mode. Courts, by contrast, are not concerned with debate in the formal sense. Their procedures call for the examination and cross-examination of witnesses, the production of evidence, and the expounding of legal doctrine. Because legal doctrine is to be expounded, the personnel of courts — the judges — are normally expected to be learned in the law, whereas legislators are not normally expected to have any special qualifications. Executives operate differently again. They seldom debate in public; they often lack formal decision rules; their personnel may or may not be qualified; they deal in papers, files, minutes, telephone calls, and committee meetings. We take these different modes of procedure so much for granted that, if we were invited in a strange country first to listen to a formal debate, then to observe men in black robes listening to argument, then to attend an informal meeting in someone's private office, most of us would know without having to be told that we had visited in turn a legislative assembly, a court, and the office of some kind of executive.[1]

What we propose to do in this chapter is to describe and compare governmental organizations in structural and functional terms, beginning with the political executive, then treating legislative assemblies and bureaucracies.

THE POLITICAL EXECUTIVE
STRUCTURE

Political executives have many names and titles, and their duties and powers also vary substantially. Some political executives are called presidents, but presidents differ in the powers they may exercise and the func-

---

[1] Anthony King, "Executives," in Fred I. Greenstein and Nelson W. Polsby, *Handbook of Political Science* (Reading, Mass.: Addison-Wesley, 1975), 5: 179.

tions they perform. Some political executives are called prime ministers or premiers; others, chairmen. Political executives also have collective titles, such as cabinets, councils of ministers, politburos, or presidiums.

In table X.1 we distinguish among political executives in two ways, according to whether they are "effective" or "ceremonial" in their activities and according to whether they are individual or collective in their structure. Executives are effective if they have genuine powers to enact and implement laws and regulations; they are ceremonial if their powers are mainly formal and symbolic.

Individual/effective political executives include the American presidency, an office with very substantial powers affecting the entire process of government. Although the American political executive includes collective bodies such as the Cabinet and the National Security Council, these bodies advise the President instead of acting as collective decision makers. The French presidency in the Fifth Republic is also a powerful individual executive, but it is not yet known how this office may develop in relation to the prime ministership and the Council of Ministers, which are both responsible to the National Assembly. Thus far, French Presidents have had the support of a majority in the National Assembly; hence the prime ministership and the Council of Ministers have tended to be subordinate to the President. The West German Chancellor is also an effective powerful executive, who may be removed only if there is a

Table X.1. *Types of Political Executives in Selected Countries*

Effective	Ceremonial
Individual	
President of the USA	Swedish King
Prime Minister of Sweden	President of W. Germany
President of France	British Queen
Chancellor of W. Germany	Japanese Emperor
British Prime Minister	Chairman of the Supreme Soviet, USSR
General Secretary of the Central Committee, USSR	President of India
President of Mexico	
Prime Minister of India	
President of Tanzania	
Shah of Iran	
Collective	
British Cabinet	British Royal Family
Japanese Cabinet	Presidium of the Supreme Soviet, USSR
Politburo, USSR	
Politburo, China	
Swiss Federal Council	

positive majority in the Bundestag favoring an alternative Chancellor. The Mexican presidency is a powerful office controlling not only the executive, but the Mexican Congress as well. The Tanzanian political executive is also dominated by an effective presidency. The Shah of Iran is an example of an effective kingship.

Whether or not a political executive is individual or collective may depend on situation and personality. In Britain in wartime the political executive tends to be "prime ministerial." Even in less troubled times strong Prime Ministers may dominate their Cabinets, but for the most part the British executive is a collective unit. The Cabinet and its committees meet regularly, with substantial agendas of important decisions, and they act on the basis of group deliberation. The Japanese political executive tends to be a collective decision-making body, as the various factions of the ruling party are represented in the Cabinet, and decision making tends to be a bargaining, consensual process. The power of the Soviet Politburo, another collective executive, seems to vary. Under Stalin, particularly in his later years, the Politburo virtually ceased functioning; under the dominating figure of Khrushchev, the Politburo met and participated in decisions; under Brezhnev, the executive seems to have become somewhat more collective. Prior to the death of Mao the Chinese political executive fluctuated from individual to collective forms. Mao periodically withdrew from direct participation, leaving decision making to others, only to return when he was dissatisfied with the course of policy and performance. The post-Mao structure of authority is still unclear at this writing.

Though we may speak of the political executive as being individual or collective, we are talking about the distribution of power and authority in it, rather than numbers. All political executives are multimembered, consisting of elective and appointive officials with policy-making power. A British Prime Minister makes some one hundred ministerial and junior ministerial appointments, and a German Chancellor may make a similar number. In the United States, President Carter, on taking office, had about two thousand political appointments to make, two hundred of which were viewed as key policy-making positions in the executive branch.

Monarchs like the British Queen and the Kings of the Scandinavian countries are principally ceremonial and symbolic officers with very occasional political powers. They are living symbols of the state and nation and of its historical continuity. Thus Britain's Queen opens Parliament and makes statements on important holidays and anniversaries. When there is an election or when a government falls, the Queen appoints a new Prime Minister. Normally she has no choice, since she picks the candidate having the support of a majority in the House of Commons;

but if there is doubt about which leader has a majority or about who leads the party, the Monarch's discretion may turn out to be an important power.

In republican countries with parliamentary systems, presidents perform the functions that fall to kings and queens in democratic and parliamentary monarchies. Thus German and Italian Presidents issue statements, make speeches on important anniversaries, greet foreign diplomats and distinguished visitors, and designate Prime Ministers after elections or the resignation of a government.

A system in which the ceremonial executive is separated from the effective executive has a number of advantages. The ceremonial executive tends to be above politics, symbolizing unity and continuity. The American presidency, which combines both effective and ceremonial functions, risks the possibility that Presidents will use their ceremonial and symbolic authority to enhance their political power or that their involvement in politics may hamper them in performing their symbolic or unifying role.

The Soviet Union and other Communist countries tend to keep separate the ceremonial and the effective executives. The assumption of the chairmanship of the Presidium of the Supreme Soviet by General Secretary Brezhnev breaks a long precedent. Normally, the Presidium has been a collegial presidency with ceremonial powers; its chairman greets distinguished visitors, opens and presides over meetings of the Supreme Soviet, and with the other members formally appoints Ministers.

Britain's royal family is an example of a collective/ceremonial executive. So many occasions call for the physical presence of the Monarch that members of the royal family — the Queen Mother, the royal consort, the Prince of Wales — share appearances. The activities of the royal family are reported daily in the press, giving a mantle of legitimacy to a great variety of events. There is much riding in carriages, parading, and ritual in British public life. The Scandinavian royal institutions are more humdrum than the British monarchy; they are sometimes called "bicycle monarchies."

FUNCTIONS

Political executives, typically, perform important *system* functions. Studies of childhood political socialization show that the first political role perceived by children tends to be that of the top political executive — the American or French President, prime ministers in parliamentary systems, and kings and queens in monarchies. In early childhood there is a tendency to identify the top political executive as a parent figure; as children mature, they begin to distinguish political from other roles and to differentiate among political roles.[2] The conduct of the political executive has some impact on the trust and confidence in the political system as a whole that young people acquire and tend to carry with them into their adult lives.

The role of the political executive in recruitment is obviously important. Presidents, prime ministers, and first secretaries of Communist parties have large and important appointive powers, not only of cabinet and politburo members and government ministers, but usually of members of the judiciary as well. Typically the political executive is the source of honors and distinctions for members of the government and private citizens — distinguished service medals, orders of Lenin, knighthoods and peerages, and prizes of various kinds.

The political executive plays a central role in political communication; and the top individual within it, the crucial one. Presidential messages, speeches, and press conferences; prime ministerial speeches in parliaments or in the public arena; statements of cabinet members in parliament, congress, and before various publics; speeches of party leaders at Communist party congresses — all may communicate important information regarding past, present, and future trends of domestic and foreign policy. These high-level communications may take the form of appeals for sacrifice and support, improved performance in various sectors of the society and economy, and the like.

Political executives are of central significance in the performance of the *process functions*. They may serve as advocates of particular interests, as when a president supports the demands of minority groups, environmental groups, or the business community, or when a prime minister supports the interests of pensioners or depressed regions. Departmental secretaries and ministers typically speak for particular interests such as labor, business, agriculture, children, minority groups, and so on. Presidents or cabinet members may play crucial roles as interest aggregators as they seek to build coalitions favoring particular pieces of legislation. Typically the political executive is the most important agency for policy making. The executive normally initiates new public policies and, varying with the division of powers between the executive and the legislature, has a substantial part in their adoption. The political executive also oversees the implementation of policies and can hold subordinate officials accountable for their performance.

Whatever *policy* dynamism there is in a political system tends to be focused in the political executive. A bureaucracy without a political executive typically only implements the policies already on the books;

[2] See chaps. II and IV.

without the direction of politically motivated ministers, bureaucracies tend toward inertia and conservatism. The decision of a president, prime minister, cabinet, or politburo to pursue a new course of action in the areas of foreign policy or defense, fiscal policy, and welfare or energy policy will usually be accompanied by adaptations of the political executive — the appointment of an especially vigorous minister, provision of increased staff, or establishment of a special cabinet committee. Where the political executive is weak and divided, as in Fourth Republic France or postwar Italy, this dynamic force is missing — the initiative may pass to the permanent bureaucracy and powerful interest groups (and legislative committees in the case of Italy), and general needs, interests, and critical problems may be neglected.

The political executive consists of the ministers and departmental secretaries for all policy areas; its policy thrust will be reflected by its composition. New departures in foreign policy or welfare policy may be reflected in the formation of new agencies or ad hoc policy committees, in new appointments to the political executive, in cabinet reshuffles or politburo changes, or sometimes in the direct assumption of responsibility for a policy area by the chief political executive.

ASSEMBLIES
STRUCTURE

Almost all contemporary political systems have assemblies, variously called chambers, houses, senates, diets, soviets, and the like. As of 1971, out of some 130 independent countries, 108 had such governmental bodies; and since that time another half dozen countries have instituted them.[3] Thus, regardless of their powers, there seem to be substantial reasons for having such agencies in contemporary governments. Multi-membered bodies that proceed by formal deliberation and voting, assemblies are generally elected by popular vote and hence are accountable — at least formally — to the citizenry. Thus they are, at the minimum, legitimating agencies, and their almost universal adoption today suggests that in the modern world a legitimate government must at least formally include a representative popular component.

The structure of assemblies varies from country to country. Their membership tends to number in the hundreds, though smaller countries (for example, Iceland, Senegal, and New Zealand) may have as few as forty or fifty members. Roughly, one can say that the larger the population of a country, the larger the size of its lower legislative chamber (see table X.2). Thus China has 888 members in its legislative Yuan, and the

[3] Jean Blondel, *Comparative Legislatures* (Englewood Cliffs: Prentice-Hall, 1973), pp. 144 ff.

Table X.2. *Characteristics of Legislative Bodies in Selected Countries*

Country	Size of lower house	Bicameral	Federal system
China	888	No	No
USSR	750	Yes	Yes
Britain	630	Yes	No
Italy	630	Yes	No
India	525	Yes	Yes
W. Germany	500	Yes	Yes
France	485	Yes	No
Japan	467	Yes	No
Poland	460	No	No
Turkey	450	Yes	No
USA	435	Yes	Yes
Brazil	409	Yes	Yes
Mexico	210	Yes	Yes
Kenya	170	No	No
Venezuela	133	Yes	Yes
Tanzania	107	No	No

Source: Adapted from Jean Blondel, *Comparative Legislatures*, appendix A, pp. 144 ff.

Soviet Union has 750 members in its Supreme Soviet. But the ratio of size to population is not without exceptions. Table X.3 shows that the legislative bodies of Kenya, Tanzania, and Zambia are small, but India — with many times the population of Britain and Italy — has a smaller lower legislative chamber than either of those countries. Nevertheless, the relationship between size of legislature and population suggests an effort to "represent" populations — the larger the population, the more representatives.

Of the 108 countries having legislatures, 52 had more than one chamber. In Europe, parliaments developed out of "estates," bodies representing different sociopolitical groups intermittently called together by kings or other hereditary rulers for purposes of consultation and revenue. On the European continent, these preparliamentary bodies might have had three or four chambers. In France, for example, there were three estates: the higher clergy, the higher aristocracy, and the so-called Third Estate, representing other classes. In England, estates were early organized in two chambers — the lords, both spiritual (the bishops) and temporal, seated in the House of Lords, and the knights and burgesses elected from the counties and boroughs to the House of Commons. But this basis of parliamentary organization persists today only in England, where the House of Lords is still dominated in numbers by the hereditary aristocracy.

Countries have a bicameral (two-chamber) assembly organization for two basic reasons. The countries organized along federal lines represent the federal units in one of the two chambers; the other chamber is usually elected from constituencies based on population. Even in unitary systems, bicameralism is a common practice, with a second chamber either elected or appointed (or partly elected and partly appointed) from constituencies other than those represented in the second branch. Larger countries and ethnically and religiously heterogeneous countries typically have a second chamber in which regional, ethnic, or religious interests are assured of representation. Bicameralism in these governmental systems is related to the protection of minority interests and the separation of powers, rather than to federalism. The second chamber breaks up the process of policy making and provides for longer and more cautious consideration of legislation.

The American system, in which the Senate and House of Representatives are practically equal in power, is an unusual case. In most bicameral systems, one of the two chambers is dominant, and the second (for example, the British House of Lords or the French Senate) tends to play a primarily limiting and delaying role. The formal constitutions of such countries as the Soviet Union, Brazil, and Mexico provide for strong second chambers, but this simply reflects the legal, and not the effective, situations. In all three of these countries the political executives are the dominant agencies, and the legislative bodies are primarily used as legitimators of governmental action.

Assemblies also differ in their internal organization in ways that have important consequences for policy making and implementation. There are two kinds of internal organization in assemblies and parliaments — party organization and formal organization (presiding officers, committees, and so forth). A consensual two-party system may function differently in a presidential government than it does in a parliamentary government. Parliamentary parties in most European systems are "disciplined" parties in the sense that members of the legislature rarely vote in opposition to the instructions of party leaders. In parliamentary systems, cabinets generally hold office as long as they can command a majority of the votes of the members of the assembly. Deviating from party discipline, therefore, means risking the fall of the government and the necessity of new elections. These risks and the party discipline they encourage also tend to prevail, though to a lesser extent, in countries where multiparty systems exist or where cabinets and governments are formed from party coalitions.

In presidential systems, the political executive and members of the assembly are elected for definite terms of office, and the fate of the party and of its members is less directly and immediately involved in voting on legislative measures. In American legislative bodies, party discipline operates principally with respect to procedural questions like the selection of a presiding officer or the appointment of committees. On substantive legislative and policy issues, Democratic and Republican members of Congress and state legislators are freer to decide independently whether or not to vote with party leaders. A comparison of roll-call votes in the American Congress and the British House of Commons would show much more consistency in party voting among British representatives than among their American counterparts.

All assemblies have a committee structure, some division of labor permitting specialized groups of legislators to deliberate on particular kinds of issues and to recommend action to the whole assembly. Without this kind of sublegislative organization it would be impossible to handle the large flow of legislative business. But the importance of committees to the legislative process varies from one extreme, where the committee system is relatively weak (the British case), to the other, where committees are so important that they sometimes preempt the power of the whole legislative body by simply failing to report legislative proposals to the assembly (the American case). The committee systems of countries like France and West Germany fall between these extremes. Italy has been an interesting case from the point of view of the powers of legislative committees. It is a parliamentary system with a weak and unstable Cabinet. Because of Cabinet instability, legislative committees have been given the power, which is frequently exercised, of actually enacting measures without reference to the whole legislative body.[4]

The power of legislative committees generally varies with the relative power of the assembly and the political executive. A parliamentary government with a strong and stable cabinet system usually has weak committees. In effect, the cabinet decides whether or not a bill will be enacted into law, and the parliamentary chamber usually adopts the bill without basic changes. Where rule-making power is divided, as between a separately elected executive and a legislative assembly, the committee organization is likely to acquire relative stability in its membership, expertise in one field, and considerable influence on policy.

In general, there has been a trend toward increasing committee specialization in legislative bodies, corresponding to the emergence of specialized bureaucracies. These committees seek to oversee and in some measure control the activities of these specialized administrative agencies and to participate in the enactment of legislation in these areas. This trend toward the formation of specialized legislative committees has

---

[4] See Joseph LaPalombara, *Politics Within Nations* (Englewood Cliffs: Prentice-Hall, 1974), pp. 130–31.

occurred even in Communist countries, in particular the Soviet Union and Poland, though they tend to be concerned with minor amendments to government legislation.

FUNCTIONS

Legislative bodies may have system, process, and policy functions. Their role in the making of constitutions and other decision rules and the parts they play in recruitment, socialization, and communication are their system functions. Their involvements in interest articulation and aggregation and in policy making and implementation are process functions, whereas their committee specializations and their partisan and issue groupings suggest their policy functions.

When one compares assemblies on the basis of their importance as political and policy-making agencies, the United States Senate and House of Representatives, which play a very important role in the formulation and enactment of legislation, are at one extreme; the other extreme is represented by the Supreme Soviet in the Soviet Union, which meets infrequently and does little more than to listen to statements from Soviet political leaders and to legitimate legislative decisions already made elsewhere. Roughly midway between the two is the House of Commons in Britain, where legislative proposals are sometimes initiated or modified by ordinary members of Parliament. In parliamentary systems of government, decisions regarding public policy and legislation are typically made by the cabinet or ministers (who are, to be sure, chosen from the members of the parliamentary body); the assembly primarily debates, amends, and formally enacts legislation.

Assemblies perform a wide variety of functions other than policy making. The British House of Commons contributes importantly to the creation of popular attitudes and values affecting government and politics. Most noteworthy political events in Britain occur in the House of Commons — statements by the Prime Minister or Cabinet Ministers, attacks on the government by the opposition, questioning of Ministers, debates on the current issues and policies, and critical votes. The centrality of the House of Commons in the British political system and the importance attached to its activities by the communications media mean that the political values, practices, and substantive decisions of the House of Commons are constantly passed on to the population. Beyond specific information on issues and votes, British citizens are thus informed of basic attitudes characterizing the relationship between government and opposition, of appropriate kinds of behavior for political leaders in their relations with one another, and of approved limits on governmental power. The United States Senate, House of Representatives, and state and local assemblies contribute to the political socialization of American citizens, affecting basic political attitudes and values. But since political and governmental power is shared by national, state, and local agencies and among assemblies, executives, and courts, the impact of any one of these bodies is more limited and the total effect more dispersed and conflicting than is true in Britain. The Soviet Union's soviets are much less significant as agents of political socialization. Their meetings are less frequent, and there is little — if any — debate, except in the local soviets. The principal image transmitted by the soviets is that the people's deputies accept unanimously, without debate, decisions made by the party leadership.

Assemblies are even more important in the socialization of political leaders. Many American political leaders spend some part of their careers in Congress, although parliamentary service is not as important as it is to British Ministers, who are chosen from among the Members of Parliament usually after long years of service. In the Soviet Union, political executives are also members of soviets, but this experience has far less importance than do membership and experience in the Communist party organization and the bureaucracy.

Assemblies may perform valuable roles in the recruitment of political leaders. Members of the British Cabinet are usually selected from the House of Commons after long years of service as "back-benchers" or junior ministers. If the cabinet in a parliamentary system loses its majority, it usually resigns, or the assembly is dissolved and new elections are called. Indeed, any weakening of the majority in parliamentary systems is often associated with some shift in the composition of the cabinet and the ministry in efforts to meet the dissatisfaction of the majority party or coalition.

In presidential systems like the United States, the recruitment function, though still important, is performed differently than in parliamentary systems. Membership in legislative bodies at the state and national levels may lead to higher political office, but not as frequently as in parliamentary systems. Four out of the last seven American presidents came from the United States Senate. But President Eisenhower was elected after a distinguished career in the army; Roosevelt's prior political experience had been as Assistant Secretary of the Navy and as Governor of New York; and Carter served as Governor of Georgia. Under the American system of separation of powers, the Senate has to approve the President's nominations to higher office in the executive and the judiciary.

Although Communist political leaders are typically elected to soviets, membership in these bodies is not particularly relevant to political advancement. More important is performance in party committees and bureaus or valuable service in the bureaucracy.

Many assemblies influence the policy-making process by expressing the interests of different economic and social groups in the population and by combining these interests into policy alternatives. Legislative bodies often include interest group blocs that act as advocates for, and that bargain and form coalitions with, other groups for particular policies. Often interest groups are represented in particular legislative committees and hence are in a position to advance or oppose legislation affecting them. Almost no interest articulation and aggregation occur in the Soviet Union's Supreme Soviet or republic soviets. In local soviets, however, issues pertaining to local affairs are sometimes permitted to surface and to become the subject of debate.

In the actual formulation and enactment of legislation, the American Congress is of greater importance than the British House of Commons; Soviet assemblies have little, if any, importance in these respects. The American Congress and the British Parliament are involved in the implementation of policies; both bodies inquire into and investigate the performance of administrative agencies, although in different ways. The investigative powers of American congressional committees give them more influence than their counterparts in the British House of Commons. In Britain, control of administrative performance and practice is handled in several different ways: select committees have special responsibilities in these areas, and members of the House of Commons may regularly ask questions about administrative efficiency and performance that the appropriate Ministers are required to answer. The British, following the Swedish example, have instituted a parliamentary commissioner (an ombudsman) who is responsible to the House of Commons and who must hear citizens' complaints regarding failures or improprieties of administrative performance in individual cases. In the Soviet Union, criticism of administrative performance occurs in a limited way in the local soviets. At the central level, control is exercised over administration through the Secretariat of the party Central Committee and other party bodies.

Some assemblies engage in rule adjudication, although in rather special ways. In Britain, the House of Lords constitutes the highest formal court of judicial appeals. In fact, however, the judicial function of the House of Lords is performed by the Lord Chancellor — head of the judiciary and presiding officer of the House of Lords — and nine "law lords" who are appointed to perform this particular function. In the United States, when crimes are committed by public officials, impeachment proceedings may be invoked, in which the House of Representatives serves as the indicting body and the Senate as the trial body. Using their powers of investigation, congressional committees often conduct seemingly judicial proceedings, in which they may compel people to testify, hold individuals in contempt, and impose punishments.

This brief comparison of the functions performed by assemblies should set to rest the simplified notion that "assemblies legislate." All assemblies have some relationship to policy making, but it is rarely a substantive one; the political importance of these bodies lies in this limited relationship to policy making as well as in the great variety of other political functions they perform.[5]

ROLE IN DEVELOPING COUNTRIES

Recent studies of legislatures in developing countries suggest that these bodies, usually neglected in "Third World" literature, deserve some description and analysis. One such study suggests that these bodies are sometimes important as (1) goal-setting agencies, (2) conflict managers, and (3) contributors to national integration. Boynton and Kim point out that some third world legislatures actually have (or have had) some influence in the modification of legislation proposed by the political executive.[6] This surely would be the case in India. They also cite the Kenyan and Iranian legislative bodies as having had some policy-making impact in the past, but acknowledge that this is rare in developing countries at present.

With regard to the management of conflict, Boynton and Kim make greater claims for third world legislatures, arguing that the mere existence of representative legislative bodies accords some legitimacy to different interest groups and ideological tendencies. A number of their case studies of third world legislatures illustrate how these bodies may facilitate bargaining and negotiation among such groups. Finally, the point is made that legislatures in the third world may contribute to national integration. One of the most common activities of third world legislators is communication with their constituents and the transmission of constituent complaints and needs to other governmental agencies and the public. Thus, previously parochial groups are brought into contact with central governmental institutions, and to the extent that there is some response, they may accord loyalty and support to the central political system.[7]

Robert Packenham, summarizing the recent literature on legislative bodies in developing countries, suggests several conclusions. He argues that legislatures in developing countries tend to be ideologically more conservative bodies, more inclined to resist modernization than popularly elected executives and even nonelective authoritarian elites. But these legislative bodies also may on occasion challenge arbitrary executive authority, serve as special interest advocates, resolve conflicts, and en-

---

[5] See Blondel, op. cit., pp. 12 ff.
[6] G. R. Boynton and Chong Lim Kim, *Legislative Systems in Developing Countries* (Durham, N.C.: Duke University Press, 1975), pp. 16 ff.
[7] Ibid., pp. 21 ff.

hance national integration. The conservative impact of third world legislatures is in part the consequence of the disproportionate representation of privileged groups and social strata in these legislative bodies.

Packenham also points out that the contribution of legislatures to development and modernization varies with the level of development. In earlier stages they tend to resist national integration and effective penetration. At later stages of development, legislatures may contribute to stability by providing means of reconciling and accommodating the interests of social, economic, and ethnic groups. He concludes his analysis by pointing out that there is no clear-cut answer to the question of the role of legislatures in developmental processes: in some developmental contexts they are conservative and disruptive, whereas in others they may be dynamic and integrative in their effects.[8]

BUREAUCRACY, POLICY MAKING AND IMPLEMENTATION
THE HIGHER CIVIL SERVICE AND POLICY MAKING

In an analysis of policy making in Britain, F. M. G. Willson states: "The policy-making centre of British government . . . consists of a group at the most 3,500 strong, of whom only 100 are politicians or in any sense 'party political' appointees. These figures can be reduced to a nucleus of some 350, of whom not more than 50 — and probably nearer 30 — are 'party political.' " [9]

Willson makes out a persuasive case for the importance of the higher civil service in Britain. He argues that Her Majesty's Government consists of some one hundred "front-bench" MP's, about twenty of whom serve in the Cabinet, the remainder acting as Ministers, junior ministers, and parliamentary secretaries in charge of the government departments. This relatively small group of political policy makers confront around three thousand permanent higher civil servants, who are largely recruited as young men and women directly into the higher civil service from the universities. They spend their life careers as an elite corps, moving about from Ministry to Ministry, watching governments come and go, and becoming increasingly important as policy makers as they rise into the top posts. Some three hundred of these are permanent secretaries, deputy secretaries, or undersecretaries in charge of particular departments, and they remain in frequent contact with Ministers. Willson claims that policy making in Britain is carried on by this combined political-execu-

[8] Robert A. Packenham, "How Much Do Legislatures Help Development?" Paper presented at the Conference on Legislatures and Development, Carmel, Calif., August 1975.

[9] F. M. G. Willson, "Policy-Making and the Policy-Makers." In Richard Rose, ed., *Policy-Making in Britain* (New York: The Free Press, 1969), p. 360.

Table X.3. *Political Power and Partisanship of Higher Civil Service in*
               Selected European Countries

Partisanship	Political power	
	Weak	*Strong*
Low	Switzerland	France
	Netherlands	Sweden
High	Belgium	
	Italy	
	Poland	

Source: Adapted from Dogan, *Mandarins of Western Europe*, p. 13.

tive and top-level civil service group, pointing out that in "the larger
mixed policy-making group there tend to be perhaps fifty people spread
over Whitehall who together can carry any case through. The art of
getting one's policy proposals accepted is the art of manoeuvering for the
support — active or passive — of that crucial two-and-one-half score." [10]

The importance of the permanent higher civil service is not unique to
Britain, though perhaps it has been most fully institutionalized there.
Mattei Dogan speaks of these higher civil servants in some modern
democratic societies as constituting a kind of "mandarinate" — a group
of high permanent officials having professional esprit de corps and en-
joying policy-making power.[11]

Dogan attributes the growing importance of these corps of higher civil
servants to a number of historical developments: the increasing scope
and power of modern bureaucracies, the declining power of parliament,
the trend toward increasing centralization and integration of bureaucracies, and the increasingly technical character of modern government.
Most statutes enacted by modern governments take the form of broad
grants of power, leaving to higher and experienced civil servants the task
of formulating regulations.

Comparing the roles of higher civil servants in a number of continental European countries (table X.3), Dogan distinguishes between
those in which "civil servants are very powerful but not politicized
(France, Sweden); . . . others [in which they are] not really powerful
but very politicized (Belgium, Italy, Poland); and . . . still others [in
which they are] neither powerful nor politicized (Netherlands, Switzer-

[10] Ibid., p. 368.
[11] Mattei Dogan, ed., *The Mandarins of Western Europe* (New York: John Wiley,
1975), pp. 3 ff.

land)." [12] The United States would fall into the relatively weak/nonpolitical category. Administrators who in Britain, France, and Sweden would be permanent higher civil servants are mainly presidential appointees in the United States, even though most of them are technically qualified for the positions they hold. Despite this difference, in the American system as well there is something like a mandarinate — higher permanent civil servants in such agencies as the Internal Revenue Service, the Central Intelligence Agency, the institutes of health, the office of the Attorney General, and the Departments of State, Defense, Interior, Agriculture, and Commerce — whose members play an important role in the policy making of their specialized agencies.

In broad terms, the power of these higher civil servants is based on their long tenure, experience, and technical knowledge in particular areas of government work. New policies and legislation have somehow to be reconciled with the old, and these higher civil servants possess this accumulated experience. Normally this creates a conservative tendency among these higher civil servants, hence the term *mandarinate*. In actual fact the substantive impact of the higher civil service on public policy may be primarily conservative, or technocratic and innovative within professional limits, or usually some of both. In Britain, France, and Sweden — where the higher civil services are organizationally mobile and are "generalists" in their skills — there may be a "don't make waves" philosophy favoring the maintenance of the status quo. In the United States — where the higher civil service that does exist is made up of specialists (for example, military officers, diplomats, medical experts, scientists, and engineers) — their impact is in favor of the values and interests of their particular professions and governmental departments. However, the stereotyped image of the higher civil service as a mandarinate overlooks the fact that much significant legislation has been, and is, initiated by civil servants devoted to conservation, welfare reform, tax reform, educational and scientific development, and the like.[13]

Higher civil services may have corporate and hierarchic structures, as in Britain, or may be quite fragmented, as in the United States. The Permanent Secretary of the Treasury, the Cabinet Secretary, and the Permanent Secretary of the Civil Service in Britain are the top civil service posts; their incumbents have some control over the careers and placement of the lower ranks. In the United States these officials are departmentally fragmented; they cannot be spoken of as a corps.

In Communist countries one may distinguish between the top party

12 Ibid., p. 13.
13 See Hugh Heclo, *Modern Social Politics in Britain and Sweden* (New Haven: Yale University Press, 1974), pp. 301 ff.

bureaucrats (the *apparatchiki*) who staff the secretariats of the Communist parties and the top officials of the various ministries and government agencies. The party Secretariat is directly under the control of the Politburo of the Central Committee. It is the guardian of the party line as laid down by the Politburo and is the instrument of the political executive in enforcing party policy on the line ministries of Communist governments. Most students of Communist politics have pointed in the past to the conflict between the ideological propensities of the central party elites and the rational-technocratic propensities of the officials of the government ministries. A recent study of Communist elites concludes that there has been a trend toward the "emergence of a technical-managerial stratum of political leaders . . . and a declining importance of ideological considerations in decision-making" and recruitment.[14] This would suggest that the political executive (the Politburo) uses the party Secretariat as a broadly supervisory corps and as a means of reconciling the claims of the various ministries with the general goals of the top party elite. A factional conflict producing a change in the Communist political executive presumably would be accompanied by changes in the party Secretariat and the ministries consistent with the goals of the new controlling faction. But since this turnover is usually limited in scope, one must assume that many higher officials in the party and ministerial bureaucracies in fact are able to maintain some neutrality vis-à-vis party factions, adapting themselves as factions come and go.

THE POLITICAL CULTURE OF HIGHER CIVIL SERVANTS

Higher civil servants in various countries differ in their attitudes toward politics and the role of civil servants. A recent study of the attitudes of higher permanent officials in three democratic countries — Britain, West Germany, and Italy — shows that British administrators accept pluralistic-competitive politics and believe that it is their duty to carry out the policies of the duly elected majority party. The Italian administrators were far less tolerant, viewing partisanship as harmful to the public interest and themselves as more competent to judge the public interest than politicians. Responses of German administrators were somewhere in between. The trend among younger bureaucrats seems to be toward greater acceptance and appreciation of democratic and political control over bureaucratic performance.[15] Studies like this show that

---

14 William A. Welsh, "Communist Political Leadership: Conclusions and Overview," in Carl Beck et al., *Comparative Communist Political Leadership* (New York: David McKay, 1973), p. 305.

15 Robert Putnam, "The Political Attitudes of Senior Civil Servants in Western Europe," *British Journal of Political Science* 3 (July 1973): 15 ff.

bureaucracies have different political cultures based on, among other things, the differences in historical experience, the groups from which administrators are recruited, and the effectiveness of the political agencies of government.

The trend in the political culture of higher civil servants in Western democracies is in the direction of a greater acceptance of and responsiveness to democratic politics. The older senior bureaucrats of European democracies reflect the political culture of the predemocratic state; the younger ones have adapted to a pluralistic and political conception of the national interest. In Communist countries there has been a tendency toward the development of a pragmatic-technical culture among higher public officials. But if there is a common culture among all top bureaucrats it is conservative, based on their interest in the maintenance of, and their avoidance of disturbance in, their enormous organizations. One writer, speaking about the British higher civil service, comments that the "bureaucratic spirit is predisposed above all toward routine processing, toward reconciliation of diverse opinions, and toward a harmony tantamount to an almost unswerving bias in favor of the status quo." He describes bureaucrats as "virtuosi at the patient, untiring, undramatic processing of problems by means of standard procedures; they take a dim view of experiments or indeed any departure from the habitual and tested practices that have underpinned their organization in the past." [16] Suleiman remarks that this characterization could quite appropriately be used to describe the French higher civil service.[17]

BUREAUCRACY AND IMPLEMENTATION

The higher civil servants discussed above are only the tip of the iceberg of the permanent officialdom of modern polities. Modern societies are dominated by large organizations, and by far the largest organizations in these societies are the governmental bureaucracies.

Table X.4 reports the percentage of workers employed by the government in a number of countries in or around 1960. The figures are for public sector employment as a whole, including central and local employees, military personnel, and public service enterprise employees (the post office, nationalized industries, collective farms, and the like). The figures are enormous, ranging into the millions for larger modern countries, constituting almost the entire labor force in some Communist countries, but accounting for a major part of modern sector employment even in such developing countries as Kenya and India.

[16] Michael Gordon, "Civil Servants, Politicians and Parties," *Comparative Politics* 4(1) (January 1971): 43.
[17] Ezra Suleiman, *Politics, Power and Bureaucracy in France* (Princeton, N.J.: Princeton University Press, 1974), pp. 386–87.

Table X.4. *Size of the Government Bureaucracy: Percentage of Workers Employed by Government*

Country	Year	% in agricultural sector	% in nonagricultural sector	% in all sectors of economy
USSR	1959	14[a]	96	59
Bulgaria	1956	6	92	37
Britain	1962	2	26	25
France	1960	–	22	17
USA	1960	1	16	15
W. Germany	1960	–	–	14[b]
Japan	1960	1	14	10
Kenya	1960	–	–	9[b]
India	1960	–	–	5[b]

Source: Adapted from Frederic L. Pryor, *Property and Industrial Organization in Communist and Capitalist Nations* (Bloomington: Indiana University Press, 1973), pp. 46–47.
[a] Agricultural workers who work private plots are placed in the private sector, even though they spend a majority of time in cooperative or state farm work and the land is owned by the government. The Soviet figure thus greatly understates the government role. Agriculture is much less collectivized in the Eastern European nations.
[b] For these nations, percentages are estimated (by doubling the percentage employed by government in relation to total working-age population, as given in Bruce Russett, *World Handbook of Political and Social Indicators* [New Haven: Yale University Press, 1964], p. 70).

Robert Putnam asks the question,

Can there really be much doubt who governs our complex modern societies? Public bureaucracies, staffed largely by permanent civil servants, are responsible for the vast majority of policy initiatives taken by governments. Discretion not merely for deciding individual cases, but for crafting the content of most legislation has passed from the legislature to the executive. Bureaucrats, monopolizing as they do much of the available information of shortcomings of existing policies, as well as much of the technical expertise necessary to design practical alternatives, have gained a predominant influence over the evolution of the agenda for decisions. Elected executives everywhere are outnumbered and outlasted by career civil servants. In a literal sense the modern political system is essentially "bureaucratic" — characterized by the "rule of officials." [18]

The importance of bureaucracy is only suggested by its size. A functional analysis may suggest why this governmental organization has acquired its enormous and problematic significance. We have often

18 Putnam, "Political Attitudes of Senior Civil Servants," p. 17.

stressed that most political agencies and institutions perform a number of different functions. The bureaucracy is almost alone in carrying out a crucial political function — the enforcement or implementation of laws, rules, and regulations in specific cases. In a sense, bureaucracies monopolize the output side of the political system. Occasionally, of course, policy makers take the law into their own hands. In the Soviet Union, the trial and execution of Secret Police Chief Lavrenti Beria is alleged to have been carried out by his colleagues in the Presidium. The establishment of the "plumbers" unit in the Nixon White House, and their carrying out of what are normally police functions, is another example of policy makers taking implementation into their own hands.

In addition to this near monopoly of rule enforcement, bureaucracies greatly influence the processes of rule making. As we have suggested, most modern legislation is very general and can be effectively enforced only if administrative officials work out regulations elaborating the policy adopted by the political branches of government. The extent to which a general policy is carried out usually depends on bureaucrats' interpretations of it and on the spirit and effectiveness with which they enforce it. Moreover, much of the adjudication in modern political systems is performed by administrative agencies, whether organized as independent regulatory bodies or as units in regular operating departments.

We discussed in chapters VII and VIII how bureaucratic agencies may serve as articulators and aggregators of interests. Agriculture, labor, defense, welfare and education, and other bureaucratic departments may be among the most important spokesmen for interest groups. And when an agricultural department obtains agreement on policy among different agricultural pressure groups, or when a labor department draws together competing trade unions around some common policy, bureaucrats are performing a significant interest-aggregating function.

Finally, bureaucracies are instrumental in performing the communication function in political systems. Even in democratic systems, the bureaucracy is one of the most important sources of information about public issues and political events. News reporters are constantly knocking at the doors of administrative officials in search of the latest information on all spheres of foreign and domestic policy. Although an aggressive press in a modern democratic society may force considerable information out of the bureaucracy, bureaucrats clearly have some control over the amount of information they divulge and the way it is interpreted. The decisions made by a political elite, whether executives or legislators, are also based considerably on the information they obtain from administrative agencies. Similarly, interest groups, political parties, and the public are dependent on the information transmitted by administrative officials.

The truth of the matter is that modern, complex, interdependent so-

Table X.5. *Typology of Controls for Bureaucratic Responsibility*

	Formal	*Informal*
External	Directly or indirectly elected chief executive: president, prime minister, governor, etc. Elected legislature: congress, parliament, city council, etc. Courts Ombudsman	Public opinion Press Public interest groups Constituencies Competing bureaucratic organizations
Internal	Representative bureaucracy where legally required Citizen participation where legally required Decentralization	Perception of public opinion (anticipated reaction) Professional standards Socialization in the norms of responsibility

Source: Taken from Mark V. Nadel and Frances E. Rourke, "Bureaucracies," in Greenstein and Polsby, op. cit., 5: 416.

cieties cannot get along without bureaucracies, and it also seems to be practically impossible to get along with them. The title of a recent book, *Implementation: How Great Expectations in Washington are Dashed in Oakland,* expresses this dilemma.[19] Public policies are statements of intent enacted by the political executive and the assembly. They allocate resources and designate responsibility for the realization of these goals. But the realization of this intent depends on the bureaucracy and the responsiveness of the social groups affected by the policies. Policies may be lost in the thicket of bureaucratic infighting or twisted out of recognition by bureaucratic misunderstanding or opposition.

Creating and maintaining a responsive and responsible bureaucracy is one of the intractable problems of modern and modernizing society — capitalist or Socialist, advanced or backward. It is a problem that can never be solved in any thoroughgoing way, but only mitigated or kept under control by a variety of countervailing structures and influences.

Nadel and Rourke suggest the variety of ways that bureaucracies may be influenced and controlled externally or internally, through governmental and nongovernmental agencies and forces (see table X.5).[20] The

[19] Jeffrey Pressman and Aaron Wildavsky (Berkeley and Los Angeles: University of California Press, 1973).
[20] Mark V. Nadel and Frances E. Rourke, "Bureaucracies," in Fred I. Greenstein and Nelson W. Polsby, op. cit., 5: 416.

major external governmental control is, as we have suggested, the political executive. Although formally presidents, prime ministers, and ministers have the power to command subordinate officials and to remove them for nonperformance of duty, there is actually a mutual dependence and reciprocal control between political executives and bureaucracies. The power of the political executive is typically expressed in efforts at persuasion; only rarely does it take the extreme form of dismissal or transfer. Centralized budgeting practices and administrative reorganization are other means by which the political executive controls bureaucracy. The reallocation of resources among administrative agencies and the changing lines of authority may bring bureaucratic implementation into greater conformity with the aims of the political executive.

Legislative assemblies and courts also exercise significant external controls over bureaucracy. Legislative committee investigations, questions put to administrative agencies by members of parliamentary bodies, judicial processes controlling administrative excesses — all may have some effect on bureaucratic performance. The recent invention and rapid diffusion of the institution of the ombudsman is another indication of the problem of the control of bureaucracy from the perspective of injury or injustice to individuals.[21] The ombudsman in the Scandinavian countries, Britain, West Germany, and elsewhere is a special office that investigates individual claims of injury or of damage to individuals by governmental action, offering a procedure more expeditious and less costly than court action and reporting to the legislative body for remedial action.

The variety and kinds of controls we have been discussing operate among the advanced industrial democracies. Authoritarian systems lack many of these controls, particularly the external ones of elected political executives and legislators, independent courts, the media of communication, and interest groups. Communist systems seem particularly to be prone to bureaucratic inefficiency and conservatism, and their social costs must even be greater in view of the greater size of the public sector and greater scope of governmental activities. The principal controls are the agencies of the Communist parties such as the Politburo, the Central Committee and its Secretariat, and the Control Committee. But in the absence of free and competitive elections, autonomous interest groups, and a free press, the effectiveness of these controls is limited.

Thus "bureaucracy," in the sense of inefficiency and inertia, is endemic in all modern societies. It is truly a dilemma since people are unlikely to

---

[21] See D. C. Rowat, ed., *The Ombudsman: Citizen's Defender* (London: Allen and Unwin, 1965).

invent any schemes for carrying out large-scale social tasks without the organization, division of labor, and professionalization that bureaucracy provides. Its pathologies can only be mitigated. The art of modern political leadership consists not only in the prudent search for appropriate goals and policies, but also in an attempt to learn how to interact with the massive and complex bureaucracy — how and when to press and coerce it, reshuffle it, terminate its redundant and obsolete parts, flatter and reward it, teach it, and be taught by it.

PART IV

Public Policy

CHAPTER XI

The Performance of Political Systems

PUBLIC POLICIES express the goals that have emerged from the political process. They reflect the societal outcomes desired by the policy-making coalition and the means by which leaders think those outcomes can be achieved. For example, a housing policy may set minimum housing standards for a society and may specify the role that the political system is to play in achieving those standards. This role may range from total construction of most housing units by agencies of the governmental bureaucracy, as in the Soviet Union; through substantial fiscal encouragement of private efforts by tax exemptions and loan guarantees, as in the United States; to an absence of political intervention in housing.

But there is always a substantial gap between policy intention and policy consequences. There are two major reasons for this gap, the first of which was discussed above: policies pass through an implementing process and are changed in that process. The policy implementation function limits the innovative capability of policy makers. Except under unusual leadership or crisis conditions, the existing administrative programs, which have already achieved legitimacy and support, will take up most available resources. Implementation structures are often staffed by individuals who will resist policies they oppose or who are open to corruption and control by other groups. And the complexities of implementation may simply overload the capacity of the administrators.

The second major reason for the gap between policy intention and societal outcome is that policies interact with the social, economic, and cultural processes of the domestic and international environments that they are supposed to affect. The immediate *outputs* of the conversion process are authoritative actions of taking, giving, compelling, and communicating between the political system and its environments. Political decision makers attempt to use these actions to bring about various social consequences. But the interaction between the performance of the polit-

ical system and the environment it wishes to shape is often poorly
understood by policy makers, or it is subject to unpredictable external
factors.

For example, despite the great theoretical contributions and empirical
research of contemporary economists, the outputs used by policy makers
to combat inflation and unemployment often have unanticipated or
mixed consequences. Increasing taxation or reducing the money supply
through changing interest rates may dampen inflation, but simultaneously increase unemployment beyond acceptable levels. Cutting government expenditures may have the same unpleasant, mixed outcome. Direct
wage and price controls seem to create numerous economic distortions
in both the long run and the short run. And pleas to business leaders
for price restraint or to union leaders for wage restraint are often
ignored.

In many other policy areas, the relationships between intent and policy
outcome are even less well understood. Following the disastrous human
and economic consequences of the nation's Vietnam policy, on one hand,
and the numerous problems that have arisen in housing and welfare, on
on the other, Americans are by now sensitive to the fact that there is
much slippage between the intended and the actual consequences of
public policy. Moreover, even if the social and economic consequences of
policies have been anticipated, the goals and preferences of individuals
and groups in the society may have been only poorly reflected in the
original policy-making process. Some groups are mobilized to action only
after experiencing the consequences of policies. Thus in the case of
busing to overcome racial segregation in the schools, the policy decisions
were made by the courts and followed by pressure group mobilizations
intended to modify their decisions.

In figure XI.1 we offer a diagram of the political system, spelling out
in greater detail the performance side of the political process. Analytically, we can distinguish five phases: *policy making, policy implementation, policy outputs, policy outcomes,* and *feedbacks.* Having already
discussed some process aspects of the first two phases, we shall turn to
the outputs, outcomes, and feedback consequences. Given the various
uncertainties, the policy process may be best understood as a search, or
a process of trial and error. A particular policy output may be seen as a
trial or a test to be pursued, modified, or replaced by other tests as information regarding the outcome of policy initiatives is fed back into
the political system. As suggested by figure XI.1, these feedback loops
report progress or failure to all phases of the political process. The outcome of a policy may produce new political demands or allay old ones,
may increase or decrease support, may eventuate in amendments to old

Figure XI.1. *The Performance of Political Systems*

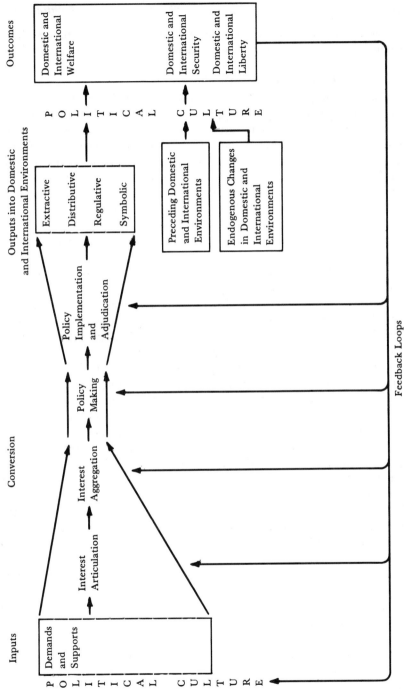

policy or adoption of new policy; and then the entire process begins again.

TYPES OF POLITICAL OUTPUTS

Comparison of political performance in the domestic and international environments can be approached in terms of four categories of outputs. Surely one salient category of political system performance is the extraction of resources from the domestic and international environments: money, goods, persons, or services. The extractive performance of the political system can be measured by the kinds of objects extracted, by the amounts extracted (both in absolute terms and in relation to resources), and by the groups affected by such extractions.

A second aspect of political system performance is its distributive activity. Comparisons can be based on what is being distributed — economic goods; services, such as education, health, sanitation, or recreation; and other values, such as status, prestige, or sense of community and safety. Other questions to be answered are what proportion of the total social product is being distributed by the political system, as opposed to other social systems, and what groups are — and are not — the beneficiaries of these distributions. Finally, charting these distributive patterns over time can provide a dynamic perspective.

A third significant category of performance concerns the regulation of human behavior. Every political system engages in some set of regulatory activities. For example, it punishes crime, compels performance of duties and obligations, licenses activities, regulates weights and measures, and so on. Performance in this dimension differs from one political system to another according to (1) the number and kinds of actions regulated, (2) the groups being regulated, (3) the procedural limits on enforcements, and (4) the types and severity of sanctions used to enforce compliance. Although one must not underestimate the complications involved in efforts to measure regulative performance, it should be possible to develop approximate measures of regulative performance over time for a single political system and to compare one system with another according to these regulatory patterns.

A fourth category of political system output is symbolic performance. We refer here to political speech, political rite and ritual, and political iconography. Much of the speech of political leaders takes the form of appeals — to historical memory; to the courage, boldness, wisdom, and magnanimity embodied in the nation's past; or to ideological values like equality, liberty, and community. This kind of symbolic output is intended to enhance other aspects of political system performance, that is, to make people pay their taxes more readily and honestly, comply with the law more faithfully, or accept sacrifice, danger, and hardship. Political systems differ in the extent to which they have reserves of the kind which are described above and upon which their political leaders can draw through exhortation.

Symbolic performance may take the form of promises of future accomplishments and rewards, and here again political systems differ in the confidence that populations have in their leaders and institutions, a confidence based in part on previous performance. Another aspect of symbolic performance touches the emotional, quasi-religious aspects of political systems. National holidays and celebrations, venerated persons, and monuments constitute significant aspects of symbolic performance. Reverence for these rituals, persons, institutions, and monuments is an important political system resource.

In considering these categories of political outputs, one must recognize the complexity of their interrelations and distinguish clearly between the concepts of *policy* and *output,* as defined here. The concept of policy implies a set of ends and means, for only rarely does a policy rely on a single means or category of output. For example, taxes intended to produce revenue may be primarily extractive. But an effective system of taxation is dependent on a mixture of regulation and exhortation as well: failure to pay taxes may be penalized by fines and prison sentences, but at the same time citizens are urged by political leaders to file honest tax returns. Thus, at least three output categories — extractive, regulative, and symbolic performance — will typically be used in the implementation of a tax policy. Moreover, the consequences of a tax policy will usually be complex, affecting different groups, as well as society at large, in various direct and indirect ways. Although the immediate ends of tax policy may be to obtain resources for implementing welfare and security programs, the incidence of taxes will directly shape the activities and welfare of various groups. As relationships between extraction and social outcomes have become more clearly understood, tax policy is debated and evaluated in complex, multilevel terms of means and ends. Will a particular tax or system of taxes produce adequate revenue to meet planned distributions? Is its incidence on the population equitable? Is it productive of future welfare and revenue in the sense of contributing to economic growth?

Similarly, American energy policy, which is intended to alter energy use behavior to conserve resources, has relied primarily on extractive and distributive inducements, as well as on symbolic exhortation, as the means of altering this behavior. In 1977 the Carter administration proposed an energy policy consisting primarily of financial incentives and disincentives: heavy taxes on "gas-guzzling" cars, rebates for gas-economizing cars, tax credits to industries converting from gas and oil to coal, tax credits to home owners for insulating their homes, and higher taxes on gas and oil. The aim of this policy was regulative; the means, however, were extractive, distributive, and symbolic. There was very little of a specifically regulative nature in this package of energy policy, save the penalties imposed for filing dishonest returns and reports. However, alternative policies that were being considered in the event of an energy crisis relied more directly on governmental regulative outputs, such as allocation of scarce energy supplies and the rationing of gas and oil. And the implications of both types of policies for outcomes other than energy conservation, outcomes such as economic growth and infringement on individual liberty, were hotly debated.

Even apparently straightforward policy programs such as unemployment insurance, old-age assistance, and provision of medical care are based on mixed extractive-distributive outputs and are backed up by regulative and symbolic outputs. Much welfare activity is based on what are called "transfer payments." Old-age assistance programs usually derive their resources from extractions or taxes imposed on employers and employees and distributed to persons on reaching a given age and meeting certain other qualifications. Violations of the statutes or regulations governing these programs may be penalized by fines or prison sentences, but public authorities also exercise moral pressure to deter individuals from infractions.

Despite these complexities of political outputs and their relation to policy, it is still useful to analyze and compare the political performance of countries in extractive, distributive, regulative, and symbolic terms. In the first place, the governmental acts of taking, giving, compelling, and communicating are the basic ingredients of policy and implementation that are combined in substantive policies in the complicated ways we have suggested.

In the second place, data on political performance are normally reported in these terms. Even though they leave much to be desired in accuracy, detail, and comparability, nations do report on their revenues and expenditures and, to a much less satisfactory extent, on crime, public order, and law enforcement. Consequently, the measures and comparisons of output we make in this chapter constitute a beginning in characterizing levels, magnitudes, and directions of governmental impacts. In the chapter that follows we will consider the outcomes in the general fields of welfare, safety, and liberty.

This kind of broad comparative analysis cannot take the place of substantive comparative policy analysis in specific fields such as income maintenance, taxation, medical care, educational opportunity, energy conservation, environmental protection, and crime prevention. Aggregate national comparisons can provide only sweeping profiles of governmental activity and its consequences in different kinds of political systems.[1]

In this and subsequent chapters we shall be reporting a great deal of quantitative data on governmental performance for advanced industrial countries and developing ones; for democratic, authoritarian, and Communist societies. These data are taken from the reports of international bodies such as the United Nations, UNESCO, and OECD (Organization for Economic Cooperation and Development), from national government reports, and from scholarly studies and data compilations. Since most of these data are based on national estimates and compilations, and since the standards and reliability of data gathering vary from country to country, we cannot guarantee their accuracy. They should be read and interpreted with caution.

EXTRACTIVE PERFORMANCE

Resources of some kind are extracted by all political systems, even the most rudimentary, in the form of obligatory service to the society. When primitive bands go to war, particular age sets among the males, or all able-bodied adults, may be required to contribute to the effort. Elders are often expected to give of their time in settling disputes, whereas all family groups may be obliged to contribute to efforts beyond the capabilities of a single family or kinship unit, as in construction of housing. Such direct extraction of service is found in even the most complex of modern-day states in the forms of military duty, other obligatory public service (jury duty, for instance), or compulsory labor imposed on those convicted of wrongdoings. Pillage is a common form of international extraction, legitimated in modern international law as spoils of war. Powerful nations may also impose trading requirements on smaller or less affluent countries, resulting in the funneling of resources from the weaker to the stronger.

What are the dimensions to be examined, then, in comparing the extractive performance of political systems? First, one must determine the absolute amount of resources that each political system is able to collect. Then, that figure is divided by the population of the country to obtain the per capita level of extraction. A third measure of extractive performance is based on how much of the national product is taken — for

---

[1] For more substantive treatments of comparative policy analysis, see Hugh Heclo, *Modern Social Politics in Britain and Sweden* (New Haven: Yale University Press, 1974); Arnold J. Heidenheimer, Hugh Heclo, and Carolyn Adams, *Comparative Public Policy* (New York: St. Martin's Press, 1975); Richard L. Siegel and Leonard Weinberg, *Comparing Public Policies* (Homewood, Ill.: Dorsey Press, 1977); Cynthia Enloe, *The Politics of Pollution in a Comparative Perspective* (New York: David McKay, 1975).

example, total taxes in a country as a percentage of its gross national product.

TAXATION

In modern polities the most common form of extraction is taxation. It is intriguing to speculate on the conditions under which taxation first appeared. What knowledge we have suggests that this device may originally have developed as a substitute for the disorganized pillage of other peoples:

> At the moment of the last campaign of Genghis Khan at Kanau, a Mongol general observed to him that his new Chinese subjects would be of no use to him, since they were not suited to war, and that consequently it would be better to exterminate the whole population — nearly 10 million souls — in order at least to benefit from the land that would be converted to pastures for the cavalry. Genghis Khan was considering this advice when Ye-liu Chu-ts'si . . . showed the Mongols . . . the advantages one could derive from fertile countries and industrious subjects. He explained that in raising taxes on the lands and imposing tariffs on merchandise, 500,000 ounces of silver, 80,000 pieces of silk, and 400,000 sacks of grain could be collected each year. And he carried the day. Genghis Khan charged Ye-liu Chu-ts'si with establishing an appropriate tax system. . . . To this end the conquered parts of China, until then considered a wasteland for arbitrary pillaging, was divided in the beginning of the year 1230 into 10 regular departments with a personnel of Mongol functionaries and educated Chinese.[2]

Even taxation of the subjects within a political system sometimes began in the same way. In England,

> the chief and oldest type of direct land taxation was the Danegeld, which had been levied and paid to buy off the Danes; indeed, direct taxation began in this somewhat humiliating form. Canute, the Danish invader, continued the tax, in spite of the extinction of its original purpose.[3]

There may also have been circumstances in which some other form of need, such as flood control, made the subjects of a regime willing to accept the burden of regular tax assessments. But such burdens are never equally distributed, and even within a single society they are apt to have constituted the means by which a dominant class or status group began to draw on the resources of the less powerful.

Figure XI.2 shows the total amount of revenues raised by governments — central, state, and local — in a number of contemporary nations. Man-

[2] Gabriel Ardant, *Théorie Sociologique de l'Impôt* (Paris: Librairie Fayard, 1971), 1: 30–31.

[3] B. E. V. Sabine, *A History of Income Tax* (London: George Allen and Unwin, 1966), p. 11.

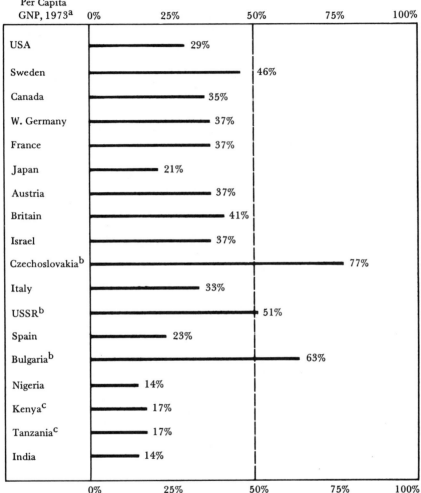

Figure XI.2. *Governmental Extractive Performance: Taxes, Social Security Contributions, and Profits and Interest from State Holdings as Percentage of Gross Domestic Product 1970*

Source: United Nations, *Yearbook of National Accounts Statistics 1973.* (New York: United Nations, 1974).

[a]World Bank, *World Bank Atlas* (Washington, D.C., 1975), p. 3.

[b]Source: Richard A. Musgrave, *Fiscal Systems* (New Haven: Yale University Press, 1969) p. 43. Estimates are for 1963 or 1964. Because of the very great differences in economic structures, comparisons between Communist and less centralized nations should be considered only very rough approximations.

[c]Source: Donald G. Morrison, Robert C. Mitchell, John N. Paden, and Hugh M. Stevenson, *Black Africa: A Comparative Handbook* (New York: The Free Press, 1972), p. 110.

datory social security contributions of employers and workers are included, since these are an important part of extracted revenue in many modern societies. The figure shows that even among the wealthiest nations there are substantial differences in the ratio of governmental revenue to gross domestic product.[4] Sweden takes about 44 percent of the domestic national product in the form of revenue; Britain, around 40 percent; Austria, Israel, France, West Germany, Canada, and Italy, a third or more. The United States took in 1970 only about 29 percent, while Japan and Spain extracted less than 25 percent. At the very bottom in extractive efforts come the very poor nations, such as India, Kenya, Tanzania, and Nigeria, taking only about 15 percent. In general, it is easier for the political system to extract greater percentages of resources — as well as greater absolute amounts — from a developed industrial economy.[5] In less developed, agrarian societies, in which most individuals are living at the subsistence level, it is difficult both to extract much of their income and to sustain the administrative structures that maintain such extractive capability. Indeed, S. N. Eisenstadt argues that the appearance of some "free-floating" resources was an essential factor in the emergence of the first great historical "bureaucratic empires." [6] The strategic problems in development created by such constraints are discussed below in chapter XIII.

Beyond the constraints of development, policy objectives and strategies play a major role in shaping the level and form of resource extraction. Considering the Socialist states of Czechoslovakia, the Soviet Union, and Bulgaria, one finds that the government extracts over 50 percent of the economic resources of the society.[7] And, as we shall show below, the im-

---

[4] We have used GDP in the table, rather than gross national product, because it is reported in statistics for more nations; the figures are very similar in these cases. For the sake of reasonable simplicity in discussion we have also not presented here the forms of government deficit financing through borrowing or inflationary policies; a full-scale treatment of resource extraction and its impact will have to do so, however.

[5] Richard Musgrave, *Fiscal Systems* (New Haven: Yale University Press, 1969), provides a useful review of historical evidence in this century; see chaps. 5 and 6. Also see Harold Wilensky, *The Welfare State and Equality* (Berkeley and Los Angeles: University of California Press, 1975). Of course, some income bases, such as mining or oil production, may be made subject to extraction much more easily than others. But the average government revenue as a percent of GNP among the black African nations in 1968 was only 19 percent. Even the avowedly Socialist regime in Guinea extracted only 32 percent, in contrast to the "command" economies in Eastern Europe (Morrison et al., *Black Africa*, p. 110).

[6] S. N. Eisenstadt, *The Political Systems of Empires* (New York: Free Press of Glencoe, 1963).

[7] Musgrave, op. cit., p. 43. Figures for the Socialist states are for 1963 or 1964. Due to the very different economic and political systems and accounting bases, comparisons should be made only at a very general level and with due caution. Moreover, the figures for both Socialist and non-Socialist countries are based on information provided by their respective governments and should be accepted only provisionally and cautiously.

pact of governments on the flow of resources in Socialist societies is even greater than the large extractive figures would indicate.

Having determined the aggregate levels of extractive performance, one would want to assess the *incidence* of extraction. That is, how is the burden distributed in each of the countries considered? Not surprisingly, the incidence of taxation has been intimately related to the distribution of political power. In the extreme example of the Mongol suzerainty over China, the Mongols had all the political power, and the Chinese paid all the taxes. Indeed, examination of the great political struggles throughout history, especially the landmark victories of democratization, reveals that the issue at stake has more often been taxation than participation. The nobles who met with King John at Runnymede to produce the Magna Carta were not concerned with participation, but with protection from arbitrary tax levies. The origins of the French Revolution are to be found in part in the fiscal privileges of the nobility and clergy and in the heavy indirect taxes imposed by the French monarchy; these were replaced after the revolution, at least in principle, by a system of progressive taxation.

As we have already suggested, taxation has varied objectives other than merely extracting resources for financing programs. An important instrument of income redistribution, it has also become a major fiscal tool for controlling inflation and for stimulating growth and employment. And taxes have often been designed to discourage the use of products — oil, tobacco, and alcohol, for example. Conversely, tax exemptions may be granted to stimulate certain types of behavior, such as charitable contributions or preferred forms of investment.

Perhaps the most familiar form in modern times is the personal income tax. Income taxes can vary in the degree to which they take greater, smaller, or equal proportions from individuals of various incomes. A tax that takes greater percentages from those with higher incomes is called *progressive;* one that takes a larger slice of the income of the less affluent is known as *regressive.* An income tax that takes an equal percentage from all individuals regardless of their income level (for example, 20 percent of all incomes) is known as a *proportional* tax. Consumer sales taxes, which take a fixed percentage of the purchase price, tend to be regressive, since persons with lower incomes may spend a larger proportion of their income on the taxed items.

The value-added tax — a form of taxation widely used in recent years, especially in Western Europe — is also regressive. In simple terms, this is a tax imposed on a product at each stage of its production and sale. Each firm pays a tax on the basis of the difference between the price at which it purchases a product (or its components) and the price at which it sells the product. The cumulative taxes paid by each firm are added to the purchase price paid by the ultimate consumer, who in effect reimburses each firm for the share that it paid.[8] A value-added tax is very efficient in that it is easier to collect a tax from a limited number of producing firms than from a multitude of consumers; and it may be easier to control for tax evasion than an income tax. As it is more hidden from the purchaser's view, it is also sometimes believed to be more politically acceptable to taxpayers, but its regressive quality makes it controversial.

In table XI.1, total governmental revenues for seventeen nations are divided into four categories: direct income taxes; indirect taxes (including value-added and turnover taxes, as well as property and sales taxes); social security contributions; and interest, rents, and profits earned by governments from economic and fiscal enterprises. Income taxes, both individual and corporate, are progressive in these nations, while indirect expenditure taxes tend to be regressive; and the progressiveness of social security contributions depends on the percentage paid by employers. Britain's total revenue is more heavily dependent on expenditure taxes than is American revenue, although its income tax bears more heavily on higher incomes. Switzerland may have the most progressive system of extraction of the nations in the table, with more than 43 percent taken in direct taxes and over 23 percent in social security contributions, a large portion of which is paid by employers. An accurate assessment, however, would depend on factors not indicated by the table: the progressiveness of the income tax and the degree to which employers' social security contributions and corporate income taxes can be passed along to the consumer in higher prices. The very poor nations of India and Nigeria have limited social security contribution programs and rely heavily on various excise and sales taxes.

In the Socialist nations, the major source of revenue has been a turnover tax, which is levied on goods in the production process and, which, like the value-added tax, is hidden from the consumer and tends toward regressiveness. An average of 40 to 50 percent, sometimes as much as 90 percent, of the price of the product is taken in taxes. Other major income sources are "profits" from state-run industries and various social insurance contributions required of individuals. As one can see in table XI.1, none of the Socialist nations shown — the Soviet Union, Czechoslovakia, and Bulgaria — uses individual income taxes as a large revenue producer. The Soviet Union has used direct taxation primarily to discourage certain activities — doctors and lawyers with private practices, priests, artisans not in cooperatives, farm income from private plots of land, and the like. Income equalization effects have been attempted primarily through direct governmental regulation of wage and salary rates

---

[8] Bernard P. Herber, *Modern Public Finance* (Homewood, Ill.: Richard Irwin, 1971), pp. 199–201.

Table XI.1. *Elements Constituting Total Government Extractions, as Percentages, 1970*

Nations in order of per capita GNP, 1973	Direct taxes[a]	Indirect taxes	Social security contributions		Profits, interest, from state enterprises, etc.	Total
			Total	Employers' part[b]		
USA	45%	33%	20%	(9.5%)	2%	100%
Switzerland	43	29	23	(21.5)	5	100
Sweden	45	27	21		7	100
Canada	41	43	8		9	101
W. Germany	28	37	31	(17.4)	4	100
France	18	39	39	(28.7)	2	98
Japan	42	36	18	(11.3)	4	100
Austria	33	43	22		1	99
Britain	38	40	15	(7.3)	7	100
Israel	32	45	16		7	100
Czechoslovakia	10	39	31		20	100
Italy	19	39	35		7	100
USSR	7	38	22		32	99
Spain	20	41	32	(27.5)	8	101
Bulgaria	6	49	28		17	100
Nigeria	22	56	9		12	99
India	21	68	–		11	100

Sources: United Nations, *Yearbook of National Accounts Statistics 1973* (New York: United Nations, 1974). The reader is reminded that comparisons with Communist nations are only very rough estimates, given both the data and the very different economic structures involved. See Musgrave, *Fiscal Systems*.

[a] Primarily income taxes.

[b] Data on employer contributions of social security taken from Central Statistical Office, *Social Trends* (London: HMSO, 1972), p. 183.

Figure XI.3. *Personal Income Tax Rates in Eight Nations*

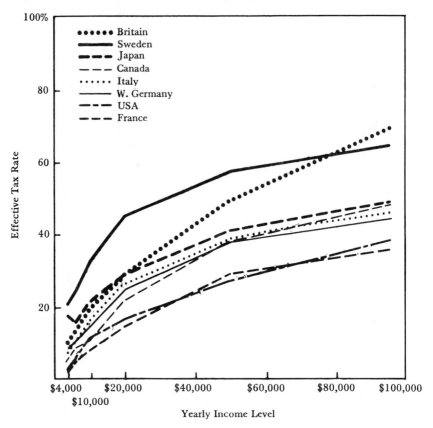

Source: Musgrave, *Fiscal Systems*, pp. 182-184.
Note: Effective tax rates (the ratio of total tax liability to total income) are computed as the percentage of wage and salary income of a married taxpayer with two dependents in the early 1960s. Yearly income levels show equivalent purchasing power in dollars.

and through the provision of public benefits, rather than through progressive taxation.[9]

While table XI.1 provides a picture of the extent of reliance of various countries on different forms of revenue extraction, it does not indicate how progressive or regressive the respective tax burdens are. Although in general such data are very limited, figure XI.3 shows the effective in-

[9] In addition to the general discussion in Musgrave, op. cit., see also Franklyn D. Holzman, "Economic Organization of Communism," *International Encyclopedia of the Social Sciences*, 3: 146 ff.

come taxes imposed on wages and salaries in eight nations. Britain imposes the highest rates at the upper end of the scale, its 70 percent of the highest incomes (after deductions) exceeding that of Sweden. In contrast, France imposes only a 36 percent tax on an income of $100,000. At the middle-income ranges, Sweden imposes the highest taxes, followed by Britain. Levels in France are generally the lowest, although the pattern in the United States is quite similar. The other four nations fall closely together in the middle, both in level and in rate of progressiveness.

The effective tax rate on salary and wage income is, of course, far from being the whole picture. One exception to the general income tax scales is the treatment of capital gains — income received from the sale of capital assets. In the United States, capital losses are first subtracted from the amount earned, and the difference is taxed at only half the normal rate. As this type of income accrues more frequently to the wealthy, the effect is to lower the progressiveness of the tax system as a whole.[10] Due to various exceptions, moreover, in 1967 in the United States there were 399 individuals with incomes over $100,000 who paid no tax on a combined income of over $185 million and 23 persons with incomes in excess of $1 million who paid no tax on a combined income of $95 million.[11] Even more significant in reducing general tax progressiveness is the impact of sales, payroll, and property taxes. Pechman and Okner show that total tax burdens for Americans increase only from about 20 percent in the $3,000–5,000 income range to about 32 percent in the $50,000–100,000 range.[12] The progressive income tax is substantially counterbalanced by the regressive taxes at other levels. The data in table XI.1 suggest that many other national tax structures are even more regressive.

MILITARY SERVICE

Nations also extract services from their populations; jury and military duty are illustrations in modern societies. Here again, nations differ in the degree to which they require these services and in the incidence of these burdens and duties among groups in their populations. Courts may discriminate against social and ethnic groups in the recruitment of juries, and exemptions from military duty may have a similar bias. Volunteer military services recruit more heavily among the poor and disadvantaged; where there is compulsory conscription, those pursuing higher education or having special skills may be exempted.

---

[10] Herber, op. cit., pp. 142–43. Also see Heidenheimer, Heclo, and Adams, op. cit., chap. 8.
[11] Herber, op. cit., p. 147.
[12] Joseph A. Pechman and Benjamin A. Okner, *Who Bears the Tax Burden?* (Washington: Brookings Institution, 1974), pp. 57–65.

Table XI.2. *Military Recruitment in Selected Nations, 1965*

Nations in order of per capita GNP, 1965	Total number	Number per thousand of working-age population
USA	3,000,000	25.9
Sweden	181,000	35.2
Canada	120,000	10.3
France	550,000	17.9
W. Germany	450,000	11.6
Britain	424,000	12.1
Czechoslovakia	235,000	25.6
Israel	250,000	163.9
USSR	3,150,000	22.4
Austria	25,000	5.4
Italy	390,000	11.5
Japan	250,000	3.7
Bulgaria	152,000	27.4
Spain	250,000	12.4
Mexico	68,000	3.2
Yugoslavia	247,000	20.2
Brazil	200,000	4.5
Egypt	180,000	11.3
China	2,500,000	6.6
India	1,000,000	3.7
Kenya	3,000	.6
Nigeria	9,000	.3
Tanzania	1,000	.2

Source: Charles L. Taylor and Michael C. Hudson, *World Handbook of Political and Social Indicators*, 2d ed. (New Haven: Yale University Press, 1972), pp. 38 ff.

In table XI.2 we offer data on the extent of military recruitment in a variety of nations. Israel stands out in the extent of military extraction, having more than 16 percent of its working-age population in the military services. Surprisingly, a neutral power — Sweden — is second in the impact of military service on its population. Nations actively involved in international politics, such as the United States and the Soviet Union, are also heavily burdened, though proportionately not as heavily as smaller countries, such as Czechoslovakia and Yugoslavia. Among the larger, economically advanced countries Japan is conspicuous for the small scale of its military establishment. At the small end of the extractive continuum of military service are the African nations of Kenya, Nigeria, and Tanzania.

DISTRIBUTIVE PERFORMANCE

Measuring the level and incidence of extraction only reveals who pays, who serves, and how much. One must also consider who benefits. The distributive performance of the political system refers to the allocation of money, goods, services, honors, statuses, and opportunities of various kinds to individuals and groups in the society. It, too, can be measured and compared, relevant factors including the quantity of whatever is distributed, the areas of human life touched by these benefits, the particular sections of the population receiving benefits, and the relationship between human needs and governmental distributions intended to meet those needs.

Some aspects of distribution can be measured in a relatively straightforward way. For the most part, governmental expenditures constitute distributions that can be characterized according to the area of life and the groups in the population benefiting from them. One might distinguish, for example, among expenditures designed to meet material needs of individuals, such as unemployment insurance and medical care; expenditures designed to assist in their economic activities, such as insurance on bank deposits and mortgages or loans to small businesses; expenditures designed to provide collective health, safety, and recreation, such as sewerage projects, police protection, and public parks; and expenditures designed to ensure national defense and security. Governmental expenditures may also be differentiated by the social and economic groupings at which they are directed: various income levels; special sectors of the economy, such as agriculture; different regions, such as Appalachia in the United States or the Mezzogiorno in Italy; ethnic groups, such as blacks; or special institutional groups, such as the military or the political elite itself. The distributive performance of a political system is said to be increasing when the amount distributed increases and when the range of individuals and groups receiving benefits broadens. There are both aggregate and distributive aspects.

Among the questions to ask in describing and comparing distributive performance, then, are the following:

1. How large is the distributive activity of the political system? (For example, what proportion of the national product is spent in distributive activities of the political system?)

2. How does the political system allocate its expenditures among various functions and activities? (For example, how much is allocated to education, defense, health, or income maintenance?)

3. Who are the beneficiaries of these expenditures?

In the following discussion of distributive performance we shall illustrate how countries differ in these first two respects; since the third question is much more complex and the data required to answer it are less accessible, we can reflect upon it only briefly. In table XI.3 we attempt to indicate both gross levels and kinds of distributions, relative to national product, that are made by some nations on which more or less comparable data exist. The table shows the efforts made in three

Table XI.3. *Substantive and Aggregate Government Expenditures as Percentage of Gross Domestic Product, 1965*

Nations in order of per capita GNP, 1965	Public education[a]	Defense[b]	Social security and health[c]	Total of columns 1-3	Total 1965 disbursements[d]	Difference between 4 and 5
USA	5%	7%	8%	21%	27%	(6%)
Sweden	7	4	17	28	41	(13)
Canada	6	3	10	19	28	(9)
France	4	6	18	28	37	(9)
W. Germany	3	4	20	27	35	(8)
Britain	5	6	14	25	33	(8)
Czechoslovakia	5	6	17	28	77e	(49)
Israel	5	12	8	25	30	(5)
USSR	7	9	10	26	51e	(25)
Austria	4	1	21	26	36	(10)
Italy	6	3	18	27	32	(5)
Japan	5	1	6	12	20	(8)
Bulgaria	4	3	11	18	63e	(45)
Spain	1	3	4	8	18	(10)
Mexico	2	1	3	6	—	—
Yugoslavia	5	5	12	22	—	—
Brazil	2	3	8	13	—	—
Egypt	5	8				—
India	2	4	1	7	16	(9)
Kenya	4	1			13	—
Nigeria	1	1			10.	—

[a] Taylor and Hudson, *World Handbook*, pp. 30 ff. (India and Japan include private spending).
[b] Ibid., pp. 34 ff.
[c] Harold Wilensky, *The Welfare State and Equality* (Berkeley and Los Angeles: University of California Press, 1975), pp. 122–24. Includes health and social security programs, 1966.
[d] United Nations, *Yearbook of National Accounts Statistics 1969, 1970* (New York: United Nations, 1970, 1972).
[e] Musgrave, *Fiscal Systems*, p. 48. (Bulgaria is 1963; USSR and Czechoslovakia are 1964).

general areas of government activity: education, health and social security, and defense. In these substantive areas we can compare the efforts made, relative to total resources, by nations with very different economic and fiscal systems. The fifth column shows the total of efforts in these three substantive areas; and the sixth, total expenditures of all kinds.

Some specific observations can be made from this table. Examination of the expenditures on education in 1965 indicates that there is a range from 7 percent in the Soviet Union to 1 percent in Spain and Nigeria. This is one of the most important components of distributive performance, for the level of education within a population is closely related to its skill and productivity. As a political resource, education encourages persons to gain access to the political process and to demand benefits from it. Finally, education enables individuals to improve their own welfare.

Providing a broader perspective on such expenditures, table XI.4 suggests how much effort is being made by governments in various parts of the world to improve the educational levels of their populations and how this has been changing over the last decade. If one compares the 1960 column to the 1970 column, the so-called gap between the rich and poor countries is clearly reflected. Although the proportion of public expenditure going into education has been increasing in all parts of the world, it has increased to a somewhat larger extent in the developed countries than in the developing areas. In the developed countries there has been an increase in the decade from 4.2 percent of GNP in 1960 to 5.8 percent in 1970, while in the developing countries it has increased

Table XI.4. *Public Expenditure on Education as Percentage of GNP by Continents, Major Regions, and Groups of Countries*

	1960	*1965*	*1970*
World Total	3.9	5.0	5.5
Africa	3.2	3.3	4.3
North and South America	3.9	5.2	6.4
Asia (excl. USSR)	2.9	3.8	3.5
Europe	3.6	4.5	4.8
USSR	5.9	7.3	6.8
Developed countries	4.2	5.2	5.8
Developing countries	2.4	3.2	3.4
Africa (excl. Arab States)	2.6	2.9	3.9
Northern America	4.1	5.4	6.8
Latin America	2.3	3.2	3.7
Asia (excl. Arab States)	2.8	3.7	3.4
Arab States	4.5	4.3	4.8

Source: *UNESCO Statistical Yearbook* (Paris: UNESCO Press, 1974), pp. 116–17.

only from 2.4 percent in 1960 to 3.4 percent in 1970. (Nor do most poor countries have substantial private educational systems.) If one also takes into account the fact that per capita GNP in the advanced industrial nations is many times larger than in the less industrialized nations, it is clear that the third world is rapidly falling behind in educational development.

In the case of expenditures on defense, there is an even wider range of expenditure levels, from 12 percent in Israel to 1 percent in Japan, Mexico, and Kenya. Defense is one area for which the per capita wealth of the nation is a poor predictor of the magnitude of spending efforts. Nations that are locked in tense international conflicts (Israel and Egypt) or that undertake widespread efforts at international influence (the United States and the Soviet Union) make major defense efforts, even at the cost of a substantial drain on other areas and on total resources.

On the other hand, in an investigation of social welfare expenditures, including both health care and social security programs, Harold Wilensky found the level of economic development to be of primary importance.[13] As shown by table XI.3, it is difficult for the very poor nations to develop extensive welfare programs. Although only a few of the poorer nations we have been examining make available such social security data, both subjective materials and data on other poor nations indicate how little of their resources are spent on welfare programs. Of the sixteen poorest nations on which Wilensky has data — all with per capita GNP figures under $300 — the average social welfare spending was 2.5 percent of GNP.[14] Wilensky notes, however, that population explosions and life expectancy in these poorer nations mean a younger age structure, so that old-age pension needs may be more limited. The extended family often remains an important factor in caring for those without personal incomes, as does direct subsistence from family agricultural plots.

Although all of the wealthier nations make a notable effort to assist in the care of aged and unemployed citizens — a glaring need in societies with high economic interdependence, high mobility, and weakened family systems — the extent and thrust of those efforts vary. The United States, for example, makes less than half the effort of the European nations, relative to resources, to provide public health and social security benefits. In a study of the development of social policy in the United States and Europe, Arnold Heidenheimer summarized differences in the development of social insurance, public education, health services, and public housing in the following terms:

1. Public *social insurance* and some other kinds of income maintenance pro-

---

[13] Wilensky, op. cit., chap. 2.
[14] Ibid., p. 19.

grams were introduced in the U.S. with about a one-generation lag behind Europe, but then exhibited growth rates which tended to bring the scope of American programs closer to those of Europeans.

2. With regard to *public education,* the broadening of U.S. post-primary school opportunities occurred a generation earlier than in Europe, and European systems have only in the past few decades allowed their secondary and tertiary systems to enter the take-off stage.

3. With regard to *non-educational public services and benefits* in kind, such as health services and public housing, where markets have been dominated by private suppliers, U.S. programs have lagged behind European ones by as much as two generations. These programs long remained in the "non-takeoff" category, exhibiting low growth rates compared to their European counterparts.[15]

Heidenheimer explains these different patterns of growth in social policy by the different political and cultural tendencies in the American and European areas, with greater stress on educational opportunity in the United States and an earlier and greater stress on welfare obligations in European societies.

Wilensky finds also that governmental centralization and well-organized working-class movements have a positive effect on welfare expenditure efforts. Given the level of societal resources, major efforts in military expenditures and, to some degree, education, showed negative effects on welfare expenditure in sixty-four nations.[16] Interestingly enough, among the wealthier nations the Socialist systems and the modern European democracies show rather similar levels of distributive performance in the area of social welfare.[17] Once again, one can see how the combination of available resources, social needs, and coalitional preferences and strategies shape policy outputs. All political systems must make choices about how much to extract from their environments and about how and to whom to distribute those extractions; however, the wealthy systems can extract more easily and face less painful distributive decisions.

We must, however, repeat our warning about too quick a leap to inferences about policy *outcomes* from our comparative analysis of output efforts. For one thing, efforts relative to resources are not the same thing as efforts per person. In spending about 8 percent of its national product on welfare in 1966, the United States was making about as much

[15] Arnold Heidenheimer, "The Politics of Public Education, Health and Welfare in the USA and Western Europe," *British Journal of Political Science* 3 (July 1973): 316–17. See Heidenheimer, Heclo, and Adams, op. cit.; also Siegel and Weinberg, op. cit., chap. 6.

[16] Wilensky, op. cit., chaps. 3–4.

[17] Ibid. A similar conclusion is reached by Frederic L. Pryor, *Public Expenditures in Communist and Capitalist Nations* (Homewood, Ill.: Richard Irwin, 1968).

an effort in dollars per person as France, Germany, or Austria, because its per capita GNP was twice as great at that time.[18] With very substantial wealth and a high percentage effort, Sweden was outspending all other nations by far on a per-person basis. Second, one must remember that in the area of welfare — in contrast to defense, and to a much greater extent than in education — expenditures in the private sector contribute substantially to the welfare outcomes in the population. This is especially so in the United States, which has a very substantial private medical sector. Public social security programs are more progressive than private ones and may thus result in increased income transfers to the less affluent, but social outcomes depend on both public and private sectors. In the next chapter, we shall look more carefully at social outcomes of welfare and security, to which these outputs contribute.

Returning to the fifth and sixth columns in table XI.3, one can see that the combined efforts made in the three major substantive areas of education, welfare, and defense are notably affected by the wealth of the society. As we have already pointed out, it is difficult for poorer nations to extract resources for these governmental purposes. Of course, the specific patterns and amounts vary within wealth levels. Not only does Japan spend little on defense, relying on American protection and limited by treaties and its own constitution, but it also spends rather little on public welfare (due, in part, to private corporate programs). Canada also has a rather low public profile in both areas. The Soviet Union spends rather less on welfare and more on defense and education than does its fellow Socialist state of Czechoslovakia. But there is not much systematic difference between Socialist and market-oriented nations in these areas.

However, the sixth and seventh columns indicate, as did the extraction analysis, that the Socialist regimes extract and distribute much greater proportions of their societies' resources than do the market-oriented regimes. The differences between the substantive areas shown and the total budgets are accounted for by government administrative costs; a variety of minor programs of subsidies, economic spending, housing, and the like; debt payment; and government capital investment in certain areas of the economy. In the non-Socialist regimes these combined areas constitute a rather consistent 5 to 10 percent of the national product. In the Socialist regimes they account for 25 to 50 percent of the national product; the government capital investment programs, which reflect

[18] Of course, ideally we would like to know about per person effort relative to the size of disadvantaged groups in the population, such as the elderly. Moreover, some goods, such as medical care, may vary in relative expense within societies, making aggregate comparisons also somewhat misleading.

government ownership of major industrial sectors, are primarily responsible for the difference.[19] We have not broken down these figures in detail because of the great complexity and the difficulties in comparing the data. But even the rough figures point out the major differences between market-oriented regimes and "command economies" such as the Soviet Union, Czechoslovakia, and Bulgaria.

Although the figures in table XI.3 are to be treated as only the roughest estimates, being drawn from a variety of sources, this conclusion is consistent with the results of more detailed studies. Scholars such as Musgrave and Pryor have pointed out that the major difference in extraction and distribution between the Socialist and market-oriented states lies not in their substantive welfare and defense programs, but in their control over the patterns of profit, decision, and investment in economic enterprises.[20]

A historical perspective on the growth of distributive performance may also be helpful. Figure XI.4 shows the trends in public expenditure for all purposes, for all nonmilitary purposes, and for social services alone in the United States, Britain, and Germany from 1890 through the mid-1960s. The most general pattern is similar in all three systems: total governmental expenditures as a percentage of GNP rose from around one-tenth to one-third or more at the same time that wealth itself was increasing rapidly. (The national product increased 300 to 400 percent in the United States over this time span.) Except in the United States, where the defense share rose markedly after 1940, the general increase in expenditures has been most strongly affected by the growth in outlays for social services. Shown as the shaded areas in figure XI.4, this category includes education, welfare programs, social insurance, and housing and has been responsible for 66 percent of the increase in civilian expenditures in the United States, 72 percent in Germany, and 82 percent in Great Britain.[21] Economic expenditures such as highway construction, have risen even more rapidly, but constitute a much smaller share of the expenditure budget. Although one must view such figures with caution (especially given the comparability problems arising from regime changes in Germany), the broad picture is quite clear: rising public expenditures in these nations have been in large part a consequence of increasing governmental provision of social services.

---

[19] See especially Musgrave, op. cit., chap. 2.
[20] Musgrave, op. cit., Pryor, op. cit.
[21] Musgrave, op. cit., p. 93. See also Alan T. Peacock and Jack Wiseman, *The Growth of Public Expenditures in the United Kingdom* (Princeton, N.J.: National Bureau of Economic Research, 1961).

Figure XI.4. *Government Expenditures as Percentage of GNP for the United States, Britain, and Germany, 1890–1963*

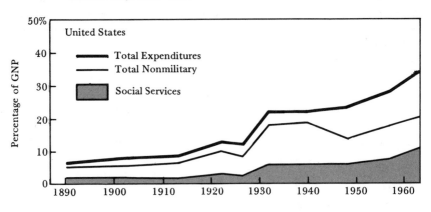

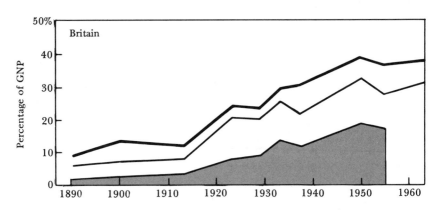

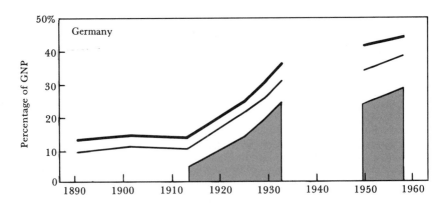

Source: Musgrave, *Fiscal Systems*, pp. 94-95.

Ideally, of course, we should like to have for all these nations more precise data on who has received the various expenditures: the ill, the unemployed, the aged, the large family, the single-parent family and so on. Under the education category we would like to see how much goes to higher education, vocational education, or primary schools. Thus, it would be possible to make comparisons in distributive performance according to our criteria of what is being distributed, how much, and to whom. In the end, we should like to make such analyses in reference to the policy propensity map of the political culture, comparing actual distributions to those preferred by various groups. Such systematic and comprehensive comparisons across nations are not possible, however, without major research efforts.

REGULATIVE PERFORMANCE

Regulative performance refers to the exercise of control by a political system over the behavior of individuals and groups in the society. The regulative activities of modern political systems have proliferated enormously in the last century or so. Industrialization and urban concentration have produced interdependence and problems of traffic, health, and public order, while growth in the size of industrial enterprises has created monopoly problems, industrial safety problems, and labor exploitation problems. At the same time, secularization has led to a recognition of the possibility of responding to these problems with governmental action. The process referred to as modernization has produced a veritable blanket of regulatory activities.

The pattern of regulation in political systems varies not only with the broad socioeconomic and cultural changes associated with modernization, but also with changes in other cultural values. Thus in recent years the scope of regulation has extended to include the protection of voting rights, the elimination of racial segregation, the prohibition of discrimination against minority groups and women in employment, the control of pollution, and the like. At the same time there has been a lightening of the regulative impact in the moral sphere — birth control, abortion, divorce, and sexual conduct.

There is a close interactive relationship between regulation and extraction: there cannot be one without the other. In an investigation of the origins of the state in Western Europe, Charles Tilly and his associates have shown how in the fifteenth to the eighteenth centuries, threatened by internal and external rivals and seeing opportunities for expansion, the successful state builders sought to develop powerful and reliable military forces.[22] This need led to the development of modern

[22] Charles Tilly, ed., *The Formation of National States in Western Europe* (Princeton: Princeton University Press, 1975).

forms of taxation, which in turn led to the emergence of a central regulative bureaucracy to ensure a productive and predictable flow of money, goods, and services for the armed forces and the other activities and functions of the emerging state. It is impossible to extract resources effectively without regulation; and it is impossible to regulate without officials and, therefore, resources to support and reward them.

ASPECTS OF REGULATORY OUTPUT

In characterizing the regulative performance of a political system, one should be able to answer the following three questions:

1. What aspects of human behavior and interaction are regulated and to what degree?

2. What groups in the society are so regulated and with what procedural limitations on enforcement?

3. What types of sanctions are used to compel or induce performance?

In table XI.5 we outline an analytical scheme for approaching the first and third of these questions. Each specifies an aspect of human interaction that is subject to political regulation; each column specifies the general form of sanction used to secure compliance. In the various cells we suggest examples of these different types of governmental regulation.

On the rows of table XI.5, we list the major categories of behavior and activity subject to government regulation, which we refer to as the *domain* of regulation. Family relations — marriage, divorce, parent-child responsibilities, and inheritance — are universal subjects of governmental regulation with differing patterns from country to country, as is personal conduct — drunkenness, vagrancy, truancy, loitering, and sexual behavior. Protection of person and property has to be viewed not only as a regulation of behavior, but also in the positive sense as a provision of security and safety. Thus, a high crime rate and a low ratio of crimes committed to criminals apprehended and punished has to be viewed as poor regulative performance.

Under the spatial mobility category we refer to traffic regulations, passport regulations, curfews, and restrictions on residence and access to transportation and other facilities such as those imposed on blacks in South Africa or formerly in the United States. The control of social mobility in modern times has taken the form of restrictions on access to education, occupation, voting, and public office. Jews were denied access to higher education in most European countries until well into the nineteenth century. In Britain it was not until the early and mid-nineteenth century that religious restrictions were lifted on admission to the universities and that Catholics, Protestant dissenters, and Jews became eligible to serve in Parliament. In Communist countries entrance into a

Table XI.5. *Examples of the Scope of Regulation and Sanctions for Compliance*

	Form of sanctions	
Domains regulated	Authorization or validation	Prescription or proscription
Family relations	Medical tests before marriage; marriage certificate required	Rule of monogamy; parental approval for marriage of minors
Personal conduct	Right to drink in public places on proof of age	Laws prohibiting disorderly conduct
Protection of person	Right of self-defense; power of citizen arrest	Laws penalizing crimes against persons
Protection of property	Right of self-defense; power of citizen arrest	Laws penalizing crimes against property
Spatial mobility	Passport for foreign travel	Restriction in access to defense installations
Social mobility	"Apartheid" control of intergroup contacts in South Africa	Access to public accommodations regardless of race
Professional and occupational qualifications	Certification for professions and trades	Laws governing withdrawal of license for unprofessional conduct
Economic activity	Licenses for sale of alcoholic beverages	Penalties for violating antipollution laws
Religious activity	Grant to churches of right to regulate marriage, divorce	Prohibition of religious activity causing nuisance to others
Political activity	Voting registration laws	Denial of right to vote to felons; fines for non-voting (Australia, Belgium, Costa Rica)

variety of statuses and roles has been denied to former members of the bourgeoisie and, to some extent, their children.

Professional and occupational qualification is commonly regulated in all modern societies, usually through certifying boards or administrative agencies. Aspects of economic activity — wages, prices, weights, measures, and coinage — have been subject to governmental control from time immemorial. Industrialization has brought with it an enormous increase in this form of governmental regulation. Industrial market economies are characterized by innumerable regulations — to control such naturally limited facilities as broadcasting channels and railways, to prevent monopolies, to protect the safety and health of workers and employees, to prevent the exploitation of labor through minimum-wage and maximum-hour rules, to prohibit interference by employers in the formation of trade unions by workers, to control the quality of goods produced. In nonmarket economies, as we have noted, regulation plays a far larger role, including decisions about types of goods to be produced and about wage, price, and investment levels.

Despite the spread of religious toleration in the last century or so, religious activity still continues to be subject to government regulation. In some Catholic and Islamic countries and in Israel, some aspects of the canon or religious law may actually be parts of the public law and may be enforced by governmental agencies. In Communist countries religious bodies are limited in the kinds of activities they can carry on, particularly as they relate to education and propaganda. The regulation of political activity includes rules pertaining to the right to vote and hold office, rules affecting the freedom of the press and other media of communication, and rules limiting the right of petition, public assembly, and association. The conduct of electoral campaigns and their financing may also be subject to regulation.

Regulation in each domain can take the forms of validation or authorization, as when the right to pursue a particular business premises have to is subject to certification, or when particular business premises have to be certified by governmental agencies as conforming to health and safety requirements. Without such certification these activities would be in violation of the law and subject to penalty. On the other hand, regulatory activities requiring individuals to do certain things stipulate *prescribed* behaviors. Males of certain ages may be required to register for military service; children are required to attend school; citizens are required to file tax returns or to serve on juries. Other specific behaviors are *proscribed* by government, ranging all the way from violating traffic regulations to engaging in acts defined by law as crimes against person and property. All of these forms are backed by coercion.

Though specifying the domains regulated and the sanctions used to secure compliance, table XI.5 still leaves important variables to be considered. For example, sanctions can vary in terms of their severity. In the case of validation much depends on the difficulty of the qualifying criteria, the size of the fines for nonconformity, and the number of offenses permitted before the withdrawal of certification. Even more important may be the question of which groups are subjected to regulations and what procedures are required before the imposition of penalties. The examples in table XI.5 suggest that various special groups may be singled out for regulation. Just as the analysis of extraction and distribution required one to consider the incidence of these on or for special subgroups, so a regulative analysis must include consideration of the effects on different groups. In a traditional society much rule making and implementation is particularistic, applying to special individuals and subgroups. In a modern society, the cultural norms often specify a universal application of the law, so all individuals are supposed to be treated equally. In practice, however, the law may be applied unequally as it relates to minority groups, and political rights may be restricted by sex, social class, or party membership. Moreover, one can distinguish between political systems in which penalties may be imposed arbitrarily and administratively, without recourse to appeal, and those in which certain guarantees are provided: the writ of habeas corpus, trial by jury, reasonable bail, and defense by counsel, such as are stipulated in the American Bill of Rights or protected by British common law. Here the application of equity in implementation and adjudication processes has important implications for the impact of regulative performance.

Finally, we must point out again the distinction between regulative outputs and the outcomes that result after those outputs are implemented in the ongoing social and economic systems of different societies. Like extractions and distributions, regulations mean different things in different external circumstances, even if the rules and their implementation appear to be identical. If lawyers are expensive, the right to counsel means something different to the poor than to the rich. Prohibition of religious parades means something different in Catholic and Protestant communities. And, as has been so long debated, the prevention of theft and other property crimes is intimately related to the ownership of wealth and its distribution, such crimes tending to increase in periods of economic depression. We can analyze the regulative output of a political system somewhat independently of these eventual outcomes. But when we come to our descriptive and evaluative assessment of policy and society in the next chapter, we shall have to consider regulative *outcomes,* as well as the intended and implemented outputs.

Having suggested briefly what facts are necessary in order to characterize the regulatory outputs of a political system, to observe how they change over time, and to compare them with outputs of other political systems, we must report that only a major research effort could supply information of this kind. There are few reliable comparative data at the present time. To be sure, certain gross differences and changes can be observed with confidence. Thus, it is quite clear that the substantive scope and intensity of regulation is far greater in Communist societies than in relatively "free" societies. One can also make some very broad distinctions regarding the availability of procedural protections for individuals as they encounter the law in different societies. In democratic Western societies one can observe several trends that have occurred in the last century or so: a decline in the severity of punishment, a decrease in the extent of regulation of personal conduct, an increase in the regulation of economic organization and activity, and an increase in equitable regulation and procedural protection.

SUBSTANTIVE AREAS OF REGULATION

Regulation of citizen behavior is performed in part by police forces. The range of tasks assigned to the police, the extent of their discretion, their internal organization and training, and the kind of image they convey to the citizenry are indicators of national regulatory patterns. David Bayley, in his comparative study of police in Britain, France, West Germany, and Italy, summarizes and contrasts these patterns.

In Britain, Bayley finds, the formal tasks of the police are narrowly defined, while their informal activities are extensive and their intrusion into politics quite infrequent. Subject to political control through Parliament and local representative bodies, the police receive primarily civilian training. He characterizes the public image and performance of the British police as "honest, approachable, trustworthy, and helpful. They are viewed with respect and an admixture of affection. Generally they work as individuals, not in groups. They carry no firearms, and are commonly non-authoritative and non-punitive." [23]

The French police are described as having extensive formal tasks, including some ordinance-making power, and as being somewhat involved in political intelligence activities. Their organization is centralized, and the control over their activities is primarily bureaucratic, rather than political. The image of the French police, according to Bayley, is that of being "efficient, indefatigable, and omniscient. They are considered individually to be brusque and rather unapproachable. They are armed, feared, and disliked, though they are not considered especially corrupt." [24]

The German police are predominantly controlled by the states rather than the federal government and, like their French counterparts, have some ordinance-making power. Subject to the control of representative legislative bodies at the state level, they have a mixed military-civilian training. Bayley reports, "German policemen are trusted and honest. They are also formal, rather rigid, and authoritarian in manner. They are not known for approachability. They are armed and do not have a reputation for effective informal mediation." [25]

In Italy police have considerable ordinance-making power in addition to their specific police duties, and they appear to be extensively involved

---

[23] David Bayley, "The Police and Political Development in Europe," in *The Formation of National States in Western Europe*, ed. Charles Tilly (Princeton: Princeton University Press, 1975), p. 341.
[24] Ibid.
[25] Ibid., p. 337.

Table XI.6. *Aspects of Correctional Systems in Selected Nations*

	Ratio of nonsentenced prisoners to total number of prisoners	*Ratio of offenders undergoing noninstitutional to institutional treatment*
Spain	35:100 (1966)	0.2:1 (1966)
France	40:100 (1961)	0.5:1 (1963)
Belgium	15:100 (1961)	0.8:1 (1963)
Japan	15:100 (1967)	1.0:1 (1967)
USA		2.0:1 (1965)
Norway		2.0:1 (1962)
Denmark	20:100 (1961)	2.5:1 (1967)
Sweden		3.0:1 (1963)
Britain	8:100 (1965)	4.0:1 (1965)
Netherlands	35:100 (1961)	4.0:1 (1965)

Source: United Nations, *International Review of Criminal Policy*, no. 26 (1974), p. 76.

in political intelligence activities. Their control is highly centralized at the national level, although little parliamentary supervision is exercised. Their training is military, and, according to Bayley, they "are considered corrupt, punitive, and unscrupulous. They are feared and disliked. One would not consider going to them for assistance except in time of great stress. They are armed." [26]

These comments of a specialist on police systems show that there may be pronounced differences in the quality of police regulation in countries in the same cultural area — differences explained by the special historical experiences that these nations have undergone. Unfortunately, the data necessary to extend these particular kinds of comparisons to police systems in other parts of the world are not yet available.

Another body of data suggestive of substantial differences in law enforcement is presented in table XI.6. The second column of the table provides the ratio of nonsentenced prisoners — prisoners awaiting trial — to the total number of prisoners in a number of countries. Obviously, long delays in awaiting trial reflect inefficiency in judicial administration and inequity in law enforcement. Performance by this standard ranges from eight per one hundred prisoners awaiting trial in Great Britain to forty in France and thirty-five in the Netherlands. In the third column of the table there is an indication of how countries differ in their approaches to crime, for the ratio of offenders undergoing noninstitutional treatment to offenders undergoing institutional treatment suggests different philosophies of crime and crime prevention. In some countries —

[26] Ibid., pp. 338–39.

Spain, France, and Belgium, for example — imprisonment of offenders as a form of punishment or deterrence is in effect the sole sanction employed. In others, such as Great Britain and the Netherlands, there are four offenders treated through probation or other forms of rehabilitation for every offender imprisoned.

These comparative data on the behavior of the police and the approach to criminality only hint at the variety of approaches to criminality, law enforcement, and punishment in various parts of the world. The substantive definition of crime, the rank order of offenses in terms of seriousness and severity of penalties, the rights of defendants, and the kind of process to which they are entitled differ from country to country and from cultural area to cultural area.

Another aspect of regulatory output is the frequency, scale, and impact of government control over political participation and organization by citizens and groups. Political systems vary from authoritarian regimes, which prohibit party organization, formation of voluntary association, and communications freedom, to democratic systems, in which these rights of organization and communication are protected. In table VI.3, we reported the results of an international survey of press freedom conducted by the University of Missouri School of Journalism in 1965. The survey showed that the economically developed democratic countries have the highest degree of press freedom, while the Communist countries included in the table — Czechoslovakia, the Soviet Union, Bulgaria, and China — are at the opposite end of the scale. Non-Communist authoritarian regimes such as Spain and Egypt are also on the minus side of the scale, while many economically undeveloped countries, such as India, Nigeria, and Tanzania, tend to fall somewhere in the middle range.

This brief review of regulatory performance suggests that the compulsory activities of political systems are quite heterogeneous. To compare countries according to their use of compulsion, one must discriminate carefully among kinds, severity, and procedures of regulation. Regulation intended to protect person and property is qualitatively different from economic regulation designed to enhance material welfare and health. Regulation of political communication, organization, and activity is still another kind of compulsion that has a significant relation to all other aspects of political performance. If the right to express disapproval of governmental activity is protected, if individuals and groups in the society have the opportunity to affect the policy process, then unsatisfactory performance can be altered. A particularly crucial aspect of governmental performance is the set of defenses against arbitrariness in the implementation of governmental action — rights to public trial, trial by jury, professional counsel, and so on. Without these procedural protections, substantive limits on governmental compulsion may be meaningless.

THE INTERNATIONAL PERFORMANCE OF POLITICAL SYSTEMS

Foreign policies, like domestic ones, consist of the same basic output ingredients of extraction, distribution, regulation, and communication. However, international interaction takes place in a very different kind of political arena with different decision rules: while there are norms of international conduct, there is no international government and bureaucracy to implement and enforce them. Nations tend to rely on self-help or the support of allies to protect their interests and integrity. There are many different kinds of foreign policies, resulting from geographical location, size, resources, culture, and ideology. Some nations follow aggressive and expansive policies, developing and deploying large military forces; others are "satisfied" powers concerned primarily with security and trade. Some nations are dependent, in the sense of vulnerability to penetration or exploitation by other nations; their foreign policies may seek to form protective alliances or to balance threatening and rival powers against one another. They may also seek foreign and international aid in order to develop their economies.

What we propose to do in this section is to illustrate differences in foreign policy behavior insofar as these are reflected in foreign trade and aid patterns, levels of military activity and expenditure, size of diplomatic establishment, and so forth.

EXTRACTION

Imperialist nations in the past have quite literally extracted raw materials and even human labor, in the form of slaves, from their colonies. In Africa, colonial authorities even introduced "head" taxes or "hut" taxes to force the populations under their control into the modern, money-based economic sector — the only way in which the mother country's extractive apparatus could be extended to tap their productive efforts.

International extractions may be based on force of arms, as victorious powers impose reparations on defeated nations, or on advantageous economic exchanges. A country that lacks the capital to invest in developing a modern economy may have to borrow the necessary funds at highly unfavorable terms from a capital-rich nation, with the latter acquiring the greater part of the return on the investment. An inordinate return on foreign investment is certainly an extraction at the expense of the country in which the investment has been made — although many countries, including the United States, began the industrialization process largely on the basis of foreign capital. What constitutes a fair return on investment of this sort is debatable and changes over time; contemporary standards are very different from the earlier ones.

Another form of international extraction is foreign aid from other nations. Table XI.7 shows the principal beneficiaries of American and

Table XI.7. *Principal Beneficiaries of American and Soviet*
Economic and Military Aid

Total Soviet aid 1954–1965		Total U.S. aid 1958–1965	
Country	Amount in millions of dollars	Country	Amount in millions of dollars
China	$16,242	India	$4,893
Bulgaria	5,197	Pakistan	2,360
Poland	2,986	S. Korea	1,819
Rumania	2,181	S. Vietnam	1,554
Mongolia	1,836	Brazil	1,476
Cuba	1,226	Turkey	1,393
Hungary	1,214	Egypt	945
N. Vietnam	1,123	Yugoslavia	917
India	1,022	Chile	826
Egypt	1,011	Taiwan	692
E. Germany	763	Mexico	651
N. Korea	752	Colombia	579
Czechoslovakia	552	Israel	551
Afghanistan	552	Italy	515

Source: Taylor and Hudson, *World Handbook*, pp. 360 ff.
Note: Includes only recipients of $500 million or more.

Russian economic and military aid during the 1950s and 1960s. Obviously, the countries listed as receiving Soviet military and economic aid are or were, for the most part, close allies and dependents of the Soviet Union, while most of those receiving aid from the United States are or were its allies and dependents. But Egypt and India have been beneficiaries of both Soviet and American aid. They have been relatively successful in extracting resources from the international environment, in the form of aid, although they may be objects of extraction in the form of trade balances and investment at high interest rates. In our discussion of international welfare outcomes, we will address the question of the *net* extractions and distributions in the international sphere.

DISTRIBUTION

International distributive expenditure includes the reciprocal sides of the trade and aid balances discussed above. If a nation provides trade on favorable terms to its partner or partners, if it provides technology, grants of money, goods, and services, or if it offers loans at low rates of interest, it is performing distributively. Distributive performance also includes commitment of money and personnel in connection with military deployments abroad, as well as expenditures for diplomatic missions, foreign information and trade agencies, and the like. As in the case of our analysis of domestic extractions and distributions, we should like to know both aggregate amounts of resources extracted and expended for these various purposes, and the countries and groups affected by them.

Domestic and international performance are quite interdependent, as are the different performance areas within each sphere. A high international distributive performance may require a high domestic extractive performance. The pressure of American taxpayers to limit foreign aid programs, especially in times of domestic recession, illustrates this point. Moreover, the interactions may be quite complicated. Government expenditures on defense, for example, may include both domestic and international distributions. Contracts to build aircraft and military equipment clearly affect the domestic national and local economies. If the military equipment is never used, the tale may end here, although it is likely that the defense force created will have important implications for international security. But if it is employed, then considerable funds may be spent directly in the international sphere, for the maintenance of occupation forces or armies in warfare. One illustration would be the huge amounts spent by the American military forces in South Vietnam, some of which was fed directly into the local economy, some of which was used for combat expenditure, and some of which sustained the occupation forces, thus feeding into the local economy indirectly.

Table XI.8 provides some examples of expenditures affecting the international arena. The second column of the table reveals something about the historical role of these nations since the beginning of the modern international system or their initiation into it. One available measure of this historical involvement is the average number of battle deaths per year of membership in the international system. Germany and the Soviet Union have quite clearly paid the highest price in lives for the pursuit of security and expansion goals, followed by China, Japan, France, Britain, Poland, Italy, and the United States, in that order. At the other extreme is Sweden, which has suffered no battle deaths during this period, but has paid a high price for the maintenance of its neutrality, as measured by the size of its military forces and its expenditures for defense purposes.

This record of battle deaths indicates past international involvement and not current performance. Some aspects of the contemporary distributions are reported in the subsequent columns of the table. The fourth column, indicating defense expenditures as a percent of GNP, shows Israel and Egypt during 1965 as among the most burdened of all the nations listed in the table, a burden that has since increased. This is, of course, a consequence of the fact that these two nations have been in a state of acute military confrontation for over a decade. The Soviet Union,

Table XI.8. *Aspects of International Security Performance in Selected Nations*

Nations in order of per capita GNP, 1965	Annual rate of battle deaths[a]	Defense expenditures in millions of dollars, 1965[b]	Defense expenditures as % of GNP[b]	Number of diplomatic missions abroad[c]	Number of diplomats serving abroad[c]
USA	4,059	$51,844	7.6	100	2,782
Sweden	0	843	4.4	64	237
Canada	861	1,535	3.2	55	388
France	13,134	5,125	5.5	98	1,152
W. Germany	41,181	4,979	4.4	88	671
Britain	8,635	5,855	5.9	96	1,403
Czechoslovakia	48	1,300	5.9	57	422
Israel	178	413	12.2	64	292
USSR	64,417	28,170	9.0	65	1,345
Italy	5,063	1,939	3.4	87	511
Japan	13,791	781	.9	71	638
Bulgaria	—	200	2.9	47	247
Spain	1,259	587	2.7	59	306
Mexico	141	153	.8	44	186
Yugoslavia	1,041	396	4.5	57	280
Brazil	725	641	2.9	60	300
Egypt	172	392	8.3	67	550
China	28,344	6,000[d]	7.9	64	292
India	263	2,077	4.2	64	497
Kenya	0	8	.9	1	2
Nigeria	0	66	1.4	3	9
Tanzania	0	6	.8	2	6

[a] J. David Singer and Melvin Small, *The Wages of War, 1816–1965* (New York: John Wiley, 1972), pp. 275 ff. Annual rate of battle deaths is computed from 1816 or the beginning of national independence, if later.
[b] Taylor and Hudson, *World Handbook*, pp. 34 ff.
[c] Ibid., pp. 357 ff.
[d] Estimate

China, and the United States also stand out here. Japan, a powerful nation in population and economic influence, has been a lower spender in the international defense area since its defeat in 1945. Of course, for analysis of relative international strength, rather than effort expended, the absolute amounts shown in the third column are perhaps the best indicator. A large and wealthy nation can wield a big international stick, even with a proportionately smaller effort.

Another measure of international expenditure, related to security but concerned as well with other aspects of international action, is the size of the diplomatic establishment. The last two columns report the number of diplomatic missions located abroad during the early 1960s and the size of their diplomatic establishments serving abroad. The United States came out highest in both respects, having one hundred missions in foreign countries, staffed by almost three thousand diplomatic officials. France was second in the number of diplomatic missions, but its staff totaled less than half the American establishment. Other major European powers — West Germany, Britain, and Italy — also had substantial diplomatic representation abroad, while the major Communist countries, the Soviet Union and China, had a smaller number of diplomatic missions, although the Soviet Union had a very large average staff for these. The new nations of Africa showed minimal involvement in the international sphere, in terms of either security expenditures or diplomatic activity.

REGULATION

Traditionally, the study of international politics has been particularly interested in international security outputs and their consequences. As in the case of the domestic regulative outputs, we are interested in the following aspects of performance:

1. What other nations are influenced in their behavior by outputs of any given nation?

2. What aspects of behavior are regulated and to what degree?

3. What kinds of sanctions or inducements are used to compel behavior of other nations: normative inducements of ideology and diplomatic negotiation, economic inducements of trade and aid, or coercive sanctions of real and threatened military action?

As in the domestic sphere, effective international regulation depends on resources and appropriate organizational structures. The tremendous defense establishments of the United States and the Soviet Union, as well as their extremely powerful positions in world trade and aid, give them great resources with which to impose their will on other nations. But as Vietnam has shown so clearly for the Americans, and Yugoslavia for the

Soviets, nations with powerful military establishments are not necessarily successful in imposing their influence on weaker countries.

Table XI.9 tells a bit about which nations have been the victims of external military interventions in the two decades following the end of World War II. Most cases involved imperialist or sphere-of-interest powers intervening to maintain control of colonial or dependent countries. Thus, in the case of the Congo (now Zaire) it was Belgium or Belgian interests that were behind the interventions in Katanga. In the case of Tunisia and Morocco, France's relationship to its North African dependencies explains the intervention, whereas in Angola and Mozambique it was independence movements based in Tanzania and the Congo and directed against Portuguese control. In the Dominican Republic and Cuba, the United States intervened, and in Hungary, the Soviet Union did. In some cases it was rival powers in conflict over spheres of influence that explain the interventions: this would be true of Yemen, where Saudi Arabian and Egyptian interests were in conflict, and of Cyprus, where Turkish and Greek nationalism clashed. Other cases in-

Table XI.9. *Victims of Military Interventions by Other Countries or Rebel Groups,*
            1948-1967

Nations	Number of interventions	
	1948-1957	*1958-1967*
Zaire	0	156
Yemen	0	79
Laos	3	67
Tunisia	33	36
Kenya	0	62
Dominican Republic	0	55
Cuba	0	44
Southern Yemen	1	39
Hungary	28	3
Lebanon	27	0
Cyprus	0	25
China	13	11
Costa Rica	24	0
Rhodesia	0	22
Ethiopia	0	20
Morocco	11	7
Angola	0	16
Mozambique	0	16
Taiwan	1	14

Source: Taylor and Hudson, *World Handbook,* pp. 124 ff.
Note: Only victims of 15 interventions or more have been included in the table.

volved attacks by tribal or ethnic independence movements, as in Kenya and Ethiopia. These data are simply illustrative of different patterns of international regulative activity.

International outputs of the various sorts are interdependent. Thus, a high international distributive performance may reduce the need for international coercion. By subsidies and favors, potential enemies may be bought off, neutrals consolidated in their neutrality, and friends confirmed in their support. Foreign aid and foreign trade discrimination may be used in this way. In contrast, a high extractive international performance — exploitation of dependent nations, monopolization of markets, or manipulation of prices — may require the increase of regulative and coercive activity. Effective international ideological-symbolic outputs may increase international extractive performance, as illustrated by India in the first decade of its independence. Within the area of international regulative performance, security diplomacy (that is, effective statements of intent, shrewd bargaining, treaty arrangements, and the like) may reduce the need to rely on coercive activities. The development of military capabilities, the deployment of forces, and the demonstration of military intent and capability may limit the actual resort to coercion or, alternatively, may actually contribute to it.

OTHER INTERNATIONAL OUTPUTS

Our review of aspects of international performance has been selective and illustrative. Some important activities are difficult to measure, others are purposely obscured. Nations gather intelligence and conduct covert operations on each other's soil. It is not easy to measure the costs and effectiveness of these operations, because these activities are concealed (though sometimes not very effectively) and the amounts appropriated are hidden under other budget categories.

The effectiveness of international communication is difficult to measure. Expenditures for these purposes, number of radio transmitters, number of persons employed in foreign propaganda activities — all may bear little relationship to the effectiveness of the communications transmitted by a nation. China commands an enormous audience without making much of a deliberate effort. Tanzania gets much international attention because of its politicosocial experimentation. The effectiveness of international communication is tied up with what a nation does, or aspires to. A revolution commands attention, possibly inspiring some groups in foreign societies and threatening others. Reactionary oppression may provoke both hostility and imitation abroad, whereas a scientific breakthrough or an important technological achievement — a Sputnik or a moon landing — may positively affect international prestige and influence.

CHAPTER XII

Outcomes and Feedback

IN CONSIDERING THE OUTCOMES of public policies and their implementation, one must distinguish between the intended and the unintended, and between the immediate and the subsequent. Even the immediate outcome of public policy deviates from the intended outcome, since factors beyond the control of politicians and bureaucrats are at play, and since their capacity to effect desired outcomes is limited by partial and inadequate understanding of social, economic, and international processes.

Thus, the yield of a tax depends on the performance of the economy, on the effectiveness of its collection, and on the attitudes of the taxpayers. If one seeks to go further in analyzing the impact of a tax, the relation to intent becomes increasingly indistinct. It is generally known that taxation affects savings, savings affect investment, investment affects economic growth, and economic growth affects the later income distribution produced by the economy. But these subsequent outcomes are the mixed consequences of tax policies, monetary policies, welfare policies, the performance of the domestic and international economies, and so on. A criminal code is intended to safeguard life and property by providing categories of offense and forms of punishment and rehabilitation. But the causes of crime and the effects of different kinds and degrees of punishment are not well understood. Increased expenditures on law enforcement and investment in criminal rehabilitation seem to have no clear relationship with crime rates.

The relationship between foreign policy outputs and outcomes is even more problematic. Foreign economic policy is dependent for its success on the policies of dozens of other countries, on the effect of the weather on crops throughout the world, on the policies of international cartels, on the conditions of international political and security relations, and the like.

Policy making and implementation are essentially a trial-and-error process. Decision, implementation, output, outcome, feedback, and decision again; these constitute the phases of the public policy process.

In this chapter we want to consider some of the immediate and important outcomes of government performance. Since students of public policy are just beginning investigation of these problems, we often do not have the data to trace the effects and consequence of outputs on societies. But we shall attempt to illustrate the direction of outcome analysis by considering several examples of welfare outcomes (particularly in areas of aggregate and distributed income, health, housing, and education), public security outcomes, and domestic political liberty outcomes and by looking briefly at welfare and security consequences in the international environment as well.

PUBLIC POLICY WELFARE OUTCOMES: INCOME, HEALTH, AND EDUCATION

One of the most important outcomes of public policy, the economic welfare of a society, has both aggregate and distributive aspects. The aggregate aspect is expressed in such measures as GNP per capita; the distributive aspect, in the degree of inequality in wealth, income, and access to opportunity. The extractive and distributive outputs of the political system interact with the outputs of the economic system in producing distributive patterns. Insofar as they affect equality, the outcomes of the distributive processes of the polity and the economy feed back into the political system either as demands for redistribution growing out of inequality or as supports in exchange for benefits. This feedback into the political system is not direct, but rather is mediated through political culture. Thus attitudes toward status and class, as well as expectations of the place of politics in shaping distributive patterns, will intervene or mediate between the outcomes of political, economic, and social processes and the feedback of demands and supports into the political system.

However these mechanisms work, the value distributions in a society are of central political importance. They are among the principal outcomes of politics and public policy, and they are among the principal conditions associated with political stability and conflict. While the actual distribution of benefits and values in a society is the product of the economic and social systems as well as the political, the political system is a peculiarly important factor because it is the most comprehensive instrument of collective goal attainment in a society and may employ compulsory means. Political processes can result in progressive or regressive taxation, or they can provide protection to the rights of workers, enabling them to organize and bargain collectively for a better share of income. Political processes can produce educational institutions that enhance the skills of the underprivileged and make it possible for them to improve their condition by making effective demands on the political system.

INCOME DISTRIBUTION

Table XII.1 provides information on distribution of income for a variety of countries at different levels of economic development, in different parts of the world, and with different kinds of political systems. Income distribution is reported before taxes, but after transfer payments (such as old-age and unemployment insurance) in the form of income. It does not include educational benefits, health benefits, or recreational amenities distributed by the political system. (In table XII.2 we shall provide information on after-tax income for a smaller group of advanced industrial societies.)

Table XII.1 demonstrates that the greatest inequalities occur in third world countries at both low and middle ranges of economic development. Thus, in Kenya and Tanzania the top 20 percent of income recipients received over 60 percent of the national income, while the bottom 40 percent of income recipients received only 10 to 13 percent. Though at higher levels of development, Venezuela, Mexico, Brazil, and Peru had similarly skewed income distributions, with more than 60 percent of the income going to the top groups. Among advanced industrial societies France stands out in income inequality with only 10 percent going to the bottom 40 percent of income recipients, and 54 percent of the income going to the top 20 percent. Two of the three Communist countries listed in the table — Czechoslovakia and Bulgaria — had substantially greater equality in income distribution than the other countries listed in the table.

From the point of view of income distribution these countries fall into three broad classes: (1) third world countries with high inequalities due primarily to the sharp differences between modernizing and traditional sectors; (2) industrial democratic societies with varied patterns of inequality partly dependent on the scale and incidence of taxation and welfare payments; and (3) Communist countries in which collectivization and wage policies produce substantial income equality.

A recent comparative study of the countries of Eastern and Western Europe from the point of view of equality indicates the same pattern seen here.[1] The Communist societies have attained markedly greater income equality than the capitalist ones, although several Western

[1] John M. Echols, "Does Communism Mean Greater Equality? A Comparison of East and West Along Several Major Dimensions" (Paper delivered at the 1976 Annual Meeting of the American Political Science Association, September 2–5, 1976).

Table XII.1. *The Size of the Pie and Its Slices: Inequality in Income Distribution for Countries at Different Levels of Economic Development*

Country	Year of analysis	Per capita GNP	Pre-tax income distribution analysis		
			% of Income to Lowest 40%	% of Income to Middle 40%	% of Income to Top 20%
USA	1970	4,850	20	42	39
Sweden	1963	2,949	14	42	44
Canada	1965	2,920	20	40	40
W. Germany	1964	2,144	15	32	53
Britain	1968	2,015	19	42	39
France	1962	1,913	10	37	54
Czechoslovakia	1964	1,150	28	41	31
Italy	1969	1,011	17	35	48
Venezuela	1970	1,004	8	27	65
Japan	1963	950	21	39	40
Spain	1965	750	18	37	46
Mexico	1969	645	11	26	64
Bulgaria	1962	530	27	40	33
Yugoslavia	1968	529	19	40	42
Peru	1971	480	7	34	60
Brazil	1970	390	10	28	62
Taiwan	1964	241	20	41	40
Philippines	1971	239	12	35	54
Kenya	1969	136	10	22	68
India	1964	99	16	32	52
Tanzania	1967	89	13	26	61

Source: All data are from Hollis Chenery et al., *Redistribution with Growth* (New York: Oxford University Press, 1974), pp. 8–9.
Note: GNP data are in 1971 U.S. dollars.

European countries are about as equal as Yugoslavia. The distributions of wealth, as opposed to income, are even more equal in the Communist than in the capitalist societies. But although the differences in income and wealth between the economically advanced Communist and capitalist societies are quite marked, the picture in other dimensions of equality is more mixed. Echols's careful survey of the literature points out that inequalities in the opportunities and treatment of men and women and in the treatment of ethnic and urban-rural groups show neither type of society to offer any particular advantage.[2]

Table XII.2 provides information about before- and after-tax income distribution, but only for a number of countries belonging to the Organization for Economic Cooperation and Development (OECD). No Com-

[2] Ibid.

Table XII.2. *Size Distribution of Pre- and Post-Tax Income
for OECD Nations*

Nation	Year	% of income to lowest 40%		% of income to middle 40%		% of income to top 20%	
		Pre-tax	Post-tax	Pre-tax	Post-tax	Pre-tax	Post-tax
Australia	1966–67	20.1	20.1	41.2	41.2	38.9	38.8
Canada	1969	15.2	16.8	41.5	42.2	43.3	41.0
France	1970	14.2	14.1	38.8	39.0	47.0	46.9
W. Germany	1973	16.0	16.8	37.2	36.9	46.8	46.1
Italy	1969	–	15.6	–	37.9	–	46.5
Japan	1969	20.2	21.0	37.3	38.0	42.5	41.0
Netherlands	1967	16.8	18.1	37.4	39.1	45.8	42.9
Norway	1970	16.5	19.2	42.6	43.5	40.9	37.3
Spain	1973–74	–	17.8	–	40.0	–	42.3
Sweden	1972	17.4	19.7	41.7	43.3	40.5	37.0
Britain	1973	17.4	18.9	42.3	42.3	40.3	38.7
USA	1972	13.8	15.2	41.3	42.0	44.8	42.9
Average	1966–74	16.8	17.7	40.1	40.5	46.9	41.8

Source: Adapted from Malcolm Sawyer, *Income Distribution in OECD Countries,* OECD Economic Outlook (July 1976), p. 14; see footnotes and appendices for sources of data.

Note: For various reasons the data here for some countries are not directly comparable with the data in table XII.1. A full discussion of comparability of income units and bases is presented by Sawyer.

munist or third world countries are included. A number of points are suggested by this table. First, taxation seems to change income distribution by only relatively small amounts, 3 percent at the very most. Hence, the distributions reported in table XII.1 for a greater variety of countries may be taken as fairly close to net income distributions in these countries. Second, the Scandinavian countries appear to have the best record of income equalization through taxation. By taxation Norway and Sweden reduced the income going to their top 20 percent by more than 3 percent and increased the income going to their bottom 40 percent by more than 2 percent. In France there was only a minute impact of taxation on income distribution. Third, there is a substantial range of income inequality among advanced industrial democratic societies with France, Italy, and West Germany at the high inequality end and Australia, Japan, Norway, Sweden, and Great Britain at the low inequality end. Canada and the United States are somewhere in the middle.

The effect of public policy on income distribution results from a combination of extractive and distributive outputs, the net effect of what the state both gives and takes. Figure XII.1, which provides a graphic summary of the net effect of all taxes and social security payments on income distribution in the United States, is a good model of what we would need to have for all countries in order to compare the impact of

Figure XII.1. *Distribution of Family Income in the United States Before and After Taxes and Transfers, 1966*

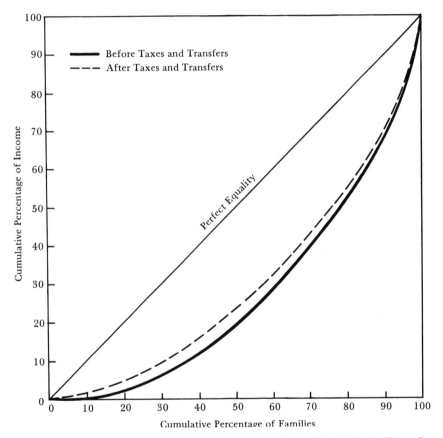

Source: From "Individual Taxes and the Distribution of Income" by Benjamin Okner. In James D. Smith, ed., *Personal Distribution of Income and Wealth*, vol. 39, Studies of Income and Wealth. Copyright © 1975 by National Bureau of Economic Research. Reprinted by permission of the NBER.

Note: The Gini coefficient is a measure of the extent of deviation of an income distribution from perfect equality. The greater the distance of the actual curve of income distribution from the diagonal, the greater the inequality. Gini coefficient, before taxes and transfers = .4595; Gini coefficient, after taxes and transfers = .3998.

governments' extractive and distributive performance on income inequality. The study from which these data are taken was based on a sample survey of 72,000 families and single individuals in the United States during the calendar year 1966 and their actual income tax returns for the same calendar year. In figure XII.1 are displayed Lorenz curves for income distribution before and after taxes and social security payments; each curve reports the percentage of the total amount of a particular value — for example, wealth or income — owned or received by different wealth and income levels.[3] In a society that distributed income perfectly equally, 10 percent of the families would receive 10 percent of the income; 20 percent of the families, 20 percent of the income; and so on. The distribution curve would be the straight line on the diagonal, the line of perfect equality. The unbroken, lower curve in the figure is the income distribution produced by the American economy unaffected by taxation and social security payments. It shows that in the United States in 1966, the 50 percent of the families at the lower income levels received only about 18 percent of the total income. After taxes had been paid and social security benefits distributed, the dotted curve shows some improvement. The lower 50 percent of income recipients netted around 22 percent of the income after governmental intervention, an improvement of roughly 4 percent.

Studies of the total effect of all taxes, including progressive income taxes and regressive sales and value-added taxes, together with welfare benefits, have been carried out in Britain and West Germany. In both cases, the combined effects were markedly redistributive, due particularly to the effects of social security payments. In Britain, after all taxes and distributions, the income of the very poorest group was more than seven times the original, and the income of the richest group was 70 percent of the original. In West Germany the poorest group's income was increased to almost six times the original amount; the most wealthy was decreased to 69 percent after government intervention.[4]

Factors that affect the extent of inequality in a society include such things as the wealth and rate of growth of the economy, the rates of enrollment in primary and secondary schools, and the rates of population growth. They also include deliberate public policies intended to affect the concentration of wealth, including agricultural land. Such data as have been compiled suggest that as national economies grow, inequality first increases and then decreases. One researcher, comparing

[3] For a more formal definition, see Hayward Alker, Jr., *Mathematics and Politics* (New York: Macmillan, 1965), pp. 35–53.

[4] Harold Wilensky, *The Welfare State and Equality* (Berkeley and Los Angeles: University of California Press, 1975), pp. 93–95.

the income distributions of developing and developed countries, points out that "the share of the lowest 40% declines sharply up to per capita income levels of $400 and then flattens out, rising steadily after per capita GNP crosses $1200. This movement is paralleled by an offsetting movement in the share of the top 20%." [5] The increasing inequality in early stages of economic development is due primarily to the introduction of a modern urban-industrial-commercial sector paid relatively high money wages in contrast to the relatively unchanged rural agricultural sector. One of the most important mechanisms affecting the structure of politics in developing societies is this tendency toward increasing inequality as they begin to industrialize and develop economically. It tends to produce an increasing income maldistribution that is associated with rising levels of political dissatisfaction and movements in authoritarian directions — either conservative-repressive regimes or authoritarian-populist regimes. We deal with these relationships in greater detail in chapter XIII.

Though population growth is accessible to political control only to a limited degree, it seems to have a strong positive relation to inequality (due to the higher birth rate among the poor) and particularly to the low share of income going to the lowest 40 percent of income recipients. The principal conclusion of one study "is that income shares are related not only to structural factors such as per capita income levels but also to variables which can be influenced by policy. The level of education and the rate of growth of population are particularly important in this context, since they indicate areas in which government action can improve distribution patterns." [6] In an investigation of inequality using rather different measures, Robert Jackman also reports the significant effects of such variables as governmental expenditures and experience with social insurance programs in reducing inequality in sixty countries.[7]

ECONOMIC AND POPULATION GROWTH

Table XII.3 provides some illustrative examples of how different political systems have been coping in the recent past with economic development, population growth, and health, all of which can be affected to some degree by public policy. The second and third columns of the table report growth in per capita GNP in 1960–1973 and percentage increase in population in 1970. Governments have some leverage over these two rates. Their fiscal policies, investment policies, foreign trade and aid

---

5 Hollis Chenery et al., *Redistribution with Growth* (New York: Oxford University Press, 1974), p. 17. Also see Robert W. Jackman, *Politics and Social Inequality* (New York: John Wiley, 1975).

6 Chenery et al., op. cit., pp. 17–18.

7 Jackman, op. cit., especially pp. 194 ff.

Table XII.3.   *Economic Growth, Population Increase, and Health Care in Selected Nations*

Nations in order of per capita GNP, 1973[a]	Annual growth rates of per capita GNP, 1960-73[a]	% annual increase in population, 1970-74[b]	Number of persons per doctor, latest available year[c]	Infant mortality rate, 1970[d]
USA	3.1	0.8	622	20.1
Sweden	3.0	–	645	11.0
Canada	3.7	1.3	613	18.8
W. Germany	3.7	0.6	530	23.6
France	4.7	0.8	–	18.2
Japan	9.4	1.3	868	13.1
Austria	4.4	0.5	510	25.9
Britain	2.4	0.2	787	18.4
Israel	5.6	3.2	351	22.9
Czechoslovakia	2.4	0.6	431	25.0[f]
Italy	4.3	0.8	502	29.6
USSR	3.6	0.9	363	27.0[f]
Spain	5.8	1.1	673	27.8
Bulgaria	6.2[e]	0.6	489	31.0[f]
Yugoslavia	4.3	0.9	864	56.0
Mexico	3.3	3.5	1,385	61.0
Brazil	3.6	2.8	1,025	110.0
Peru	2.1	3.2	1,802	75.0
Egypt	1.5	2.2	1,516	103.0
Nigeria	3.6	2.7	25,463	150.0
Kenya	3.1	3.6	16,292	155.0
Tanzania	2.8	2.7	27,572	160.0
India	1.3	2.1	4,162	130.0

[a]World Bank, *World Bank Atlas* (Washington, D.C., 1975), p. 3. There are some differences in the estimates of Soviet growth given by various sources. The World Bank estimate in column 2 may be compared with the figures of 5.5% for 1966-70 and 3.8% for 1971-75 given for the USSR by Economic Accounts Section, Production Staff, Office of Economic Research, Central Intelligence Agency, *Handbook of Economic Statistics* (Washington, D.C., 1976).

[b]United Nations, *Statistical Yearbook,* 1975 (New York: United Nations, 1976), pp. 67 ff.

[c]Ibid., pp. 839 ff.

[d]World Bank, *World Tables* (Baltimore: Johns Hopkins University Press, 1976), pp. 510 ff. The figures are infant deaths in the first year of life per thousand live births.

[e]The figure for Bulgaria is rate of real income per employed worker, 1955-1967. From Abram Bergson, "Development under Two Systems," *World Politics* 23 (July 1971): 600.

[f]Infant mortality figures for Czechoslovakia, the Soviet Union, and Bulgaria from Charles L. Taylor and Michael C. Hudson, *World Handbook of Political and Social Indicators* (New Haven: Yale University Press, 1972), pp. 295 ff.

policies, and investments in the quality of their labor forces — all have effects on economic growth rates. Population policy, on the other hand, is less directly susceptible to governmental influence, although family planning education and information programs may have some impact.

The relationship between these two rates of change is clearly suggested in the entries in the first two columns of table XII.3. Japan, Bulgaria, and Spain have exceptionally high economic growth rates and low population increase rates, while Mexico, India, and Kenya have high population growth rates that tend to lower the per capita rate of economic growth. From Mexico on down the countries with low per capita GNP have relatively high birth rates. High rates of population growth tend to be concentrated among the lower-income recipients. Thus, high rates of population increase imply increasing inequality in income distribution, with all that this means for political conflict and instability.

One extremely important question raised by table XII.3, and by our discussion of governmental performance in the last chapter, is the success of the Socialist "command economies" in achieving economic growth. Government distribution of economic investment is a distinctive characteristic of the command economies of the Soviet Union and Eastern Europe. Although the market-oriented economies, such as the United States, Britain, and Japan, do manifest substantial governmental regulation and fiscal involvement, the basic investment decisions are left to private firms and the market. The command economies in table XII.3 — Czechoslovakia, the Soviet Union, and Bulgaria — show a rather mixed performance pattern in terms of growth rates, with Bulgaria on the high side, Czechoslovakia on the low side, and the Soviet Union in the middle.

In a detailed investigation of growth performance in the 1950s and 1960s, Abram Bergson has compared the command economies of the seven COMECON nations with the market-oriented economies of the OECD nations.[8] His analysis suggests the following conclusions about economic growth in this time period:

1. The command economies did, on the average, succeed in generating substantially higher investment levels than did the market economies. (Some market economies, such as Japan, did as well.) [9]

2. However, the productivity of that investment was markedly higher in the market-oriented economies; the differences were particularly notable in nations at similar development levels.[10]

[8] The COMECON countries were Bulgaria, Rumania, Hungary, Poland, the Soviet Union, East Germany, and Czechoslovakia. The OECD countries were Turkey, Greece, Portugal, Japan, Ireland, Italy, Austria, Britain, Denmark, West Germany, France, Switzerland, Belgium, Norway, Netherlands, Sweden, Canada, and the United States.

[9] Abram Bergson, "Development under Two Systems: Comparative Productivity Growth since 1950," *World Politics* 23 (July 1971): 579–617; p. 595. Also see the literature review in Frederic L. Pryor, *Property and Industrial Organizations in Communist and Capitalist Nations* (Bloomington: Indiana University Press, 1973), pp. 325–33.

[10] Bergson, "Development under Two Systems," p. 600.

3. The overall growth rates were virtually identical for the two total sets of countries — 4.2 percent a year for COMECON and 4.0 percent a year for OECD between 1955 and 1967.[11]

4. Comparison of overall growth rates for the COMECON nations with the seven poorest OECD nations, which are at a rather similar economic development level, shows higher growth rates in the market economies. (Turkey, Greece, Portugal, Japan, Ireland, Italy, and Austria grew at an average rate of 5.2 percent between 1955 and 1967; deletion of Japan drops this to 4.7 percent.) [12]

Hence, it would seem that despite the apparent advantages (for economic growth) of total government control over economic investment, the inefficiencies of the command economy — due not only to bureaucratic centralization and information problems, but also to policy choices away from maximum profitability investments — result in slightly smaller productivity payoffs from investment. Of course, these findings do not necessarily apply in all time periods and circumstances. Nor do they necessarily apply to countries at much lower levels of economic development, although Caiden and Wildavsky have impressively illustrated some of the difficulties of attempting even centralized planning in poor nations.[13] But they indicate again the important differences between government performance and societal outcomes, warning against the assumption that government control over the economy is a solution for all social problems. And, of course, final evaluations must include societal outcomes in other areas: equity and amount of welfare, security and liberty, participation and stability.

SOCIAL POLICY: HEALTH AND HOUSING

Health care has a mixed relationship to economic growth and modernization. On the one hand, the introduction of modern epidemiological procedures and pharmaceuticals improves health and vitality, but it also tends to lower the death rate and so contributes to population increase — the introduction of "death control" before birth control. Though more children survive into adulthood in all countries as a consequence of the introduction of medications, vaccines, and sanitation procedures, in the poorer nations health care and nutrition are at much lower levels than in the advanced countries. Hence, life expectancy and vitality is lower in the poorer countries. The infant mortality rate is a good indication of general levels of health in a nation, and table XII.3 (column five)

---

[11] Ibid., p. 588.

[12] Ibid.

[13] Naomi Caiden and Aaron Wildavsky, *Planning and Budgeting in Poor Countries* (New York: John Wiley, 1974).

shows the great range associated with both general economic development and collective health efforts. In Sweden almost 99 percent of all infants live to be a year old; in the poorest African nations on which we have data, the figure is not much more than 80 percent. Similarly, the number of persons per physician (the fourth column of table XII.3) ranges all the way from the high side of over 27,000 in Tanzania, over 25,000 in Nigeria, and over 16,000 in Kenya to lows of only 351 in Israel, 363 in the Soviet Union, 431 in Czechoslovakia, and 530 in West Germany. The number of physicians available varies to some extent with the investment in and the requirements for medical education, two matters which are subject to public policy.

The dilemma of health care and development arises out of the greater capacity to influence death rates than birth rates. Evidence suggests that the acceptance of birth control hinges on values and expectations that vary mainly with involvement in the modern society and economy, where the incentives for small family size are strong and positive. The vicious circle of death control, population growth, low rates of economic development, and increasing economic inequality in poor countries does not lend itself readily to public policy solutions, though recent efforts at effective birth control measures have shown some success in China and perhaps India as well.

The reach of modern governments extends into social areas beyond these levels of population control, incomes, and health into other conditions of human life. Table XII.4 reports differences in the quantity and quality of housing available in a number of countries during the 1960s. The columns report not only the amount of space, but also the availability of running water and the proportions of dwellings that are owner-occupied. The quantity of housing during this period was clearly greatest in the United States and Britain, with well over three hundred dwellings per thousand population, and nearly five rooms per dwelling, almost all of which had running water and other amenities. But all the economically developed nations show an average of over one room per person and high quality, although one must recall that these averages conceal wide variations within nations, especially among regions and economic groups.

At the middle levels of economic development there are great variations in both quantity and quality of housing. The sharp contrast between Mexico and Spain is particularly notable. Spain provides an average of one room per person, and half of the dwellings report running water; Mexico reports only a third of that quantity, and less than a quarter of the dwellings have running water. In Israel there is high quality, but shortages of space; in Peru crowding is great, and less than one-sixth of dwellings have running water. The Latin American nations' welfare outcomes in health and housing seem to reflect the marked in-

Table XII.4. *Housing Facilities in Selected Nations*

Nations in order of per capita GNP, 1965	Dwellings per thousand persons	Rooms per dwelling	Rooms per person	Dwellings with piped water (%)	Owner-occupied (%)
USA	325	4.9	1.6	94.0	61.9
Sweden	370	3.6	1.3	94.3	35.5
Canada	262	5.3	1.4	89.1	66.0
W. Germany	292	4.1	1.2	96.7	29.4
France	351	3.1	1.1	79.8	41.5
Japan	227	3.8	.9	67.9	64.3
Austria	358	2.7	1.0	84.2	41.2
Britain	315	4.6	1.4	98.0	40.4
Israel	236[a]	2.3	.5	98.6	58.1
Czechoslovakia	278	2.7	.8	49.1	50.4
Italy	278	3.3	.9	71.6	45.8
USSR	235	2.8	.7	—	—
Spain	251	4.2	1.1	48.3	—
Bulgaria	250	3.2	.8	28.2	71.0
Yugoslavia	220	2.8	.6	—	77.5
Mexico	184[a]	1.9	.3	23.5	54.1
Brazil	189[a]	4.7	.9	27.4	60.4
Peru	199	2.3	.5	14.6	56.0
Egypt	166	3.6	.6	39.5	43.0
Kenya	204[a]	1.9	.4	—	—

Source: *United Nations Statistical Yearbook,* 1974 (New York, United Nations, 1975), pp. 786 ff. Figures for most nations are for the early 1960s; for Brazil, 1970; for Austria, 1971. Rooms per person was calculated by the authors from columns two and three.

[a] Occupied dwellings per thousand persons.

come inequalities shown by table XII.1. Not surprisingly, the very poorest nations on which we have data, India and Nigeria, have extremely limited quantities and do not provide information on such amenities as running water.

These data on housing conditions reflect a mixture of the general level of economic development and the manner and extent to which governments intervene in the provision of housing facilities. In the Soviet Union, the government dominates housing construction, and housing has long been rationed by authorities in the urban areas. As a policy matter, Soviet housing has taken second place to defense, economic growth, and education efforts. Thus, it is not surprising to find Soviet housing less plentiful than that in many nations of similar wealth. On the other hand, the very high levels of housing in the United States, Sweden, and Britain reflect three rather different governmental approaches, each carried out in a context of substantial economic wealth. A more complete

Table XII.5. *Housing Starts by Governmental and Private Sectors, 1971*

Builder	USA	Sweden	Netherlands	France	W. Germany	Britain
National County, Local governments	2.0%	3.7%	8.9%	0.6%	2.4%	46.4%
Quasi-public bodies	—	56.7	39.6	64.7	30.6	—
Private builders	98.0	39.0	51.5	34.7	67.0	53.6
Total	100.0%	99.4%	100.0%	100.0%	100.0%	100.0%

Source: Adapted from Arnold J. Heidenheimer, Hugh Heclo, and Carolyn Teich Adams, *Comparative Public Policy: The Politics of Social Change in Europe and America* (New York: St. Martin's Press, 1975), p. 72.

insight into the complex patterns of performance and consequence is provided by table XII.5, which shows the three major approaches of the market-oriented nations. In the United States there is little direct governmental housing construction, but tax benefits and massive loan guarantees (F.H.A. and V.H.A.) encourage private housing construction. In Britain, about half of all housing construction in 1971 was directly carried out by the government; half was purely private. In the other four European nations shown, a major role was played by quasi-public bodies, including utility companies with mixed public and private directorships and nonprofit, government-regulated cooperatives. Although government construction has been more limited in these nations than in Britain, government loans have played an important role even in the private sector.[14]

EDUCATION POLICY

In the preceding chapter we dealt with educational expenditures as a measure of political output. The availability of data on education makes it possible to compare policy goals, policy outputs, and policy outcomes in different nations. Education is a critical component of welfare policy, for the economic productivity of a nation is closely related to the skill and knowledge of its population. Moreover, the data suggest that a larger investment in primary school development is associated with an increased income share going to the lowest 40 percent of the

[14] Arnold J. Heidenheimer, Hugh Heclo, and Carolyn Teich Adams, *Comparative Public Policy: The Politics of Social Choice in Europe and America* (New York: St. Martin's Press, 1975), pp. 72–73, and chap. 3 generally.

income recipients, while a greater investment in secondary school development helps explain increases of the share of income going to the middle 40 percent of income recipients. Thus, the way in which a country allocates its resources in the development of primary and secondary education has a significant impact on the shape of the distribution.[15] Individual effectiveness in both political and economic life is closely associated with educational background in virtually all societies.

In table XII.6 we show the governmental education goals set in a number of nations, as indicated by the number of years children are obliged to attend school. The next set of columns displays the policy outputs in this area. The complexities of distributive analysis are indicated by our three measures: gross amounts spent on education, expenditures relative to the nation's wealth, and expenditures relative to the size of its population. We may consider the last to be a measure of expenditures relative to need, although ideally we should compare them to the school-age population. As we have already shown, some nations make a much more substantial effort in education than others. Britain and the Soviet Union, for example, do not require more school attendance than France and West Germany, but they spend much more on education relative to both their resources and the per capita needs of the population. Similarly, although Yugoslavia is a slightly poorer nation than Spain and Mexico, it spends over twice as much per capita than either of them and over three times as large a percentage of its GNP as Spain.

But of principal interest here are the outcomes of these efforts, which are reflected in the last three columns of table XII.6. The sixth column in the table shows the proportion of children between ages five and nineteen who are actually in school. This is a short-run measure of educational output, although it does not measure quality (or distribution within the population). Of course, the differing age requirements at the older teen-age levels affect these figures somewhat, but they are quite suggestive, nonetheless. In general, there is a strong relationship between per capita expenditure and percentage of children in school. The leading nations in per capita expenditures — whether they reach this level due to gross wealth, as in the case of France and West Germany, or due to effort, as in the case of Britain and the Soviet Union — show nearly three-quarters or more of their children in school. Nations spending less than $10 per pupil, whether due to extreme poverty (as in Egypt and Kenya) or due to somewhat limited resources and little effort (as in Mexico and Brazil), manage to get less than half of the group into the classroom.

---

[15] Chenery et al., op. cit., p. 17.

However, some differences in the apparent effectiveness of resource use are reflected in differences between amount spent and children in school. Japan, for example, not only makes a sizable effort relative to resources (4.9 percent of GNP), but is remarkably effective in converting its $42 per capita expenditure into a 74 percent in-the-classroom outcome. In this regard Japan does more with less funds than nations such as Italy, Israel, Czechoslovakia, and Austria. Similarly, China is notably more effective than Egypt and Brazil in converting its expenditures into classroom attendance, although here especially the figures must be viewed with caution since they are estimates. But a full-fledged public policy analysis would explain both the varying factors that explain these apparent differences in efficiency of expenditure and the policies that lead to different levels of effort.[16]

In the last two columns of table XII.6 we show the outcomes of educational policy outputs for the educational stock of these countries. The next to last column reports the proportion of literate population, while the last column indicates the median years of schooling for persons over 25 years of age. The United States and Britain exceed or come very close to reaching a median level of education required by their obligatory education laws. The adult population of Italy has a median educational level of 3.6 years as compared with a contemporary statutory requirement of 8 years of education. With 61 percent of its children aged five to nineteen in school, Italy would appear to be making progress in improving its educational stock. Brazil has lower requirements, lower expenditures, and a very low performance rate in terms of the educational level of its population.

The figures for India suggest the development problem confronting very poor countries. While by law it requires at least five to eight years in school (the minimum differs in the various Indian states), its per capita educational expenditures are very low and it appropriates only a small percentage of GNP for education. Further, almost two-thirds of India's population were illiterate as of 1965, and the median number of years of schooling for its adult population was less than one. It is an inevitable, but frustrating, fact that nations such as India find themselves in a difficult circle. They are poor nations to begin with, and their poverty stems in part from the lack of education and limited technological skills of their populations. Because of their poverty, they must expend a substantial proportion of national wealth to generate even

---

[16] We have not endeavored, for example, to examine the role of private education in this analysis, which may well account for some of the effectiveness in outcomes of government effort in some nations. According to UNESCO, for example, unsupported private education contributed some 20–25 percent to education expenditure in the United States and Spain, expenditures not shown in table XII.7.

Table XII.6. *Education: Policy Goals, Outputs, and Outcomes in Selected Nations*

		Policy Output Measures[b]		
Nations in order of per capita GNP, 1965	*Policy goals Years of obligatory education, 1970*[a]	*Absolute Millions of dollars expended on education, 1965*[c]	*Relative to resources Educational expenditures as % of GNP, 1965*	*Relative to needs Educational expenditures per capita, 1965*
USA	10-12	$36,687	5.2%	$199
Sweden	9	1,278	6.5	165
Canada	8-10	3,039	6.3	155
France	10	3,439	3.7	70
W. Germany	12	3,832	3.4	65
Britain	10	5,094	5.1	93
Czechoslovakia	9	1,087	4.9	77
Israel	11	169	4.6	66
USSR	8	22,849	7.3	99
Austria	9	388	3.6	47
Italy	8	3,112	5.5	60
Japan	9	4,111	4.9[c]	42[c]
Spain	8	244	1.4	8
Mexico	6	365	1.9	9
Yugoslavia	8	414	4.7	21
Peru	9	100	2.3	9
Brazil	4	381	1.7	5
Egypt	6	254	5.4	9
China	—	2,800[f]	3.7	4
India	5-8	1,002	2.0[g]	2[g]
Kenya	—	35	4.1	4
Nigeria	12	84	1.9	2
Tanzania	7	27	3.6	3

[a] *UNESCO Statistical Yearbook* (Paris: UNESCO Press, 1972), pp. 49 ff.
[b] Taylor and Hudson, *World Handbook*, pp. 30-33.
[c] Includes private sector—about .02% of total.
[d] Taylor and Hudson, *World Handbook*, pp. 225-228, 232-235.
[e] *UNESCO Statistical Yearbook*, pp. 49 ff.
[f] Estimate.
[g] Includes private sector—about 23% of total.

rather low levels of per capita expenditure. With such low levels of expenditure per capita, it is difficult to get very large percentages of children into school or to develop good educational facilities and teaching personnel. And they face not only the problem of educating the new generation, but upgrading the older population.

	Policy Outcomes		
Nations in order of per capita GNP, 1965	Short Run % of 5- to 19- year-olds attending school, 1965[d]	Long Run Literacy rate, 1965[d]	Level of Education Median years of schooling for persons over 25, 1960–1970[e]
USA	87%	99%	12.20
Sweden	74	100	8.11
Canada	81	99	9.48
France	73	99	4.36
W. Germany	78	99	–
Britain	87	99	9.63
Czechoslovakia	69	99	5.72
Israel	66	90	7.92
USSR	72	99	8.12
Austria	70	98	3.16
Italy	61	92	3.60
Japan	74	98	5.86
Spain	55	87	3.88
Mexico	49	65	3.92
Yugoslavia	63	77	4.08
Peru	52	61	1.96
Brazil	41	61	1.98
Egypt	43	30	–
China	46	50	–
India	38	28	0.66
Kenya	39	23	0.65
Nigeria	25	33	–
Tanzania	20	18	–

PUBLIC POLICY SECURITY OUTCOMES
SAFETY AND PUBLIC ORDER

In illustrating security area outcomes, particularly as affected by regulative outputs, we have selected for comment the outcomes of safety of person and of property and public order, two important consequences of

Table XII.7. *Murder as a Cause of Death in Selected*
            Countries, 1967

Country	Murders per 100,000 Population
Britain	1.5
W. Germany	2.5
France	1.8
Italy	1.9
Netherlands	.9
Denmark	1.0
Norway	.9
Spain	.3
Switzerland	1.6
USA	13.8
Canada	3.1
Japan	2.8

Source: Adapted from Central Statistical Office, *Social Trends* (London: HMSO, 1972), p. 179.

the regulatory side of governmental activity. The first is a measure of the extent to which people in a society are secure in their persons and property; the second estimates the extent to which there are collective threats to public order.

Despite the general increase of crime and disorder in modern societies, there is relatively little reliable comparative data. In table XII.7 we compare murder rates in a number of countries. The figure of 13.8 per 100,000 population for the United States strikes the eye. However, the United States does not have as high a murder rate as a number of Latin American countries and South Africa. Another source reports that Colombia had 36.5 murders per 100,000 population (1962); Mexico, 31.9 (1960); and South Africa, 21.8 (1960).[17]

Crime rates in most countries of the world have been increasing. For the United States a recent FBI report showed that all types of crime had increased almost threefold in the last decade (see table XII.8).

Similar increases in crime rates, but on a smaller scale, have been reported for Britain. Indictable offenses in that country have risen from an annual average of about half a million in the 1950s to more than a million a year since 1965. In France, on the other hand, the crime rate

[17] President's Commission on Law Enforcement, Task Force Report, *Crime and Its Impact: An Assessment* (Washington, D.C.: U.S. Government Printing Office, 1967), p. 39.

Table XII.8.   *Total Number of Crimes in the United States per 100,000 Population, 1966–1973*

1966	1,666.6
1968	2,234.8
1970	2,740.5
1971	2,906.7
1972	2,829.5
1973	4,116.4

Source: Department of Justice, Federal Bureau of Investigation, *Uniform Crime Reports for the U.S.*, 1973 (Washington, D.C.: U.S. Government Printing Office, 1974).

(excluding minor offenses such as traffic violations) has remained relatively stable in the period since the end of World War II.

Evidence suggests that there has been a greater rise in crimes against property than in crimes against persons:

> During the ten years 1955–1965, property crimes are reported to have doubled in France, Italy, Norway, the United Kingdom and the United States, and to have trebled in the Federal Republic of Germany, Finland, the Netherlands and Sweden, although remaining stable in Belgium, Denmark and Switzerland. On the other hand, violence against the person is reported to show less of a general trend, with an increase in the United Kingdom and the United States and a decline in Belgium, Denmark, Norway and Switzerland. A recent United States report pointed out that the homicide rate, although only one-sixth that of some other countries, is more than twice that of Finland, and from four to twelve times higher than the rates in a dozen other developed countries including Canada, England, Japan and Norway; the rape rate is twelve times that of England and Wales and three times that of Canada; the robbery rate is nine times that of England and Wales and double that of Canada; and the aggravated assault rate is double that of England and Wales and eighteen times that of Canada. The ratio of prisoners to the economically active population was five times higher in the United States than in Denmark, Japan or the Netherlands.[18]

Some information is available on crime rates in the Communist countries of Eastern Europe. Official reports in these countries claim substantial decreases in crime rates after the establishment of Communist regimes. Within the Communist period, however, there has been a considerable amount of fluctuation in criminal behavior as reported in the

[18] United Nations Department of Economic and Social Affairs, *Report on the World Social Situation* (New York: United Nations, 1971), pp. 222–23.

official statistics of these countries. In Hungary, crimes of violence against persons were reported by the Minister of Justice as having increased in the late 1960s and early 1970s, while Czechoslovakia reported increased crime rates in the period of repression after 1968, probably attributable both to the demoralization of that period and to the tough policy toward deviants. Economic crimes in Communist societies comprise misappropriation of public funds or resources for personal use and thefts of public property. Judged by published reports in the Communist press, this category of offense is endemic in Communist societies and has increased during recent years in some of them.[19]

Relating these crime rates to governmental performance presents a number of problems. In the first place, we cannot be sure of the validity of the trends we report. Nations vary in the quality of their statistics, and public policy may lead to selective and biased reporting of criminal data. Improvements in detecting and reporting of crimes — rather than increases in the crimes themselves — may explain some fluctuations. Only when we are able to adjust our data for these factors will we be able to say with confidence just how much crime has increased and what the comparative country records are.

On the whole, what evidence we have suggests that crime has increased generally in recent years, markedly among the advanced democratic countries, and most markedly in the United States — despite increased expenditures on police and law enforcement processes. There is more than one possible explanation for this decline in public safety in recent decades. The post-war baby boom produced a youth bulge in the 1960s, and there is evidence to suggest that a disproportionate share of the crime increase is related to this change in population age structure. Alternatively, the declining indoctrinative capacity of family and church in recent decades may have resulted in attenuation of respect for law and authority. Whatever the causes, the results have been an increasing discrepancy between political output and outcome in the provisions of personal safety and, associated with this discrepancy, a declining trust and confidence in the performance of government.

The incidence of riots, or spontaneous collective violence, is in part an indicator of public peace, of the ability or inability of groups in a society to resolve issues short of violence, and of the degree of citizens' satisfaction or dissatisfaction with governmental authority. But it also reflects the extent to which nations successfully impose discipline on their populations, the amount of freedom they accord them, and the

---

[19] Walter D. Connor, "Deviance, Stress, and Modernization in Eastern Europe," in Mark G. Field, ed., *Social Consequences of Modernization in Communist Societies* (Baltimore: Johns Hopkins University Press, 1976), pp. 186 ff.

amount and incidence of policing. Moreover, the incidence of riots should be viewed together with the data in chapter VIII on armed political attacks, which represent a more extreme form of the breakdown of public order.

Table XII.9 reports the incidence of riots since World War II in a selection of countries. The data have to be viewed with caution since they have been taken from the public press, which is carefully regulated in some countries, remains relatively free in others, and varies in accuracy and coverage from country to country. Shifts in the incidence of riots reported in the table vary from country to country. The figures for France and Germany represent a sharp decline from levels in the previous decade, as do those for Egypt. Most of the riots in Austria took place in a single year, 1959. On the other hand, rioting increased dramatically in

Table XII.9. *Internal Security Forces and Rioting in Selected Nations*

Nations in order of per capita GNP, 1965	Internal security forces per thousand working population, 1965	Number of riots		Riots per million citizens, 1958-1967
		1948-1957	*1958-1967*	
USA	3.5	55	628	3.2
Sweden	2.0	5	5	.6
Canada	.6	6	23	1.2
France	4.7	108	18	.4
W. Germany	3.6	67	31	.5
Britain	2.7	25	57	1.0
Czechoslovakia	3.8	39	9	.6
Israel	5.4	28	31	11.9
USSR	2.6	8	36	.2
Austria	—	18	18	2.5
Italy	4.6	217	93	1.8
Japan	2.3	89	70	.7
Bulgaria	7.3	8	2	.2
Spain	3.5	25	40	1.3
Mexico	—	48	83	1.9
Yugoslavia	3.6	17	2	.1
Peru	2.8	15	26	2.2
Brazil	2.6	35	60	.7
Egypt	6.6	66	2	.1
China	1.6	72	124	.2
India	2.1	164	332	.7
Kenya	2.6	44	49	5.2
Nigeria	.7	31	146	2.5
Tanzania	.2	0	13	1.2

Source: Taylor and Hudson, *World Handbook*, pp. 42 ff., 94 ff.

Nigeria with the breakdown of the "premobilized" democratic regime in that country, and the table reflects the beginnings of the Cultural Revolution in the increased amount of rioting in China in the 1958–1967 decade. In the United States there was an explosion of rioting in the 1960s associated with the black rebellion and the Vietnam War.

It is clear that the larger absolute numbers of riots are to be found in the larger countries. Although most of the nations in the table are large countries, there is clearly a concentration of large numbers of riots in the very large countries, such as China, India, and the United States. Obviously, the problem of keeping order among hundreds of millions of people is not an easy one. But as the shifting patterns of unrest indicate, size is certainly not the only factor shaping riot activity. On a per capita basis, as shown in the last column, the countries with the most riots in the second decade were Israel, Kenya, the United States, Austria, Nigeria, Peru, Mexico, and Italy. Cross-national comparisons must be made carefully, with regard both to the data and to the causes and impacts of relative and absolute numbers of riots.

The complexity of the relationship between security outputs and public order outcomes is suggested by comparing the second and last columns of the table. The United States and West Germany have equal security forces, relative to their population, but the riot level and rates in the United States in the second decade were about six times that of West Germany. Israel had a large security force and the highest per capita riot rate, while Britain had a relatively small internal security establishment and a low riot rate. The Communist countries of Czechoslovakia, Bulgaria, and Yugoslavia had relatively large security forces and low riot rates. Communist China, on the other hand, had a relatively small security force, an absolutely large riot level, but a low riot rate per capita. Thus, public order seems to be only marginally related to the size of police forces among these nations. The characteristics of the social and political order seem to be the important factors. Ethnic divisions in India, Kenya, Nigeria, Peru, and the United States help explain to some degree the high incidence of rioting. (See table I.1 and the discussion in chapter VII.)

Had our data included more recent years, the British figures would show not only an increase in internal security forces (with the use of the army in Northern Ireland), but also a sharp increase in the riot levels and rate. Income level, economic growth, and equity of distribution are also relevant, as are general patterns of regime control of liberty. The low riot rates in Czechoslovakia (before 1968), Bulgaria, and Yugoslavia have to be explained in some part by the political structures of these countries, which impose high penalties for public opposition and protest and which employ other organizations and institutions (especially the Communist party organization) in addition to police forces to control dissent.[20]

POLITICAL LIBERTY

We have already suggested that low riot rates in authoritarian political systems are in part the consequence of the suppression of opposition and dissent. The extent of regulation of political opposition is suggested in table XII.10, which is based on Dahl's "opportunity for political opposition" rankings for a variety of countries. Dahl's scores were computed on the basis of estimates of such conditions as: (1) the freedom to form and join organizations; (2) the freedom of expression; (3) the extent of the right to vote; (4) the right of political leaders to compete for support; (5) the availability of alternative sources of information; (6) the availability of free and fair elections; and (7) the availability of institutions for making government policies that depend on votes and other expressions of preference. It should be noted that in many cases these estimates are based on statutes and regulations rather than on the actual implementation of oppressive rules. A top ranking implies little regulation of political opposition and maximum opportunities for political opposition. Dahl himself identifies types 1 through 8 as "polyarchies." A low ranking implies substantial limits on freedom of association, communication, petition, and political participation.

As one glances down the column of rankings, it becomes evident that some of these discriminations are of questionable validity. To give such a loosely authoritarian third world regime as Nigeria roughly as low an "opportunity for political opposition" ranking as the Soviet Union overlooks the enormous differences in penetrative capacity and mobilizing effectiveness of the two countries; or the characterization of Brazil as substantially less oppressive than Egypt makes one ask questions about the validity of these measures, as does the similar scoring of Yugoslavia and the Soviet Union. The large differences between rankings for the advanced industrial democracies and those for the advanced Communist countries probably reflect a greater validity in the measures used in computing the polyarchy score. Dahl's polyarchy ranking seems to be more valid for those countries in which there is a reasonably close correspondence between policy, formal organization, and implementation.

---

20 For a systematic and sophisticated analysis of the sources of rioting and other forms of "collective protest," see Douglas A. Hibbs, *Mass Political Violence* (New York: John Wiley, 1973). Hibbs found ethnic discrimination, low economic growth rates, and non-Communist central regimes, in addition to population size, among the significant variables that were associated with higher levels of the collective protest form of violence in his final models. His analysis uses all countries, rather than our subset of examples.

Table XII.10. *Opportunities for Political Opposition in*
              Selected Nations, Late 1960s.

Nations in order of per capita GNP 1973	Opportunities for political opposition
USA	High
Sweden	High
Canada	High
W. Germany	High
France	High
Japan	High
Austria	High
Britain	High
Israel	High
Czechoslovakia	Very low
Italy	High
USSR	Very low
Bulgaria	Very low
Yugoslavia	Very low
Mexico	Moderate
Brazil	Low
Peru	Low
China	Very low
Egypt	Very low
Nigeria	Very low
Tanzania	Very low
India	High

Source: Adapted from Robert A. Dahl, *Polyarchy: Participation and Opposition* (New Haven: Yale University Press, 1971), pp. 231 ff. Dahl develops 31 scale types of opportunities for political opposition. We have here simply classified nations falling into types 1 to 8 as High; those in types 9 to 16 as Moderate; those in types 17 to 24 as Low; and those in types 25 to 31 as Very low.

OUTCOMES OF INTERNATIONAL PERFORMANCE

Two major introductory points must be made about the outcomes of the international action of political systems. The first relates to similarity: the same categories of output and outcome used in the analysis of domestic performance apply to international performance. Political systems in the international arena are engaged in extracting resources from one another, distributing goods and services to one another, compelling (and being compelled) by one another, and communicating with one another. These outputs are related to welfare and security outcomes in the international arena. The second point, however, reflects sharp contrast: the relations between outputs and outcomes are far more ambiguous and tenuous in the international sphere than in the domestic. While reality falls short of legitimate expectation, it is still true that the authority of a nation-state extends to its borders. There is a legitimate expectation that a tax will be paid, a benefit lawfully claimed, and a regulatory statute obeyed in the domestic context. But in the international arena, while there may be appeals to moral standards and while international rules may be formulated and adopted, they lack the binding quality, the expectation of enforceability, of domestic law. To use the traditional metaphor of the ship of state, if the helmsman of a vessel coming into domestic port has to contend with the reliability of his crew and uncertainty about wind and current, in international waters he has to contend not only with mortal frailty and fickle nature, but also with other ships and crews — some actively seeking to throw him off course, some clumsily getting in his way. Nowhere is the tragic irony of human affairs more evident than in the divergence between intent and outcome in the making and implementation of foreign and security policy.

The outcomes nations seek in the international arena have to do with welfare and security — an advantageous share of international trade, aid, and investment and an advantageous position of security and power. Beyond these self-centered goals nations may seek to establish international norms and institutions providing for more equitable distribution of welfare among nations and for less costly, more orderly resolution of international conflicts.

The military, economic, political-diplomatic, and other exchanges between political systems constitute a structure or system of international interaction. Within that structure the set of particular exchanges of a single political system may be referred to as its role. A role may be defined in terms of relative dominance (implied in the notion of "the great powers") and may be further characterized according to the relative emphasis on kinds of interaction. Dominance consists of some combination of military coercion, economic penetration, and political or ideological penetration. Similarly, subordination or dependence takes the form of the reciprocals: being militarily cowed or occupied, politically subverted, economically exploited, or ideologically influenced. Concepts such as "spheres of influence," or "blocs" and "orbits" suggest subsystems of the international system consisting of such dominant and subordinate nations. In the last two decades there has occurred a shift away from a bipolar international structure with the United States and the Soviet Union as dominant and competing powers, to which most of the nations of the world had somehow to relate. Instead, the present trend is increasing multipolarity and declining concentration of power.

The shifting emphases on the kinds of exchanges may constitute outcomes as important as the shifting patterns of dominance and subordination among nations. Periods of peace and détente are marked by increases in the salience and frequency of diplomatic, economic, and communication exchanges: less coercive means are used by the nations in their regulative outputs. In contrast, periods of war or tension are typified by security diplomacy, military mobilization, psychological warfare, and the like. And revolutionary periods are marked by the salience of ideologically and politically subversive exchanges, as well as by overt coercion.

WELFARE

In our analysis of welfare outcomes in international policy we are interested in, first, a nation's net balance of extractions and distributions and, second, the degree to which it is dominated in these exchanges. In chapter XI we reported the amounts of aid received from the United States and the Soviet Union by a number of countries, using a cutoff point of half a billion dollars. Although the African nations received smaller amounts of aid, they represented larger proportions of the resources available to these nations. But the proportion of a nation's GNP attributable to aid can give a misleading impression of dependence. China in the mid-1960s gave up an enormous amount of Soviet aid in the interest of pursuing its own domestic and international course. Similarly, Yugoslavia in the late 1940s was prepared to forego Soviet aid and accept the rise of Soviet hostility in the interest of its own autonomy. Yugoslavia found it possible to turn to the United States for substantial aid and still maintain a neutralist foreign policy. And as we have already pointed out, such nations as India and Egypt have been able to obtain foreign aid from both superpowers. Thus, they have managed to extract substantial resources from the international environment, in the form of aid, without surrendering their autonomy. Clearly, this is a beneficial welfare outcome for them.

Another critical welfare area is the amount of foreign trade, its composition, and its pattern. Table XII.11 reports some trade statistics for selected nations in 1965. In the second column of the table we report the magnitude of foreign trade as a percentage of GNP, which indicates the degree to which nations are dependent on international markets and sources of supply and on international economic conditions. The more dependent countries are less in control of their own welfare because their economies are more quickly and substantially susceptible to extranational fluctuations. The third column measures the extent to which a nation is dependent on a few, or even one, export products or commodities. This concentration measure is a further element in international dependence, for a country heavily dependent on one or two export commodities is subject to the special fluctuations of those specific commodity markets. Finally, the last column measures dependence on specific foreign markets

Table XII.11. *International Economic Performance in Selected Nations*

Nations in order of per capita GNP, 1965	Foreign trade as a percentage of GNP, 1965	Concentration of export commodities, 1965	Concentration of export-receiving countries, 1965
USA	7.3	.08	.07
Kuwait	67.2	.88	.16
Sweden	42.3	.09	.09
Canada	34.8	.08	.36
France	21.7	.06	.08
W. Germany	31.5	.10	.07
Britain	29.1	.09	.05
Czechoslovakia	47.1	—	.17
Israel	33.5	.20	.07
USSR	9.8	—	.07
Austria	39.6	.07	.12
Italy	25.2	.07	.08
Japan	19.7	.09	.09
Bulgaria	67.5	—	.29
Spain	22.5	.14	.08
Mexico	13.9	.09	.31
Yugoslavia	27.0	.07	.07
Cuba	51.7	.75	.25
Peru	32.5	.17	.17
Brazil	11.8	.25	.13
Dominican Republic	23.3	.35	.67
Egypt	32.7	.37	.08
China	6.0	—	—
India	9.1	.17	.10
Kenya	46.6	.23	.09
Nigeria	31.4	.18	.20
Tanzania	42.1	.23	.09

Source: Taylor and Hudson, *World Handbook*, pp. 366 ff.

Note: The concentration indices reflect the dominance of total export values by a few large products or exports to only a few countries. Technically, the index is calculated by the formula $c = \Sigma p_i^2$, where p_i is the proportion of total value of exports accounted for by the ith commodity or country.

by indicating the degree to which the value of a country's exports are accounted for by trade with a few nations. Needless to say, a country that depends heavily on foreign trade, on a few export commodities, and on a single export market is very dependent indeed. The Dominican Republic and Cuba manifest these multiple forms of international dependence. Cuba's foreign trade is more than half its GNP; its foreign exports are concentrated in one commodity, sugar; and the bulk of these exports go to a single market, the Soviet Union. (Bulgaria shows a similar pattern, although the commodities are different.) Although the foreign trade of the Dominican Republic accounts for only about one-quarter of its GNP, exports are again dominated by a single commodity, also sugar, and go largely to a single market, the United States.

At the other extreme are such undominated countries as the United States and the Soviet Union, whose economies are overwhelmingly internal, whose exports are variegated, and whose markets are unconcentrated. Two countries — Canada and Mexico — depend on the American market for more than one-third of their exports and so are peculiarly susceptible to American economic fluctuations and foreign trade policies. Kuwait and Egypt, on the other hand, are peculiarly dependent on specific commodity markets — oil and cotton.

Dependence on a single product results in vulnerability because of fluctuations in demand and supply of particular commodities. A price rise may be a bonanza; a drop in prices, a disaster. The example of the oil cartel (OPEC) suggests that international collusion in the pricing of commodities for which demand is high and relatively inelastic can convert this dependence into great advantage. In a period of increasing raw materials shortages we need to revise our image of the backward nation with only raw materials to offer in international trade, as inherently dependent and subject to exploitation by the industrial powers. Much depends on how essential the commodity is and on its distribution, the availability of substitutes, and the ability of its principal producers to take advantage of their control of the resource.

The energy crisis of the 1970s also demonstrates how dependent the modern industrial economies are on supplies of foreign oil, particularly from the Middle East. Rates of growth and inflation in such countries as Japan and France have been sharply affected by rises in the price of oil, and the Middle Eastern policies of many countries have been influenced by the oil-rich Arab countries.

Much has been written in recent years about the political, economic, and social consequences of the dependence of third world nations. The American-initiated economic development crusade of the 1960s is now widely criticized as having been primarily extractive in effect, as having deformed and distorted third world societies, and as having produced a net deterioration in their economic situation and distributive patterns. The principal villains in this process of third world exploitation are reputed to be the advanced capitalist countries, particularly the United States, and the multinational corporations based in the United States and Western Europe.

The political, social, and economic consequences of the economic interaction between the developed and the third world nations is not yet fully understood. There has been considerable variation in rates and patterns of growth among the Asian, African, and Latin American countries.

Whatever growth in GNP has occurred in most third world countries has been reduced on a per capita basis as a consequence of population increase. Modernization in third world countries has tended to produce "dual societies," nations with both a developed, modern sector dependent on foreign trade and capital and a residual rural agricultural sector benefiting little, if at all, from modernization. But the story of the effects of foreign investment in the third world is considerably more complicated than the simple, exploitative scenario described in "dependency" theories, and it is surely not the benign story told in the brochures of multinational corporations.[21]

SECURITY

The expenditures of nations in lives and treasure for foreign and security policy purposes and the thrust of their diplomacy and covert operations abroad — their international security outputs, in other words — have intentions and effects that must be sharply distinguished. As far as the intentions of foreign policy makers are concerned, their purposes may be aggressive, defensive, or creative of new international institutions and norms. Many smaller powers intend their international outputs to be purely defensive in character, maintaining military forces and practicing diplomacy for this purpose alone. The classic neutral countries — Switzerland and Sweden — have succeeded in attaining outcomes consistent with these defensive intentions. Other smaller powers have similar defensive goals, but pursue them through diplomatic and security alignments with larger powers — for example, the NATO countries with the United States or the Eastern European countries with the Soviet Union. In these cases the connection between security intentions and outcomes is greatly influenced by the policies pursued by the dominant power in the bloc.

In general, foreign and security policy decisions are only partially under the control of a single country. A nation may begin a phase of international politics with defensive security goals, but be confronted with an aggressive country and, hence, be compelled to engage in aggressive actions to maintain its security. Even as unambiguously aggressive a nation as Nazi Germany had to justify its policies to its people as responses to the aggressions or potential aggressions of other nations. The Soviet invasion of Czechoslovakia was justified in terms of a threat of capitalist penetration in the Socialist area, and the American aggressions in Cuba, Chile, and the Dominican Republic were similarly justi-

---

[21] An interesting discussion of the problem of introducing foreign capital into Latin American countries on mutually beneficial terms is to be found in Albert Hirschman. *A Bias for Hope* (New Haven: Yale University Press, 1971), pp. 225 ff.

fied in defensive terms. Thus a defensive security policy (as in the case of Israel) may turn into aggression and conquest; and a relatively innocent bystander (such as Lebanon) may be overrun, infiltrated, and drawn into outcomes having little relationship to its own policies.

Historically, this built-in tension between policy and outcome in international politics has contributed to periodic wars of increasing scale and destructiveness. This story is told in part in figure XII.2, which reports the trend in the magnitude of war over the period from 1816 until 1970. Magnitude is measured by the total number of months that nations were at war with one another during each of the years over this century and a half. The high peaks of the curve are in the present century, reflecting the multinational scope of World Wars I and II and the Korean War. The number of nations involved in war and the duration of their involvement is, of course, closely correlated with the costs of war, in terms of military and civilian casualties and the physical destruction of property, capital, and resources.

The burden of these costs is partially reported in table XII.12, which reports the deaths in battle for a selection of nations since the signing of the Treaty of Vienna in 1816 (when the modern nation-state system

Figure XII.2. *Number of Nation-War-Months Underway by Year, 1816–1965*

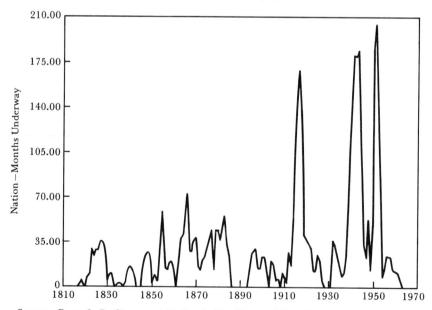

Source: From J. D. Singer and M. Small, *The Wages of War*, 1816–1965, 1972, p. 209. Reprinted by permission of John Wiley & Sons, publishers.

Table XII.12. *War Experience for Selected Nations, 1816–1965*

Nations in order of per capita GNP, 1965	Total years in system	Number of wars	Total battle deaths	Battle deaths per year
USA	150	6	608,000	4,059
Sweden	150	0	0	0
Canada	46	2	39,610	861
France	148	19	1,943,840	13,134
W. Germany (incl. Prussia)	141	6	5,353,500	41,181
Britain	150	19	1,295,280	8,635
Czechoslovakia	42	1	2,000	48
Israel	18	2	3,200	178
USSR	150	15	9,662,560	64,417
Italy (incl. Sardinia)	150	12	759,500	5,063
Japan	99	7	1,365,300	13,791
Spain	150	9	180,900	1,259
Mexico	135	3	19,000	141
Yugoslavia (incl. Serbia)	85	5	88,500	1,041
Brazil	140	3	101,500	725
Egypt	29	2	5,000	172
China	106	8	3,110,500	29,344
India	19	3	5,000	263
Kenya	3	0	0	0
Nigeria	6	0	0	0
Tanzania	5	0	0	0

Source: Singer and Small, *The Wages of War*, pp. 275 ff.
Note: These figures do not include civil wars.

may be said to have originated) or since the beginning of the nation's independence, if it took place subsequent to 1816. Battle deaths are reported as totals for the nation during the whole period and on an annual basis.

We reported battle deaths per year for these same nations in Table XI.8 as one of the international security costs of nations, along with military expenditures as a percentage of GNP and measures of diplomatic activity. Over time these costs of security policy have escalated. Most of the deaths are concentrated in the twentieth century, and what the table does not show — relatively random civilian deaths and destruction — have escalated even more rapidly. With the development of nuclear weapons, large-scale war promises to become far more destructive in lives and property and far more random in its selection of victims. Hence, it is no longer possible to view war expenditures in lives and treasure simply as security outputs. The output overwhelms the outcome, indeed becomes the outcome. Large-scale war — and smaller-scale war insofar as it holds out the prospect of escalation — no longer has a meaningful relationship to the intentions of policy makers. This notion is suggested in the concept of "balance of terror" in which nuclear powers are inhibited from embarking on war through fear that it may get beyond control with the fully irrational result of wiping out some substantial part of the populations of the participants and that of innocent by-stander countries.

The tension between security output and outcome is also suggested by the phrase "thinking the unthinkable" and by the introduction of a new measure of human battle costs, "mega-deaths," which would be appropriate in a post–nuclear war version of table XII.12. Hence, we feel justified in repeating that these data serve as a measure of outcome as well as output. As figure XII.2 indicated, until 1914 the incidence and magnitude of war seemed to bear some relationship to public policy. The victorious alliance that defeated Napoleon in 1814 viewed the Europe constituted through the Treaty of Vienna as an outcome worth the costs — in blood and treasure — of the long sequence of Napoleonic wars. Victorious Prussia under Bismarck could view the Austrian and French wars of the mid-nineteenth century as costs reasonably incurred in the interests of a unified Germany under Prussian domination. One may well note, however, that the Franco-Prussian War was in some sense a prelude to World War I, as World War I was prelude to World War II when the line between war as means and its outcome began to stretch taut. With the development and use of nuclear weapons at the end of World War II this relationship between large-scale war and national security purposes may be said to have broken.

However, even though actual resort to large-scale war is viewed as unthinkable, budget allocations for military purposes, the development of more versatile nuclear weaponry, and the deployment of such military means continue to be crucial components of the international security policy of nations, intended to maintain or alter an inherently unstable balance of terror. International disarmament efforts intended to reduce the danger that these capabilities will be utilized are still in a tentative, groping stage.

THE FEEDBACK METAPHOR

Having been first applied to the study of politics by David Easton and Karl Deutsch, the notion of feedback has come into common use in the analysis of political phenomena in recent years. The metaphor as used by Deutsch is that of a "servo-mechanism . . . a communications network that produces action in response to an input of information, and includes the results of its own action in the new information by which

Figure XII.3. *The Feedback Metaphor*

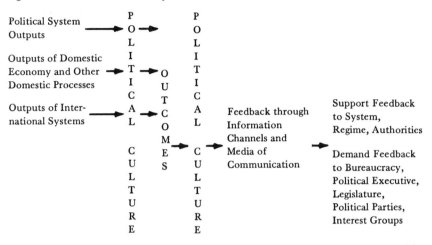

it modifies its subsequent behavior." [22] What we suggest in figure XII.3 is that the outputs of political systems combine with the outputs of other domestic systems and processes (such as the economy) and with the outputs of international systems, "passing through" political culture before they become outcomes. The effect of political culture on outcomes is by no means trivial. Compliance with the authoritative outputs of the political system is in part dependent on the "compliance propensities" of a population. The yield of taxation, responsiveness to law enforcement, and willingness to sacrifice in war, are very much a matter of feelings, values, and other attitudes current in the population as a whole or in particular groups.

After these outputs and cultural propensities combine to produce outcomes, they again pass through political culture as they produce feedbacks. The outcome of a political system's international activity may be increased international tension or war requiring sacrifice on the part of the population. Response to these outcomes will vary substantially with the depth and intensity of national loyalty. A political system may be viewed in this case as drawing on a fund of support associated with national identity, with the particular constitutional regime, or with the particular authorities then in control of the regime. This fund of support for nation, regime, and authorities may in time be overdrawn, resulting in deteriorating performance or increasing cost of performance. Thus,

---

22 David Easton, An Approach to the Analysis of Political Systems. *World Politics* 9 (April 1957): 383 ff. Karl W. Deutsch, *The Nerves of Government* (New York: Free Press of Glencoe, 1963), pp. viii, 88 ff.

political culture affects the performance side of the political system at these two phases of the process — as outputs become outcomes, and as outcomes become feedbacks — and may itself be changed in the process.

Feedback of demands resulting from these processes may be directed at any one or any combination of the political process structures — the bureaucracy, the political executive, the legislature, the political parties, and the interest groups. The responsiveness of these agencies to demands affects the reserves of support that particular incumbents or institutions accumulate or that accrue to the "legitimacy account" of the nation or the regime as a whole. The British nation and parliamentary regime in World War II could draw heavily on a legitimacy reserve that had accumulated from centuries of performance, but recent developments in Britain suggest that this reserve is not inexhaustible. The Soviet leadership in World War II found that its reserves of support were associated with Russian nationalism rather than with the Bolshevik party or the Stalin regime. The credit and credibility of particular government agencies in the United States — the presidency, Congress, and the courts — similarly fluctuate with performance. Roosevelt left the presidency with reserves of support, while Nixon had all but drained it of reserves.

As we have suggested in chapter VI, feedbacks are also affected by the specific properties of the information channels and media of communication through which they pass. There is a distinction between information channels and media of communication, the former being the direct information networks among political officials and elites, and the latter referring to the more open channels such as press, radio, and television. American Secretaries of State, for example, receive feedback on the effects of their foreign policy not only through the "diplomatic pouch," but also through the general news media. Reports of outcomes in these information channels and media of communication may be more or less accurate, more or less biased.

It is when one begins to consider the role of political culture in transforming outputs into outcomes and outcomes into feedbacks that the importance of the symbolic aspect of political performance becomes so evident. Incumbents of political roles — political elites — are in constant communication with one another, with groups of citizens, or with the citizenry as a whole. Much of what they say consists of arguments as to why other elite members, or citizens, should comply with the law or support public policy and implementation. Leaders appeal to cultural values, feelings, and beliefs in efforts to coax and persuade desired kinds of behavior among citizens. The symbolic output of political elites may appeal to the past as a way of mobilizing support for contemporary lines of public policy, or it may take the form of an appeal to the future in terms of acting consistently with traditional performance or with ideological aspirations.

Perhaps we can best illustrate the significance of symbolic performance by the use of an economic metaphor. A political system may be thought of as having both "current" and "capital" accounts. In the early postwar period West Germany seemed to have had no capital account at all. What legitimacy it acquired was based on economic performance. Recent evidence suggests that West German citizens still tend to keep the Bonn system on a short-term, current accounts basis, although there is evidence that its capital account is accumulating.

Good symbolic performance uses the right cues in efforts to draw on the captial account, if one exists, or effectively appeals to group interests, if no capital reserve is available. Where no capital exists, the costs of performance may be high and the range of leadership freedom, low. The citizens compare costs and benefits in a hard-nosed, calculative fashion, press their demands, and withhold their support to the limit. Something like this draining of psychological capital seems to have been taking place in the whole of the Western world in the last decade. (See chapter II.)

CHAPTER XIII

The Political Economy of Development

WE HAVE USED the term *political development* in earlier chapters to refer to a set of related political system, process, and policy changes that have been, or are, taking place within the larger context of socioeconomic modernization. Political development occurs in part as a consequence of this modernization, and in increasing part as its cause.[1]

Modernization in the economic sense has meant growth in productivity and more equal distribution of economic benefits. In the social sense modernization has meant a host of related transformations spelled out earlier by such social theorists as Karl Marx, Max Weber, Emile Durkheim, Ferdinand Toennies, and Talcott Parsons. These aspects of modernization include increasing division of labor and differentiation of social structure; urbanization, industrialization, and the spread of education and the mass media of communication; improved health, welfare, and social amenities.

Political development has specifically referred, first, to the rise of specialized political executive and bureaucratic agencies capable of setting collective goals and implementing them in the domestic and international environments. Second, it has been used to mean the rise of such broadly articulating and aggregating agencies as political parties, interest groups, and communication media that serve the purpose of relating groups in the population to these goal-setting and goal-implementing structures. While political development both influences and is influenced by the socioeconomic process of modernization, historically it has tended

---

[1] See the excellent review of the development literature by Samuel P. Huntington and J. I. Dominguez, "Political Development," in Fred I. Greenstein and Nelson W. Polsby, *Handbook of Political Science,* vol. 3 (Boston: Addison-Wesley, 1976), chap. 1. As we stressed in earlier chapters, of course, political development did take place to some degree in such systems as the historic bureaucratic empires and in response to a variety of challenges and goals (see especially chap. III).

to become the focal process of the larger modernizing process. Thus, for the first modernizing country, Britain, most of the initiative for innovation came from the society and the economy; the political system played a facilitating role. In the second echelon of developing countries in the Western part of the European continent (France and Germany, for example) the political system played a more important role in economic and social modernization. And among the successful later modernizers, such as Russia and Japan, the role of politics has tended to assume dominating dimensions.

THE LOGIC OF POLITICAL DEVELOPMENT

The way in which various components and levels of political development are related is suggested in figure XIII.1. That is to say, desired sociopolitical goals or outcomes — such as national security and expansion, economic growth and social welfare, and liberty — typically require increased regulative, extractive, distributive, and symbolic outputs. These greater outputs and outcomes, in turn, are dependent on the development of more specialized and effective processes for making and implementing policy and for articulating and aggregating interests. And these specialized processes are dependent on structural and cultural changes: first, the differentiation of specialized roles in political structures, such as the executive, bureaucracy, political parties, interest groups, and mass media; and, second, the spread in societies of values, attitudes, and skills consistent with these roles, in particular, readiness to comply with the law, participant propensities, and welfare expectations.

Although the specific relationships depend on the goals in question, the environmental conditions, and the existing structures, the general logic would seem to be clear: one cannot shape the outcomes without the outputs; one cannot have the outputs without the processes; and one cannot have the processes without the structures and cultural propensities. And, finally, one cannot develop or sustain these structures and cultural propensities without appropriate recruitment and socialization. This logic, which we have diagrammed in figure XIII.1, is a "synchronic" logic, which assumes that these components all come into place simultaneously and that they mutually sustain one another. But while this model spells out the interdependence of these system, process, and policy components in advanced societies, it does not tell how they developed historically.

In figure XIII.2 we take liberties with Western European history and suggest schematically how the advanced democratic countries developed their political systems. It was an adaptive process that extended over the last four centuries, one in which individual issues and challenges peaked and lent themselves to separate and partial solutions. The developments

Figure XIII.1. *Processes of Political Development: A Functional Model*

New Needs and/or New Goals of Citizens and Political Elites ⟹ Policy Development to Achieve New Goals ⟹ Process Development to Make Policies, Implement Them, and Sustain Political and Resource Support ⟹ System Development to Create the Necessary Structure and Culture Basis

New Outcomes	Require	New Outputs	Require	New Processes	Require	Adaptation
Public Security and Order		Regulative		Policy-Making Specialization		*Recruitment* into and Creation of Differentiated Structures
Economic Growth		Extractive		Policy-Implementing Specialization		Executive
Welfare		Distributive		Interest-Aggregating Specialization		Bureaucracy
Liberty		Symbolic		Interest-Articulating Specialization		Parties
International Security and Welfare						Interest Groups
						Mass Media
						Socialization into and Creation of Secularized and Supportive Culture
						Compliance and Legitimacy
						Identity
						Participant Propensities
						Policy Expectations
						Communication Linkages to Integrate the Specialized and Interdependent Roles

Note: The double arrows here signify the implication of requisites at different levels of the political system, not a sequential order.

Figure XIII.2. *Stages of Political Development: The Advanced Industrial Democracies*

System Development	Process Development	Policy Development	
		Outputs	Outcomes
Structural Differentiation			
Political Executive — I	Policy-Making Specialization — I	Regulative	Public Order and Security — I
Bureaucracy	Policy-Implementing Specialization	Extractive — I	Economic Growth
Party Organizations — II		Symbolic	
Interest Groups — &	Interest-Articulating Specialization — II	Distributive — III	Liberty — II
Mass Media — III	Interest-Aggregating Specialization — & III		Social Welfare — III
Cultural Modernization			
Compliance and Legitimacy — I			
National Loyalty — I			
Participant Propensities — II			
Welfare Expectations — III			

described as stage I took place in the "age of absolutism" — the state- and nation-building era in Western Europe, extending roughly from the beginning of the sixteenth century into the nineteenth. The process began in the crucible of dynastic, international, and religious wars of the sixteenth to the eighteenth centuries. Success in expanding and maintaining power for the Tudor, Bourbon, Hohenzollern, Hapsburg, Romanov, and other monarchs was dependent on the development of effective military and policing forces under central control and the acquisition of the economic means necessary to support these forces. In other words, the outcomes sought by these state and nation builders were the establishment and expansion of political control and prosperous economies on which they could draw in order to maintain and expand this control. For these purposes they developed cabinets and councils to set goals and make policies, military and police organizations, and the civilian bureaucracy necessary to extract resources and supplies and to regulate behavior in support of these organizations and purposes.

Though we are vastly oversimplifying historical reality, the essential point is that in Western Europe, roughly by the mid-nineteenth century, nation-states and commercial-industrial economies were in being; and the participant (power-sharing) stage and distributive (welfare-sharing) stage could take on momentum at a time when there were centralized political power and material means to share. Stages II and III in figure XIII.2 describe the related structural-cultural changes, process specializations, outputs, and outcomes associated with the historically overlapping participant and welfare revolutions of the nineteenth and twentieth centuries.[2] Thus, in Stage II, Western nations developed party organizations, interest groups, and mass media on the structural side and participant expectations and skills on the cultural side. These changes made it possible for social groups to articulate their interests and aggregate them in such a way as to share in policy making and implementation, to produce distributive outputs beneficial to them, and to contribute to libertarian and welfare outcomes.

The Western states had two centuries or more for their age of absolutism, a century and a half for their "age of democratization," and a century for their "age of welfare." The new nations must somehow telescope all three into one single age. They are under pressure, by the example of the modern states, to open channels for mass participation in decision

---

[2] For detailed discussion of political development and modernization in Western Europe and the third world see Cyril Black, *The Dynamics of Modernization* (New York: Harper & Row, 1966); Charles Tilly, ed., *The Formation of National States in Western Europe* (Princeton: Princeton University Press, 1975); Leonard Binder et al., *Crises and Sequences in Political Development* (Princeton: Princeton University Press, 1971).

making before effective central decision-making institutions have been constituted and before organizations to facilitate such participation have formed. Further, they are under pressure, by the example of the modern economies, to distribute material welfare before the capacity for the production of welfare — capital goods, managerial talent, and labor skills — has been developed. Surely state building and political development in the contemporary world must assume different proportions under the pressure of these simultaneous and conflicting demands. The need to concentrate power is in conflict with the demand for the diffusion of power; [3] and the need to extract and invest in economic growth is in conflict with the demand for increased welfare. An effective state-building strategy in the contemporary world must somehow reconcile these conflicts between political concentration and diffusion, between economic growth and distribution.

DEVELOPMENT AS A POLITICO-ECONOMIC PROCESS

The kinds of political systems that have emerged in the third world are related to different politico-economic strategies intended to resolve the tensions described above. State building and economy building are logically prior to political participation and material distribution, since power sharing and welfare sharing are dependent on there being power and welfare to share.

But third world countries have not been free to cope with the tensions of this development dialectic in terms of this logic. They have come into an international society of politically capable and economically advanced nation-states in which the salient political issues are those of participation and welfare. Thus, while the *logic* of development would suggest a prior period of state and economy building, the *politics* of development compel a simultaneous confrontation of participant and distributive demands and expectations. In some sense, the distributive demands and expectations are the most compelling of all. Among many contrasts, that which distinguishes the underdeveloped world from the developed world most sharply is its relative poverty; and among the most powerful motives animating its politics is the desire to eliminate or mitigate this condition.

It may be useful to begin our discussion of the political-economy of third world development by spelling out the requirements of a distributive growth process, since the political components may be viewed at least in part as means to that end. Once one grasps the nature of the policy requirements for a distributive economic growth process, one is

---

[3] Samuel P. Huntington and Clement H. Moore, eds., *Authoritarian Politics in Modern Society* (New York: Basic Books, 1970), pp. 13 ff.

in a position to treat the political systems of the third world as development strategies involving different orderings or emphases in confronting these challenges.

POLICY REQUIREMENTS FOR EQUITABLE ECONOMIC GROWTH

Historical and contemporary evidence suggests that there is a curvilinear relationship between economic growth and income inequality; that is, at the earlier stages of growth, inequality in income shares increases as capital is accumulated for investment and a modern economic sector emerges; it then declines as development reaches higher stages.[4] But the relationship between growth and inequality is not of such a strong and inevitable character that it is unresponsive to political intervention and public policy. Population control, education, land ownership, and fiscal and public investment policy constitute levers that may reduce inequality in the process of growth; and there are cases demonstrating that it is possible to have "growth with distribution" even short of a fully Socialist solution.[5]

The success of a development strategy combining growth with distribution depends on the probability of forming and maintaining ruling coalitions among the power groups in given societies favoring or tolerating distributive policies.[6] The kinds of coalitions and policies that are possible depend in turn on the socioeconomic structure of developing societies. The World Bank study on which this analysis draws proposes a typology of countries for purposes of illustrating the ways in which these structural characteristics constrain policy options and development strategies.

> The three dimensions of the typology were chosen on a priori grounds: (1) the relative proportions of the population in urban and rural areas, reflecting also the GNP per capita of the country; (2) the availability of land already cultivated or brought easily under the plough, whether it is abundant or scarce relative to the country's population; and (3) the degree of concentration of land ownership, whether it is high or low.[7]

This classification scheme yields eight country types (see table XIII.1). From these eight the World Bank study group selected three "arche-

---

[4] Hollis Chenery et al., *Redistribution with Growth* (New York: Oxford University Press, 1974), p. 17; S. Kuznets, "Economic Growth and Income Inequality," *American Economic Review* (March 1955): 1–28; Irma Adelman and Cynthia Morris, *Economic Growth and Social Equity in Developing Countries* (Stanford: Stanford University Press, 1973).

[5] Chenery et al., op. cit., chaps. 2, 4.

[6] Chenery et al., op. cit., chap. 3.

[7] Ibid., pp. 93 ff.

Table XIII.1. *Developmental Starting Points in the Third World*

Availability of land and concentration of ownership	Degree of urbanization			
		High		Low
Abundant land High concentration	I	Latin American type (Mexico, Brazil, Peru, Colombia)	V	(Rhodesia)
Abundant land Low concentration	II		VI	Sub-Saharan African type (Tanzania, Sierra Leone)
Scarce land High concentration	III	(Caribbean)	VII	South Asian type (India, Pakistan, Indonesia)
Scarce land Low concentration	IV	(Taiwan, South Korea)	VIII	(Bangladesh)

Source: Adapted from Hollis Chenery et al., *Redistribution with Growth* (New York: Oxford University Press, 1974), pp. 93 ff.

types" encompassing "the bulk of the population in poverty" in the developing world and illustrating different combinations of urbanization-industrialization levels, land ownership, and land availability patterns. Type I is the Latin American variety, exemplified by Mexico, Brazil, and Peru and characterized by high urbanization-industrialization, abundant agricultural land relative to population, and high concentration of land ownership. Type VI, the African variety exemplified by Tanzania and Sierra Leone, is characterized by low urbanization-industrialization, abundant land, and low concentration of land ownership. Type VII, the South Asian variety that includes India, Pakistan, and Indonesia, is characterized by low urbanization-industrialization, scarce land, and high concentration of land ownership.

In an effort to extend and illustrate the typology discussed by the World Bank study group we present table XIII.2, which adds two East Asian cases — Taiwan and South Korea (their type IV) — exemplifying more or less free economies in which effective distributive policies have been pursued. In the columns of table XIII.2 we include measures of urbanization, industrialization, economic growth, population density, concentration of land ownership, and patterns of income distribution. Together, tables XIII.1 and XIII.2 should illustrate how basic socio-economic conditions constrain policy options and political strategies.

Table XIII.2. Socioeconomic Conditions of Selected Developing Countries

Country	% of population in cities of 100,000 and over, 1960 [a]	% of labor force in agriculture, mid-1960s [b]	Number of persons per Km² of agricultural land, 1950-1965 [c]	Concentration of land ownership, Gini Index, 1955-1965 [d]	GNP per capita, 1972 [e]	% of growth in GNP per capita, 1965-1972 [e]	% of income in late 1960s to [f] Lowest 40%	Middle 40%	Top 20%
LATIN AMERICA									
Mexico	16	59	42	69	750	3	10	26	64
Brazil	26	57	65	85	530	6	10	28	62
Peru	15	55	58	93	520	1	7	33	60
AFRICA									
Tanzania	2	95	23	—	120	3	13	26	61
Sierra Leone	5	75	39	—	190	2	10	22	68
SOUTH ASIA									
India	9	68	275	52	110	1	16	32	52
Pakistan	7	73	399	65	130	2	18	38	45
EAST ASIA									
Taiwan	30	49	1397	46	490	7	20	40	40
South Korea	23	51	1320	39	320	4	18	37	45

Note: Figures are rounded to nearest whole number.
[a] Charles L. Taylor and Michael C. Hudson, World Handbook of Political and Social Indicators (New Haven: Yale University Press, 1972), pp. 219 ff.
[b] Ibid., pp. 332 ff. For Tanzania and Sierra Leone, Donald Morrison et al., Black Africa: A Comparative Handbook (New York: Free Press, 1974), pp. 37 ff.
[c] Taylor and Hudson, World Handbook, pp. 303 ff.
[d] Ibid., pp. 267 ff.
[e] World Bank, World Bank Atlas (Washington, D.C., 1973).
[f] Chenery et al., Redistribution with Growth, pp. 8-9.

Reading across the rows of table XIII.2, one can see that Mexico has a sizable urban-industrial sector with some 16 percent of its population as of 1960 living in cities of 100,000 and over. By 1970 the population residing in cities with 20,000 and over accounted for more than half the total population. It has a relatively high and growing GNP, which has been cut roughly in half on a per capita basis through population increase. Population density on agricultural land is relatively low, while land ownership and income are highly concentrated. The lowest 40 percent of the population receive only 10 percent of the income, while the highest 20 percent get more than 64 percent of the income. Brazil and Peru are quite similar to Mexico except that land ownership is even more concentrated.

The two African cases — Tanzania and Sierra Leone — are far less urbanized and industrialized than the Latin American countries and are also characterized by low population densities on agricultural land and substantial income inequalities. Though comparable data are not available, land distribution in Tanzania and Sierra Leone is less concentrated than in the Latin American countries. The South Asian cases have a much higher population density on agricultural land, a somewhat larger urban sector than the African cases, and a somewhat more egalitarian income distribution than either the African or Latin American varieties.

What kind of policy mix is likely to produce an equitable growth trend in these types of societies? The World Bank study suggests that for both the rural and urban sectors of all three country types there are several common policy components.[8] In the first instance, coping with the distributive problem calls for population control. Population increase, since it is highest among the rural and urban poor, has the effect of nullifying resource reallocations and economic growth. Hence, any policy directed toward growth and distribution must set a high priority on population control. A second common policy component is education directed toward enhancing the skills, productivity, and effectiveness of the rural and urban poor. A redistributive educational policy will have to stress primary education and training in vocational skills and to include extension services in the rural sectors.

A third common component for rural and urban sectors of all three types of societies is the effective delivery of health care in both its preventive and curative aspects, a kind of policy realizable only through the development of paramedical services, improved nutrition, and a deliberate effort to bring these benefits to the rural and urban poor. Finally, a fourth component of policy — one that exhibits differences on the rural

[8] For a more general discussion of the mix required for a growth plus distribution policy see Chenery et al., op. cit., chaps. 6, 7.

and urban sides — is the more effective delivery of public works and infrastructural elements to the poor. In the rural context improved infrastructure includes roads and access to water, while on the urban side improved delivery of public works to the poor would include road and sanitation improvements, better transportation between poor neighborhoods and places of work, urban land use reform, and cheap housing. Productivity among the rural poor would be enhanced by improved inputs — better seeds, fertilizers, and agricultural implements. In contrast, on the urban side public policy would favor labor-intensive industrialization and subsidies to small enterprises in order to absorb the urban unemployed and marginal workers, rather than the high-technology industrialization that tends to create privileged enclaves and sharper income inequalities.

Though there is a common core of distributive policies for the rural sectors in all three types of societies, variations in population density and concentration of land ownership call for different kinds of land reform. In the Latin American case the combination of low density of population on agricultural land and high concentration of its ownership among a privileged *latifundia* suggests the solution of dividing the large estates and making land available to farm laborers and subsistence farmers on acceptable terms.

This land reform solution is less suitable in the South Asian case, in which the ratio of rural population to agricultural land is such that general land division would result in a shift of rural laborers into the status of sub-marginal farmers with little net reduction in poverty. Here the solution seems to call for a combination of labor-intensive industrialization to draw excess population away from the land, limitation on farm size to mitigate gross inequalities, and improved inputs into the agricultural areas to increase productivity.

In the African societies exploitation of land is limited by tribal patterns of land use and ownership. Much of the land is uncultivated. Political difficulties aside, an economic solution calls for land registration, the stabilization of holdings, and the colonization of new areas. Agricultural productivity would be enhanced by infrastructural development — roads and irrigation — and by improved inputs of seeds, fertilizers, and the like. In general, the delivery of education, health, farming techniques, and agricultural inputs would be facilitated by land reforms that include cooperative and communal features, in which the social setting encourages the acceptance of new norms and skills.

An effective growth-cum-distribution policy has to take into account the interaction of the urban and rural sectors. A deteriorating countryside compounds the poverty problem of the cities as the rural poor emigrate to the urban slums. A policy directed at rural poverty would retard this rate of urban migration, and a policy directed toward the reduction of both rural and urban poverty would reduce pressure in both contexts, while strengthening internal markets for agricultural and industrial products.

POLITICAL REQUIREMENTS AND CONDITIONS

In the cool language and logic of economics an equitable growth policy — one that would be deliberately equitable and would not rely on ultimate and uncertain trickle-down processes — seems reasonable and attainable. But when we convert these economic policies into the political structures and processes required to enact and implement them, the great difficulty of the development problem becomes clear. The complex of policies discussed above involves the transfer of assets (as in land reform and nationalization); the upgrading of skills and vitality through education, health, and nutrition measures that are dependent on redistributive taxation; and investment policies intended to integrate the urban and rural poor into the productive economy. All these measures involve the reallocation of resources from the politically powerful to the politically weak.

Such reallocations have rarely been effected peacefully; and when they have taken place quickly, the human costs have often been high. In the state-building processes in the West, resources were extracted from the weak and concentrated through warfare and coercion. The economy-building processes in the West were accomplished through the enclosure movement and through low wages, long hours, child labor, exploitation of colonial labor and markets, and the like. The political enfranchisement of the urban and rural poor occurred in the context of threatened or actual civil war; and the conversion of the state into an instrumentality of mass welfare likewise was accompanied by conflict and resistance.

If one is seeking a low-cost, equitable growth policy for the third world, neither the liberal capitalist model nor the Socialist revolutionary model has much to offer. Hirschman's "reform-mongering" model, which predicted a nonrevolutionary distributive coalition from a four-fold set of actors — reactionaries, conservatives, progressives, and revolutionaries — confronted with the threat of revolutionary disorder, has failed to match reality in the third world.[9] The social and political structures and cultures in these areas do not produce the kinds of political elites and bargaining culture in which progressives, seeking to combine free insti-

[9] Albert Hirschman, *Journeys Toward Progress* (New York: Doubleday & Co., 1965), chaps. 4, 5.

tutions with equitable growth, are able to draw conservatives, who are fearful of revolution, into an alliance in which they are prepared to adopt substantial social reforms.

Hirschman's exercise in "reform-mongering" was offered at a time when liberal incremental solutions to the problem of economic development still seemed possible in some parts of the third world; indeed, they appeared to be the preferred policies of most of the third world elites themselves. After World War II, most of the new nations of Asia and Africa adopted — at least in the formal sense — democratic and parliamentary institutions, universal suffrage, and the rule of law. Similarly, in the older nations of Latin America the prestige of parliamentarism and democracy was high. American policy makers and scholars tended to shut their eyes to the scale and complexity of the problems confronting the new nations, even though it was quite evident that they were going to have problems. This development euphoria was fueled by changes then taking place in the industrialized West: living standards in the 1950s and 1960s were rising; the welfare state was at hand; the working classes were becoming affluent, acquiring durable goods, improved housing, and access to education and health care. Economic growth, participation, and democratic stability seemed to be going hand in hand.

This was the period that proclaimed the "end of ideology," and social science research contributed to this illusion. Many influential studies demonstrated that there was a high correlation between industrial productivity, education, and communication on the one hand and stable democratic politics on the other.[10] Social scientists were measuring these relationships in the post–World War II period. Had they examined the relationship between industrialization and democratic stability in nineteenth- and early twentieth-century Europe, they would have found that the relationship between economic growth, equality, and democratic stability was ambiguous at best.

In this ahistoric, optimistic mood American policy makers and scholars spelled out a policy of incremental modernization in which the leaders of the new nations, with foreign and particularly American aid, would begin investing in industrialization, modern education, transportation, and communication. This socioeconomic modernization would produce an ever increasing standard of living for the population as a whole, and a democratic, stable nation-building process would be initiated. Expectations were that these goals of economic and social development, increased

10 See Daniel Lerner, *The Passing of Traditional Society* (New York: Free Press of Glencoe, 1958); Karl W. Deutsch, "Social Mobilization and Political Development," *American Political Science Review* 55 (September 1961): 493–514; Seymour M. Lipset, "Some Social Requisites of Democracy," *American Political Science Review* 53 (March 1959): 69 ff.

welfare, improved governmental capacity, and democratic participation could all be pursued simultaneously and that they constituted a kind of benign dialectic — each contributing positively to the other. In Packenham's words: "All good things go together." [11]

A number of important considerations had been overlooked. These new and developing nations were set in a very different world and exposed to very different influences and conditions than prevailed at the time of Western modernization. In the first place, modern epidemiological, pharmaceutical, and medical technology jumped the development barrier and introduced death control before birth control. The declining death rate was coupled with a high birth rate, producing a population explosion particularly among the poor. Any rate of economic growth was bound to be reduced on a per capita basis by population growth; and since this growth was concentrated among the poor, it accentuated the problem of inequality in the process of economic growth.

Second, the model of development that the third world was exposed to by the modern media of communications was an affluent, participant society. Thus the demands to which third world leaders had to respond were for industrial growth, welfare, and participation on the part of rapidly growing populations. Further, these demands came at a time when many newly independent countries had not even become nation-states and had no efficient bureaucracies, capacity to govern, or widespread sense of national loyalty and commitment.

Third, although the liberal Western model was the most influential in the early years after World War II, it soon had to compete with the revolutionary model of the Soviet Union, China, and Cuba. In this model economic growth and popular welfare could be realized only through a revolutionary dialectic in which the traditional ruling and exploiting classes were eliminated. Growth would be reconciled with equality through coercive and expropriative measures.

Just as socioeconomic conditions differed substantially among third world countries, so, too, did their political characteristics as they embarked on modernization efforts in the 1950s and 1960s. In the sub-Saharan African type of political system the contenders for political power consisted of leaders of independence movements, bureaucratic officials recruited and trained by the various colonial powers, and tribal elites of the traditional sector. In Latin America the post–World War II development decades began with well-established nation-states having relatively large urban-industrial sectors. The contenders for political power, though varying in significance from one Latin American country

11 Robert Packenham, *Liberal America and the Third World* (Princeton: Princeton University Press, 1973), pp. 123 ff.

to the next, included urban industrial elites, rural landowning elites, bureaucratic-technical elites, and political party elites ranging across the whole spectrum from conservative to left-revolutionary tendencies. In the South Asian type of socioeconomic context, the same types of elites were present, but the rural traditional components were more significant in numbers and influence.

THIRD WORLD DEVELOPMENT STRATEGIES

Table XIII.3 seeks to compare and contrast the principal development strategies followed by third world nations in the last three decades. The first column compresses under single headings the system-process-policy categories elaborated in figures XIII.1 and XIII.2. The first item, governmental capacity, includes the formation of political executive and bureaucratic agencies capable of making policy and implementing it in the society and, in particular, of maintaining public order and sustaining legitimacy. Item two, political participation, implies the formation of political structures — such as parties and interest groups — that are capable of mobilizing and aggregating popular demands for public policy. The third item refers to the degree of economic growth in the aggregate sense; and the fourth, distribution, refers to the degree to which the benefits of growth are equally shared. The five types of development strategies described in the table are scored low, medium, or high for these four aspects of politico-economic development. The scores in the columns are for the class of development strategies and should be viewed as tendencies of policy, structure, and aspiration, not as accurate descriptions of particular countries. After providing some examples that explicate the general classification of strategies, we shall suggest some of the variability in the use and success of these strategies in the third world.

DEMOCRATIC POPULIST STRATEGY

The most common strategy of development adopted by the nations of the third world in the first decade or so after World War II was the democratic populist pattern.[12] In most of the new nations of Africa and Asia the forms of parliamentary democratic regimes were instituted, and in Latin America the prestige of democracy was also high. The United States and the former colonial powers of Western Europe embarked on programs offering grants and loans to third world nations for development and modernization purposes and, on the whole, encouraged them to introduce democratic and parliamentary regimes and market economies.

---

[12] Our discussion of development strategies and their consequences is influenced by S. P. Huntington and Joan Nelson, *No Easy Choice: Political Participation in Developing Countries* (Cambridge: Harvard University Press, 1976), chap. 2.

Table XIII.3. *Development Strategies in the Third World*

Aspects of political-economic development	Democratic populist	Authoritarian-technocratic	Authoritarian-technocratic-equalitarian	Authoritarian-technocratic-mobilizational	Neo-traditional
Governmental capacity	L	M-H	M-H	H	L
Participation	M	L	L	*	L
Growth	L-M	M-H	M-H	H	L
Distribution	M	L	M-H	H	L

Note: L = Low; M = Medium; H = High.

*The forms of participation in the authoritarian-technocratic-mobilizational systems emphasize controlled mobilization, not citizen participation in articulation and aggregation. There is citizen involvement—but in a qualitatively different fashion.

The performance of most of these populist regimes fell short of expectations in several ways. First, in the competitive regimes at low levels of modernization, the political process has in fact tended to be dominated by those few groups having the resources and skills for political participation. Hence, the distributive, and even the participatory, goals went largely unrealized. And despite rather low participation, the low levels of governmental capacity made it difficult to implement policies and sustain support among the elites themselves, with consequent instability. Second, in the somewhat more developed populist systems, either mobilization by counter-elites or gradually increasing participatory pressures led eventually to a need to satisfy the promises of participation and distribution. In practice, this meant massive redistribution of both political power and economic resources — which was bitterly opposed by the holders of each — and, therefore, led to an intense and destabilizing political conflict. Moreover, distribution without growth not only was a source of intense conflict, but actually impeded the accumulation of the capital needed to finance future growth. Conflict was also economically disruptive.

The African populist regimes collapsed one after the other during the 1960s, giving way to control by what were essentially political machines, regardless of their formal legal characteristics.[13] In the later 1960s many of the civilian governments were swept aside in military coups that merely substituted military-dominated machines. From a development perspective these democratic experiments in sub-Saharan Africa fell vic-

13 Henry Bienen, "One Party Systems in Africa," in Huntington and Moore, *Authoritarian Politics in Modern Society,* pp. 109 ff.

tim to the prior requirements of nation-state building and economic growth, in other words, the creation of concentrations of power and economic capacity. The experience of Ghana may illustrate this populist developmental phase. During the Nkrumah period (both before and after his seizure of power) real GNP per capita failed to grow, income inequality increased, foreign exchange reserves declined sharply, government borrowing increased sharply, and foreign exchange reserves were depleted.[14] Economic performance in Ghana has not notably improved under its military regimes with the exception that government borrowing has decreased and the foreign exchange situation has improved.

The Latin American democracies collapsed in the tensions between established rural landowning and urban industrial elites, on one hand, and populist movements pressing for access to power and a more equitable distribution of benefits, on the other. Where these populist movements and elites threatened to take or actually took power (as in the Brazil of Goulart and the Chile of Allende), there occurred rising political tension and disorder, inflationary tendencies, land seizures, and so on. In turn, these produced crises in which the military overthrew the existing governments and suspended constitutions.[15]

Similar developments took place in South and Southeast Asia. Prior to the military coup of 1966, Indonesia under Sukarno was embarked on a leftist trend. Though opposition parties were not repressed, the Indonesian Communist party was growing in strength and influence, and business enterprises were being nationalized. Per capita GNP declined, there was a serious inflation problem, and income inequality increased from 1959 to 1966.[16] The experience of India in this period suggests the outcomes of the populist development strategy. During the period 1960–1972, India's per capita growth rate was just a bit over 1 percent, and the share of income going to the poorest 40 percent of income recipients declined from 20.2 to 13.1 percent.[17] The inability of India to cope with its massive problems contributed to the suspension of liberties and the

[14] See J. Clark Leith, *Foreign Trade Regimes and Economic Development: Ghana* (New York: National Bureau of Economic Research, 1974), p. 6; Kodwo Ewusi, *The Distribution of Monetary Incomes in Ghana* (Legon: Institute of Statistical, Social and Economic Research, University of Ghana, 1971), pp. 30–31.

[15] For an analysis of the shift from populist to bureaucratic authoritarian regimes in Latin America, see Guillermo O'Donnell, *Modernization and Bureaucratic-Authoritarianism* (Berkeley: University of California, Institute of International Studies, 1973), pp. 53 ff.

[16] Thomas E. Weisskopf, *The Political Economy of Development in Non-Revolutionary Asia* (Paper prepared for a conference of SSRC-ACLS Joint Committee on Contemporary China, San Juan, Puerto Rico, 1976).

[17] World Bank, *World Bank Atlas* (Washington, D.C., 1973); Shail Jain, *Size Distribution of Income* (Washington, D.C.: World Bank, 1975), pp. 50 ff.

state of emergency in the final years of Indira Gandhi's prime ministership. During this period of suppression and power concentration, efforts were made to increase governmental effectiveness, to improve economic performance, and to deal with the problem of inequality. The willingness to hold competitive elections and the defeat suffered by Indira Gandhi and the Congress party in 1977 suggest that despite poor performance, the Indian parliamentary regime and the commitment to a populist strategy have deep roots and are supported to some degree by effective political structures. The performance dilemmas remain.

We do not wish to suggest that all third world attempts at a democratic populist strategy have been unsuccessful. Writing in the late 1960s, Dahl listed fourteen third world countries as polyarchies or near-polyarchies.[18] Although the regimes in Chile, Uruguay, the Philippines, and Cyprus were overthrown during the 1970s, some relatively successful cases of populist strategies remain. Further, these populist systems are quite dissimilar in culture, economy, and performance.[19] As we have noted, India is particularly deviant in that its parliamentary institutions seem to have survived in the face of poverty, low growth rates, increased inequality, and a brief authoritarian interlude. But its future is far from certain, despite the relatively strong civil service and party structures that have carried it so far. Venezuela, because of its oil resources, has one of the highest levels of per capita GNP in Latin America and an impressive record of economic and cultural modernization. Its oil windfall helps explain its ability to sustain competitive politics, but the deliberately accommodative efforts of its elites have also played a key role.[20] The persistence of peaceful democratic politics in Costa Rica seems to be a consequence of the strength of its own traditions, as well as the result of the great cultural homogeneity and high growth rate (4.1 percent, from 1965 to 1972). Turkey and Malaysia have moderate levels of GNP per capita and quite good growth rates, but their democratic tendencies seem to be at least as much the consequence of their own historical experiences. Turkey embarked on a course of modernization under the authoritarian regime of Ataturk after World War I, then opened itself up to competitive politics by leadership choice after his death. Having defeated

[18] Robert A. Dahl, *Polyarchy: Participation and Opposition* (New Haven: Yale University Press, 1971), p. 248.
[19] Dahl's original list included Costa Rica, India, Jamaica, Lebanon, Malaysia, Trinidad, Turkey, Venezuela, Colombia, and the Dominican Republic, in addition to Chile, Uruguay, the Philippines, and Cyprus. Most such classifications also include Sri Lanka, whose politics clearly fit the populist model. Each of these systems is worthy of investigation, although we can discuss only a few of them here.
[20] See Stephen Blank, *Politics in Venezuela* (Boston: Little, Brown, 1973); and Daniel Levine, *Conflict and Consensus in Venezuela* (Princeton: Princeton University Press, 1973).

a guerrilla Communist movement while still a British colony, Malaysia has remained on a more or less democratic course in the last decades. Both countries have experienced serious violence and internal conflict, with military intervention constituting a frequent element in Turkish politics, and with ethnic divisions troubling Malaysia.

These cases of surviving, more or less democratic, regimes serve to illustrate the point that modernizing processes in the third world are not necessarily associated with authoritarian regimes. They also suggest the possibility that some of the authoritarian regimes in the third world may return to competitive democratic politics.

AUTHORITARIAN-TECHNOCRATIC STRATEGY

The kinds of regimes which replaced these first experiments with democracy may be subsumed very broadly under the four remaining categories in table XIII.3. They all have in common the elimination of competitive popular participation. In the authoritarian-technocratic strategy, emphasis is placed on increasing the order-maintaining and economic-growth-facilitating capacities of the government. It tends to foster economic growth by establishing tax and investment policies favorable to industry, by disciplining labor, and by offering profitable investment opportunities to foreign capital. While they may achieve growth in per capita terms, the benefits in increased income are skewed in favor of the rich.

Brazil provides a good illustration of this tendency. McNamara pointed out that in the decade of the 1960s, per capita GNP increased at an annual rate of 2.5 percent in Brazil. However, "the share of the national income received by the poorest 40 percent of the population declined from 10 percent in 1960 to 8 percent in 1970, whereas the share of the richest 5 percent grew from 29 percent to 30 percent during the same period. In GNP terms the country did well. The very rich did well." [21] Figure XIII.3 shows the increasing inequality in the Lorenz curves for Brazil in 1960 and 1970. Under the military regime in post-1964 Brazil, all political parties were dissolved, then replaced by official government and opposition parties. Civilian political leaders were deprived of their rights, freedoms of press and association were sharply curtailed, and elections were limited to the choice of members of powerless legislative bodies. Thus, Brazil in effect is an authoritarian regime run by military officers and civilian technocrats in the bureaucracy.[22] Tax, investment,

---

[21] Robert S. McNamara, *One Hundred Countries, Two Billion People* (New York: Praeger, 1973), p. 103.

[22] Philippe C. Schmitter, "The 'Portugalization' of Brazil," in Alfred Stepan, *Authoritarian Brazil: Origins, Policies, and Future* (New Haven: Yale University Press, 1973).

Figure XIII.3.   *Lorenz Curve and Gini Coefficient of Income Distribution in Brazil, 1960 and 1970*

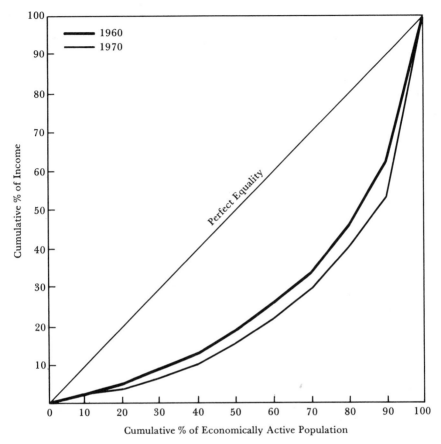

Source: Shail Jain, *Size Distribution of Income* (Washington, D. C.: World Bank, 1975), pp. 15-16.
Note: Gini coefficient, 1960 = .5046; Gini coefficient, 1970 = .5770.

wage, and foreign economic policies have been employed in combination to produce an extraordinary rate of economic growth, accompanied by a decline in the rate of inflation, but also by increasing income inequality.[23]

The post-populist regime in Indonesia has also moved in an authoritarian-technocratic direction, as political participation and freedoms of press, party, and association have been sharply curtailed. Similarly, eco-

23 Albert Fishlow, "Some Reflections on Economic Policy," in Stepan, ibid., pp. 97 ff.

nomic policy produced an improved rate of economic growth of almost 3 percent per annum in the period 1966–1972, along with increasing income inequalities.[24]

The countries following this development strategy produce a kind of dual society of privileged, urban middle-classes and backward and exploited peasants and workers. To maintain order the authoritarian elites introduce a coercive apparatus to repress demands for equality and participation. Thus the authoritarian-technocratic regime encourages material growth, but is indifferent about its distribution. It leaves most members of the society relatively untouched by modernization and suppresses their protests.

The political dynamic of this transition from populist democracy to authoritarian regime is captured in a metaphor suggested by Albert Hirschman. He asks one to imagine a tunnel with two lanes of traffic, both going the same way. The traffic has come to a halt. Horns are honking, and people are asking from their cars, "What's the trouble up ahead?" Suddenly one lane begins to move. Everyone is happy and relieved, although only one lane is moving. The people in the lane that is still stopped think, "Well, there is some movement; our turn will come soon." It goes in this way for a while until the people in the stopped lane become impatient, lose faith in the prospect of their lane's ever moving, and the chorus of horns begins.[25]

The authoritarian-technocratic regimes "relieve" the polity and the economy of developing nations from this pressure of frustrated expectations by suppressing protest, that is, by disconnecting the horns of the cars in the blocked lane. However, long-term instability is inevitable. The strategy depends on growth, but that very growth and the accompanying increase in inequality will eventually heighten pressure for involvement.

AUTHORITARIAN-TECHNOCRATIC-EQUALITARIAN STRATEGY

The third strategy — the authoritarian-technocratic-equalitarian — is a more equitable variant of the second. It also disconnects the horns of protest in the blocked lane of Hirschman's tunnel, but it permits traffic in the blocked lane to move a bit and slows down vehicles in the fast lane. From the perspective of political structure this kind of regime suppresses political parties or radically limits their activities, and it exercises control over the media of communication and interest groups. The two powerful governmental agencies are the political executive and the bureaucracy. Two examples about which we have sufficient information

[24] Weisskopf, op. cit., pp. 53–54.

[25] Albert Hirschman, *The Declining Tolerance of Income Inequality in Third World Nations,* Princeton University, International Finance Section, vol. 81 (November 1973).

are Peru and South Korea. Both are military regimes, and both have pursued a distributive economic policy, in Peru within the framework of a "social" economy, and in South Korea within the framework of a market economy with substantial governmental intervention.

Since the seizure of power by the military in 1968, Peru has deliberately sought to devise a new system of political economy, one drawing upon the Catholic corporative tradition. The Peruvian military have adopted a left-oriented ideology and assumed responsibility for implementing it. Its inclination is partially explained by its revulsion with the bloody suppression of peasant rebellions that took place in the backward rural regions in the early 1960s. In the mid-1960s the military leadership instituted a program of officer training and indoctrination stressing the social-reformist and ideological responsibilities of the armed forces. Drawing on Latin American Catholic doctrines and traditions, the Peruvian military adopted a corporatist-collectivist model of reform. The first steps taken were the nationalization of foreign oil interests, the expropriation of large agricultural estates, and the formation of peasant cooperatives. Larger industries have been required to provide for worker participation in company management and profit sharing.

According to one analysis of Peru, the military "are deliberately attempting to bypass the Western democratic framework of multiple political parties and self-mobilized competitive interest groups in order to institutionalize the citizen's relationship to the system through an arrangement in which hierarchical political organizations are set up along functionally determined sectoral lines, largely at the initiative of the central government." [26] In an important analysis of the Peruvian experiment Alfred Stepan refers to it as an "organic-statist" regime. He describes the twofold effort being made by the Peruvian military leaders: first, to connect economic functional groups with the governmental bureaucracy in a partly collectivized economy, and, second, to provide for two-way communication between the government and grassroots functional units (such as farm and industrial cooperatives) through a representative corporative organization. Called the National Social Mobilization Support System (SINAMOS), this organization was intended as a representative political structure that would provide the sole vehicle of citizen participation and would assure that divisive and conflictive political parties, as well as self-interested pressure groups, were prevented from exploiting the needs and interests of ordinary people. [27]

The plans for this sociopolitical revolution in Peru have run into

26 Kevin J. Middlebrook and David Scott Palmer, *Military Government and Political Development: Lessons from Peru* (Beverly Hills, Calif.: Sage Series in Comparative Politics, 1975), p. 7.

27 Alfred Stepan, *The State and Society: Peru in Comparative Perspective* (Princeton: Princeton University Press, 1977), chap. 8.

major difficulties. The corporatist structure has failed to assimilate demands in an orderly way, and SINAMOS is being reconsidered and reorganized. Similarly, the growth rate of the economy has been slow, while worker and peasant dissatisfaction has been increasing. There have also occurred shifts in the top leadership of the junta. It is impossible to forecast at this point the probable future of the Peruvian experiment and its effort to work without a mobilizing political party and with a minimum of coercion. Whatever its future may be, its land reforms and experiments with social property and worker participation have put Peru on a distributive course not easy to reverse.[28]

Social reforms in South Korea had their origins in World War II and the Korean War. The expulsion of the Japanese after World War II made possible a land reform under American auspices that resulted in a substantial reduction in tenancy in 1947. Tenancy was practically eliminated in 1950 when large Korean-owned landholdings were divided. A further redistribution of capital — accompanied by social disruption and increased social mobility — resulted from the Korean War.

After the Korean War a major effort at educational improvement succeeded in raising the literacy rate from 30 percent to 80 percent; secondary and higher education enrollment also increased significantly. Utilizing substantial American aid and pursuing a labor-intensive development strategy, Korea tripled its per capita GNP during a ten-year period — from $100 in the early 1960s to $300 in 1972. At the same time, wealth and income distribution are among the most equalitarian in the developing world.

Though elections, some political party competition, and some press freedom are tolerated, South Korea has been, in essence, an authoritarian regime under the control of the military for the last fifteen years. Most of the Cabinet members and top administrative officials have been military officers in inactive status. A military background is also shared by many of the higher-ranking civil servants, chairmen of legislative committees, and directors of government corporations, large industries, and banks. The large and powerful Korean army, kept large by the threat from the north and with American support, thus supplies the principal cohesive and directive force in Korea. Unlike the Peruvian military, the Korean officer corps has no explicit political ideology. Its incentives seem to be primarily a mix of nationalism, service loyalty, power, and patronage. Korea's rapid rate of growth in industrialization, urbanization, and education has not been accompanied by the development of stable polit-

[28] See Stepan, *State and Society*, chap. 8; Middlebrook and Palmer, op. cit., pp. 43 ff. See also Alain Rouquie, "Military Revolution and National Independence in Latin America," in Philippe C. Schmitter, *Military Rule in Latin America* (Beverly Hills, Calif.: Sage Publications, 1973), pp. 15 ff.

ical parties, trade unions, or a consensual political culture. There have been three experiments with democratic republican constitutions, the first of which was dominated by Syngman Rhee and lasted until 1961, when a brief second republic was constituted. The third republican adventure was suspended by President Park and replaced by a regime that accorded broad powers to the presidency – including power to appoint one-third of the membership of the Assembly and control over the courts – and provided no limits on the number of presidential terms.[29]

South Korea's policy of distributive economic growth is explained by several factors: the major early land reforms; the upgrading of skills through rapid educational development; the pursuit of a labor-intensive, export-oriented industrial strategy; and American advice, support, and pressure. Rapid industrialization of this kind has reduced pressure on the land and brought an increasingly large proportion of the Korean population into the modern urban-industrial economy.[30] Figure XIII.4 suggests the equalitarian income distribution that has been achieved.

AUTHORITARIAN-TECHNOCRATIC-MOBILIZATIONAL STRATEGY

The fourth development strategy is exemplified primarily by the Communist countries, but to a lesser extent as well by such countries as Mexico, Taiwan, and Tanzania. The Communist regimes use their political parties as instruments of popular mobilization and penetration of the society and as means for the making and implementation of public policy. In table XIII.3 we suggest that their strategy stresses the development of governmental capacity and a form of participation that does not lend itself to the same kind of scoring as is used in the other cases. Because people are mobilized in the implementation of policies formulated by the party elites, rather than in the making of policies, it is a form of mobilized or structured participation. The economic record of third world Communist regimes is mixed. The three countries for which we report data – China, North Korea, and Cuba – have followed thoroughgoing distributive policies providing relative income equality and equality in the provision of services. Growth rates have been relatively high in China and North Korea, averaging almost 5 percent in North Korea and just under 4 percent in China during 1960–1973.[31] In Cuba a policy of radical redistribution has been accompanied by a negative growth rate

---

[29] Se-Jin Kim, *The Politics of Military Revolution in Korea* (Chapel Hill: University of North Carolina Press, 1971); Jonngwon A. Kim, *Divided Korea* (Cambridge: Harvard University Press, 1975), chaps. 2, 4, 6, 9; C. J. Eugene Kim and Young Whan Kihl, *Party Politics and Elections in Korea* (Silver Spring, Md.: Research Institute on Korean Affairs, 1976), part 1.

[30] Irma Adelman, "South Korea," in Chenery et al., op. cit., pp. 285 ff.

[31] *World Bank Atlas*, 1975, p. 3.

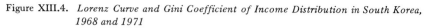

Figure XIII.4.   *Lorenz Curve and Gini Coefficient of Income Distribution in South Korea, 1968 and 1971*

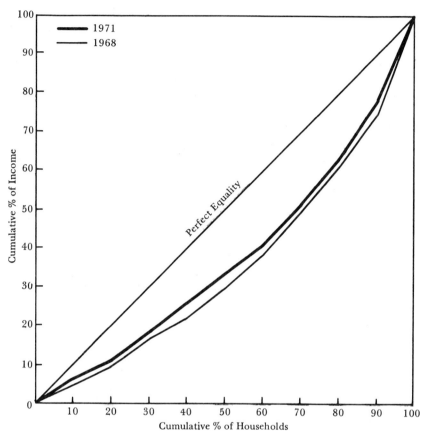

Source: Jain, *Size Distribution of Income*, pp. 65, 66.
Note: Gini coefficient, 1968 = .3045; Gini coefficient, 1971 = .2718.

(−1.1 percent) during the same period. The poor growth rate in Cuba during this period seems in part to have been attributable to poor management — lack of effective planning procedures, ineffective accounting, and failure to relate material incentives to labor productivity.[32] Communist regimes have their own version of conflict between growth and distribution: too much stress on equality may reduce productivity; growth seems to require the provision of wage and salary differentials in order to enhance productivity.

[32] Chenery et al., op. cit., pp. 262 ff.

The non-Communist technocratic-mobilizational cases differ substantially from the Communist model. The Mexican case might be called an "arrested" mobilizational system, the Tanzanian example is one of "proto-mobilization," and the Taiwanese system is one of "preemptive" mobilization. Mexico and Taiwan have preserved substantial private economic sectors, while Tanzania has nationalized more of its economy.

The Mexican regime took a mobilized equalitarian course during the Cárdenas phase of the revolution (from the mid-1930s until the early 1940s), when the Party of the Institutionalized Revolution (PRI) was formed, and trade unions and peasant organizations were encouraged and assimilated into the party. Land reforms and increased worker incomes reduced inequalities at that time.[33] Since the 1940s the mobilizational-equalitarian impulse has become primarily symbolic, and the dominant party has served as a cooptative, preemptive system, sharply restricting the activities of other political parties, repressing dissent, and following policies primarily benefiting the privileged sectors of the population. While growth per capita from 1960 until 1972 averaged over 3 percent per year, the benefits of growth have gone more substantially to the upper-income groups. Figure XIII.5 shows that income inequality increased during the period 1963–1969.

Taiwan, like Korea, is an example of an American client state that has achieved a remarkable rate of economic growth accompanied by an exceptionally equalitarian income distribution. (See figure XIII.6.) It has been estimated that American aid more than doubled the rate of growth of the Taiwanese economy.[34] American influence was also partly responsible for the equalitarian distributive policy, by stimulating the various land reforms, and supportive of the labor-intensive and export-oriented industrialization. The threat from mainland China also provided strong incentives for a distributive growth policy.

The Taiwanese political system is dominated by a single political party, the Kuomintang (KMT), which has adapted itself to the Taiwan setting by combining authoritarian control on a national level by the mainland refugees with some participation of the indigenous Taiwanese at the provincial and local levels.[35] The Kuomintang controls almost all the seats in the National Assembly, and party membership is a requirement for positions in the national bureaucracy. Party membership has

---

[33] Wayne A. Cornelius, "Nation-Building, Participation, Distribution: The Politics of Social Reform under Cárdenas," in Gabriel A. Almond, Scott C. Flanagan, and Robert J. Mundt, eds., *Crisis, Choice and Change: Historical Studies of Political Development* (Boston: Little, Brown and Company, 1973), pp. 478 ff.

[34] Neil Jacoby, *U.S. Aid to Taiwan* (New York: Praeger, 1973), pp. 151–52.

[35] Hung-chao Tai, "The Kuomintang and Modernisation in Taiwan," in Huntington and Moore, op. cit., pp. 406 ff.

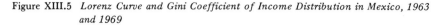

Figure XIII.5   *Lorenz Curve and Gini Coefficient of Income Distribution in Mexico, 1963 and 1969*

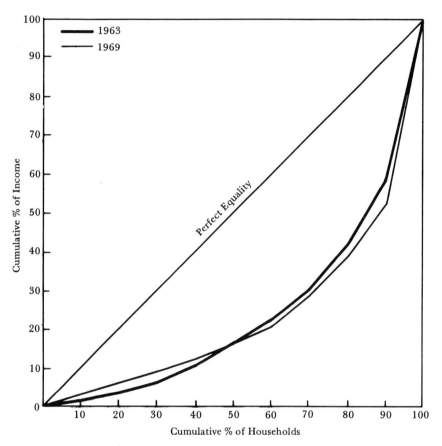

Source: Jain, *Size Distribution of Income*, p. 77.
Note: Gini coefficient, 1963 = .5390; Gini coefficient, 1969 = .5827.

risen sharply and has drawn increasingly from the indigenous Taiwanese. Minor parties are permitted to run candidates at the local and provincial levels, but the KMT substantially preempts the political arena. Taiwanese politics has been dominated by the fear of mainland China and the myth of the return of the KMT to the rule of all of China.

If Mexico is an arrested mobilization regime and Taiwan a preemptive one, then Tanzania may be described as a proto-mobilization regime. The leadership proposes to transform Tanzania into a Socialist society operating through a one-party system and permitting some electoral competition. Much of the economy has been nationalized, including

Figure XIII.6. *Lorenz Curve and Gini Coefficient of Income Distribution in Taiwan, 1953 and 1972*

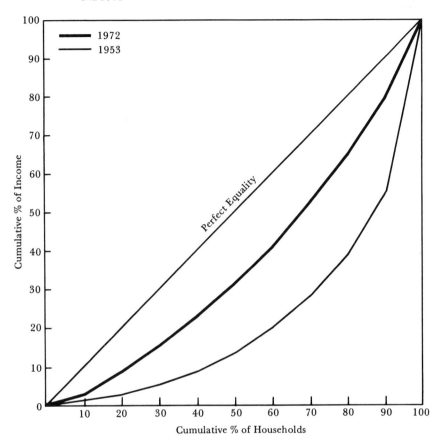

Source: Jain, *Size Distribution of Income*, pp. 108–109.
Note: Gini coefficient, 1953 = .5762; Gini coefficient, 1972 = .2843.

the major banks and insurance companies and many manufacturing and commercial enterprises. Around one-third of the population lives in co-operative (*ujamaa*) villages, and the official goal has been to organize the entire population in such villages by the late 1970s. Salary levels for governmental officials and skilled urban workers are regulated in order to control inequality.[36]

The experiment in rural collectivization has been disappointing, turn-

---

[36] Michael F. Lofchie, "Agrarian Socialism in the Third World," *Comparative Politics* 8 (April 1976): 479 ff.

ing Tanzania into an agricultural importing country and depleting foreign exchange and other reserves. Currently the regime has been encouraging private farming and large-scale agriculture as emergency measures without modifying its ideological aim of an agrarian Socialist countryside. In part the difficulties with the establishment of cooperative villages have been the consequence of the incapacity of the Tanzanian party organization (TANU) to penetrate and indoctrinate the countryside effectively. More often than not, the traditional tribal organizations have taken over and subverted the local units of TANU. As figure XIII.7 shows, Tanzania has been moving toward increasing income equality. A

Figure XIII.7.   *Lorenz Curve and Gini Coefficient of Income Distribution in Tanzania, 1967 and 1970*

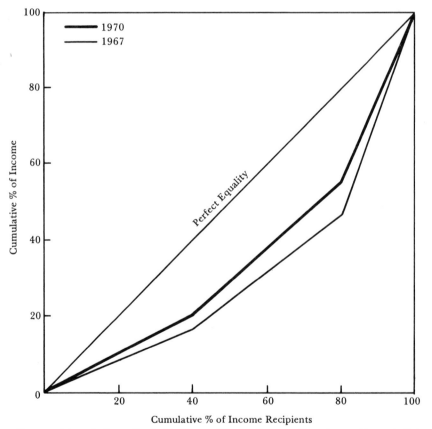

Source: Adapted from Reginald Green, "Some Country Experience: Tanzania," in Chenery, et al., *Redistribution with Growth*, p. 269.
    Note: Gini coefficient, 1967 = .42; Gini coefficient, 1970 = .35.

Lorenz curve for the mid-1970s would show the effects of more recent measures to equalize income. However, the Tanzanian growth rate has declined following the efforts to establish cooperative villages in the countryside, particularly in the most recent period.

NEO-TRADITIONALISM

The last category in table XIII.3 — the neo-traditional strategy — is primarily to be found in sub-Saharan Africa, although there are examples in other third world areas.[37] These largely static authoritarian regimes are characterized by low growth rates, low urbanization-industrialization, and low literacy. They are called neo-traditional or "neo-patrimonial" because they have survived into the modern era with their traditional social structures and cultures largely unchanged.[38] In these countries the principal modern development has been the introduction of modern military institutions and technology, which in many cases has enabled groups of officers to seize and maintain power. Where this has not oc-curred, civilian groups have established control through political ma-chines operating through the traditional tribal and village structures of the countryside. Aristide Zolberg and Henry Bienen have drawn atten-tion to such reversions to traditionalism in the African context.[39] The sequence described by these scholars involves the establishment of new "nations" by independence movements, the assimilation of the leaders and the activists in these movements into the growing bureaucracy, the inability of the bureaucracy to penetrate the countryside effectively, the result being a largely static polity and society. The elite maintains cohe-sion through a system of patronage, spoils, and privileges distributed among urban interest groups and tribal elites. Where such inter-elite cohesion breaks down, violence and instability are commonplace.

More anomalous are the oil kingdoms and sheikhdoms of the Middle East — Iran, Saudi Arabia, and Kuwait, for example. Their control over a scarce and valuable resource has enabled them to attain extraordinarily high rates of economic growth and to follow policies of rapid technical modernization, often accompanied by distributive and mass welfare poli-cies. They have been able to accomplish this without revolutionary

---

[37] Paraguay and Ecuador are Latin American examples of neo-traditionalism gov-erned by military juntas and large landowners, with low GNP and low rates of eco-nomic growth.

[38] See S. N. Eisenstadt, *Traditional Patrimonialism and Modern Neo-Patrimonialism* (Beverly Hills, Calif.: Sage Publications, 1973), chap. 4; and Gunther Roth, "Personal Rulership, Patrimonialism and Empire Building in the New States," *World Politics* 20 (January 1968): 194 ff. See also Ali A. Mazrui, "Soldiers as Traditionalizers," *World Politics* 28 (January 1976): 246 ff.

[39] Aristide Zolberg, *Creating Political Order* (Chicago: University of Chicago Press, 1966); Bienen, "One Party Systems in Africa."

Table XIII.4. *Economy and Polity in Sub-Saharan Africa*

Country	GNP per capita, 1972[a]	Annual growth in GNP, 1965-1972[a]	% of Wage earners[b]
Gabon	490	—	18
Zambia	380	−0.1	12
Ivory Coast	340	4.1	10
Ghana	300	1.0	10
Congo People's Rep.	300	1.4	17
Senegal	260	−0.7	8
Liberia	260	4.0	12
Cameroon	200	3.8	7
Sierra Leone	190	1.8	7
Kenya	170	4.1	12
Togo	160	3.3	3
Central African Republic	160	2.3	11
Uganda	150	2.0	6
Nigeria	130	5.4	2
Sudan	120	−1.1	10
Tanzania	120	2.9	8
Dahomey	110	1.7	3
Zaire	100	3.9	17
Malawi	100	2.9	6
Niger	90	−5.1	3
Guinea	90	−0.3	4
Chad	80	1.6	3
Ethiopia	80	1.2	3
Somalia	80	1.1	3
Mali	80	1.3	3
Upper Volta	70	0.6	3
Burundi	70	1.1	8
Rwanda	60	2.1	7

[a] *World Bank Atlas* (1973).
[b] Lynn Fisher et al., *Black Africa Handbook* (New York: Free Press, 1972), p. 37.

changes in political structure, combining traditional patrimonial patterns of rule with bureaucratic organization staffed partly by foreign experts, but increasingly by native, foreign-trained technicians. This remarkable blend of traditionalism and modernization can be explained only by the windfall of oil riches. As economic, cultural, and military modernization proceeds in these countries, conflict between surviving traditionalism and technocratic-rational tendencies would seem to be inevitable. But as long as the oil windfall is available to be drawn upon, the traditional elites

| Country | % of Income to[c] | | | Political characteristics[d] |
	Top 20%	Middle 40%	Lowest 40%	
Gabon	67.5 (1968)	23.7	8.8	One party, civilian
Zambia	57.1 (1959)	27.0	15.9	One party, civilian
Ivory Coast	57.1 (1970)	32.1	10.8	One party, civilian
Ghana	— —	—	—	One party, military
Congo People's Rep.	— —	—	—	One party, mobilizational
Senegal	64.0 (1960)	26.0	10.0	One party, civilian
Liberia	— —	—	—	One party, civilian
Cameroon	— —	—	—	One party, civilian
Sierra Leone	68.0 (1968)	22.4	9.6	One party, civilian
Kenya	68.0 (1968)	22.0	10.0	One party, civilian
Togo	— —	—	—	One party, military
Central African Republic	— —	—	—	One party, military
Uganda	47.1 (1970)	35.0	17.1	No party, military
Nigeria	— —	—	—	No party, military
Sudan	50.1 (1963)	36.0	13.9	No party, military
Tanzania	57.0 (1967)	29.0	14.0	One party, mobilizational
Dahomey	50.0 (1959)	34.5	15.5	One party, military
Zaire	— —	—	—	One party, military
Malawi	52.9 (1969)	32.1	15.0	One party, civilian
Niger	42.0 (1960)	40.0	18.0	One party, civilian
Guinea	— —	—	—	One party, mobilizational
Chad	43.0 (1958)	39.0	18.0	One party, civilian
Ethiopia	— —	—	—	No party, military
Somalia	— —	—	—	No party, military
Mali	— —	—	—	No party, military
Upper Volta	— —	—	—	One party, military
Burundi	— —	—	—	One party, military
Rwanda	— —	—	—	One party, civilian

[c] Chenery et al., *Redistribution with Growth,* p. 11; Sudan and Malawi data from Jain, *Size Distribution of Income.*
[d] Fisher et al., *Black Africa Handbook.*

are in a position to respond to popular demands and expectations and to coopt the new technocratic elites into the ruling circles.[40]

In table XIII.4 we provide economic and political information on the political regimes of sub-Saharan Africa. The countries toward the top of the table are those in which GNP is relatively high. These countries at

[40] See James A. Bill and Carl Leiden, *The Middle East: Politics and Power* (Boston: Allyn & Bacon, 1974), chaps. 5, 6.

the top (note Gabon, Zambia, Ivory Coast, Senegal, Sierra Leone, and Kenya) display high income inequality, reflecting the general tendency toward inequality in the early stages of economic development. Though their growth rates in the most recent period vary, their higher GNPs per capita and high inequalities in income reflect the development of a dual society — a modern urban-industrial-literate sector and a traditional countryside in which the dependence on subsistence agriculture persists.

Moving toward the bottom of table XIII.4, one encounters countries with low GNPs, very low growth rates, relatively small industrial-commercial sectors, and predominantly military authoritarian regimes. These are the countries that fit into the neo-traditional category, for only superficial changes have taken place, primarily in the small urban sector. Tanzania, the Congo People's Republic, Guinea, Ethiopia, and the recently independent, former Portuguese colonies of Mozambique and Angola are the proto-mobilization regimes of sub-Saharan Africa. We have already reviewed the Tanzanian record; Mozambique, Angola, and Ethiopia are too recently established for comment. The experience of Guinea illustrates the possibility that a mobilizational regime at a very low level of development can easily deteriorate into neo-traditionalism. Since its independent establishment in 1957, Guinea has been a one-party, "Marxist" regime, but its growth rate since 1960 has been zero and, in the more recent period 1965–1972, actually negative.[41] Not only is there "no easy choice" between the competing values at stake in the strategies of development, but the realization of any of them over a substantial time span is extremely difficult.

[41] *World Bank Atlas,* 1973.

CHAPTER XIV

Political Goods and Political Productivity

OUR APPROACH to political analysis leads us from process, to performance, to evaluation. Goal-oriented activity is what these processes are all about. Inputs are intended to generate outputs, outputs are intended to produce outcomes, and outcomes create states of goal attainment or frustration. It makes no sense to terminate political analysis at the point of structure and process or even of output, since we are left with the questions of whether or not the output achieved its intended outcome and whether or not the outcome can be said to represent a production of goods. But before proceeding to our discussion of political values and goods, we need to make a distinction.

Political processes are saturated with values, purposes, and objectives. In our earlier treatments of political socialization and political culture, we showed that induction into political process and political purpose was the essence of the first and that value standards and expectations constitute very important components of the second. The feedback processes furnish information to the various actors in the political arena about the degree to which their goals are being attained and their value standards and expectations are being implemented. This kind of evaluation, however, is "internal" to the particular polity — culture-centered and ideology-centered. The particular goods sought and produced are given time- and place-bound weights; goods important in one system may be given a low value in another or not even acknowledged as goods at all. In such a context we are talking about the members of a particular polity with their particular conceptions of, and priorities among, goods.

When we talk about comparative political productivity, we are affirming the possibility of an outside and relatively unbiased evaluation. To do this satisfactorily for ourselves and others, we have to work from a comprehensive set of political goods that avoids a biased comparison. This kind of comparison of political systems in productivity terms meets a very real need. Ordinary people have the ability to reach above the everyday pursuit of their own welfare in search of some valid judgment of the virtue of their institutions, processes, and policies. Their perspectives may vary; they may be able only to compare today's performance with yesterday's. Or they may be able only to compare political productivity as it affects their community and those of their immediate neighbors, their occupation or locality with those of others. Or, indeed, with increasing education and the spread of information through the media of communication, growing numbers of ordinary people may seek and succeed in making quite cosmopolitan comparisons of nation with nation and ideology with ideology.

For professional political scientists the comparative study of political performance ought to be a central concern. Though this obligation has not been met effectively, several recent efforts suggest that it is becoming increasingly acknowledged.

APPROACHES TO POLITICAL EVALUATION

Three recent contributions to the political science literature illustrate this growing commitment to move beyond process into the comparative analysis of performance and productivity: Robert Dahl's study of polyarchy, Eckstein's work on political performance, and Roland Pennock's suggestive analysis of political goods.

Dahl's study of polyarchy uses a two-dimensional scale to rate more than one hundred contemporary political systems (see chapter XII). One dimension is the extent to which people in modern nations participate in the political process; the other is the extent to which individuals and groups may compete with one another for access to and influence over policy-making processes. Dahl justifies his polyarchy scale on the grounds that this type of polity distributes political influence widely in societies and, hence, represents more interests and is more responsive than other kinds of systems.

Two points may be made about Dahl's theory of polyarchy. First, the theory tends to stress "process values" — the degree of participation and competition in policy making — though competition in policy making is possible only in a political system that provides the classic substantive liberties of communication, association, and assembly. Thus Dahl's polyarchy extends into liberty, but does not extend to the whole of it. In the second place, Dahl seems to be moving toward a pluralist approach to political valuation.[1] But while he stresses again and again that polyarchy optimizes only a limited set of political values, he does not tell us what

---

[1] Robert A. Dahl, *Polyarchy: Participation and Opposition* (New Haven: Yale University Press, 1971).

values other types of regimes may seek and attain. Dahl's study is a contemporary relativist version of an earlier, powerful liberal faith that affirmed the moral superiority of participation and open political competition over all other forms of political process. Until recently this belief in the absolute virtue of participatory, pluralist political systems so dominated Western political science that it was simply taken for granted. In our own treatment of evaluation we view these polyarchal values in the context of other political goods.

While Dahl's polyarchy scale stresses participatory and competitive process values, the work of Eckstein and his associates stresses stability and survival. Their four criteria of performance boil down to questions of survival at relatively low cost.[2] If a political system lasts long, has a low level of collective violence, is widely accepted by its members, and copes relatively effectively with the problems of leadership recruitment and budget making (which they call "decisional efficacy"), then it rates as a good performer.

But neither the Dahl approach to comparative evaluation nor the Eckstein approach effectively confronts the substantive issue of what values or goals are produced by political systems. The polyarchy criteria sidestep the issue by inferring this productivity (with the exception of some aspects of liberty) from process; and the Eckstein-Gurr approach avoids the issue by defining performance without regard to policy consequences. They acknowledge that they may be giving good marks to a polity that produces unsatisfactory outcomes stably and efficiently. In terms of our three levels of analysis, one tends to focus on process, the other on system. Neither develops a policy-level analysis.

In an important article published some ten years ago Roland Pennock introduced the concept of political goods. Political goods are the consequences of political action,

> consequences for the people, for the society as a whole, or for some subset other than the polity, as for instance, the economy or the family. We are indeed still dealing with the attainment of political goals, but the focus of attention is upon those goals that satisfy "needs" — not just needs of the state as such, matters that will enable it to persist, but human needs whose fulfillment makes the policy valuable to man, and gives it its justification.[3]

Pennock lists and defines the principal political goods as security, justice, liberty, and welfare. Considering the political system in both its domestic

2 Harry Eckstein, *The Evaluation of Political Performance: Problems and Dimensions* (Beverly Hills: Sage Publications, 1971); and Ted Robert Gurr and Muriel McClelland, *Political Performance: A Twelve-Nation Study* (Beverly Hills: Sage Publications, 1971).
3 J. Roland Pennock, "Political Development, Political Systems, and Political Goods," *World Politics* 18 (April 1966): 420.

and international aspects, he views its productivity in terms of these political goods.

Our own approach to political valuation has been influenced by Pennock's creative suggestion. Its virtue is that it approaches valuation through substantive productivity, in addition to process or system properties. What needs or wants is a political system meeting, how effectively, and at what cost? Pennock locates political goods primarily at the outcome phase of political processes. Outputs are intended to produce political goods, but the real test is in the outcome. Does a pattern of political output intended to increase security really have that effect? Or does a welfare program really enhance it? Productivity is actual, not intended, productivity.

The crucial question in Pennock's formulation is the relationship between the products of the political system and the needs they are presumed to be meeting. To be a good, a political product has to be valued by its "consumers." Pennock does not go so far as to assert a natural law position, that the desire for welfare, security, liberty, and justice are immanent properties of human nature, or of man in society. Instead, he bases the validity of these goods on assertions that they are commonly sought by or expected of political systems and that they are widely acknowledged as the legitimate obligations of political systems: "The maintenance of order and . . . security . . . appears to be almost a universal objective of political organization and activity, and it is certainly one of the principal values it supplies." [4] Similarly, the modern state has assumed an obligation to foster the material welfare of its citizens, even though the extent and character of this obligation varies from country to country and from time to time. In the area of justice he argues, "We recognize that a political system is developing as it acquires standards, machinery, and modes of procedure that facilitate judgments based on full and accurate information, that treat all cases alike, and that protect society with a minimum of degradation and a maximum of rehabilitation for its deviant members." [5]

Finally Pennock makes a case for liberty as a political good: "Some freedom to move about and to make choices in the areas of one's interests is a desideratum for virtually all sane human beings. . . . clearly a major purpose of 'law and order' is to make it possible for people to enjoy a predictable environment and to be free and feel free to exercise their own choices." [6]

We agree with Pennock that if we are going to be value pluralists, then we must indeed put all the values on the table and not consign to a

[4] Ibid., p. 421.
[5] Ibid., p. 424.
[6] Ibid., p. 425.

kind of moral vacuum those systems which come out with low scores on polyarchy or stability. Pennock's fourfold classification of political goods includes Dahl's polyarchy values tucked away in his definition of liberty and, to some extent, Eckstein's approach in his definition of security. But it also encompasses other political goods that nonpolyarchies or unstable systems may produce effectively.

Pennock recognizes the tensions among these political goods: security and liberty, welfare and liberty, security and justice, or welfare and justice may be in conflict; more of one may imply less of the others. Further, the level of development and capacity of a political system affects its ability to produce these goods. And environmental threats and problems may set limits on the kinds and volumes of political goods that may be produced. We will return to this problem of the tensions and conflicts among political goods at a later point.

POLITICAL GOODS AND HUMAN NEEDS

Since Pennock rests his notion of political goods on the proposition that they meet or respond to human needs, the question of needs deserves more attention. Here again, mainstream political science observes near silence about human needs and politics. The occasional political scientist who talks about needs and their implications for politics is likely to be quickly shushed on the grounds that all one really can know about are wants or demands and that these vary widely from time to time and from place to place. In part this silence is due to the multiplicity of theories of human nature that were advanced in the natural law doctrines of earlier political philosophers, who tended to select theories of human nature and needs to fit the social and political institutions they preferred. In part it was the consequence of the ideological confrontations of World War II, in which theories of human nature or "natures" were used to justify grotesque inhumanities. A political science based on evidence had to begin with what could be observed in all its variety, and searching for what might be widespread or even universal in this evidence could lead only to falling into this natural law swamp, or worse. Relativism and empiricism regarding needs and values became the dominant point of view.

Harold Lasswell deals with the question of goods in the form of a classification scheme. Identifying eight base values — power, wealth, respect, affection, skill, enlightenment, well-being, and rectitude — he presents them not as a universal set of human needs, but as "an exhaustive category list . . . to make it easier to make valid comparisons from one context to another." [7]

[7] H. D. Lasswell, *Psychopathology and Politics* (New York: Viking Press, 1960), p. 279; and *Power and Personality* (New York: W. W. Norton, 1948), pp. 16 ff.

Abraham Maslow ventured more boldly, arguing the universality of human needs set in a sequential or hierarchical order. First-order needs are those having to do with people's physiological nature — the needs for food and shelter. The need for physical safety is also primary, but seems to be less urgent and basic than the need for food, since hunger may lead to the assumption of physical risks. When these needs are met, the higher-order needs of love, belonging, and esteem assume importance, followed by self-actualizing needs such as artistic and intellectual experience and creativity.[8] With minor amendments Davies accepts Maslow's formulation and illustrates its implications for political behavior with research and information drawn from many contexts.[9] Inglehart uses the Maslow scheme to suggest hypotheses about generational change in political attitudes in Europe since World War II.[10]

Finally, in his examination of natural law theories in political philosophy, Paul Sigmund concludes that the affirmation of universal principles of social and political organization based on human nature is not revivable in its earlier form. In its place he suggests a conception of universal needs and potentialities that grant moral legitimacy to aspects of political process and public policy. Sigmund begins, as Maslow does, with the basic needs for subsistence and safety; he treats higher-order goods, which include equality, freedom, affection, and community, as potentialities: "These are some of the human needs and potentialities by which social, political, and economic institutions may be evaluated. The use of these goals as standards preserves something of the attempt of natural law theory to develop universal and objective norms related to human nature." [11]

Pennock's fourfold set of goods is consistent with those of Maslow and Sigmund. Thus security, welfare, and freedom appear in all three formulations, as they do in Lasswell's base values. Justice as defined by Pennock is related to Maslow's "esteem," Lasswell's "rectitude," and Sigmund's "equality."

A SYSTEM, PROCESS, AND POLICY APPROACH
TO POLITICAL GOODS

Pennock's article was an appeal to students of political development to push forward into the ethical implications of their work, to move from process to output and outcome consequences, and to consider these

---

[8] A. H. Maslow, *Motivation and Personality* (Oxford: Oxford University Press, 1938), pp. 80–98.

[9] James C. Davies, *Human Nature in Politics* (New York: John Wiley, 1963), chap. 1.

[10] Ronald Inglehart, *The Silent Revolution: Changing Values and Political Styles Among Western Publics* (Princeton: Princeton University Press, 1977), chap. 3.

[11] Paul E. Sigmund, *Natural Law in Political Thought* (Cambridge: Winthrop Publishers, 1971), pp. 209 ff.

from an evaluative perspective. We wish here to respond to his invitation, moving to a more systematic approach in order to evaluate types of political goods within the framework of our general analysis. We treat welfare, security, and liberty as in part the outcomes of governmental acts of taking, giving, compelling, and exhorting. Welfare is in part an outcome of governmental acts of extracting and distributing resources, while liberty and security have to do with the forms, range, and extent of governmental compulsion. In chapter XII we attempted to compare the welfare, security, and liberty outcomes of a number of political systems. In addition to these policy goods, however, there are important system goods of stability and adaptation and important process goods of participation, compliance, and procedural justice that must be incorporated in our general evaluative perspective.

In table XIV.1 we schematize our approach to political productivity and take the first step to operationalize these political goods as they manifest themselves in both the domestic and international environments. The table provides a classification for all types of political goods, without assumptions about hierarchies of human needs or any implications for the relative weighting of these goals. The general classes and subcategories of political goods can include all those aspects valued by individuals generally and can allow us to compare political cultures and political outcomes in given societies from the perspective of each type of value.

The categories and examples of political goods in table XIV.1, then, can provide us with a check list of the possible ethical perspectives from which we might consider political productivity. However, the table also suggests a kind of research program, sets of questions with direct implications for ethical evaluation. Such a program might include questions like the following:

1. Which kinds of goods do people value, with what intensity, and under what conditions? What risks and deprivations are they willing to bear in the present to attain various future values?

2. How can we measure and compare the productivity of different political systems with regard to each type of good?

3. What are the tradeoffs between different value types? To what extent are security and liberty, for example, values that cannot both be simultaneously maximized?

4. What are the tradeoffs that limit the productivity of different types of goods in given situations? At a given level of wealth, for instance, what choices must be made between education and social security or between equality and security?

5. What are the tradeoffs from a dynamic point of view? Must future welfare be purchased at the cost of current welfare, current equality, or current liberty — or all three?

6. Under what conditions can some goods act as multipliers for others,

Table XIV.1. *The Productivity of Political Systems*

Classes of Political Goods		Domestic Goods	International Goods
System goods	System maintenance	Regularity and predictability of processes and content	Regularity and predictability in international interaction
	System adaptation	Structural and cultural adaptability in response to domestic environmental challenges and opportunities	Structural and cultural adaptability in response to international environmental challenges and opportunities
Process goods	Participation	Instrumental activity for domestic outputs Activity directly productive of sense of efficacy and dignity	Instrumental activity for foreign outputs Activity directly productive of sense of efficacy and dignity through patriotic or international input
	Compliance and support	Instrumental (sanction-avoiding) compliance with law Fulfillment of duty, opportunities for service, achievement	Instrumental (sanction-avoiding) performance of military and other foreign duties Opportunities for patriotic service and/or international service
	Procedural justice	Equality before the law Equitable procedure	Respect for international law and procedure Encouragement of procedural justice abroad
Policy goods	Welfare	Growth per capita; quantity and composition Distributive equity	Growth; creation of externalities Distributive equity; facilitation of trade, growth, and welfare abroad
	Security	Safety of person and property Public order	National security Contribution to international conflict resolution
	Liberty	Freedom from regulation Protection of privacy	Respect for the autonomy of other nations Encouragement of domestic liberty abroad

such that stability improves welfare goods, or participation also brings compliance?

In earlier chapters we have already discussed some of these problems from a purely descriptive point of view. Here we shall try to indicate some of the critical issues for an evaluative analysis.

DOMESTIC SYSTEM GOODS

First, a word or two about the logic of the threefold classification. There is more to political productivity than policy goods. For productivity to be sustained, system maintenance is required in the form of effective socialization and recruitment into system roles. Increased political productivity calls for structural and cultural adaptations. Thus the development of specialized bureaucracies and agencies may increase the production of security, welfare, and procedural justice, just as the development of political parties, interest groups, and the media of communication may increase the production of liberty and welfare. From this "capital improvement" perspective, institutional maintenance and development do not directly produce political consumer goods, but they make them possible at continued or improved rates, and perhaps at lower cost. As in the economy, the maintenance and improvement of "political plant" calls for a regular allocation of resources for these purposes and for extraordinary rates of capital investment for purposes of adaptation. Both may reduce productivity of policy goods in the short run in order to increase it and improve its composition in the long run.

The notion of adaptation has at least two aspects. The first of these is the capacity to change structure and performance in order to cope more effectively with environmental challenges and opportunities. The second is the aspect of efficiency, of benefits in relation to costs. The payoffs to consumers of system goods from this perspective are instrumental and indirect. There is also a larger sense in which system maintenance and adaptation provide direct consumer goods in the form of a sense of regular order and in constructive responses to challenge. The sense that things are in their proper place on earth and in heaven may be a direct output to consumers. The world acquires a familiar structure and process to which people can adapt — the social orders, ranks, and role incumbents behave appropriately. Interruptions and serious deviations in these routines and behaviors create uneasiness and arouse anxiety; there is a decline in the productivity of orderliness.

Similarly, the occurrence of system challenges and threats — wars, rebellions, or economic disasters — creates a generalized need for adaptiveness and creativity. And political systems that "do something" about threats and challenges benefit political consumers directly, allaying feelings of anxiety and urgency. Thus, system maintenance and adaptation are not only instrumental to productivity, but may be directly productive of political consumer goods.

It goes without saying that the system goods of order and adaptation are in conflict; even when adaptation is incremental, it is accompanied by some loss of regularity, predictability, and productivity. Furthermore, adaptive efforts may fail or may fall short of transformations that can be stabilized. But assuming a constructive adaptation, one may view the conflict or tradeoff between order and adaptation as two related curves with order declining as adaptation rises, then rising again as the adaptation rate declines.

DOMESTIC PROCESS GOODS

Process goods are produced at both input and output phases: participation in the formulation of public policy, and compliance and procedural justice in its implementation and enforcement. In their narrower significance, participation and compliance are instrumental; their value as goods depends on their effectiveness in bringing about desired policies. Participation brings important issues to the political process and supports friendly coalitions. Compliance with the law avoids sanctions and penalties and encourages implementation of supported policies. Procedural justice is related to the equitable enforcement of the law.

But participation is also a direct consumer good, even though it occurs in the political process and not among the policy outputs, save in those situations in which access to participation is itself the subject of policy. People who participate effectively in political decisions may acquire a sense of political efficacy, of influence, or of dignity. Wherever one places the satisfactions of self-expression and achievement in a hierarchy of human needs, one must recognize their importance to many people and give political participation the status of a good when it enhances them. Even individuals who fail to achieve their particular policy goals may receive satisfaction from having made the attempt or from receiving response and attention from political leaders.

Similarly, compliance with the law may in a narrow fashion involve only actions of citizens and subjects who behave appropriately because of actual or threatened sanctions. Policies specify fines, imprisonments, and deprivations of rights and privileges. But the relation of citizens to the implementation of policy may, and indeed often does, go beyond compliance in this narrow and instrumental sense. The actions of governments may attempt to tap powerful impulses within citizens to fulfill duty and to live up to obligation. Governments may offer opportunities for service, achievement, or glory. In his inaugural address President Kennedy called upon such impulses to serve and sacrifice when he said, "Ask not what your country can do for you; ask what you can do for your country." The impulse to serve collectivities is a powerful one, which manifests itself particularly in crises, although not only then. A polity that successfully draws on these needs or impulses may lower its implementation costs or maintain a level of productivity beyond the face value of its capacities. A humdrum polity, or one that pursues unpopular policies, thwarts these impulses and may even convert them into political withdrawal, or alienation, thereby increasing the costs of performance and/or lowering its productivity.

Procedural justice is the set of conditions, limits, and processes required in the enforcement of the law upon individuals and their property. While it applies in situations in which individuals directly encounter the law, general societal knowledge of the equity and justice of law enforcement is a more general process good contributing to the sense of safety and predictability and the confident exercise of liberties and rights. Procedural justice normally implies equality of treatment before the law and provision of equitable procedure in its enforcement. The requirement of warrants before persons or premises may be searched and the rights to reasonable bail, counsel, habeas corpus, trial by jury, appeal to higher courts, and reasonable punishment may have the effect of raising the costs of law enforcement and delaying the imposition of sanctions. But without them substantive liberty is endangered. A bill of rights that is full of guarantees and specified freedoms may mean little or nothing if persons accused of violations of the law do not have effective access to the means of defense. But access to the judicial process to protect rights from infraction or to guarantee that sanctions are imposed equitably is not equally distributed in societies. Procedural justice thus has both magnitude and distributive aspects that must be taken into account in any measure of political productivity. The relations of procedural justice to compliance with the law and to public safety and order are complex. On the one hand, a more punctilious procedure raises the costs of law enforcement and lowers the probability that a violator of the law will be apprehended and punished. On the other hand, a system of justice with a reputation for fairness and equity may encourage compliance with the law. Needless to say, the law enforcement process is only one of the variables that affect public safety and order in societies.

So one must add to Pennock's set of goods these process-related consumption goods of efficacy and dignity, fulfillment of obligation and service, and sense of procedural equity. And they are often related to each other and to the system and policy goods as well. Figure XIV.1 suggests how satisfaction of compliance and effective participation may go together in a responsive, participatory political system, reinforcing each other and maintaining the stability of the system.[12] It also suggests how

---

[12] For some data on positive associations of this kind in several democracies, see Gabriel Almond and Sidney Verba, *The Civic Culture* (Princeton: Princeton University Press, 1963), pp. 247 ff.

Figure XIV.1. *Effective Participation and Voluntary Compliance: A Reinforcing Relationship of Process Goods*

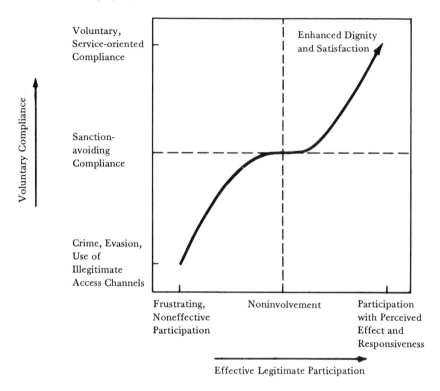

frustrating, ineffective participation or deliberate exclusion from involvement may go with evasion of compliance and use of illegitimate violence and coercion. Much of the appeal, surely, of the concept of democracy lies in the hope of developing a political system in the upper-right-hand quadrant of the figure, where the successful exchange of participatory demand, response, and satisfying support provides system, process, and policy goods to its citizens. The disappointment of such an ideal can, thus, be especially bitter to excluded minorities.

DOMESTIC POLICY GOODS: WELFARE

Let us begin our consideration of policy goods with welfare. In chapters XI and XII we have presented welfare data for a variety of countries. Building from and drawing upon this data, we can indicate the possibilities and problems for an ethical evaluation of welfare development. Of course, we recognize that political systems distribute honor, status, and aesthetic and moral satisfactions as well and that these nonmaterial benefits may be substituted for material welfare benefits. But the material considerations will suffice to illustrate the analysis.

In the data on welfare outcomes that we have considered – including income, health, education, and housing – one fact stands out above all: material well-being is greater in countries with high levels of gross national product per capita. In the wealthiest countries citizens enjoy better health, have more physicians available to them, have more housing space, can read and write, and can buy more consumer goods than in the poorest countries. Not surprisingly, it is better to be rich than poor.

However, an evaluative perspective on welfare must begin, not end, with the facts of economic productivity. High levels of economic productivity cannot be achieved overnight; they are in part a consequence of cultural, social, and technological patterns in which political forces interact with the environment, but seldom control it. International dependence, historical development, and natural resources play critical roles in bringing nations to their present wealth levels. An evaluation of the contemporary political system must consider its dynamic effects on wealth, as well as levels attained. From this point of view, the data in table XII.3 on growth rates are highly relevant to evaluation of welfare.

Consideration of the dynamics of growth, as well as of the levels of economic development, seems essential to a productivity analysis. Yet, it immediately raises two serious problems: (1) the effectiveness of the political system in shaping growth, and (2) the evaluation of immediate welfare consumption versus future welfare consumption. No one is really entirely sure how the political system can most effectively bring about economic growth in different situations. This question is an empirical one, but it has enormous evaluative consequences because attaining higher future levels of productivity almost invariably means giving up some present consumption. One increases economic productivity through investment: building and replacing plants, encouraging research, constructing new machinery, or implementing new agricultural techniques. National income spent for these purposes cannot be spent on health, housing, social security, and many other welfare purposes.

Figure XIV.2 shows a pair of tradeoff curves (production-possibility curves) that illustrate the point. In 1970, countries A and B are at the same general productivity levels: they produce the total levels of goods and services of $350 per capita, while country C produces $850 per capita. The tradeoff lines show the possible ways the countries could use this capacity to produce various mixes of consumption or investments. Country A consumes more of its output, while country B trades off more present consumption against (hoped for) future consumption, putting more of its production into investment. In 1980, a decade later, country B has found its investment paying off. It has grown at about 6 percent per year

Figure XIV.2. *Production Possibility Tradeoffs: Consumption or Investment?*

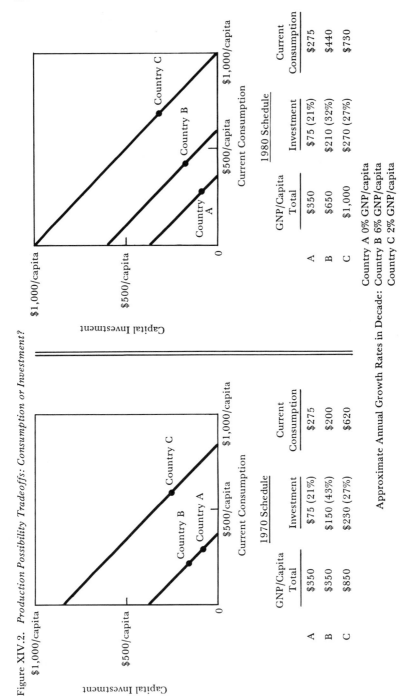

1970 Schedule

	GNP/Capita Total	Investment	Current Consumption
A	$350	$75 (21%)	$275
B	$350	$150 (43%)	$200
C	$850	$230 (27%)	$620

1980 Schedule

	GNP/Capita Total	Investment	Current Consumption
A	$350	$75 (21%)	$275
B	$650	$210 (32%)	$440
C	$1,000	$270 (27%)	$730

Approximate Annual Growth Rates in Decade: Country A 0% GNP/capita
Country B 6% GNP/capita
Country C 2% GNP/capita

Source: Adapted from Paul A. Samuelson, *Economics* (New York: McGraw Hill, 1967), p. 23. Hypothetical dollar amounts have been added for illustrative purposes.

and is able to consume more than static country A, while still continuing a fairly high investment level for the future. Illustrating popular wisdom — "them that's got, gits" — wealthy country C has been able to maintain more investment and more consumption than either poor nation and to increase its welfare lead over country A at little discomfort to its citizens. The ethical problem of evaluating the productivity of country A and country B at the first time period is somewhat intractable, as it depends on which generation is to enjoy more benefits. All we can do is point out that both aspects must be considered.

However, the critical practical aspects of the problem are also evident. If country B's investment scheme failed, as many investment efforts have failed in developing nations (especially the huge efforts for a single dramatic push, like China's "great leap forward"), then it might end up a decade later still at the level of country A — and have experienced years of welfare sacrifice for its citizens in the interim. Less dramatically, if country A uses its investment money more effectively, it may gain as much growth as country B, at less short-term costs to its citizens. In chapter XII we reported the findings of Bergson on growth in command and market economies in the middle-level wealth range. His findings indicated that the command economies of Eastern Europe had put more income into investment, on the average, than the comparable market economies, but, at least in that time period, had not managed to attain faster growth rates. While one must be cautious in drawing inferences to other situations and time periods, this pattern implies a net loss in welfare performance for the command economies, although the differences are not great.

Our consideration of the evaluation of welfare productivity cannot end here, for the problem of equity deserves discussion. Table XII.1 showed that countries differ greatly, even at the same level of economic development, in the shares going to different income groups in their populations. This analysis could be extended to consider smaller groups and the special problems of regional and ethnic minorities as well. But the table clearly indicated that among the wealthiest countries, France gave a markedly smaller share to its lowest 40 percent than did Britain; among those at the next level, Italy provided a far less equitable distribution than Czechoslovakia, but was much more equitable than Venezuela; and so on, down the list. Analyses of health, housing, and educational outcomes show somewhat similar patterns, within and across general income levels.

Equity considerations, too, are complex. First, we encounter again the problem of present and future welfare. Thinking only of individuals, for the moment, we would like to know how much economic mobility exists in the population. How likely is it that some of those presently in the bottom 40 percent will rise into the top group in the next decade? How is such mobility perceived; what importance do citizens attach to it; how should we evaluate it? If citizens were high risk takers, they might prefer to live in a society with greater income differentials, but also with a chance to rise to the top, rather than in a society in which such opportunities were not available. In terms of the total system, there is the question of relationship between equality and growth. Is economic growth encouraged by a concentration of income in the hands of the wealthy, who are more likely to save (invest) it than to use it for food and housing? At what levels and in what type of political system is this true? [13]

Even when equity is considered at a particular time, there is more to the figures in table XII.1 than meets the eye. From an ethical point of view, income is closely bound up with the freedom to dispose of that income as one chooses. Here we are thinking not merely of the question of liberty, but also of the uses of personal income. One determinant is the wealth of the nation; in a wealthy economy more types of goods may be available, along with possible services, medical technology, public goods like parks and roads, and the like. Even with a smaller income share, more consumption possibilities may appear. Another aspect is related to the command economy and the control over production. Although the Socialist command economies of Czechoslovakia and Bulgaria gave a more equitable share of the national income to their lower classes than did comparable market economies, the national planners decreed low production of consumer goods. The housing figures in table XII.4 provide one indication; the long consumer lines and great delays in obtaining such consumer goods as appliances and automobiles, as well as serious quality problems, provide other evidence. Moreover, the table of income distribution shows income before taxes; we have already seen that in the command economies the governments collect very large portions of the national revenue, usually through regressive turnover taxes and similar means, much of which is plowed back into investment. To gain a clearer understanding of relative equity and productivity, we need much better information on living standards of various social groups in these different nations. And the question of present and future welfare would remain.

Let us consider one final problem in welfare productivity: tradeoffs and multipliers in allocating present types of public expenditures. Figure

[13] The need for incorporation of such empirical questions into evaluative analysis is clearly identified in John Rawles, *A Theory of Justice* (Cambridge: Harvard University Press, 1971), and has played an important role in most classical philosophy.

Figure **XIV.3.** *Production Possibility Tradeoffs: Education or Health and Social Security?*

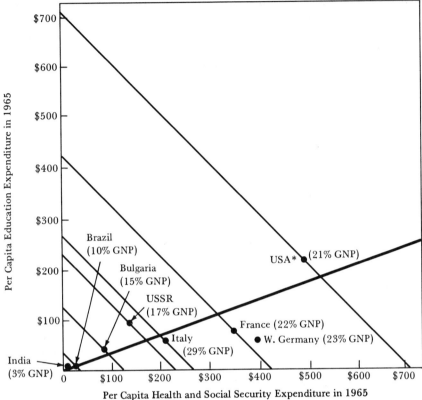

Sources: Table XI.3; Charles L. Taylor and Michael C. Hudson, *World Handbook of Political and Social Indicators* (New Haven: Yale University Press, 1972).

Note: Total commitment is assumed to be fixed. Rising diagonal line represents a 1:3 tradeoff between education and health-social security.

*USA data includes 29% private education spending and 69% private health-social security spending. From Frederic L. Pryor, *Public Expenditure in Communist and Capitalist Nations* (Homewood, Ill.: R. D. Irwin, 1968), pp. 142, 162, 200.

XIV.3 shows some production possibility curves resulting from the assumption that a nation's ruling coalition decides (on the basis of available resources, alternative needs and demands, various preferences, and so forth) to allocate a fixed amount of the GNP to education and welfare. Having made that decision, leaders must now decide how much to allocate to each good. We show the possible tradeoffs between education, on one hand, and health and welfare, on the other, as a line of production-possibilities. The line is drawn from the extreme of 100 percent to health and welfare at the bottom of the figure to the exact opposite, 100 percent to education at the top of the figure. (Such lines are usually drawn as outward-bending curves, due to the inefficiencies of complete tradeoffs at the extremes — for example, schoolteachers may make poor welfare workers. But for simplicity we show a straight line here.) The actual position of the nation on that line in 1965, taken from chapter XI, is indicated with a dot and the name of each country, as well as the percentage of its GNP which that line reflects. For the United States, we show combined public and private spending, as it is this mix that affects welfare. Due to absence of data, other nations show only public spending; but for those included, most education, health, and welfare spending is publicly financed.

On first inspection, one sees again that it is better to be rich. The United States gets both more education and more welfare than other nations. Indeed, its education spending alone is more than the total Indian GNP per capita. But one can also note the varying tradeoffs between these two welfare areas.[14] The figure shows a dotted line marking the average tradeoff of 5 percent of GNP on education and 15 percent on health and social security — a 1-to-3 ratio. The United States spends relatively more on education; its position on its tradeoff curve is further up toward the education end. The Soviet Union is even a bit further toward the education end of its tradeoff curve; France and Germany, on the other hand, traded off education for more welfare spending. Italy and Bulgaria are very close to the 1-to-3 ratio, although Italy spends a larger proportion of GNP on the two welfare goods. For the very poor nations, one can see very clearly that the total effort per citizen in the combined areas is quite limited, regardless of the tradeoff chosen. However, Brazil chose relatively more social security; India, more education.[15]

Two additional points should be made in considering these tradeoffs: (1) education and social security, especially in nations with extensive social security programs, go to very different parts of the population; and (2) education often has a multiplier effect on future welfare productivity, as well as being a desirable consumption good. Both tradeoff needs and future productivity multiplier effects are relevant to an ethical assessment of allocative decisions.

[14] The discussion here assumes that expenditures result in actual welfare in both areas. Of course, we already know that the output-to-outcome effects vary substantially in different nations. The education expenditure and outcome data from table XII.6 provided one example.

[15] These data, we should emphasize, are from the mid-1960s and capture the policy tradeoffs in Brazil during the period of competitive populism before the 1964 military coup.

DOMESTIC POLICY GOODS: SECURITY

Security as a domestic political good consists of two components: safety of person and property against crime, and public peace and order. Just as welfare is a mixed product of the polity and the economy, security is the mixed product of social and political processes. If family, church, community, school, and the like fail to inculcate law-abiding propensities, the law enforcement processes of the polity become heavily loaded. Infractions of public order — demonstrations, riots, terrorist acts, and guerrilla warfare — are usually associated with ethnic, religious, and social conflict, with unpopular public policies, or with failures of public policy to deal with serious grievances. If the distributive processes of the polity and the economy are perceived as inequitable, then the propensity to obey the law may attenuate. Persons with little or no stake in a society or with powerful feelings of injustice, discrimination, or hopelessness (whatever their source) may be willing to incur the risks of crime or to become involved in collective attacks on public order. Such actions may be, and usually are, harmful of innocent parties, and they may create general anxieties regarding personal safety. Thus, insecurity of person and of property and public disorder must be entered into any political ledger in negative terms, regardless of the state of material welfare.

Although not very much is known about the varied causes of general crime, there is a good deal of information about causes of political conflict. Different manifestations of public order breakdown may affect citizens in different ways. A large, property-destructive riot may directly affect more citizens than a terrorist bomb. But the many victims of the riot are not as severely affected as those few hit by the bomb. Despite the various causes of perceived deprivation and the important organizational underpinnings that shape political conflict (which we discussed particularly in chapters VII and VIII), the general relationship between level of welfare and level of security is fairly clear. As is indicated in figure XIV.4, conditions of high general welfare, including equality (or at least well-being) of all population segments, are associated with lower levels of intense domestic political violence. Whether one measures the condition of the poorer classes and deprived ethnic groups by income shares and levels, education, or health, these very general relationships appear. The line in figure XIV.4 is generally a positive one, whatever its exact shape. Even with many exceptions created by value conflicts and the like, the static relationship between welfare and security is probably positive and reinforcing.

However, what is true for static relationships is not necessarily true for dynamic relationships or marginal changes. As we have suggested in our welfare discussion, the rates of growth and improvement in material conditions may be a critical factor in evaluating welfare outcomes. But

Figure XIV.4   *Welfare Levels and Political Security Levels: Empirical Relationship between Two Static Measures.*

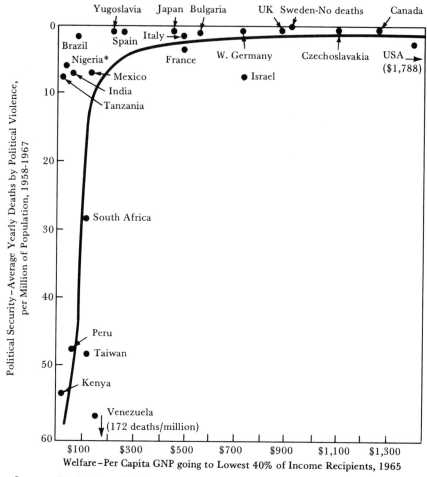

Sources: Deaths by political violence from Taylor and Hudson, *World Handbook*, pp. 110 ff. Welfare variable calculated from table XII.1.

*Nigeria figures are for 1958-1962 only. For 1958-1967, the estimate of deaths is 9,153 per million per year in Nigeria, reflecting the disastrous civil war.

there is some evidence that growth rates may be associated with increased political violence and lower security.[16] In periods of change and turbu-

[16] See Mancur Olson, "Rapid Growth as a Destabilizing Force," *Journal of Economic History* 23 (December 1963): 529–552. Empirical evidence is, however, contradictory. See the studies reviewed by Douglas A. Hibbs, *Mass Political Violence* (New York: John Wiley, 1973), pp. 31–36. Hibbs's own quantitative analyses found rate of economic growth negatively related to collective protest, not systematically related to internal war at a significant level.

lence, some groups are typically threatened, while others lose position. And as we showed in chapter XII, the common pattern in economic development is for inequality to increase at the early middle stages, exacerbating relative deprivation. For these and other reasons, achievement of superior and more equitable welfare levels may constitute a long-range solution to security problems, but in transition periods the conflicts and demands may decrease security. For decades and longer, there may be negative dynamic tradeoffs. A standard promise of military regimes and of Communist ideology is to avoid such security threats through greater coercive control — a tradeoff of liberty for security, as a temporary or indefinite practice. In conflict-torn nations, the appeal to security values may be difficult to deny.

DOMESTIC POLICY GOODS: LIBERTY

The concept of liberty that we use here refers to the exemption and protection of spheres of activity from external interference and the protection of privacy. This is sometimes viewed as the negative, "freedom from" meaning of liberty that is associated with constituent, statutory, or customary limits on governmental power. But it is more than a simple set of inhibitions of governmental action, since infractions of liberty and privacy may be initiated by other private individuals, groups, and organizations. As a political good, liberty may be fostered by governmental intervention in private actions, for example, when private parties interfere with the liberty of others. Much of the recent legislation regarding racial segregation may be understood in these terms. Denial of residential rights or tenancy on the part of property owners, restrictions on access to employment, private interference with exercise of political rights, and so on — all constitute denials of the liberty of one group of citizens by other groups of citizens. In this case, government circumscribes the autonomy of some in order to accord it to others.

In an age of computerized data banks and rapid dissemination of information, the problem of privacy and its protection assumes a new magnitude. These technological developments place the political goods of welfare and security into a special state of tension with liberty, in the sense of privacy. The facilitation of criminal justice that these new information technologies make possible, or the increased efficiency and productivity in the economy that they allow, has to be set off against the loss of privacy resulting from the accumulation of sometimes obsolete, inaccurate, or misleading information readily available to users, regardless of their ability to evaluate it.

Although the technology of the twentieth century may pose special tensions for the relationship between liberty and security, the confrontation between them has been a classic dilemma in political philosophy. At the logical extremes, at least, there seem to be negative tradeoffs between liberty and security, and no ready ethical answer dictates the most appropriate balance between them. Political development and economic riches provide no obvious solution to this problem. At some point, liberty for some individuals threatens the security of others. The logical and ethical dilemma does not, however, obviate some very important empirical questions about the relationships between security and liberty, and welfare as well, under specific conditions. For part of the problem of liberty concerns the use that citizens wish to make of it, and part of the problem of security concerns who shall enforce it.

In figure XIV.5 we attempt to suggest some of the differing tradeoff conditions for liberty and security. We show possible liberty-security

Figure XIV.5. *Security and Liberty Tradeoffs in Different Social Tension Conditions*

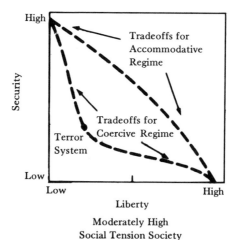

tradeoff curves in three different societies. Society A is a "low tension" society: for whatever reasons, citizens are relatively satisfied with their welfare conditions and do not perceive fundamental value conflicts. Likely, the society is culturally homogeneous, and perhaps it manifests high levels of wealth and equality or low expectations of them. Overall, there is still a negative relationship, a tradeoff relationship, between liberty and security. At the extreme right, the extreme liberty end of the curve, security drops sharply as personal and property rights become exposed to the covetousness, the cunning, and the physical strength of others. But in such a low tension society, even with a rather minimal sacrifice of liberty, citizens can obtain a great deal of security; and for a wide range of liberty levels there is no change in security. Indeed, at the middle liberty ranges, the short-run relationship may even be positive; a decrease in liberty may create tensions as political equality is threatened, causing security to decline rather than rise. And in general, it is possible for citizens in such a society to enjoy very substantial amounts of both liberty and security.

The second society shows a very different set of tradeoff possibilities. Here, ethnic, class, or political value differences and inequalities create great tensions. After a substantial amount of liberty appears, the society collapses at least temporarily into civil war, and security vanishes completely. Moreover, even with very great sacrifices of liberty, it may be impossible to attain high amounts of security. As citizens in such troubled areas as Northern Ireland are too well aware, even the imposition of military patrols, checkpoints, and continual security searches cannot guarantee security against terrorist actions. And at some point the very efforts of the regime to sustain security impinge on citizen security, as everyone is suspected of being a security threat and may face detention, or at least harassment, because of it. Even the best tradeoffs, whether the preference is for security or liberty, are not very happy ones.

Finally, in the last example, we look at two kinds of tradeoff curves, depending on regime policies within a moderate tension society. The top curve suggests a very responsive, equitable, and justice-oriented regime. Due to the threats of tension, there is a tradeoff between liberty and security of a continuing sort; and the desired position on the curve will depend on which is more valued: avoidance of strife or maintenance of freedom of action. The lower curve suggests a very coercively oriented regime, determined to maintain its own security through various levels of terror. At its worst, the massive application of terror tactics – against even high-level officials in the government, not to mention millions of citizens – and a context of constant police and party intervention, complete censorship, and travel control destroy liberty, but provide little security. The uncontrolled actions of the regime itself undermine any security for its citizens. The Soviet Union under Stalin may provide an example. In less extreme forms, the authoritarian military or civilian regime may use imprisonment without trial, torture, and secret murder as tactics against suspected opponents of the regime. Minority groups are particularly vulnerable to such security threats from their own governments. Although there is no simple set of statistics that can easily measure the insecurity created by such regime policies, the toll can be a dreadful one. One of the grim ironies of modern political life is the situation in which the disturbing daily tensions of a conflict-ridden democracy are replaced by the tensions of life under a terror-oriented authoritarian government that has overthrown its predecessor and diminished liberty in the name of security. Strikes, riots, and demonstrations are replaced with capricious arrest and broken lives.

With regard to the relationships and tradeoffs involving liberty and welfare, we must confess that very little is known about the possibilities. It is tempting to suggest a rather positive general relationship between liberty and stable welfare, if only because high welfare systems may more likely enjoy that low social tension condition which makes possible substantial amounts of both security and liberty. But, on the other hand, in countries striving for welfare improvement, the tensions that undermine security make liberty difficult to sustain. Such nations may also need high levels of security to support stable development and redistribution programs and must be willing to sacrifice a good deal of liberty for their sake. Above all, however, so much depends on the deliberate policy choices of the ruling coalitions in low liberty countries that generalization is difficult. Decisions about alternative welfare policies and their beneficiaries are critical.

The empirical range available to ruling coalitions in low liberty countries is suggested by considering the cases of South Africa and Bulgaria. In the case of Bulgaria, as we have shown, the regime has managed a good record of economic growth, apparently quite equitable income distribution, and low domestic violence. It is primarily in the Socialist command economies (but in such authoritarian-technocratic countries as Taiwan and South Korea as well) that substantial income equality is found at the middle levels of economic development. These welfare goods have been obtained at the cost of liberty, and perhaps of some individual citizen security, under authoritarian control. In South Africa, on the other hand, one also finds a suppression of liberty, especially for the black majority, although freedoms of travel and political expression have also been increasingly circumscribed for whites. Here domestic violence has been rather high, as was shown in figure XIV.4, and government harassment of potential dissidents has made individual security less likely. Above all, a generally good record in growth and wealth has been accompanied by the worst distributive record of any nation for which we have data: the bottom 40 percent of the population received only 6 percent of the national income.[17] And despite a relatively high per capita GNP, the literacy rate in the 1960s was only 35 percent, an incredibly low figure for a nation of this wealth.[18] Clearly, the lack of liberty implies no guarantee of equality.

INTERNATIONAL GOODS
INTERNATIONAL POLITICAL GOODS

The outcomes related to the actions of political systems in their international environments may also be viewed in terms of productivity. The domestic policies of nations have impacts abroad simply by example. Domestic stability and adaptability, patterns of participation, compliance with and resistance to law, procedural justice, growth in technology, improvements in welfare, security and rebellion, the growth or contraction of liberty — all may be incorporated, adapted, or resisted abroad.

These outcomes by example, by demonstration effects, are part of a nation's international productivity, and they may contribute to or detract from the productivity of other nations and of the international political system as a whole. The industrial revolution in England and the American, French, Russian, and Chinese revolutions had enormous impacts on domestic and international political order and set in motion substantial adaptive reactions in the farthest reaches of the globe.

INTERNATIONAL SYSTEM GOODS

Whether intended, partly intended, or unintended, the international goods produced by nations must be specified in system, process, and policy terms. (See table XIV.1.) We spoke of a nation as having an international role, a set of patterned transactions and interactions over time, the result of exchanges with other nations of security, diplomatic, economic, and symbolic outputs. Insofar as the regularity and the predictability of the international political system are goods, they are dependent on member nations' playing of appropriate roles, adhering to treaties, functioning appropriately as trading partners, maintaining or avoiding military deployments, and so forth. That is, order and predictability are goods even though the order that is being maintained may leave much to be desired. The full account of productivity can come only when this order is balanced against the requirements of adaptability and against the process and policy characteristics of other national outputs.

17 Hollis Chenery et al., *Redistribution with Growth* (New York: Oxford University Press, 1974).
18 Charles L. Taylor and Michael C. Hudson, *World Handbook of Political and Social Indicators* (New Haven: Yale University Press, 1972).

It is not difficult to make the case today for the importance of system adaptability as an international good. The development and spread of nuclear and missile capabilities, population growth, resource depletion, environmental deterioration, and increasing inequality among nations and groups of nations all constitute pressing challenges and threats calling for the creative adaptation of national political systems. At the most basic level, perhaps most of the new nations, and surely many of the older ones, are too small and too poor in resources to develop viable economies. Regardless of size and level of social and economic development, the nation-state system confronts challenges that may result in catastrophic losses of life and productivity if not met creatively and quickly. Military technology contains inevitable destabilizing potentialities, which may seriously upset the balance of terror and deterrence. The spread of this military technology similarly seems to raise these risks. A world industrial economy confronting resource depletion must move in the direction of conservation and technological adaptation. And a world in which welfare is so unequally distributed among nations and groups of nations — and in which this inequality promises to increase — is inherently unstable and steadily becoming more so. One cannot escape the conclusion that the system good of adaptability has to be given a greater weight than that of system maintenance in the emerging world system. And one must recognize that those nations which take creative steps and risks in the direction of formulating more appropriate norms of national conduct and of shaping supranational institutions are more productive of political goods than those which define their roles in simple system-maintenance or conventional national-interest terms.

INTERNATIONAL PROCESS GOODS

Process goods have instrumental and directly expressive aspects on the international side as well as the domestic. Participation has an instrumental relation to foreign policy: signing a petition, attending a demonstration, or writing a letter to a politician regarding foreign and military policy is intended to support that policy or to change it. The foreign policy output is the intended good. But the act of participation in foreign policy making may be a direct consumer good as well, contributing to a sense of efficacy and dignity in relation to foreign affairs; and the political system that permits this participation may be productive of these participation goods.

In the compliance and support aspects of international process goods, performance of military or other duties (for example, observance of customs laws) may have the simple avoidance of punishment as its goal; or, as in a volunteer army, the service may be in exchange for pay, interesting work, opportunities, and the like. But nations may also draw on powerful patriotic impulses for national service or on interest in achievement and glory in the nation's service. In addition, some nations permit citizens to travel abroad freely, to affiliate with international associations, and to comply with and support the policies of international bodies intended to affect the structure of international politics. As an international political good, procedural justice refers to the respect shown by a nation for existing international norms and procedures and for their further development. It also refers to efforts to foster internal procedural justice and human rights within foreign nations.

INTERNATIONAL POLICY GOODS

Nations may be evaluated for their contribution to international welfare again in terms of both growth and distribution. Technological improvements occurring in one nation or group of nations become positive "externalities" to other nations. The costs of developing these improvements are borne by the inventing nation. The importing nation may benefit from a bureaucratic process or technology even when licensing or other charges are imposed, when they lack the supporting economy and culture to generate innovations of these kinds by themselves. Thus, technological and organizational innovation represents a contribution to international welfare even without deliberate distributive efforts. But the terms under which a nation or a corporation within it makes such innovations available to foreign countries may be more or less distributive. Thus, the international welfare performance of a political system may be evaluated in terms of distributive equity. Does it facilitate trade on equitable terms; does it directly contribute to technological development abroad? Does it act generously in helping nations to improve their educational capacities or to increase the skill and productivity of their labor forces? Is it responsive to famine and other disasters abroad?

Nations allocate resources, recruit and train personnel, deploy armed forces abroad, send and receive diplomats, negotiate and conclude treaties, and conduct military operations and war in their "national interests." The conception of national interests may range from conquest and expansion at one extreme to policies intended to resolve conflicts without recourse to war at the other. The net contribution of a nation to international security is very difficult indeed to compute. Men act as though there are "just wars," that is, wars productive of good. If there are productive wars, it follows that there are kinds of peace that are unproductive. A colony seeking its freedom, a dominated and exploited country seeking to attain autonomy, or a stability-oriented nation seeking to contain the expansion of an aggressive power are trading off security for other goods, such as liberty, welfare, or procedural justice, or are accepting the threat to security today for a greater security tomorrow. The cost of war has always been such that its productivity is problematic. Even where just wars are successful — the colony frees itself, the exploited country gains its autonomy, or the expansive country is contained — one has to subtract the human costs from the benefits accruing to the survivors. And there is no arithmetic that does this satisfactorily.

But wars initiated with productive goals normally attain ambiguous results at best; a just war may establish an unjust peace. Hence, to what may be an unproductive outcome one has to add the human cost of the war and the probable human costs and unproductive outcome of the future just war intended to undo the unjust peace. Modern military technologies render calculations of these kinds grotesque. All that can be said with conviction about international security productivity in the contemporary world is that those nations which make sustained efforts at international conflict resolution and are willing to take some risks of their own national security in the process may be contributing to political productivity.

In an era in which nuclear powers are deterred from large-scale war since they cannot escape catastrophic destruction themselves, a novel situation has set in: smaller powers can assert autonomy vis-à-vis vastly more powerful nations. National honor and pride receive a lower weighting at a time when fostering them involves unacceptable risks. As a consequence of these trends, there may have been a net increase in liberty in the international context. Interferences in the autonomy of small nations by large nations tend to be confined to the immediate environs of these nations or to be based upon explicit or implicit acknowledgments of special relations and exemptions. Beyond the deterrent effect of the risks of escalation, other factors that may have contributed to increasing restraint of the great powers include improved international communication, visibility, and even rising international moral standards. On the other hand, this deconcentration of power in the international arena may have produced a decline in international security and an increase in the probability of smaller wars and rebellions, leading to larger-scale confrontations.

In the international context, liberty as a good has two aspects. It refers to the respect shown by one nation for the autonomy of others; it also refers to the efforts of one nation to enhance internal liberty in foreign countries. Needless to say, these two aspects of liberty may be in conflict, as in the case of a nation that employs sanctions in efforts to defend human rights in a foreign country that denies them to its citizens (such as South Africa). Efforts to defend liberty abroad may also come into conflict with international security and welfare, as in the case of a nation that employs military or economic measures in seeking to deter an aggressive nation from violating the autonomy and intervening in the internal affairs of weaker nations.

TRADEOFFS AND OPPORTUNITY COSTS

Economists often sum up the wisdom of their science by saying that there is no such thing as a free lunch. A distribution of benefits may reduce maintenance expenditures and increase future costs. Part of the cost of producing a product may be "externalized," passed on to future generations or to the people downstream. Even in the pub or the bar to which their metaphor refers, the free bread and cheese bear some relationship to the price or quality of the beverages. What we have said so far about the productivity of political systems should make it clear that politics is no refuge for free-lunch seekers and that the costs incurred in politics may be far grimmer than in economics. If economics is the dismal science, then politics is the tragic one.

We have tried to show how useful it is to conceive of political productivity in economic terms, that is, in terms of trading off political goods one for the other, or of counting into the costs of one kind of productivity the lost opportunity to produce another kind. We have also stressed the constraints on productivity and the kinds of political goods that cannot be produced at all without prior investment in productive facilities. Surely the analogies from economics are most suggestive, but they are only analogies.

In political science there is no way of converting units of liberty into units of safety or welfare. And since politics often involves ultimate coercion and life itself on a large scale, it is important to acknowledge that one can never calculate the value of a political outcome gained at the cost of human life. People act in history as though they have such conversion criteria; but all that professional political scientists can do is to point to regular or recurring aspects of such conversion phenomena. Under what conditions, in what contexts do people demand welfare in exchange for liberty and justice, or risk life in exchange for liberty, justice, or welfare? Such an investigation is unlikely to yield a clear set of regularities. These conversion rules will vary from culture to culture and from time to time. As in economics, there is something like a principle of marginality operating in politics. This defines points at which the utility of political goods diminish — points, for example, at which order and safety become replaceable by liberty, points at which equality is replaceable by liberty, or liberty by equality. The advantage of a clear-cut ideology is that it provides people with what appear to be sound utility-weighting schemes and orderly sequences of action leading to value optimization. But there is no ideology, just as there is no political science, that can really solve these problems objectively. There is no "bottom line" in politics, just subtotals of goods and their costs, and this is the moral schema that one must use in comparing the productivity of political systems, or developmental strategies.

DEVELOPMENT STRATEGIES AND POLITICAL PRODUCTIVITY

In chapter XIII we discussed and provided illustrations of five politico-economic development strategies: populist, technocratic-authoritarian, technocratic-authoritarian-equalitarian, technocratic-authoritarian-mobilizational, and neo-traditional. The democratic populist strategy was described as high in aspiration and in the creation of expectations, but as low in performance. Without a productive economy and effective governmental and political institutions, participation and distributive expectations are frustrated. Many of these populist regimes have collapsed through inability to confront and resolve the painful tradeoffs between growth and distribution or between order and participation.

The technocratic-authoritarian strategy places a high priority on political order and economic growth, trading off political participation, procedural justice, distributive welfare, and liberty. The instability inherent in this strategy is the rising cost and difficulty of maintaining order and repressing demands in a situation of increasing inequality.

The technocratic-authoritarian-equalitarian strategy opts for a combination of political order, economic growth, and distributive welfare, trading off political participation, some procedural justice, and some liberty. The instability inherent in regimes opting for this strategy is that in the absence of an organized political movement, the improvements instituted by these regimes stimulate demands for increased participation and welfare. Thus the cost of maintaining order rises, and the regime must move in one of two directions — either increasing direct suppression through police and/or military action or resorting to some form of organized political movement that might transform it into an authoritarian mobilizational regime. This dilemma is reflected in the Peruvian experiment with corporatism and in the intermittent alternation of constitutional and military regimes in South Korea.

The technocratic-authoritarian-mobilizational strategy seeks to combine political order, mobilized political participation, and economic growth at the cost of competitive participation, procedural justice, and liberty. Regimes pursuing this course may follow an equalitarian strategy — as in the case of the Communist countries, Taiwan, and Tanzania — or a growth-and-inequality strategy — as in the case of Mexico. They may pursue an economically collectivist strategy, as in the case of the Communist countries and potentially Tanzania, or remain within the framework of a mixed economy, as in Mexico and Taiwan.

The neo-traditional strategy stresses system maintenance and political order and marks time on other aspects of modernization. The outstanding exceptions here are those third world countries which are in effect forced into a pattern of rapid change through the possession of a scarce and valuable resource such as oil. Rapid economic growth as a consequence of this kind of situation compels political adaptation of a bureaucratic-technocratic sort. The very magnitude of the wealth generated may move these societies in distributive directions as well.

Those modernizing regimes which place a high value on welfare distribution generally resort to some form of capital asset redistribution, such as the collectivization of the economy in Communist countries or the major land redistributions and the encouragement of small labor-intensive industries in South Korea and Taiwan. While the South Korean and Taiwanese cases may be explained in part by their having been American client countries in a threatening and unstable international environment, the Peruvian case demonstrates that this strategy may be initiated in consequence of internal pressures and decisions and in direct conflict with the United States. Similarly the Tanzanian case demonstrates that the mobilization-collectivization strategy may be followed by countries that are independent of outside Communist pressure. The choices of third world countries are constrained, but by no means determined, by the cold war and the international environment.

The mobilization regimes are a mixed bag from the point of view of productivity. Even the Communist mobilizational systems differ substantially. While they all stress economic equality and growth, they vary in the extent to which they restrict liberty, permit participation, and provide procedural justice. Thus Yugoslavia, though less egalitarian than the Soviet Union, is more libertarian, more participatory, and more equitable in its judicial processes. Mexico, having been an egalitarian mobilizational regime, has now moved in the direction of inequality, as its mobilization is preemptive rather than dynamic. Insofar as it permits a private sector, it enhances the economic liberty of a limited stratum of the population. And insofar as it tolerates limited opposition, it offers some participation in its mix of goods. Through more thoroughgoing redistribution of wealth, Taiwan seems to offer a more productive mix of growth, equality, order, and liberty than Mexico. Tanzania is perhaps too early along the course of development to judge and seems to have reached a point at which its goals of growth and equality are in increasing conflict with liberty, participation, and procedural justice.

The case of Tanzania raises an important issue in the analysis of political performance. For an accurate evaluation one must do more than compare one regime with another; one must also examine the productivity of a particular regime over time. Thus Tanzania, prior to independence and embarkation on its present course, was a British colony, a congeries of small tribal communities based largely on a subsistence agriculture economy. The applicability of such concepts as liberty, equality, and procedural justice to societies of this kind is seriously open to question. Our theory of political goods does not travel well in traditional societies. One can speak of a tradeoff of liberty, equality, and procedural justice in the transition from democratic to authoritarian government (in Brazil, for example). But in the transition from traditionalism to modern processes and performance, evaluation is much trickier. Political science does not yet really know how to do that.

ADVANCED INDUSTRIAL SOCIETIES AND POLITICAL PRODUCTIVITY

During the last several centuries, the nation-states of the West have been experiencing a high rate of "political growth." This growth has accompanied the economic growth of the industrial and technological revolutions, affecting and being affected by it. The indicators of political input (political participation and mobilization) and political output (rates of extraction, extent and variety of regulation and distribution) all show rising curves in the nineteenth and twentieth centuries. If we view productivity as outcome in the sense of human satisfaction with domestic political performance in the West, the modern era would surely also show rising levels of welfare — life expectancy, health, education, housing, income maintenance, access to recreation, and the like; of liberty in the sense of effective rights of participation and organization; and of procedural equity.

Given these rising levels of political and economic performance in Western countries, one needs to explain the contemporary mood of disillusionment, the declining levels of political legitimacy, and the increasingly common view that modern liberal society has become "ungovernable." This malaise in Western democratic countries has both economic and political components. Economically, there are three kinds of disillusionment. First, there is a distributive disillusionment. High levels of economic productivity, rapid rates of growth, and substantial governmental efforts to distribute these values and opportunities more equitably still leave substantial parts of populations in relative poverty, and the problem seems to be an intractable one.

Second, the very assumption of the feasibility of economic growth continuing at the same rates as in the past has come into question in the last decade. The great engine of modernization in the last two centuries was technological innovation, producing an ever-increasing level of productivity and material welfare. The principal ideologies of the West — liberalism and Marxism — both shared this assumption of an ever-growing material product. In the late 1960s and early 1970s the assumption that such a pattern of growth was sustainable given population increase, the depletion of natural resources, and the pollutive burden on the environment resulting from industrial processes began to be challenged, first by a few "alarmist" voices and then by the more sober mainstream of expert opinion.

And third, arising out of a sense of glut and redundancy rather than impending depletion, there emerged in the same period among the educated affluent classes the beginnings of a revulsion against the material-technical content of welfare, symbolized in the phrase the "quality of life." Here the concern was not so much with the inherent limits to material growth set by the population-environment balance, but with the material emphasis of the growth and development package itself. The intellectual, middle-class bearers of these views, relatively small in number though highly visible and vocal, had had too much of material growth, and now began to question its costs in aesthetic and moral values.

Thus, economic growth in the advanced democratic societies was under attack as being inequitably distributed, as running beyond its material base, and as preempting other values more important to human happiness. On the political side there is a comparable malaise, a paradox of system, process, and policy development associated with declining political satisfaction and legitimacy.

One of the popular topics among Western political scientists is "ungovernability." The notion of the ungovernability of modern political systems refers mainly to two sets of conditions. The first is the surfacing of a new set of political problems which are both menacing and difficult to solve. At the international level these include the arms race, nuclear proliferation, resource depletion, and pollution, all of which are beyond the capacity of any single nation to control. Domestically the problems involved in the conflicts among environmental, conservational, and growth values, and in the trade-offs among growth, inflation, and unemployment, are similarly threatening and intractable.

The second aspect of ungovernability is a set of attitudinal and value changes which on the one hand have set higher standards of political productivity and on the other undermine the effectiveness and coherence of the policy-making process. The more educated and informed electorates of advanced industrial societies no longer accord "diffuse legitimacy" to the nation-state and its political leaders. The latter are held to a short-tether performance legitimacy, with constituencies tending to expect quick results. The cohesion of party organizations and interest groups has declined, and populistic, confrontational political techniques are increasingly employed outside the framework of these institutions. Special interests and extremist ideological groups have discovered how vulnerable advanced, industrial societies are to strikes, unconventional pressures, and acts of terror.

Despite growth in output and performance in recent decades in advanced industrial societies, one can speak of a crisis of productivity; a set of dilemmas of adaptation; a groping for new norms, institutions, and policies, new powers and divisions of power, providing mankind with a more versatile set of arrangements and rules for dealing with the threatening problems of the modern world.[19]

In the advanced Communist societies, the problem of political productivity has somewhat different dimensions. The Marxist-Leninist ideological program promised material abundance and human emancipation once the era of "Socialism" was well under way. Though increased welfare and productivity have been attained, and inequality substantially reduced, there is no material abundance, and no signs of attenuation of powerful and oppressive state apparatuses. The chances for further improvements in material welfare seem good; but the prospects for increases in public liberty and procedural equity seem remote.

These countries adopted or were forced to adopt solutions to their problems that were highly productive of the particular goods of growth and equality. The means they used and the organizations they contrived may have been effectively directed toward those goals, but they may have precluded or indefinitely postponed further productive adaptations once the first goals had been attained. Thus, the Soviet Union and the Eastern European countries have surely succeeded in increasing their productivity and their distributive performance in the last decades; but if they should now wish to accede to growing demands for participation, liberty, and procedural justice, the structure of their institutions and the interests that are associated with them stand in the way. There is such a thing as solving a problem too well, overinstitutionalizing the solution, solving it in such a thorough way as to foreclose growth and adaptation. Looser solutions, although perhaps less productive in the short run, may be more adaptive and hence more variedly and creatively productive in the long run.

---

[19] For discussion of the issues and problems of advanced industrial society see among others Samuel P. Huntington, "Postindustrial Politics: How Benign Will It Be?" *Comparative Politics* 6(2) (January 1974), pp. 163 ff; Daniel Bell, *The Coming of Post-Industrial Society* (New York: The Free Press, 1973); Ronald Inglehart, ed., "Policy Problems of Advanced Industrial Society," *Comparative Political Studies* 10(3) (October 1977).

Index

Abrams, C. J., 159
Achievement-oriented recruitment, 133–136
Adaptation (adaptability)
  domestic system goods and, 399–400
  as international good, 416
  structural innovation through, 139–140
Administrative officials, 70–71. *See also* Civil servants, higher
Advanced industrial societies, productivity and, 422–424
Advantaged, the. *See also* Educated, the
  elite recruitment channels and, 124
  participant attitudes of, 118–120
Affective component of attitudes, 26
Almond, Gabriel, 90, 100
Anderson, Kristi, 27–28
Andrews, William R., 155–156
Anomic interest groups, 172–173
Apter, David, 99, 165
Armed forces, 57, 58. *See also* Military organizations
Assemblies. *See* Legislatures
Associational interest groups, 175–177
  as interest aggregators, 204–205
Astiz, Carlos, 144
Attitudes, 14. *See also* Political culture; Socialization
  cognitive, affective, and evaluative components of, 26
  consistency, 26–27
  distribution of, 28–30
  of participants, 35
  political behavior and, 25
Authoritarian political systems, 45. *See also* Totalitarian systems
  communication structures' autonomy in, 149–150
  concentration of powers in, 237

Authoritarian political systems (*cont.*)
  participation in, 37, 116
  secularization and, 48
  structural classification of, 73–76
  symbolic involvement roles in, 122–123
Authoritarian-technocratic-equalitarian strategy, 378–381, 420
Authoritarian-technocratic-mobilizational strategy, 381–387, 420
Authoritarian-technocratic strategy, 376–378, 420
Authorities, definition of, 34
Authority, territorial distribution of, 233–237
Autonomy, subsystem
  developmental typology of political systems and, 72–76
  communication structures and, 149–152

Barnes, Samuel H., 27
Bayley, David, 312, 313
Bergson, Abram, 311
Bienen, Henry, 222, 387
Blau, Peter, 60–61
Boulding, Kenneth, 165
Boundaries of political systems, 5, 6
Boynton, G. R., 269
Budget making, policy coordination and control and, 247–250
Bureaucracy, 57
  communication and, 146–147
  as elite recruitment channel, 124
  information distortion and, 163–164
  policy implementation and, 274–279
  recruitment into, 109
  responsive and responsible, 277–278
  secularization and, 50
  as socialization agent, 99–100

425